GAME OF THRONES

PRIMA Official Game Guide

Written by Michael Searle

CONTENTS

HOW TO USE THIS GUIDE

In *Game of Thrones*, two unlikely heroes—Mors Westford, a sworn brother of the Night's Watch, and Alester Sarwyck, a self-exiled prince of Riverspring—become entwined in the politics and power struggles of a vengeful queen. Many years ago, the two heroes fought side by side. Now events will force Mors and Alester to do so again, but will they fight on the same side once the truth of their past is fully revealed?

THE WORLD OF WESTEROS

Learn more about Westeros, from its 700-foot-tall wall that defends the land from the wildlings to the throne room of the Red Keep, where the royal Lannister family shapes the fate of all under their rule. Dive into combat basics as you discover how to slow down time and choose the best tactics to win the day. Examine the game's world map, achievements, and much more.

MORS WESTFORD

Everything you want to know on "the Butcher," including his Night's Watch background, stance preferences, Skinchanger powers, combat moves, and more.

ALESTER SARWYCK

Everything you want to know on the red priest, including his mysterious background, stance preferences, Rh'llor powers, combat moves, and more.

THE WALKTHROUGHS

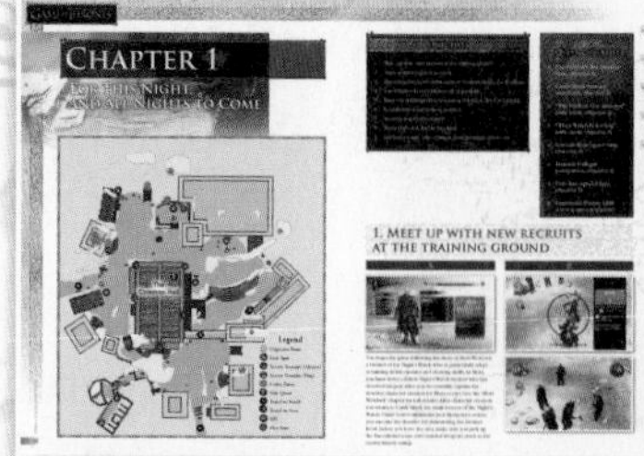

A chapter-by-chapter breakdown of gameplay. Each walkthrough chapter details all the maps in the area, quest objectives, key items, pivotal companions and NPCs, and comprehensive hints and tips to defeat each foe and unlock every game secret.

SIDE QUESTS

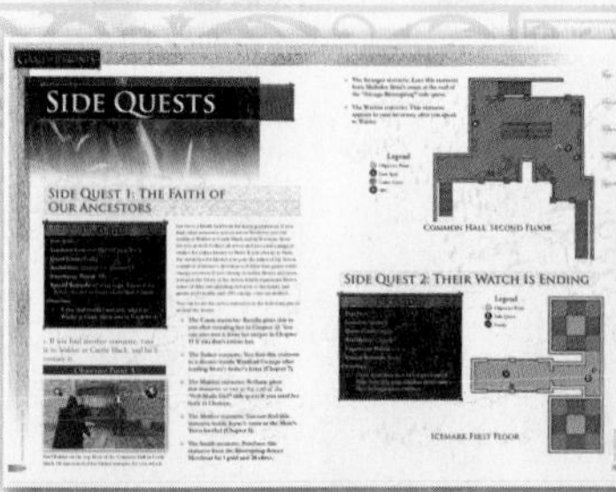

For those who want to explore Westeros completely, this chapter gives you the full scoop on all the game's side quests. If you want to take a break from the main quest, you can interrogate suspicious brothers in Castle Black, or seek out hidden treasure in the Gift, or even stop a serial killer.

The World of Westeros

IN A WORLD where a season can last generations, winter and its ill omens descend on Westeros. Mors Westford, a sworn brother of the Night's Watch, defends the Wall from wildling raiders and only has thoughts of defending the land and protecting the honor of his brotherhood...until he meets a young woman with a fateful past. Alester Sarwyck returns from a 15-year self-imposed exile to the East only to discover his once-proud family and kingdom lie in near ruin. In *Game of Thrones*, you play through alternating story lines involving Mors Westford and Alester Sarwyck. These story lines eventually converge in an epic tale of betrayal and brutality, honor and heroism.

Adventuring in Westeros

As you follow the stories of Mors and Alester, you will explore the world of Westeros. There are many unique locales and many areas within each main location. Here are the four places where you will spend most of your time: Castle Black, Riverspring, King's Landing, and Castlewood.

Castle Black

Castle Black is the heart of the Night's Watch and the cornerstone of the Wall's defense. Mors Westford begins his adventures here. Though a strong fortress against the perils north of the Wall, there is much duplicity and treachery lurking in the Night's Watch camp.

Riverspring

Riverspring is the ancient home to the Sarwyck family. Alester returns to this city at the beginning of his adventure. The kingdom mourns many recent losses, and the city has fallen on hard times. Because Alester has been abroad for 15 years, he walks as a stranger among those he once knew.

The Westeros Map

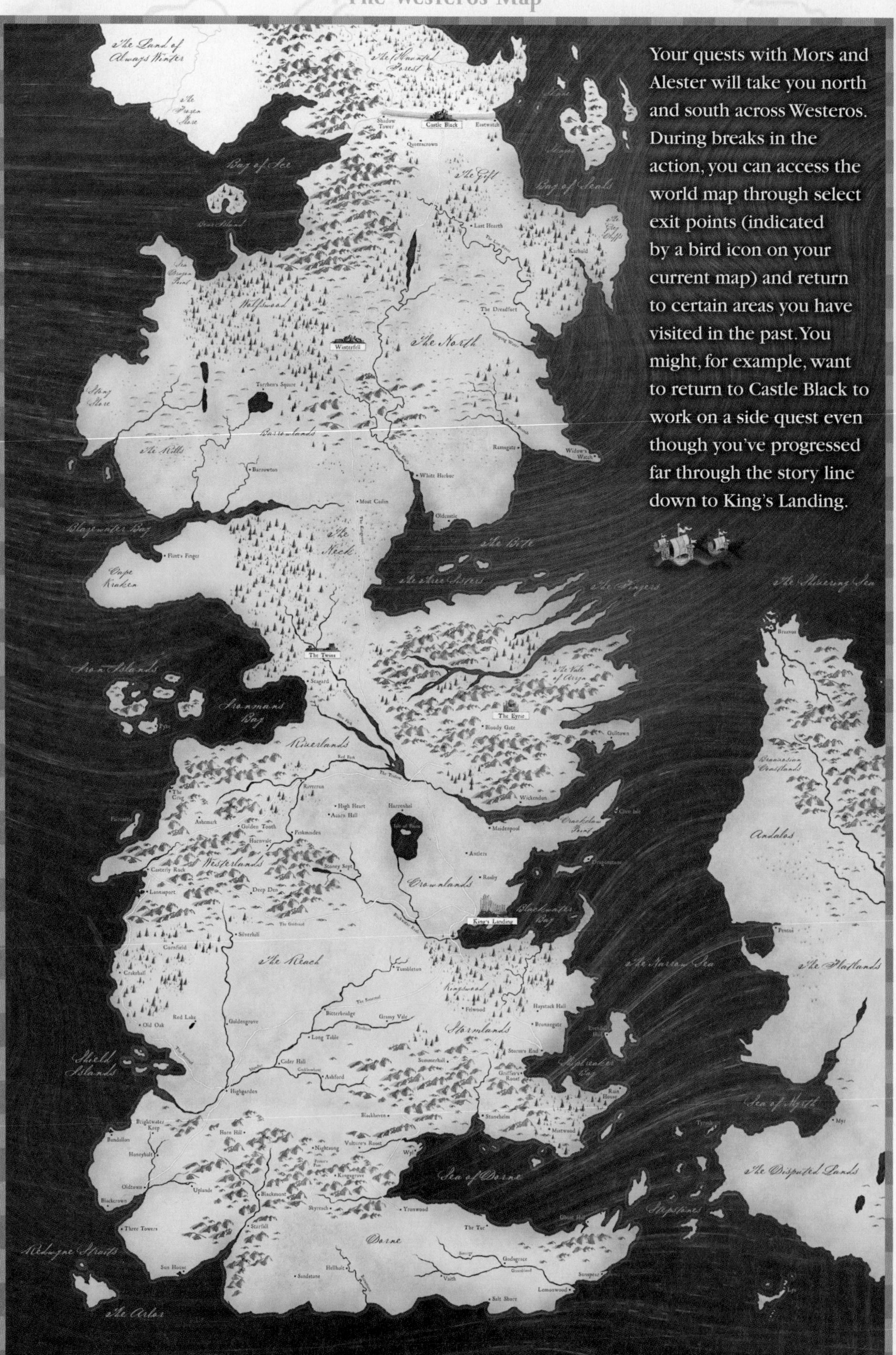

Your quests with Mors and Alester will take you north and south across Westeros. During breaks in the action, you can access the world map through select exit points (indicated by a bird icon on your current map) and return to certain areas you have visited in the past. You might, for example, want to return to Castle Black to work on a side quest even though you've progressed far through the story line down to King's Landing.

King's Landing

The biggest city in the game, King's Landing holds the royal palace of Queen Cersei Lannister, along with countless shops, alleys, and even dungeon corridors. Even as far away as the Wall, Mors will find events leading him to King's Landing; Alester's family struggles lure him there too.

Castlewood

Lord Harlton's fortress sits in the woods away from courtly affairs. A friend of Alester's father, Lord Harlton holds secrets tied to the mysteries surrounding the Sarwycks. Alester will visit Castlewood in search of answers.

Combat Display

With a single glance at your combat display, you can see your character's health, energy, Action Queue, and Active Stance. Become familiar with the icons and their functions, especially the health and energy bars—you'll be checking your character's status often.

Health represents your life in the game. As the green bar above your character portrait drops, you lose health. If your health reaches zero, your character is knocked out. If all characters in your party become knocked out, you lose. Armor improves your health score, and certain abilities increase your health regeneration, which can help in close fights. Keep in mind that it's possible to sacrifice a party member for the greater good—say, to deal maximum damage to a target before falling in combat—but it's only worth the risk if the rest of the party survives.

Energy

Energy represents your endurance in a fight and determines how many abilities you can activate during the battle. As you add abilities to your Action Queue, the yellow energy bar decreases; if you reach zero, you can't add any more abilities to your queue. Certain abilities, however, will increase your energy regeneration, which allows you to get off more abilities in a fight. Also, you can gain energy back by executing a recover energy order during combat; it takes up a spot in your Action Queue, but it's well worth it if you're low on energy and aren't desperate to swing your weapon.

Action Queue

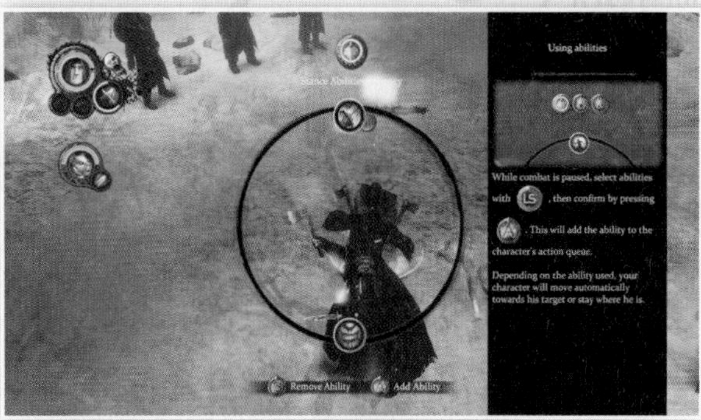

You can give up to three actions to characters. As you order each action, it will slot to the right in the character's Action Queue; they will activate in the order you execute them. Think about the battle and how your character's abilities should execute—it takes planning. For example, you don't want to activate your damage resistance as your final action after you've taken a beating. You may also want to set up combos, such as using a Bleeding attack first, followed by an attack that deals extra damage to Bleeding opponents.

Active Stance

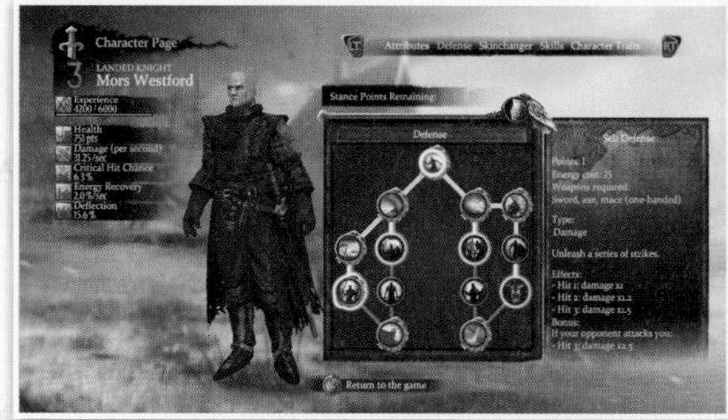

Early in the game, you won't have to worry about your Active Stance icon much; you only have one stance until Level 7. After you pick up your second stance, always check to make sure that your Active Stance is appropriate for the current battle tactics.

COMBAT

Whether you're chasing deserters through the Icemark or exploring the streets of King's Landing, enemies confront you at seemingly every turn. You'll first practice your combat moves in Castle Black, and you will perfect your favorite maneuvers and stance ability combos as you adventure along. In most fights, you'll want to stick with the following standard combat progression.

Precombat Preparation

You have two weapon slots with two spots each. Depending on your preferred stance, make sure your equipment is properly set before each battle. For example, if you're a Hedge Knight, you want to equip a two-handed weapon, while a Landed Knight would need a one-handed weapon and a shield. You can use other weapon configurations, though it's not advisable; if you don't have the proper configuration, you won't have access to your stance abilities, which will cripple your combat options.

You do have flexibility, though, with two weapon slots. You can set the first slot for your stance ability and set the second slot for ranged attacks or a really powerful weapon that doesn't fit with your main abilities. Switch back and forth as necessary.

When selecting weapons and spending your skill points, think about armor types. Cutting weapons (swords, axes) do more damage against light armor, perforating weapons (polearms, daggers) match up best against medium armor, and blunt weapons (maces, war hammers) land more damage against heavy armor. If you know the relative strength of enemies in the area, you can choose weapons to match their estimated armor. If you're not sure, choose the best DPS (damage per second) weapon for your first weapon slot, then add a ranged weapon to your second slot to hit enemies from long range or stock up on a blunting weapon to better smash down tougher enemies with heavy armor.

Slow It Down

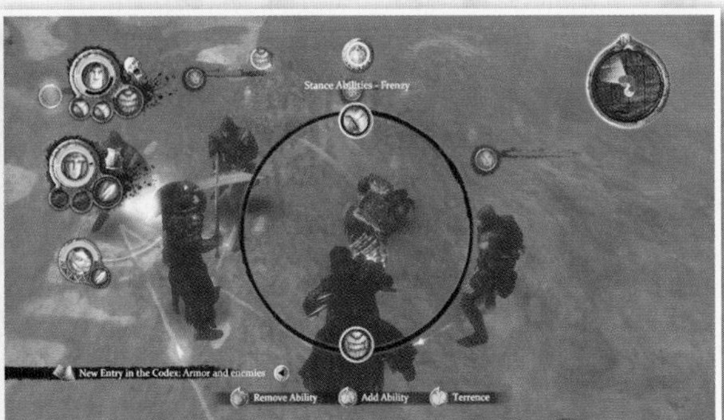

As soon as you enter combat, you should engage Active Pause. This slow-motion setting serves double duty: It gives you time to survey the entire battlefield to plan your tactics and allows you to select your stance abilities effectively without having to rush in the heat of real-time battle. Normally, you will target the nearest enemy, or possibly the leader in a big group battle. Don't forget that you can easily change your targeting: A green circle equals the selected target; a red circle equals the target being attacked. You may also want to alter which foe you go after. For example, if you're a Landed Knight, consider engaging the strongest foe so you can defend better with your shield. A Sellsword may want to jump from one target to the next and cut down wounded enemies so they don't linger on the battlefield. You might also shift your targeting to an enemy whose armor your weapon matches up better against.

Control Your Main Character

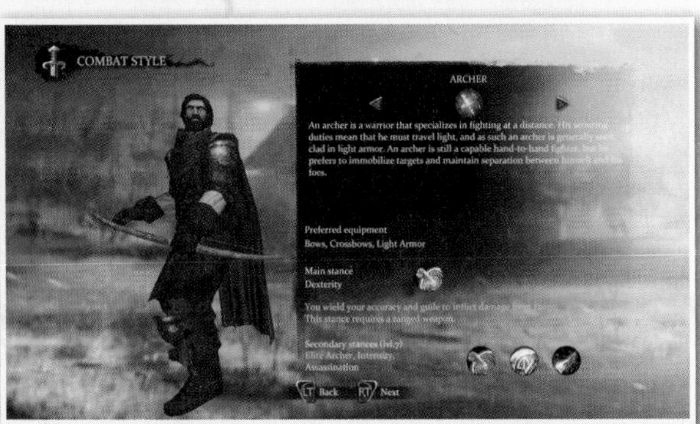

Glance often at your current character's combat display. The green bar represents your health; the yellow bar shows your energy. Below those, the Action Queue orders your next three actions so you can plan out a few moves into the combat.

Maximize your character's stance abilities for each combat. Match effects against vulnerable enemies as often as possible. For example, if a foe has a Bleeding effect on it, strike with an ability that increases damage to Bleeding foes. If an enemy begins a complex action (displayed in a circle to the right of their action bar), choose an interrupt ability to disrupt the attack. Generally, stacking three abilities in the Action Queue will drain all your energy (or come close to expending it all), but that's okay if you can remove a powerful enemy from the fight. You also regenerate energy during combat; swing several normal attacks while you gain back energy and then queue up another big ability.

Activate Secondary Character Abilities

In a group, after you've queued up your main character's three abilities, remember to rotate through your other characters. As you did with your main character, target enemies with your most appropriate stance abilities and coordinate your attacks on the enemy. When playing Mors, don't forget about his dog's abilities. The Hound can be a fearsome addition to the assault, especially if you have it immobilize an opponent while Mors deals with another aggressor.

Flasks Before Failing

You have four slots on your belt for flasks. Fill these with

different substances at alchemist shops—they give you special combat abilities such as healing or temporary invulnerability. Once you equip a flask, it appears on the Flash Ability Wheel, and you can add a flask action to your queue during Active Pause just as you would one of your stance abilities.

Attacking Your Enemies

Now all that's left is to take down your enemies. Combat can go quickly if you wish to battle in real-time, or you can watch it all unfold in slow motion through Active Pause. To put together the best plan of attack for each battle, factor in your strengths and the enemies weaknesses, and analyze the terrain and how it will affect movement. It won't be long before enemies fall to your blades like wheat during harvest.

Enemies and Armor

Using the right weapon in combat can mean the difference between delivering a blade clean through your adversary's stomach or receiving a spiked mace to your face. Your enemy's armor displays on the left side of the health bar, and if they're an elite opponent, you'll see a skull above the armor. If you see a red skull above your enemy's armor circle, look out! Red means boss enemies—the toughest foes in the game.

See the picture here for each armor and opponent difficulty type:

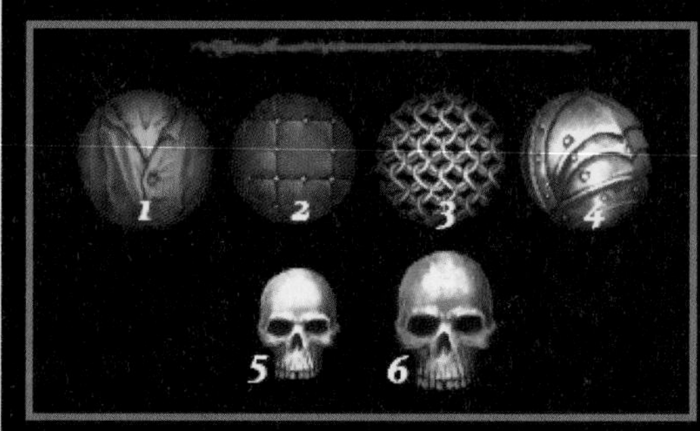

1. No armor
2. Light armor
3. Medium armor
4. Heavy armor
5. Elite opponent
6. Boss

OPTIONS MENU

Check the Options menu for all your needs outside of combat. You can review your inventory, character page, current map, codex entries, and quest log from the menu.

Inventory

Access your weapons, belt items, armor, jewels, and quest objects on your Inventory page. If you want to alter your equipment, simply click on the desired object and it will be added to your active slot or be swapped with an item already in that slot. A small character portrait in the top left shows you which character has that particular item equipped (if at all). You can also peruse item stats by scrolling over the item, and you can set which weapons you want in your weapon slots or which belt items you want in your flask slots.

Character Page

The character page displays your current character's attributes, stances, special powers, skills, and traits. You can always go here if you want to spend any points you've earned from leveling up. You can also see your scores for experience, health, damage (per second), critical hit chance, energy recovery, and deflection. Consider new equipment and purchasing new skills if you want to alter any of these stats.

Map

Look at your map often as you navigate unknown areas. It provides invaluable clues to your current whereabouts and quest objectives. If you're in an area with multiple levels, you'll see the floors displayed to the map's right. On the left, you'll see all the map icons, including primary quest locations, secondary quest locations, Warg hints (if you mark a spot with Mors's dog), dog treasure (if Mors's dog locations contain hidden loot), doors, stairs, shops, and talking NPCs (word balloons).

Codex

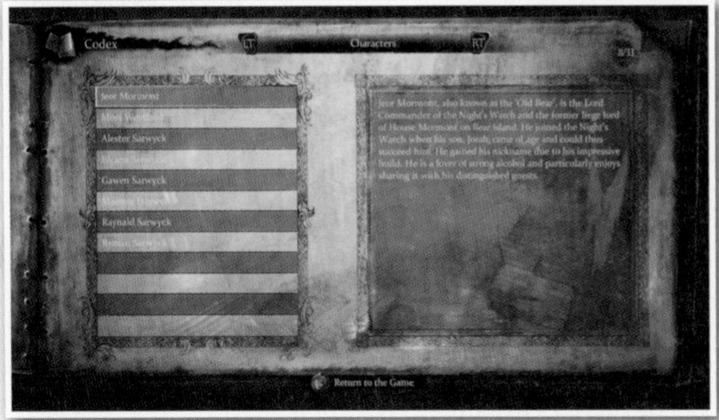

The Codex gives you tons of background story information to fill in the tales of Mors and Alester, and occasionally, you'll need to read a Codex entry to help you solve a quest (such as a riddle). Some Codex entries trigger automatically when you complete a task or enter a new area. Other Codex entries must be found. Look for a Seal of Knowledge to unlock a Codex entry; after you gain the Codex entry, feel free to sell the Seal of Knowledge for a little more pocket change to spend at the next merchant.

Quest Log

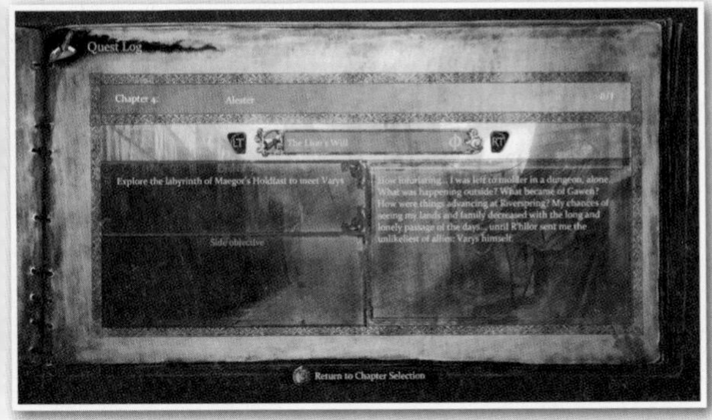

If you want clarification on your active quests, check the Quest Log. It shows you the primary quest and any secondary quest (side quests) that you are on. You can read a quick recap of where you are in the story line to the right, and a list of your current quest objectives are listed to the left.

ACHIEVEMENTS

NOTE

See the appendix at the end of the guide for complete details on all achievements.

Rewards are more than coins in a chest; accolades also comes in the form of your achievements. You gain titles from completing tons of things, such as finishing a chapter or finding all the corrupt brothers of the NIght's Watch. There are more than 50 achievements that reward you for completing story-related, secondary objectives, secondary quests, and game-related deeds.

To gain achievements for the story-related events, you simply have to complete the associated game chapter. For example, when you complete chapter 1, you receive the achievement "Winter is Coming," and when you complete chapter 12, you receive the achievement "As High as Honor." You also gain achievements for finishing Alester's and Mors' stories.

Secondary objectives are a bit trickier to achieve. During certain situations in chapters, if you perform a particular action, you can earn a special achievement. For example, in chapter 1, you can earn the "Disciplinarian" title if you choose the dialogue option "I'll show them who's in charge here" during the recruit training and then win the first two fights. In chapter 2, if you protect the nobility during the riots you earn one title ("Know Your Place") and if you protect the people during the riots you earn a separate title ("Man of the People").

There are only five secondary quest achievements. By completing tasks such as sending 10 recruits to the Wall with Mors ("Endless Watch"), finding all the statues of the Seven ("Devout Follower"), and emerging triumphant in the final arena combat in the sewers beneath King's Landing ("The Greatest") you can earn some of the achievements for side quests.

You'll have a lot of fun tracking down all the gameplay-related achievements. You can use Mors' dog to sniff out five secret objects for "Fetch!" or discover 10 secret items with Alester's special R'hllor powers for "R'hllor Sees All." Once you earn one golden dragon you gain "Golden Touch," and if you kill 400 enemies you receive the title "Accomplished Warrior." The list of entertaining achievements goes on and on; there are so many that you'll be able to replay *Game of Thrones* over and over, always discovering something new.

THRONES AND BONES

From the thrones of kings and queens to the fallen bones of your enemies, your journey will take you across the world of Westeros. Mors Westford begins in the icy refuge of Castle Black, while Alester Sarwyck returns to his home city of Riverspring at the start of his adventure. Eventually, the two collide on a single quest that threatens the lives of those they care about and may doom them both. It's an epic story, so enjoy the ride as you master the fighting skills of these two worthy heroes.

Mors Westford

Mors's Story

Fifteen years ago, Mors Westford took the Black. Because he disobeyed a direct order from his liege, Tywin Lannister, Mors was forced into service with the Night's Watch or he would have been executed under the order of his former lord. Knowing Tywin Lannister's unforgiving nature, Mors hid his wife and daughter in a secluded cottage far from prying eyes and asked his best friend to watch over them. He hasn't seen his family since and has devoted himself to the brotherhood that patrols the Wall and guards the southern lands from unspeakable evils to the north. Mors's honor and unwavering loyalty to the Night's Watch are the pillars of his life now.

Attributes

There are five attributes that affect combat, loot, health, energy, skill learning, and bargaining with merchants. Which attributes you spend more points on will depend heavily on your starting profession and your preferred play style. For example, if you want to go all-out offense, load up on strength, which improves your damage (both normal and critical) and increases your damage resistance. However, if you want to be more well rounded, you might pour points into intelligence, which aids your energy recovery, increases the amount of skill points you earn each level, and improves your chances of negotiating with merchants.

Strength

This is a vital attribute for almost any profession or play style. It enhances your normal damage, increases the multiplier for your critical damage, and bulks up your damage resistance so you suffer less damage from incoming attacks. When in doubt, spend points in strength.

Agility

If you want to attack faster, spend points in Agility to increase your attack speed. Hit chance also goes up, which means you'll miss less and will more consistently deal damage over the course of combat. If you're thinking defense, your deflection score goes up with Agility; this isn't as reliable as sinking points into Health through endurance, but it gives you a percentage chance to reduce damage taken by two-thirds or to make a dodge (see the "Luck" section).

Luck

Luck is better than you might think at first glance. It increases your dodge chance, and you can avoid damage if you successfully dodge attacks. Your critical hit chance also improves, and that extra damage can prove pivotal in a battle if you take out enemies quickly through damage spikes caused by critical hits. As an added bonus, your loot chance increases, which adds to your chances of finding additional objects inside loot spots.

Endurance

If you're looking to toughen up your character, and almost everyone should, drop points into Endurance. Each point increases your Health score, which makes it more difficult to kill you. Health recovery also helps you regain the edge in longer battles. The Energy cost of all your abilities is also lowered—another benefit not to be overlooked.

Intelligence

Intelligence does a little bit of everything. You gain Energy recovery, add to the skill points you earn each level, and increase your bargaining chance. Though it's nice to negotiate lower prices with merchants, you'll generally find the best items through questing, so you won't do too much shopping at merchants. Skill points are good, but you get a minimum of 10 points each level anyway, and by game's end you'll have maxed out in a couple of categories without any help. Overall, intelligence is the least critical attribute.

CLASSES

Mors can choose from three classes: Landed Knight, Hedge Knight, and Magnar. There are benefits for each profession. If you like using a one-handed weapon and shield, choose Landed Knight; if you like wielding a two-handed weapon, choose Hedge Knight; and if you enjoy fighting with a weapon in each hand, choose Magnar.

Landed Knight

A Landed Knight values defense over attack, and thus his initial stance keys around defense, and the ability to wear heavy armor makes him difficult to kill. You can tweak many aspects of your class, though you won't be able to use two-handed weapons or dual-wield without serious penalties.

The Defense stance starts off with the Self-Defense ability, which allows you to retaliate with three consecutive strikes for increasing damage. As a bonus, if your opponent attacks during this time, you deal even more damage on your final strike. With your second stance point, you must choose between offense and defense (left side of the tree) or commit to defense for both yourself and your allies (right side of the tree).

On the left side of the skill tree, you must take Daze Strike next. This interrupt is useful for disrupting your opponent's actions and dealing light damage. With your third point, your choice splits again on the left side: You can take either Fighting Spirit, a passive ability that increases damage for all your allies, or Massive Strike, which smashes any close opponents and knocks down any foe who had previously been immobilized.

Under Fighting Spirit, the Stalwart Defender ability increases your dodge and critical hit chance when fighting three or more enemies. Under Daze Strike, Massive Strike smashes any close opponents and knocks down any foe who had previously been immobilized. Once you have all your other abilities on the left side, you can choose Shield Strike. Your top offensive ability does a little bit of everything, as it upends a foe with a violent shield blow (damage), disrupts your opponent's action (interrupt), knocks your foe to the ground if he has no shield, and stuns him for a short duration regardless.

Over on the right side, you must purchase Taunt after Self-Defense. For a moderate duration, Taunt forces all nearby opponents to attack you and leaves your allies free to counterattack or recover. You then have a choice: Resistance, which temporarily increases damage resistance for a short duration, or Tactician, which significantly increases damage for you and your party if surrounded by three or more opponents.

Under Resistance, you can take two more abilities: Physical Strength, which increases your resistance to stun and knockdown effects, and Clenched Teeth, which improves Health recovery for each critical hit you receive. Under Tactician, there is only one ability: Flawless Armor. While recovering, your damage resistance increases and gives you a chance to catch your breath.

Once you take all the abilities on the right side, you can choose Quick Fix. It allows you to "patch up your armor" in combat, which translates into a small heal. If you can't stock up on healing flasks, this is a very valuable ability. If you have the money to buy your flasks, it's probably best to pick up some of the offensive abilities first and add this later (as well as some of the other passive abilities on this side of the tree).

Hedge Knight

The Hedge Knight wields a two-handed weapon with power and impunity. You are slower in battle, but when you land blows, they tend to put enemies down. You can tweak many aspects of your class, though you can't use a sword/shield combination or dual-wield without serious penalties.

The Domination stance begins with Devastation, which performs a massive strike against all opponents in front of you. From there, you can choose the left part of the tree or the right. If you go left, you gain some attacks and damage-increasing abilities. If you go right, you gain more attacks, stun and knockdown effects, and some defensive abilities to keep you in the battle longer.

Pierce is the first ability on the skill tree's left side. It deals light damage but causes your opponent to bleed (even longer against foes with medium armor). Next, you must choose The Sight of Blood, which increases damage and attack speed with each of your kills.

If you continue down the chain under The Sight of Blood, you gain Add Injury to Injury (minor attack that becomes a moderate attack if your opponent is Bleeding) and Massacre (a wild swing that strikes all enemies in front of you). If you branch out from The Sight of Blood to the left, you can pick up Butcher (extra damage to stunned or knocked down enemies) and Born to Fight (significantly increases your critical hits).

On the tree's right side, Earthquaker is your first ability. The area interrupt shakes the ground and stuns all nearby opponents for a short duration. If you continue down the chain from Earthquaker, you gain Headbutt (damage and short stun effect), Upheaval (knock your opponent to the ground with a violent blow), and Death from Above (minor attack that becomes a major attack if your opponent is knocked down).

If you branch off to the right of Earthquaker, you first gain Hard Head, an ability that makes you more resistant to stun effects. Under Hard Head, you can gain Unflinching (chance to resist knockdown effects) and Ferocity (increases your stun and knockdown durations).

Generally, you'll want to choose some of the attacks from the tree's left side first, though Earthquaker is a great interrupt against multiple opponents. Born to Fight is a great ability, but you have to go deep into the tree to get it, while some of the abilities on the right side are situational, revolving around stun and knockdown, so it really depends on how you want to set up your character.

Magnar

A Magnar is a scary, offensive juggernaut with a weapon in each hand. He might not have the power of the Hedge Knight's two-handed weapon, but the Magnar's combo-reliant abilities can deal just as much damage over time in a fight. You can tweak many aspects of your class, though you won't be able to use a sword/shield combination or two-handed weapons without serious penalties.

The Frenzy stance starts off with Slash, a standard attack that causes your opponent to bleed. Since many abilities trigger off Bleeding, it's a fine attack to kick off combat.

You can then choose the skill tree's left side (more offensive abilities) or right side (general effects).

On the left side, Vicious Hit is your first ability, an attack that deals significantly more damage and stuns if your opponent is Bleeding. Under Vicious Hit, you can pick up Warrior's Aura (increases critical hit chance every time you interrupt an opponent) and Cutthroat (a brutal attack if your opponent doesn't dodge it).

If you branch left from Vicious Hit, you can gain Rage (attack all enemies in front of you) and Flurry of Blows (three attacks that increase in damage and interrupt). Once you have all abilities on the left side, you can train Victorious Assault, a merciless attack on an opponent who has been knocked down.

On the right side, Revenge is your first ability. When you receive a critical hit, your next attack will inflict Bleeding on your foe. Under Revenge, you can pick up Bloody Frenzy (increased damage and attack speed for the whole party) and Fury (significant boost to your damage and attack speed, but you lose control of your character if your health drops below 50 percent). In order to counterattack the Berserk penalty on Fury, you must learn all the abilities on the right side and then take the final ability, Self-Control.

If you branch to the right of Revenge, you can gain Tough Nut (increases damage resistance with each critical hit received), Tireless (energy cost decreases as your health drops), and Trance (energy recovery improves when you have less than 50 percent health).

Both sides of the Magnar tree have intriguing possibilities. If you want to take the sure route, spend more points early on in the tree's left side and stock up on extra attacks. If you want to roll the dice, you may deal more damage on the tree's right side with Blood Frenzy and Fury, but you may lose more than control—your life!—when you go Berserk. If you plan to Fury a lot, spend all your points on the right side first so you can unlock Self-Control to nullify Fury's potentially severe penalty.

Comparing Mors's Classes

Name	Combat Preference	Weapons	Armor	Main Stance	Secondary Stances
Landed Knight	One-Handed Weapon/ Shield	Swords, Maces, Short Blades	Heavy	Defense	Elite Knight, Domination, Frenzy
Hedge Knight	Two-Handed Weapon	Swords, Maces, Polearms	Heavy	Domination	Elite Warrior, Defense, Dexterity
Magnar	Dual-Wielding	Axes, Hammers, Short Blades	Medium	Frenzy	Berserker, Domination, Intensity

STANCES

Depending on your starting class, you must choose Defense (Landed Knight), Domination (Hedge Knight), or Frenzy (Magnar) for your initial stance. At Level 7, you earn a secondary stance. You can choose Landed Knight's secondary stance from Elite Knight, Domination, or Frenzy. Hedge Knight has access to Elite Knight, Defense, or Dexterity. Magnar can choose from Berserker, Domination, or Intensity.

Defense (Landed Knight Starting Stance)

Three-quarters of the skill tree concentrates on building up defense. The other quarter works in some attacks, generally focusing on disrupting your opponents' actions. If you want to be the one who takes a pounding from the enemy, pick up this stance.

Domination (Hedge Knight Starting Stance)

Focused on a two-handed weapon, Domination loads up on abilities that inflict great damage with stunning and knockdown effects to complement the increased damage. There's some defense here, but mostly in the form of "kill before they kill you." If you want to wield the biggest weapons on the battlefield, Domination is a good place to start.

Frenzy (Magnar Starting Stance)

The Frenzy stance also focuses on offense, but it's the two-handed variety and relies more on speed and precision than massive blows. Many abilities deal extra damage and trigger an effect (Bleeding, increased Attack Speed, stunning, etc.), but you have to set up a lot of combos, which takes valuable time in combat, or you risk going berserk and losing control of your character.

Berserker (Mastery)

Your incredible will and pain tolerance allows you to perform remarkable feats in combat. As you increase in proficiency, expect to improve combat damage, attack speed, and critical hit chance. You can also pick up a bonus to luck and energy.

Dexterity (Secondary Stance)

Your projectiles are deadly attacks at range. Because you would rather your enemies stay at a distance, you have various Immobilization and stun effects to make sure foes don't close on you. If you like slinging arrows and causing carnage from the perimeter, the Dexterity stance is definitely for you.

Elite Knight (Mastery)

The ultimate training for a knight prepares your body for the difficult trials of combat. You can gain bonuses to health, energy, and endurance, or you can opt for a better health recovery and health replenishment per kill at the highest level. If you use a shield, you gain several improvements, or you can study how to punish foes with Bleeding.

Elite Warrior (Mastery)

The ultimate training for a warrior develops many of your other abilities. You can improve your damage resistance, strength, and energy. You can add extra effects to abilities such as Earthquaker (adds damage on top of stun) or Massacre (knocks down opponents instead). You can even choose to ignore the effects of Hemlock, Blindeye, and Manticore's venom.

Intensity (Secondary Stance)

Your smooth and swift maneuvers set you up to counterattack with precision or capitalize on effects like knockdown and Bleeding. If you like to adjust on the fly and react to what the enemy throws at you, Intensity offers a lot for you.

SKILLS

You can spend skill points on your weapon categories—cutting, perforating, and blunt weapons—and armor. Your class's preferred weapon types, highlighted in green, give you two points for every one skill point you spend; white types are one for one. Unless you want to customize a particular weapon type, it's best to spend your points on your preferred weapon types and get more each level.

Try to balance your points between the cutting, perforating, and blunt weapons so you're ready for any enemy armor type. If you gain a special weapon that you want to wield for a while, sink more points into that weapon type to bolster its effectiveness. Spend points on your weapons first. Once you max out your primary weapon, you can think about spending points on armor to beef up your defense.

TRAITS

Traits are divided into strengths and weaknesses. Each strength has a value associated with it (from one to four); the more powerful abilities have the higher values. You can take up to three strengths for your character, but you must take an equal value's worth of weaknesses to balance it out. For example, if you take Born Leader and Gifted (six points), you must take six points' worth of weaknesses, such as Hematophobia (3), Clumsy (2), and Allergic (1).

Review all the traits to see which ones appeal to your class and play style. Some standouts include Born Leader, which increases damage for all your allies; Gifted, which gives you two extra skill points per level; and Brute, which has a chance to stun your opponent with each attack. Of course, your class might determine a better trait, such as Bruiser (extra damage with two-handed weapons) for a Hedge Knight. After you pick your traits, you'll have to match them with weaknesses; this is no easy feat, since they're all disadvantages, and some can kill you at the wrong moment in a fight.

NOTE

Some traits unlock through your deeds in the game. Check your character page frequently to see if you've acquired any new strengths.

WARG POWERS

Mors is a rare breed: a Warg. He has a special telepathic link with his dog, which means he can see and act through his dog while his human body remains stationary. Once you unlock the Warg ability, you can give the dog commands and access the Skinchanger abilities.

Mors's Dog

The dog is more than a "best friend"; he's a great ally. During combat, Mors always has his dog at his side, so it's like having an extra ally in every fight. Early on, the dog hassles enemies for minor damage, but once Mors gains his Skinchanger abilities and can command the dog, the canine becomes a valuable team member. You can use the dog's initial Attack ability at any time in combat; all the other dog abilities share a common cooldown, so use them sparingly and efficiently.

Perhaps the dog's most valuable asset is his stealth. As long as Mors stops moving, you can switch point of view to the dog and see things through his eyes. Scouting an area becomes much easier with the dog, who is difficult to detect, prowling the perimeter and noting enemy positions.

TIP

If you switch back to Mors from the dog, your map will be marked with a Warg hint in the spot where the dog last stood. This is an excellent way to mark where scents end up and where potential ambush points lie.

Even better, in Stealth mode, the dog can assassinate enemies without raising the alarm. If you can sneak up on a single enemy, you can pounce on him and rapidly hit the Damage button to deliver a deadly blow. Be careful, though: If an enemy sees you, the attack fails and the alarm goes up, putting defenders on high alert.

Many times during your quests, you'll need to track down an enemy or an NPC. The dog can smell the various scents in the area and follow their trails. Each scent has a different color: yellow for the main scent you've targeted, green for secondary scents, and blue for scents that lead to hidden treasures. While tracking, move slowly and scan for watchful enemies.

If the scent seems to disappear and you get lost, simply backtrack till you last found the scent and look carefully for the trail. Sometimes the trail continues through doors or into areas that the dog can't reach without help from Mors. In those cases, switch back to Mors; a Warg hint will be marked on the map to follow and the dog will immediately return to Mors without incident (even if he passes through enemy territory, he won't trigger an alarm while returning to Mors). Think about tracking on a quest objective if you're unsure of your targeted NPC's location; the dog can pick up scents almost anywhere and follow them to their source.

NOTE

Drop into "scent mode" frequently in areas to search for hidden treasure. It will help bolster your inventory, and there are certain spots in the game where you must find a secret item to continue.

Skinchanger

Mors's bond with his dog gives him Skinchanger powers. Everyone begins with the dog's general Attack ability. After that, you can choose the tree's left or right side. The left side offers more canine attacks; the right side gives you more passive abilities that strengthen the dog.

The first ability on the left side, Immobilize, is one of your best. You command your dog to bite a foe's leg and distract him for a short duration. It serves as an interrupt to break an opponent's upcoming action, and it allows Mors to fight bigger groups since the enemies can't all gang up on him with the dog immobilizing one of them. Under Immobilize, you must take Remove Shield, which disarms a shield from a foe.

Now you have three choices that branch out from Remove Shield. If you continue down the Remove Shield chain, you get Disarm (remove an enemy's weapon) and Sharp Fangs (adds Bleeding to Throat Lunge, Remove Shield, and Disarm). If you branch left from Remove Shield, you can gain Cave Canem (increased kill speed during stealth assassinations) and Fighting Dog (a massive bonus to the dog's damage). If you branch right from Remove Shield, you can give the dog the Takedown ability (knock down a foe) and Throat Lunge (major damage attack if the enemy doesn't have a shield).

The first ability on the right side, Energy, complements all abilities: your abilities recharge faster. If you continue down the chain from Energy, you gain Wild (whole party recovers Energy faster), Intimidation (scares a foe in place for a short duration), and Barking (increased durations for Wild and Intimidation).

If you branch to the right of Energy, you can pick up Harassment (recharge all abilities if the dog kills an opponent), Toughness (a big bonus to the dog's health), and Reflexes (increased Deflection).

In general, you'll want to load up on the tree's left side first to give your dog many combat options. As you earn more points and have plenty of attacks, shift over to the right side and begin to build the dog into a formidable killer.

Sensing Mood

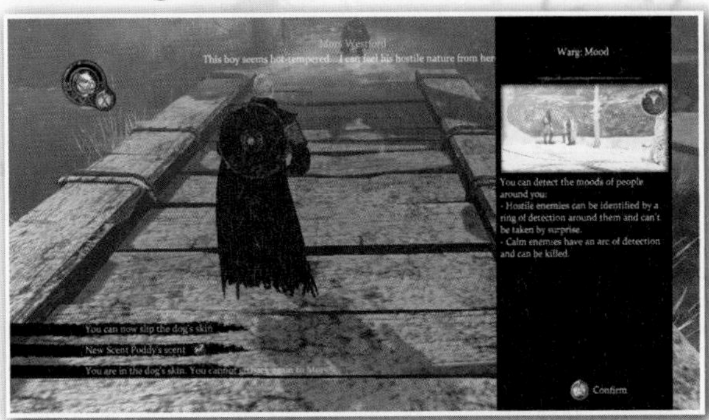

A Warg can sense the mood of people around him. Hostile enemies can be identified by a ring around them and can' be taken by surprise. Calm enemies have an arc of detection and can be killed if you sneak up on them.

Mors in Combat

Your class choice will dictate your primary battle practices. Here are your four main combat configurations, though there are many variations when you factor allies, enemy position, and terrain into your tactics.

The Defensive Stalwart

As a Landed Knight, you won't deal as much damage as the other two classes, but you won't take as much damage either. You'll generally want to charge the toughest enemy and hold his attention with a constant barrage of attacks or with your Taunt ability. Given that you can soak up damage more than most, it's fine if enemies begin to swarm you, so long as your less-durable allies can inflict their fair share of damage. If you find yourself getting knocked out often at early levels, invest more points on the right side of your skill tree. Otherwise, use Self-Defense against normal targets, Massive Strike against large groups, Daze Strike to interrupt an action, and Shield Strike to flatten powerful enemies without shields.

The Smasher

The Hedge Knight pounds foes with vicious two-handed attacks. Against single opponents, open with Pierce to cause Bleeding and follow up with Add Injury to Injury for extra damage against Bleeding foes. Devastation works great against crowds, and if you can earn Born to Fight, all your attacks have a better chance to go critical. Though you'll likely want to concentrate on the left side of your skill tree, don't forget to put one point into Earthquaker so you have an area interrupt that can thwart key enemies' actions in progress.

The Slicer

No matter your preferred tactics, a Magnar can open with the standard Slash attack and take advantage of the Bleeding state in which it leaves the opponent. Follow up with Vicious Hit to punish a Bleeding opponent with extra damage and a stun effect. Seize the opportunity to use Cutthroat against wounded foes; if it succeeds, you deal massive damage and cause Bleeding and a knockdown effect. Victorious Assault can compound the damage and give you some health back in the process against foes knocked down by Cutthroat. Your Flurry of Blows ability triggers a series of three attacks of increasing damage—a fine choice at almost any time in the battle. On the right side of your tree, the Blood Frenzy/Fury combo will turn you into a damage-dealing monster. Unfortunately, unless you earn Self-Control, too, you lose control of your character and there's no telling what will happen then.

CAUTION

When you pick up new weapons, be careful that you don't equip an item that disrupts your stance. A two-handed weapon in the hands of a Magnar is nowhere near as deadly as in the hands of a Hedge Knight.

The Tag Team

Mors and the dog form a great team. Even when Mors doesn't have other allies in the party, he always has his dog to distract, stun, and knock down enemies. Against single opponents, go for maximum damage attacks for Mors and the dog. Against two or more opponents, order the dog to immobilize one enemy while Mors goes after the others. Depending on the circumstance, you can order the dog to disarm a foe's weapon or shield, or scare them out of combat for precious seconds. Think of Mors and the dog as a single combat entity and your attacks will be much more thorough and deadly.

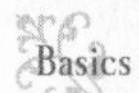

Alester Sarwyck

Alester's Story

Fifteen years ago, Alester fled Westeros. Unable to come to grips with the sins of his past, Alester journeyed across the sea to the Free Cities and embraced the religion of R'hllor. As a red priest, Alester has returned to his home, Riverspring, to attend his father's funeral. Like it or not, the game of thrones has caught up with him, and Alester must now make difficult choices that will either save or doom his kingdom and family.

Attributes

There are five attributes that affect combat, loot, health, energy, skill learning, and bargaining with merchants. Which attributes you spend more points on will depend heavily on your starting profession and your preferred play style. For example, if you want to go all-out offense, load up on Strength, which improves your damage (both normal and critical) and increases your damage resistance. However, if you want to be more well rounded, pour points into Intelligence, which aids your energy recovery, increases the amount of skill points you earn each level, and improves your chances of negotiating with merchants.

Strength

This is a vital attribute for almost any profession or play style. It enhances your normal damage, increases the multiplier for your critical damage, and bulks up your damage resistance so you suffer less damage from incoming attacks. When in doubt, spend points in strength.

Agility

If you want to attack faster, spend points in Agility to increase your attack speed. Hit chance also goes up, which means you'll miss less and more consistently deal damage over the course of combat. If you're thinking defense, your deflection score goes up with Agility; this isn't as reliable as sinking points into health through endurance, but it gives you a percentage chance to reduce damage suffered by two-thirds or to dodge (see the "Luck" section next).

Luck

Luck is better than you might think at first glance. It increases your dodge chance, and you can avoid damage completely if you successfully dodge attacks. Your critical hit chance also improves, and that extra damage can prove pivotal in a battle if you take out enemies quickly through damage spikes caused by critical hits. As an added bonus, your loot chance increases, which adds to your chances of finding additional objects inside loot spots.

Endurance

To toughen up your character, which almost everyone should do, drop points into Endurance. Each point increases your health score, which makes it more difficult to kill you. Health recovery also helps you regain the edge in longer battles. The energy cost of all your abilities is also lowered—another benefit not to be overlooked.

Intelligence

Intelligence does a little bit of everything. You gain energy recovery, add to the skill points you earn each level, and increase your bargaining chance. Though it's nice to negotiate lower prices with merchants, you'll generally find the best items through questing, so you won't do too much shopping at merchants. Skill points are good, but you get a minimum of 10 points each level anyway, and by game's end you'll have maxed out in a couple of categories without any help. Overall, Intelligence is the least critical attribute.

CLASSES

Alester can choose from three classes: Water Dancer, Sellsword, and Archer. There are benefits for each profession, though if you like to take advantage of your opponents' weaknesses, choose Water Dancer; if you like relying on stealth and timing to kill your enemies, go with Sellsword; and if you enjoy pelting your foes with projectiles, choose Archer.

Water Dancer

Based on speed, balance, and agility, a Water Dancer's sword fighting cuts away at an opponent's weak spots until they fall. Though you wear light armor, your formidable offensive skills overmatch almost any foe. You can adjust many aspects of your class, though you won't be able to use two-handed weapons without serious penalties.

The Intensity stance begins with the Fierce as a Wolverine ability, a better-than-average attack that reduces the hit chance of your opponent's next strike. As with all stance skill trees, you can choose to pour more points into the left side or the right. The left side offers more offensive abilities, while the right side focuses on defense.

Your first ability on the tree's left side is Light as a Feather, which allows you to immobilize an opponent for a short time and deal a moderate amount of damage. If you continue down the chain from Light as a Feather, you pick up Quick as a Snake next, which strikes all enemies surrounding you for normal damage. Beneath that, you gain Calm as Still Water, a blow that deals less-than-normal damage but knocks down your opponent for a short time. Calm as Still Water sets up both abilities connected to it: Opportunist performs an automatic critical hit against a knocked down opponent, and Sting of the Manticore deals double damage and bleeds your foe for a short time.

If you branch off to the left of Light as a Feather, you can learn some passive abilities to improve damage dealing. First, Vicious Circle increases critical hit chance with each critical hit performed. Next, Cocksure increases attack damage after each successful dodge.

On the tree's right side, you must take Retaliation first. This ability allows you to drop into a defensive position and improve Deflection, increase damage for each incoming attack, and increase damage for each successful dodge. Directly under Retaliation, Strong as a Bear is an interrupt that deals slightly-above-average damage but stuns the target for a short duration.

If you branch off to the right of Retaliation, you can pick up Bully, which taunts your enemies to rush at you. Teamed up with Bully, Smooth as Summer Silk increases your Deflection percentage and your ability to dodge during the Bully duration. Next down the chain, Anticipation further increases Deflection for each attack received, and, lastly, Recuperative Defense enables you to deflect enemy attacks even while using the Recovery action in combat.

Sellsword

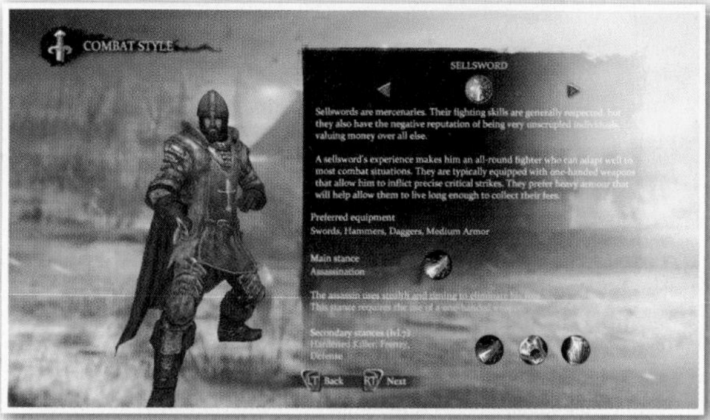

A Sellsword's experience as a mercenary prepares Alester well for most combat situations. They wear the toughest armor of all of his class choices and typically wield a one-handed weapon to inflict precise critical strikes. You can adjust many aspects of your class, though you can't use two-handed weapons without serious penalties.

The Assassination stance starts off with Sneak Attack, an ability that punishes an opponent with heavy damage if that foe isn't attacking you. The left side of your skill tree concentrates on poison and stun effects, while the right side has a variety of abilities that range from Bleeding to temporary invulnerability.

On the tree's left side, Poisoned Weapon sets up the poison chain with Hemlock, an attack that poisons; it also increases attack speed and improves hit chance. Beneath Poisoned Weapon, Apothecary allows you to apply various poisons to your blade. Contagion, the last ability in the poison chain, enables your poison to spread to a second opponent in the area.

Branching off to the left from Poisoned Weapon, Blinding Dust is an excellent defensive ability: It stuns an opponent for a short duration and interrupts any enemy action in progress. Under Blinding Dust, Guile gives a bonus to damage against opponents who are stunned, knocked down, or fighting one of your allies. Continuing down the chain, Savage Strike hits your opponent with a vicious blow for heavy damage, and Pommel Strike deals heavy damage with a chance to disarm your opponent.

On the tree's right side, Deterring Strike forces your current foe to switch to a teammate. It allows you to avoid damage, but you must have an ally in the fight to use it. Below Deterring Strike in the chain is Assassin's Dance, a passive ability that grants a bonus to critical hit chance and critical damage. Below that, Thirst for Life increases your dodge ability when your health is low, and Unbowing gives you a short burst of invincibility when you fall under a quarter of your health.

Branching off to the right on Deterring Strike is Vicious, a passive ability that gives you a chance to inflict the Bleeding state on an opponent who isn't fighting you. Finally, Precision Strike falls under the Vicious ability and causes moderate damage over time.

Archer

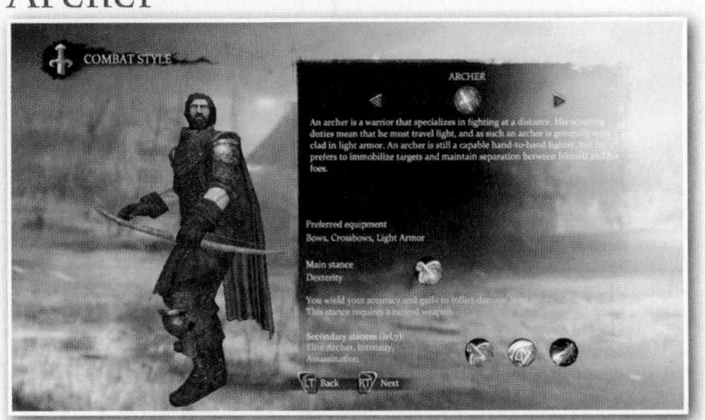

Where most of the other classes prefer up-close-and-personal combat, the Archer specializes in fighting from a distance. Because you wear light armor and your melee abilities won't excel until higher levels, Archers should linger on the outskirts of a battle and let allies charge into the fray. You can adjust many aspects of your class, though you can't use one-handed or two-handed melee weapons without serious penalties.

The Dexterity stance begins with Paralyzing Powder, a clutch defensive ability that immobilizes an enemy in front of you for a short duration and allows you to put some distance between you before the next attack. Look for more offensive abilities on the tree's left side and a mix of attacks, defense, and quicker reload abilities on the right side.

On the left side, you start off with Poisoned Missile (apply Hemlock to your projectile and increase attack speed and hit chance) and the must-take Impact (chance to immobilize with each attack). If you continue down the chain under Impact, you can gain Head Shot (major damage to target and knockdown) and Explosive Missile (massive damage to all enemies in the immediate impact area). If you branch out to the left from Impact, you have access to Target Practice (increased attack speed against immobilized targets) and Focus (take time to regain energy while targeting an opponent).

On the tree's right side, Rapid Fire kicks things off. Your attack speed increases on a single enemy, but the effect ends if you miss your foe. If you continue down the chain from Rapid Fire, you can pick up Smoke Bomb (force enemies to target an ally instead of you), Discourteous Kick (a moderate attack that causes Bleeding), and Chirurgeon (extra critical hit chance on Bleeding foes and each critical hit immobilizes your opponent for a short duration).

If you branch out to the right of Rapid Fire, the passive ability Sequential Shot increases the hit chance for each attack carried out on the same target, plus you score a critical hit every five attacks on that same foe. Under Sequential Shot, Deft Reloads increases reload speed and Skilled Marksman increases aiming speed.

Comparing Alester's Classes

Name	Combat Preference	Weapons	Armor	Main Stance	Secondary Stances
Water Dancer	One-Handed Weapons	Swords, blunt projectiles, Short Blades	Light	Intensity	Master Water Dancer, Dexterity, Frenzy
Sellsword	One-handed weapons	Swords, hammers, Short Blades	Medium	Assassination	Hardened Killer, Frenzy, Defense
Archer	Ranged weapons	Bows, crossbows	Light	Dexterity	Elite Archer, Intensity, Assassination

STANCES

Depending on your starting class, you must choose Intensity (Water Dancer), Assassination (Sellsword), or Dexterity (Archer) for your initial stance. At Level 7, you earn a secondary stance. You can choose Water Dancer's secondary stance from Master Water Dancer, Dexterity, or Frenzy. Sellsword has access to Hardened Killer, Frenzy, or Defense. Archer can choose from Elite Archer, Intensity, or Assassination.

Intensity (Water Dancer Starting Stance)

Your smooth and swift maneuvers set you up to counterattack with precision or capitalize on effects like knockdown and Bleeding. If you like to adjust on the fly and react to what the enemy throws at you, Intensity offers a lot for you.

Assassination (Sellsword Starting Stance)

You'll use any tactics necessary to survive, including poisoning, blinding an enemy with dust, and stabbing someone in the back. Your attacks are deadly if you can keep opponents from focusing on you. If you like to sneak into combat and deal the killing blow with your enemy's back turned to you, pick up the Assassination stance.

Dexterity (Archer Starting Stance)

Your projectiles are deadly attacks at range. Because you want enemies to stay at a distance, you have various Immobilization and stun effects to make sure foes don't close on you. If you like slinging arrows and causing carnage from the perimeter, the Dexterity stance is definitely for you.

Defense (Secondary Stance)

Three-quarters of the skill tree concentrates on building up defense. The other quarters works in some attacks, generally focusing on disrupting your opponents' actions. If you want to be the one who takes a pounding from the enemy, pick up this stance.

Elite Archer (Mastery)

For anyone specializing in Dexterity, Elite Archer is the natural extension. Your first ability, Point Blank, increases your effectiveness against melee enemies, and your last gives you a little bit of everything: increased critical damage, hit chance, deflection, and energy recovery. In between, you can learn how to fire faster or more accurately.

Frenzy (Secondary Stance)

The Frenzy stance also focuses on offense, but it's the two-handed variety and relies more on speed and precision than massive blows. Many abilities deal extra damage and trigger an effect (Bleeding, increased Attack Speed, stunning, etc.), but you have to set up a lot of combos (which takes valuable time in combat) or risk going Berserk and losing control of your character.

Hardened Killer (Mastery)

The talents of slaying your opponents come naturally to you. You can become an expert in poisoning or learn how to gain the early advantage over your foe in combat. You can enhance your energy reserves, your damage, and even your intelligence. At the higher levels, you become brutally efficient and master the ultimate survival techniques.

Master Water Dancer (Mastery)

You react and respond to your opponents even better as a Master Water Dancer. It starts with a bonus to agility, and you can go on to gain improvements to your dodge ability and energy reserve. You can also specialize with extra effects on certain abilities, such as adding damage and increased Bleeding to Sting of the Manticore.

SKILLS

You can spend skill points on your weapon categories—cutting, perforating, and blunt weapons—and armor. Your class's preferred weapon types, highlighted in green, give you two points for every one skill point you spend; white types are one for one. Unless you want to customize a particular weapon type, it's best to spend your points on your preferred weapon types and get more each level.

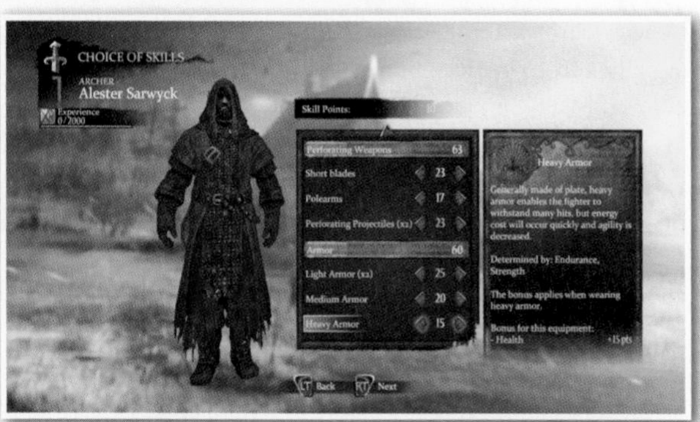

Try to balance your points between the cutting, perforating, and blunt weapons so you're ready for any enemy armor type. If you gain a special weapon that you'll be wielding for a while, sink more points into that weapon type to bolster its effectiveness. Spend points on your weapons first. Once you max out your primary weapon, you can think about spending points on armor to beef up your defense.

Traits

Traits are divided into strengths and weaknesses. Each strength has a value associated with it (from one to four); the more powerful abilities have the higher values. You can take up to three strengths for your character, but you must take an equal value of weaknesses to balance it out. For example, if you take Born Leader and Gifted (six points), you would have to take six points' worth of weaknesses, such as Hematophobia (3), Clumsy (2), and Allergic (1).

Review all the traits to see which ones appeal to your class and play style. Some standouts include Born Leader, which increases damage for all your allies; Gifted, which gives you two extra skill points per level; and Brute, which has a chance to stun your opponent with each attack. Of course, your class might determine a better trait, such as Dexterous (increased hit chance with ranged weapons) for an Archer. After you pick your traits, you'll have to match them with weaknesses—this is no easy feat, since they're all disadvantages, and some can kill you at the wrong moment in a fight.

Note

Some traits unlock through your deeds in the game. Check your Character Page frequently to see if you've acquired any new strengths.

R'hllor Powers

As a red priest devoted to the god R'hllor, Alester has some magical abilities that have a great impact on the story line and your chances of survival in combat. Once you unlock your R'hllor abilities, you can light targets on fire, generate heat to recover health and energy faster, and even discover secret passages through the guidance of your lord above.

R'hllor Abilities

At the top of Alester's R'hllor powers is Flaming Weapon, the simplest form of Alester's fire-based weapon abilities. You must have a flask of flammable oil to set Alester's weapon on fire with Flaming Weapon; if so, the weapon stays alight for 10 seconds and can set enemies on fire with each attack.

If you branch to the left, Accelerated Combustion increases the burn rate on an opponent who is already on fire. Next, you can choose from two abilities: Ignition (inflicts more damage and quickens the Accelerated Combustion ability) and Explosion (causes an explosion on a burning opponent that also stuns him).

Under Ignition, the potent Wildfire Weapon allows you to set your weapon on fire with wildfire, which inflicts greater damage than normal fire and spreads twice as quickly to nearby targets. Try to unlock Wildfire Weapon at an early level to take advantage of its powerful damage potential.

Under Explosion, Inferno increases the damage from Explosion and spreads it over a larger area. Below Inferno, Vial of Last Resort triggers when you are knocked out and leaves a blast of wildfire behind that affects nearby enemies.

In order to reach R'hllor's Blade, you must first have Ignition and Explosion. You'll want this early, too, since it allows you to set your weapon alight without using flammable oil. Now you can use your power at any time and not have to worry about conserving on flammable oil flasks. Under R'hllor's Blade, R'hllor's Fire improves the duration of your Flaming Weapon attack.

On the trees right side, Regenerative Heat increases your health and energy recovery times. Continuing down the chain under Regenerative Heat, R'hllor's Flames increases the length of Regenerative Heat, and Flame of Life allows you to revive a knocked out ally to 30 percent health. If you branch to the right of Flame of Life, Breath of Life revives a knocked out ally to 50 percent health and Rebirth automatically revives Alester to 25 percent health after his first knockout each fight.

If you branch to the right of Regenerative Heat, Incombustible gives you a huge defense against fire damage, cutting the amount of damage you might take from fire in half. Under Incombustible, Dazzling Light blinds nearby enemies; they will have trouble distinguishing allies from opponents.

Secret Passages

R'hllor has blessed Alester with a special sight that allows him to see secret areas. At any time, you can call upon R'hllor's vision to show you hidden passages and items. After your hands ignite in fire, scan around the area and look for a new item marker (glowing green circle). It might be a hidden item that you're looking for to complete a puzzle, or it might be a wall sconce that you can pull to open a secret passage. When you run into a dead end where you think there shouldn't be one, call up on the Vision of R'hllor to show you the way.

Alester in Combat

Your class choice will dictate your primary battle practices. Here are your four main combat configurations, though there are many variations when you factor allies, enemy position, and terrain into your tactics.

The Acrobatic

Killer

As a Water Dancer, you can play it offensively or defensively. If you go for offense, you'll want to hit enemies with Calm as Still Water to knock them down. Follow up with Opportunist for a critical strike and Sting of the Manticore for major damage and Bleeding. On defense, Light as a Feather can always immobilize an enemy if you need to put some space between you. However, Retaliation is your go-to defensive ability, as it allows you to increase your ability to deflect enemy blows and counterattack with enhanced damage; the more enemy attacks, the better your counterattack. Several abilities, such as Anticipation and Recuperative Defense, aid in your acrobatic defense.

The Assassin

The Sellsword works best if he isn't the center of attention. Let your allies engage the enemies first, and if you can sneak around and attack enemies who aren't targeting you with abilities such as Sneak Attack, Guile, Assassin's Dance, and Vicious, you'll rule the contest. When you need to inflict extra damage on tougher foes, rely on some of your poison abilities. To get out of danger, Blinding Dust temporarily stuns a single enemy and Deterring Strike sends enemies away from you and toward your allies. Now you're set up all over again for another Sneak Attack.

The Marksman

The Archer has several combat strategies to waylay enemies. He can use poison arrows to whittle down health totals. He can trigger Rapid Fire and tap into abilities like Sequential Shot, Deft Reloads, and Skilled Marksman to pelt the enemy with multiple projectiles. Explosive Missile blows away a small group of foes, and Impact gives the Archer the skill to immobilize enemies and take advantage of their hesitation. If enemies get too aggressive, Head Shot, Smoke Bomb, or Discourteous Kick will put them in their place quickly.

CAUTION

When you pick up new weapons, be careful that you don't equip an item that disrupts your stance. A bow in the hands of a Sellsword is nowhere near as deadly as in the hands of an Archer.

The Tag Team

Later in the game, Mors and Alester form a merciless team. No matter what class you pick for each, these two are your best warriors and will cleave through almost any foe in seconds. However, some class combinations are better than others. For example, if you want to benefit from ranged/melee tandem, choose Archer for Alester and Hedge Knight for Mors. Alester (and Mors's dog) can immobilize targets while Mors pounds them with his massive two-handed blows. If you want to combo in melee, Mors as a Magnar can Bleed targets with Slash and Cutthroat, and Alester as a Sellsword can finish them off with abilities that capitalize on Bleeding with Precision Strike. Mors as a Landed Knight can Taunt enemies while Alester cripples them from behind. There are countless possibilities, so experiment and be creative with powers at your disposal.

CHAPTER 1

FOR THIS NIGHT, AND ALL NIGHTS TO COME

CASTLE BLACK

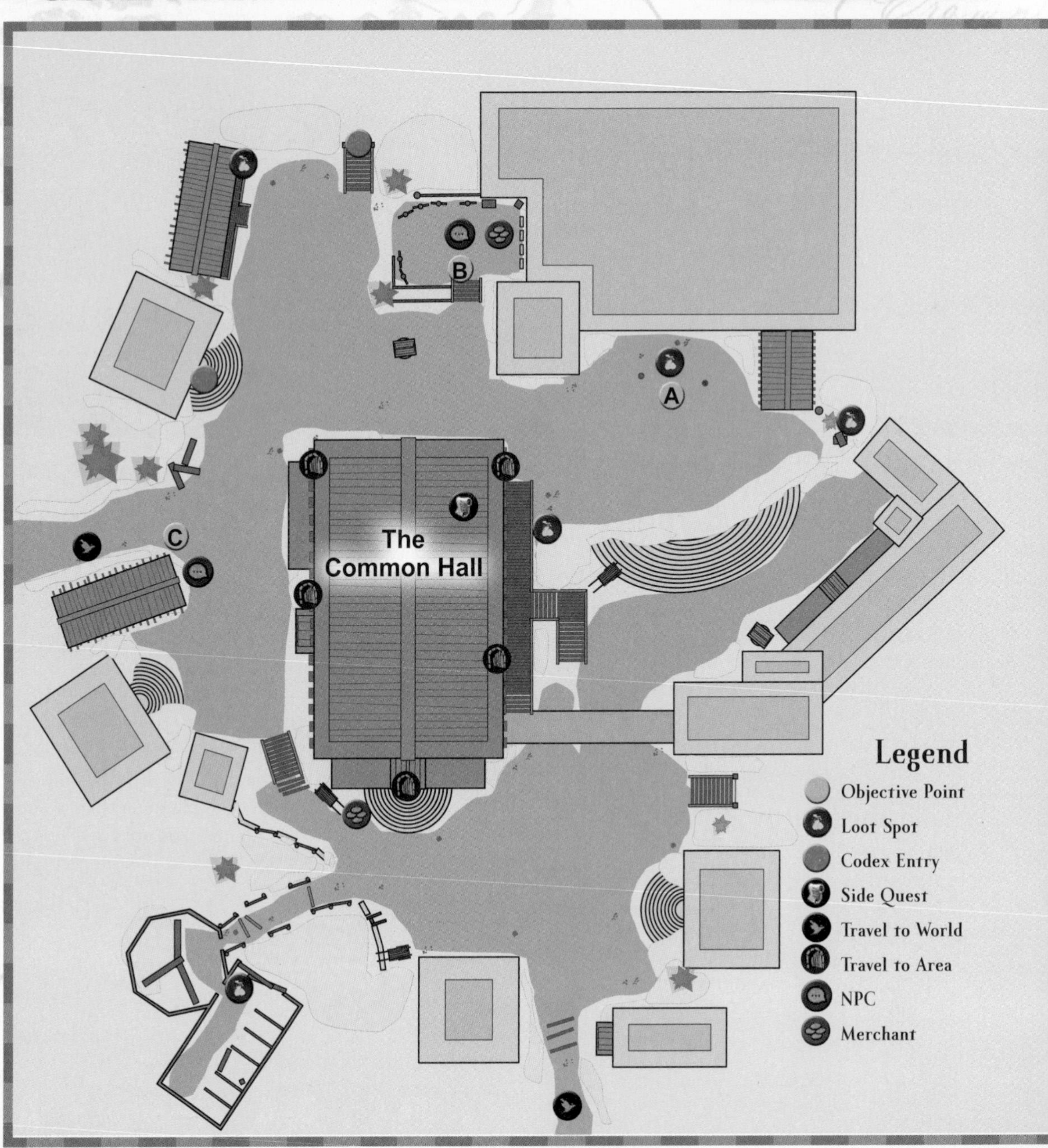

Objectives

1. Meet up with new recruits at the training ground
2. Track down Cregan at Icemark
3. Find Cregan's patrol in the ruins of Icemark before the wildlings
4. Use Cregan's keys to explore all of Icemark
5. Keep the wildlings from reopening the Great Door of Icemark
6. Lead Poddy to the lookout position
7. Set your dog on the archers
8. Battle Gorn in a duel to the death
9. For honor's sake, take down as many wildlings as you can

Quest Checklist

- Executioner's Axe (special item, objective 1)
- Castle Black Steward (merchant, objective 2)
- "The Faith of Our Ancestor" (side quest, objective 2)
- "Their Watch Is Ending" (side quest, objective 3)
- Icemark Keys (quest item, objective 4)
- Terrence Celtigar (companion, objective 4)
- Flint Axe (special item, objective 5)
- Experience Points: 1,500 (upon quest completion)

1. Meet Up with New Recruits at the Training Ground

Objective Point A

You begin the game following the story of Mors Westford, a brother of the Night's Watch who is particularly adept at hunting down enemies and cleaving skulls. As Mors, you hunt down a fellow Night's Watch brother who has deserted his post. After you successfully capture the deserter, character creation for Mors occurs (see the "Mors Westford" chapter for full details). After character creation, you return to Castle Black, the main fortress of the Night's Watch. Under Lord Commander Jeor Mormont's orders, you execute the deserter for dishonoring the brotherhood. Before you leave the area, make sure you pick up the Executioner's Axe (two-handed weapon) stuck in the nearby bloody stump.

Objective Point B

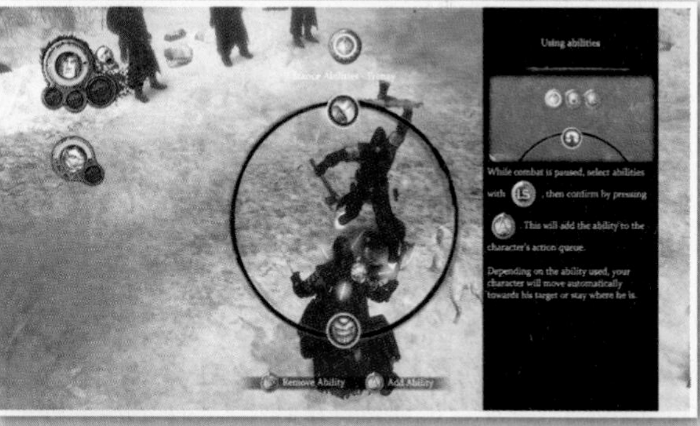

You have several young recruits in your charge, so it's off to the training ground to give them a bit of combat training. When you arrive, the combat tutorial begins (players new to the game's combat get trained while the new recruits get trained). The tutorial runs you through the basics of combat as you fight in a one-on-one battle against a single recruit and then face off against two recruits in a group battle. For the detailed ins and outs of combat, see the "Combat" section of the "The World of Westeros" chapter.

Book Watch: The Wall

The Wall is 700 feet tall and guards Westeros against the perils and horrors of the north. In the novel *A Game of Thrones*, supernatural events occur in the Haunted Forest north of Castle Black; at the same time, two members of the Night's Watch, Will and Ser Waymar Royce, come face-to-face with the Others. In the game, the Others are only rumors whispered by the new recruits of the Night's Watch, though there is frequent action against the wildlings who harass those who guard the Wall.

2. Track down Cregan at Icemark

Objective Point C

Lord Commander Mormont will interrupt the end of your skirmishes with the new recruits. Another brother of the Night's Watch, Cregan, has betrayed his vows and murdered a boy at Castle Black. Unfortunately, Cregan led a patrol to Icemark earlier in the day, so Mormont charges you with hunting down Cregan for answers. Three of the new recruits—Ronnet Hill, Terrence Celtigar, and Poddy—will accompany you to Icemark.

NOTE

Even though your three recruits journey with you to Icemark, you cannot control them. They will act on their own accord until later in Icemark when Celtigar officially joins the party.

The recruits leave to get ready for their first mission beyond Castle Black. In the meantime, you can explore the rest of the castle grounds. Visit the Castle Black steward at the training ground to buy basic weapons and sell anything you don't want to keep for the long haul. Before you leave the Castle Black steward, ensure that your weapon slots match your Stance. For example, a Hedge Knight wants a two-handed weapon for your primary slot, a Landed Knight wants a one-handed weapon and shield, and a Magnar needs two weapons.

After you leave the training ground, search for minor loot hidden around the buildings, and enter the Common Hall if you want to talk to Walder about the "The Faith of Our Ancestors" side quest. When you're ready to leave Castle Black, seek out your three recruits huddled on the outskirts of the castle and leave via the nearby exit.

TIP

Before you leave for Icemark, visit the Common Hall at the center of Castle Black. Here you can talk with some of your fellow brothers, listen to the goings-on in the castle, and pick up side quests for Mors.

Side Quest: The Faith of Our Ancestors

Enter the Common Hall at the center of Castle Black if you want to pick up "The Faith of our Ancestors" side quest. Walder waits for you up on the top level and will give you the quest if you're interested in it. Your fellow brother does restoration work on pieces of art and has done an exquisite job of beautifying one of your family heirlooms. For more details on collecting the other statues and completing the quest, see the "Side Quests" chapter at the end of the walkthrough chapters.

Icemark (Ground Floor)

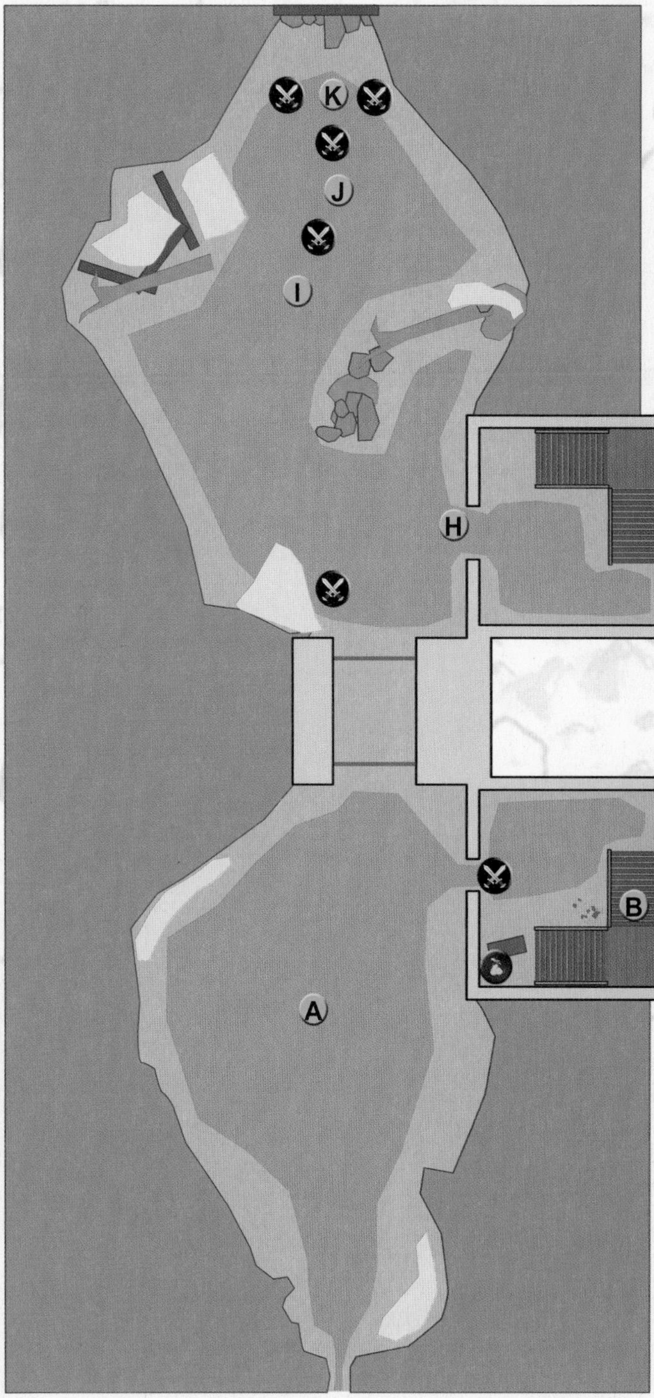

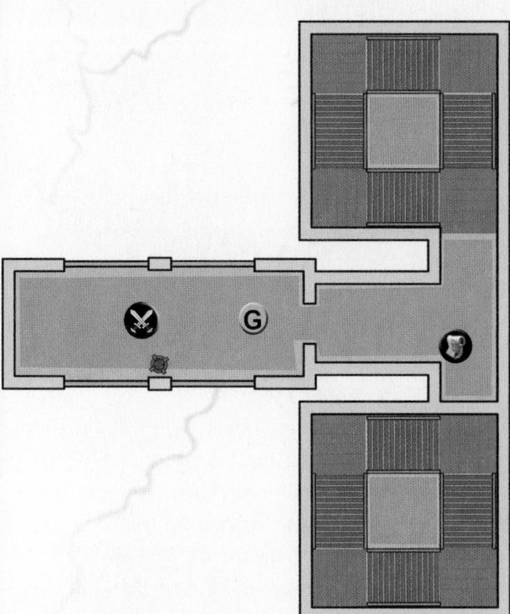

Icemark First Floor

Legend

- Objective Point
- Loot Spot
- Codex Entry
- Side Quest
- Enemy
- NPC

ICEMARK SECOND FLOOR

Legend

- Objective Point
- Loot Spot
- Codex Entry
- Side Quest
- Enemy
- NPC

3. FIND CREGAN'S PATROL IN THE RUINS OF ICEMARK BEFORE THE WILDLINGS

Objective Point A

When you reach Icemark, proceed across the icy plain. An open door to your right leads into the fort, but before you can explore much farther, a wildling charges out at you. Slow down combat and choose your abilities before the wildling reaches you. As you take the wildling on, your recruits will surround him and the battle will be over with minimum effort.

TIP

You heal back up to full health and energy after each battle. Don't hold back and conserve abilities unless you know it's going to be a long battle against multiple opponents.

Objective Point B

Climb the stairs inside the fort. More wildlings confront you on the landing above. This fight is more challenging, as it's a group battle. For maximum damage, engage the closest enemy and try to match a perforating weapon against the wildlings' medium armor. Tap into some of your special abilities to bring the first wildling down quickly while your companions deal with the second one. If you move fast enough, you can help them fell the second enemy.

Objective Point C

Head down the corridor after you slay the second set of wildlings. You'll find Cregan in the next room; alas, the wildlings have gotten to him first. He lies mortally wounded amid slain brethren. Before his dies, he warns you to leave this place before the wildlings overwhelm your small party; however, you can't leave if there's a chance of disrupting the wildlings' plans in Icemark.

Side Quest: Their Watch Is Ending

Cregan and his four men are dead. Collect the four A Ranger's Personal Belongings items around Icemark to complete the quest and prevent the wildlings from desecrating the dead. For more details on recovering the belongings and completing the quest, see the "Side Quests" chapter.

4. Use Cregan's Keys to Explore All of Icemark

Objective Point D

Take the Icemark Keys quest item from Cregan's dead body. You can also pick up a small flask, which you can fill with different substances at an alchemist to give you combat effects like healing and poison. Now it's time to explore the rest of Icemark.

CAUTION

Save here! The next battle against the wildlings will be a challenge. It's best to save your progress so you don't lose it.

Objective Point E

Open the door in the room and exit into the outdoor courtyard. One of your brothers burns on the stake in the middle of a large bonfire surrounded by wildlings. As you enter the courtyard, combat begins and you can now control both Mors and the young recruit Celtigar. There are many wildlings, so fill Mors's Action Queue with abilities before switching over to Celtigar and doing the same. If you team up on the enemy, you'll cut them down quickly enough to slay them all before they can kill Mors.

Companion Role Call: Terrence Celtigar

Stats:

- **Strength:** 6
- **Agility:** 6
- **Luck:** 6
- **Endurance:** 4
- **Intelligence:** 7

Class: Landed Knight

Stance: Defense

Abilities: Resistance, Self-Defense, Targeted Strike

Weapons of Choice: Andal Glaive (1H sword), Worn Small Wooden Shield

Description: You can control Celtigar as a member of the party in the battle with the wildlings after you find Cregan. As a Landed Knight, Celtigar uses the Defense Stance. Rely on Self-Defense as Celtigar's go-to ability: He strikes three times, each increasing in damage. If Celtigar is attacked during the barrage, he strikes for even more damage with his final attack. Celtigar's Targeted Strike ability can interrupt an enemy's action, and he deals increased damage (three times as much damage against Bleeding opponents). If the wounds start piling up on him, Resistance increases Celtigar's damage resistance by 50 percent and keeps him in the battle longer.

After the battle, take a breather and recover any spoils of war from the dead bodies. You can retrieve a Belongings quest item from the poor brother in the bonfire if you're looking to complete the "Their Watch Is Ending" side quest.

You fight two huge wildlings next. Open the door in the courtyard and prepare for major bloodshed. As the two wildlings enter the courtyard, one of them heaves an ax that catches Ronnet Hill in the forehead. He dies instantly (there's nothing you can do about this—it's part of the cutscene). The three remaining party members (plus Mors's dog) must beat the tougher wildlings. Slow combat down and use Celtigar's Targeted Strike (and possibly an Interruption ability from Mors, if he has any) to disrupt the wildlings' big attacks. So long as you don't let them gang up on Mors, you can win the battle.

When the two wildlings fall to the ground, you can torture the one who is still alive for information about his leader's plans. They plan to open the Great Door at the base of Icemark and let an army of their kindred through the Wall's defenses. Before leaving the area, grab the wildling's Flint Axe, which is probably an upgrade to your one-handed cutting weapons.

TIP

Mors gains the new trait Expeditious if you torture the fallen wildling for information.

5. Keep the Wildlings from Reopening the Great Door of Icemark

Objective Point F

Enter the door from which the two wildlings appeared and descend the stairs. Battle the wildlings you find there to continue on your mission to prevent the wildlings from opening the Great Door. This is your main objective for the rest of your adventure in Icemark, though you'll perform other combat-related tasks before the end.

TIP

If you're working on the "Their Watch Is Ending" side quest, detour down the path leading out of the courtyard before you enter the door where the two wildlings appeared. Collect belongings from another dead brother.

6. Lead Poddy to the Lookout Position

Objective Point G

As the danger increases, the cowardly Poddy begins to panic more and more. Finally, Mors has enough of it and instructs Poddy to serve as an archer to cover them from the balcony. Dispatch the two wildlings guarding the balcony and set Poddy up for your added defense.

TIP

When Mors earns Level 2, open your Character Page and immediately spend your skills on your Skinchanger talent. Once the dog's abilities are unlocked, you can now command it to aid you in combat.

7. Set Your Dog on the Archers

Objective Point H

Descend the stairs to the ground floor. Wildling guards will immediately attack as you exit the tower into the snow-covered plains in front of the Great Door. Teamed up with Celtigar, you should win over these guards without breaking much of a sweat.

Objective Point I

Continue farther out onto the plains until you trigger the wildling attack. You'll be surrounded by wildlings, so it's crucial that you work with Celtigar to beat down the enemy. During the fight, a small tutorial will pop up on enemy strength and armor types. Pay close attention to each enemy's armor type in the battle; if you can match your weapons to the correct armor (i.e., cutting for light armor, perforating for medium armor, blunt for heavy armor), you will increase your damage per strike, which could prove the difference against so many enemies.

After you defeat the wildlings at the Great Door, enemy arrows will begin pelting you from above. Mors quickly realizes that something has happened to Poddy and you no longer have ranged support from above. Command the dog to attack the archers so that you can concentrate on the major battle ahead.

8. Battle Gorn in a Duel to the Death

Objective Point J

In his overconfidence, Gorn challenges you to a duel to the death. You are about evenly matched with Gorn; however, if you use your Stance abilities wisely, you can prove victorious. Interrupt his big attacks if you can, and any additional damage you can do (such as Bleeding) will drop his health total faster than his blows can drop yours.

Even as you dispatch the initial wildlings at the Great Door, the wildling leader, Gorn, springs an ambush on you. He has you hopelessly surrounded and orders his archers to kill Celtigar. There is nothing you can do as Celtigar drops to the ground, several arrows through his chest.

9. For Honor's Sake, Take Down as Many Wildlings as You Can

Objective Point K

Unfortunately, defeating Gorn doesn't get you out of the jam. The remaining wildlings fall on you to avenge their leader. There are simply too many of them. You decide to take down as many as you can before dying an honorable death.

Just as the end draws near and your wounds bring you to the brink of unconsciousness, a band of Night's Watch archers arrives atop the fortress. They rain arrows down on your foes as you black out and the cold claims you.

Chapter 2

For All the Days Gone By

Quest Checklist

- Tyrek (NPC, objective 1)
- Riverspring Steward (merchant, objective 4)
- Harwyn (NPC, objective 4)
- Ryman Sarwyck (companion, objective 5)
- Riverspring Potions Merchant (merchant, objective 5)
- Riverspring Blacksmith (merchant, objective 5)
- Riverspring Armor Merchant (merchant, objective 5)
- The Smith (side quest item, objective 5)
- Rapier (special item, objective 5)
- Experience Points: 1,825 (upon quest completion)

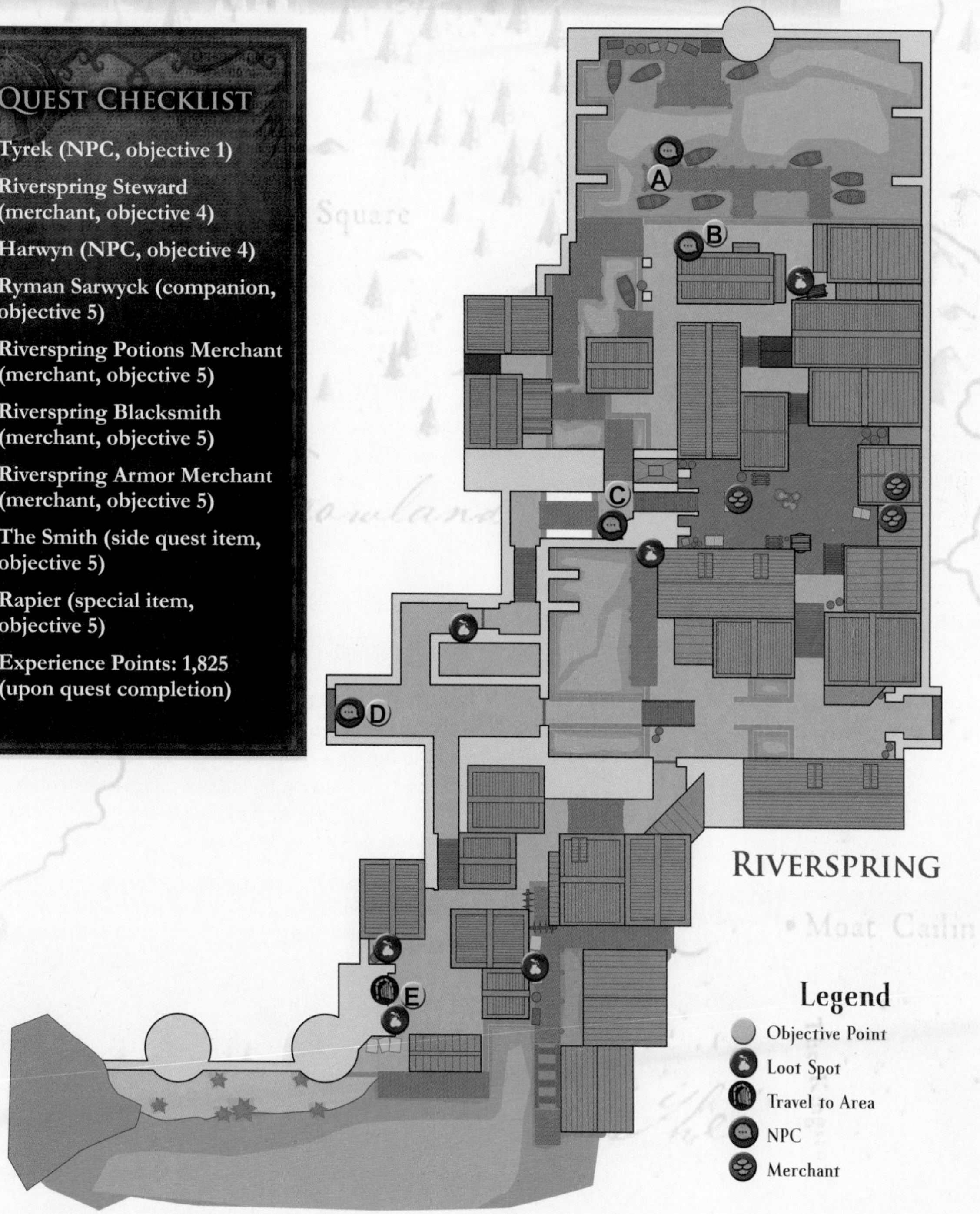

Square

A
B
C
D
E

RIVERSPRING

Moat Cailin

Legend

- Objective Point
- Loot Spot
- Travel to Area
- NPC
- Merchant

Objectives

1. Go to Riverspring Castle to attend your father's wake
2. Follow Maester Harwyn to Riverspring godswood
3. Pay homage to your father, Lord Raynald Sarwyck
4. Find Harwyn to discuss your lands' troubles
5. Walk the streets of Riverspring and try to ease the situation
6. Meet Harwyn inside Riverspring Castle and talk to him about your brother Gawen
7. Return to your chambers and make contact with your temple

1. Go to Riverspring Castle to Attend Your Father's Wake

Objective Point A

In Chapter 2, you're introduced to Alester Sarwyck, eldest son of Lord Raynald Sarwyck. Alester has returned to his home after a 15-year absence at the request of his old maester Harwyn, who has asked Alester to attend his father's funeral. As the ferryman, Victor, guides you into the city of Riverspring, you take on the role of Alester Sarwyck as he journeys back into the problems and power struggles of his family's kingdom.

Victor drops you off at the docks. He tells you of the hard times that have befallen Riverspring since your disappearance 15 years ago. Ultimately, you need to find the castle gate, but you have some important stops along the way.

Objective Point B

Look for an animated speaker on the far side of the docks. The rabble-rouser Tyrek has the locals in an uproar about their unfair treatment, and he rallies for a bloody revolt. You can speak to them and try to calm Tyrek down, but he won't listen to your appeals to decency. However, you'll meet him later during the riots, so now you know who you're dealing with.

Objective Point C

Continue walking toward the southwest part of the city. In the middle of the map, the Riverspring armor merchant will start up a conversation as you pass by. He explains the differences among the main weapon types: cutting (best against light armor), perforating (best against medium armor), and blunt (best against heavy armor).

Objective Point D

The castle gates are in the map's far southwest portion. When you arrive, you can't get in; the city guard's orders are to keep everyone out during the funeral. You ask for Maester Harwyn, but before the guards can summon him, Ryman Sarwyck, captain of the guard, arrives. Ryman immediately recognizes you, but he isn't happy to see you. Ryman feels you abandoned your family and so you have no claim to paying respects.

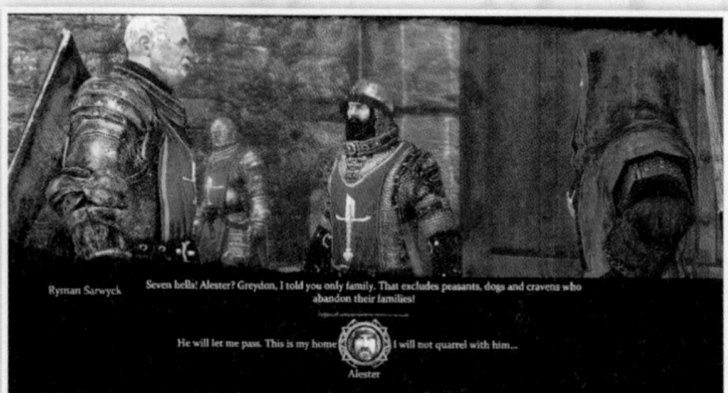

When Ryman insults you, the dialogue choice pops up with, "He will let me pass. This is my home" or "I will not quarrel with him..." If you choose the first option, it will come to blows. Ryman will draw his weapon and you'll battle until Maester Harwyn arrives and breaks up the fight. Neither can actually die in the fight; Harwyn won't let it go that far. If you choose the second option, Ryman is still angry, but he'll let you in without a fight.

Book Watch: Red Priest

Alester left Westeros 15 years ago to reinvent himself and found R'hllor, his one true god. The red priests who worship R'hllor are a rare sight in Westeros, though they have formed a dominant religion across the sea. In *A Game of Thrones*, we first hear about the red priests when we meet Daenerys and Viserys Targaryen in the Free Cities. As Daenerys gazes out her window, she hears the red priests singing as they light their night fires and perform their rituals.

Objective Point E

Maester Harwyn leads you to the funeral at the godswood. Follow along and listen to him as he updates you on the current state of affairs.

2. Follow Maester Harwyn to Riverspring Godswood

Riverspring Godswood

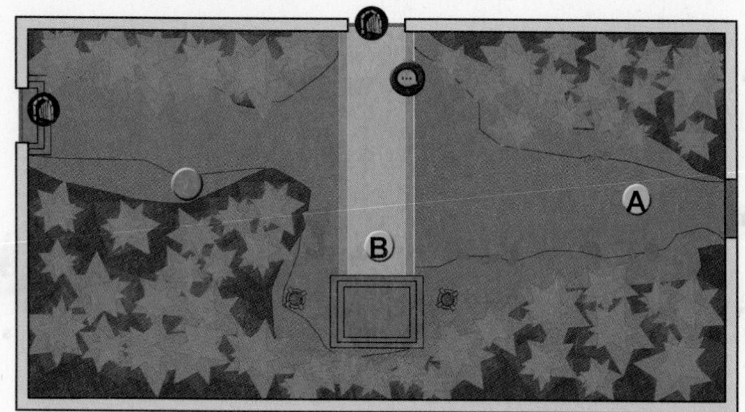

3. Pay Homage to Your Father, Lord Raynald Sarwyck

Objective Point A

You enter the godswood in the middle of your father's funeral. As you gaze on the ceremony from afar, your sister Lady Elyana Sarwyck approaches. She mistakes you for a stranger, and when you reveal yourself as her long-lost brother, she angrily dismisses you to pay your respects to your father and says that you'll talk later.

Objective Point B

Walk up to the dais when you are ready. You offend some when you perform the "last kiss," a respectful tribute that the priests of R'hllor use. You can even get into a philosophical discussion about it with Ravella near the door before you leave (this gives you the Septons/Septas Codex entry). There's also a gate to the Tunnels Under Riverspring off to the side, but you can't enter until you have the keys to the castle.

NOTE

Notice the man in the green robes as you climb toward your father's coffin. He'll be in the crowd intently watching you later. This is Lord Harlton of Castlewood, and he will play an important role in the chapters to come.

Courtyard of Riverspring Castle

A
B
C

Legend

- Objective Point
- Loot Spot
- Travel to Area
- NPC
- Merchant

4. Find Harwyn to Discuss Your Lands' Troubles

Objective Point A

Enter the courtyard and look for Harwyn ahead. There are a few talking crowds in the courtyard after the funeral, but none of their conversations concern you.

Objective Point B

Before you visit Harwyn, stop in at the Riverspring steward. He's stocked up with standard melee and ranged weapons if you need anything. If you picked up anything in the streets of Riverspring that you don't want to use in combat, you can sell it here.

Objective Point C

Speak with Harwyn. You talk about your sister Elyana and how you should proceed regarding her impending marriage to your half brother, Valarr. Harwyn also tells you that he believes your father was murdered with an almost undetectable poison. Before you can continue the conversation, however, the guards burst in and report that the city has erupted in rioting.

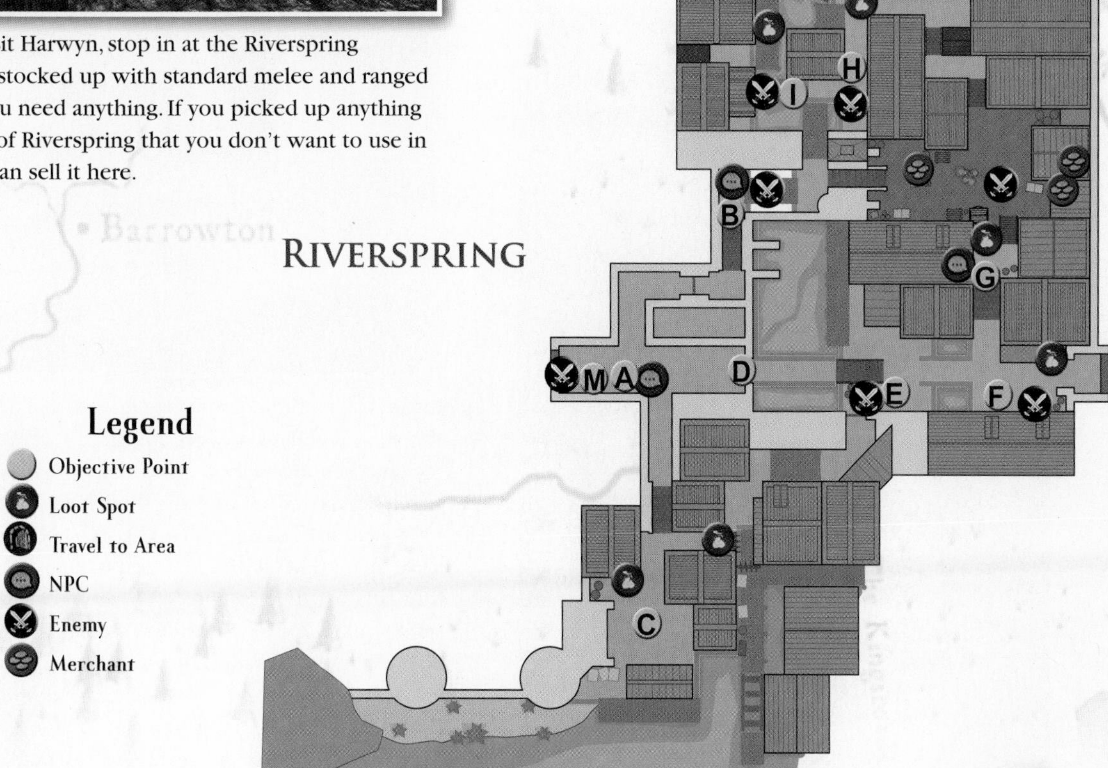

5. Walk the Streets of Riverspring and Try to Ease the Situation

Objective Point A

You need to talk with Ryman Sarwyck first. He's just outside the castle gate at the first intersection. You tell him you want to accompany his patrol as they investigate the riots. Throughout the city, you'll have opportunities to choose arms or diplomacy to quiet the conflicts. By the end of the riots, the people, nobles, and city guard will respond to your actions and voice their opinions of you as a potential ruler.

Companion Role Call: Ryman Sarwyck

Stats:

- Strength: 5
- Agility: 4
- Luck: 4
- Endurance: 6
- Intelligence: 4

Class: Landed Knight

Stance: Defense

Abilities: Daze Strike, Quick Fix, Taunt

Weapons of Choice: Battle Mace (1H), Sarwyck Shield

Description: Ryman joins you during your first fight in Riverspring. He's a tough old brawler with a sword and shield; rely on him to bear the brunt of the attacks as you pick off enemies around him. Ryman can Taunt enemies away from Alester, and if he gets in trouble, Quick Fix gives him a health boost to stay in the battle. His patented attack is Daze Strike, which doesn't deal that much damage but does interrupt opponents' actions and stun them.

Objective Point B

Before you go through the gate into the main streets, you should deal with two closer encounters. To the north, seek out Benfrey, a city guard who has townsfolk barricaded behind a door. He tells you that the mob is ready for violence, and you're given two dialogue choices: "It's safer to leave them there" or "It's inhuman to keep them locked up." If you choose the first choice, the mob remains contained and harmless. If you go with the second choice to open the door, the mob pours out. They won't listen to reason, and you have a big battle on your hands. It's nothing you and Ryman can't handle, and if you want a little extra experience, cut them down; however, keep in mind that it will affect how the people think of you when the rioting ends.

Choices in Riverspring

The many choices you can make as you roam the streets of Riverspring will influence what happens in the climactic final encounter. You will either fight Tyrek alone, fight Tyrek with friends, or not fight Tyrek at all based on the following actions:

Side with the nobles more than any other faction (fight Tyrek with friends)

- **Pay the ransom at the port**
- **Dole out harsh judgment during the riots**
- **Fight the rebels in the marketplace**

If you side with the nobles, a special merchant linked to the nobles appears in Riverspring near the docks in Chapter 4.

Side with the peasants more than any other faction (avoid fight with Tyrek)

- **Ask the hostages to pay themselves**
- **Be kind during the judgement**
- **Convince the rebels to leave the marketplace with food**

If you side with the peasants, a special merchant linked to the average townsfolk appears in Riverspring in the marketplace in Chapter 4.

Side with the guards more than any other faction (fight Tyrek alone)

- **Kill the hostage-takers at the port**
- **Be fair during the judgement**
- **Threaten the rebels in the marketplace with your crossbowmen**

If you side with the guards, a special merchant linked to the guards appears in Riverspring in the castle's courtyard in Chapter 4.

Objective Point C

Next, take care of the encounter south of the main gate. The city guards have rounded up four suspects who they believe should be executed for crimes during the rioting. You intervene before the executions start, and you can question each villager and guard pair to determine the real story in each case.

Speak with Alyn first. He's accused of killing a man in the port during the riots. Alyn knew that the guard was killed with an axe, but he claims to not have been there. You can deduce that he must be guilty, as he would not know how the guard died if he was not present. Sentence him to the dungeons or have him executed.

Next, question Little Leo. He was seen standing over the body of a dead guard. When you interrogate the guard further, you learn that there was dried blood on Little Leo's knife. There would be fresh blood on the knife if he had just committed murder, so the best course is to free him.

Third in line is Brusco. He's a known criminal in the port and has been arrested before for misdeeds. This time it appears as if he wasn't involved in the rioting, but the guards have brought him in under that pretext to deal with his criminal activities. You have a choice: execute him for his past sins, throw him in the dungeons to avoid more unruliness in the future, or let him go free.

Finally, question Mellara. The guard accuses her of burning down his house during the riot; however, when you get to the bottom of the story, the guard raped Mellara's sister in the confusion. You should have the guard arrested and let the woman go.

TIP

If you avoid jailing anyone during the riots, townsfolk with give you gifts later as you walk the streets of Riverspring. If you jail townsfolk, you can speak with them in the Riverspring jail cells and ask them later to fight with you in Chapter 12.

Objective Point D

Travel to the main gate. The rioters surround the gate on the far side and complain about starvation in the streets. You can tax the nobles to pay for more food (making the nobles unhappy), threaten them with force (making the townsfolk unhappy), or distribute the castle's extra food (making the townsfolk happy).

CAUTION

If you hand out food at the gate or during negotiations with the rebels in the marketplace, you will not receive the Tytos Lannister's Shield in Chapter 9 when you return to Riverspring.

No matter what you choose, the mob will disburse and you can continue deeper into the city.

Encounters are marked on your Riverspring map. Word balloons are optional encounters; those marked with a scroll are mandatory to progress the story line.

Objective Point E

To the right as you exit the bridge after the main gate, a group of armed townsfolk are attacking a city guard. As soon as you approach, they turn and attack you. Have Ryman use Taunt to draw their attention while you swiftly cut down a couple of them and make it a more even fight. With minimal weapons and armor, they shouldn't prove too difficult.

Objective Point F

In the next courtyard, more rioters attack the city guard. Go with a similar attack pattern: Ryman takes on the largest group with Taunt and Daze Strike, while you pick off any stragglers with your better abilities. Since these battles are relatively small and short, don't worry so much about conserving energy—take down your targets quickly so they can't gang up on you.

When you drop the final enemy, you'll be given a choice to show mercy or not to their leader, Big Bludgeon. If you show mercy, your approval with the townsfolk will increase.

Objective Point G

As you approach the market square, a city guard named Hother hides in an alcove to the left of the stairs. He explains that there is a huge mob in the market square below, and the guards with their crossbows would be no match for charging pitchforks, so they were forced into hiding. You order the guards to the rooftops with a threat of force if needed.

Two sides argue in the market square whether to riot or not. You step into the middle of the heated discussion and have three choices: intimidate them with the crossbowmen, suppress them with your melee weapons, or offer them food. If you want to avoid combat, offering food is your best option. You can give them the food from the castle, and then the townsfolk will ask you to swear by the Seven Gods on it. This brings up a dialogue choice: "They are not my gods," "I swear by R'hllor," or "Well, if that's what he wants to hear..." If you choose either of the latter choices, you will avoid combat and disburse the mob. If you choose the first option, the mob attacks.

Prepare for a potentially deadly situation if you incite combat. Per standard procedure, Ryman should engage the largest group, but he won't last long without serious

help. Prioritize wounded enemies to take them quicker and remove their attacks from the equation. If Ryman is failing, take control and immediately activate Quick Fix for a health boost. Rely on your stuns, knockdowns, and immobilize effects to even the odds. After a long fight, collect any loot from the bodies. Before you leave the market square, check out all the merchants' wares. If you have enough coin, you might want a weapon or armor upgrade. Later, you'll likely want to return to stock up on flasks and potion supplies for the difficult journey ahead.

TIP

The Riverspring armor merchant sells the Smith statuette. It's too expensive for you to buy now, but return later when you can afford it and collect the statue as one of the many you need to fulfill "The Faith of Our Ancestors" side quest.

Objective Point H

You witness a mugging in progress here. Speak with the thug Habert and you can pacify the situation with your faith and understanding.

Objective Point I

Continue west to the next encounter. More rioters have attacked the city guard, and only one is left. Intervene to save the guard and take down the rioters. After the battle, search the bodies for loot, including a Rapier, which should be an upgrade to your existing one-handed weapon.

Objective Point J

Head to the docks where more violence is occurring. It's a smaller battle, though these thugs are a little better armed. After the fight, you can choose to show mercy on the leader and improve your standings with the townsfolk.

Objective Point K

You meet up with a man here who has lost his family in the rioting. He's contemplating suicide. If you talk to him about R'hllor, you give him hope. He decides not to jump and considers religion as an answer to his despair. He also becomes a red priest merchant in Riverspring Godswood after the chapter 4.

Objective Point L

Head east along the docks. A group of rioters threatens the nobles who attended your father's funeral. You can either try to calm them down or outright attack them. If you negotiate, you can let them take the nobles' jewels or ask Ryman to give them his coin pouch. Both will bribe the rioters to release the prisoners; otherwise, you have another large-scale battle on your hands.

CAUTION

If you refuse to negotiate with the hostage-takers, Rosamund Peckledon dies. When you arrive at the Red Keep, Garrison Moreland will insult you rather than herald your praises.

Objective Point M

Return to the castle gates. Tyrek wishes to speak with you about his revolt. You know from your past dealings with the man that he's dead set on leading the townsfolk against the current order. No matter your words of wisdom, violence is inevitable.

To prove your honor, you order Ryman to stand aside and you battle Tyrek and his lackeys yourself. Stun or immobilize as often as possible to reduce incoming attacks, and switch to cutting weapons to maximize your damage against their light armor. One has no armor, so target him first and bring him down quickly. Switch to the other lackey and drop him before they can team up on you too badly. Leave Tyrek for last and throw your best abilities at him. You may need to execute a Recovery move in the middle to regain energy for your more potent abilities, which is fine so long as you don't have multiple foes slashing away at you.

With some superior tactics, you'll triumph and bring Tyrek to his knees. Kill him here to get some light armored gloves (your teammates are healed when you dodge an attack). Send him to jail and you'll get a trinket during chapter 12 (you inflict more damage with low health). Finally, the riot is quelled and you can return to the castle to speak with Harwyn about your brother.

Riverspring Castle First Floor

Legend

- Objective Point
- Loot Spot
- Codex Entry
- Side Quest
- Enemy
- NPC

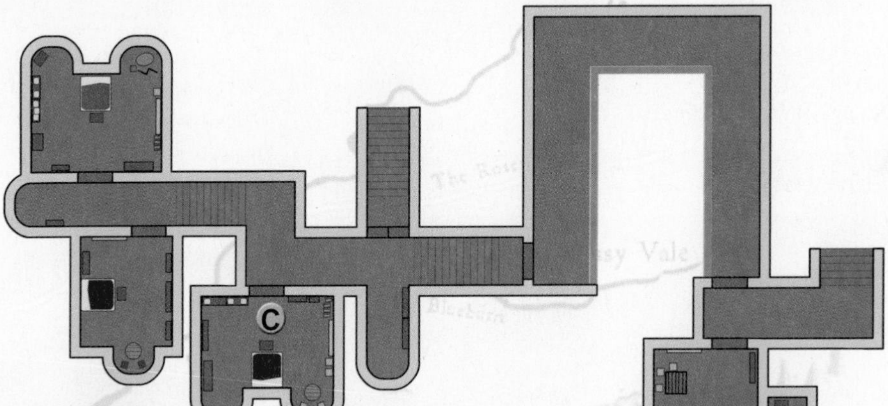

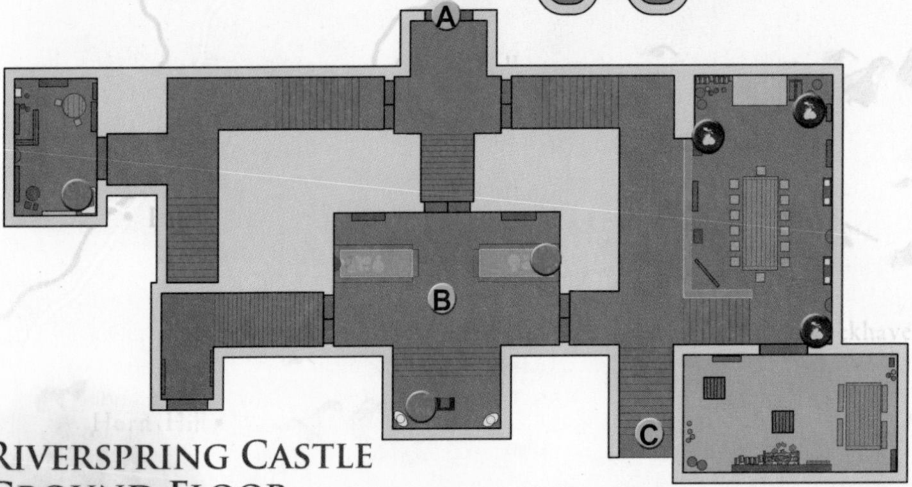

Riverspring Castle Ground Floor

6. Meet Harwyn inside Riverspring Castle and Talk to Him about Your Brother Gawen

Objective Point A

Elyana intercepts you at the entrance to the castle and voices her concerns about your current course of action. You reassure her that your goals are the same and that you intend to speak with Queen Cersei Lannister to get Riverspring back in the good graces of the ruling family.

Objective Point B

Harwyn waits for you in the castle throne room. You talk of your little brother's mysterious disappearance and his possible involvement in your father's death. Harwyn mentions that Gawen used to frequent King's Landing often, so that's your next destination.

7. Return to Your Chambers and Make Contact with Your Temple

Objective Point C

Head to your bedchamber upstairs in the castle. You use the fireplace fire to contact your fellow red priest Betharios. You update him on happenings and reassure him that you will not be leaving the order. Instead, you will seize your kingdom back and leverage your position as ruler of Riverspring to spread the word of R'hllor.

In a symbolic gesture, you put away your red robes and don armor befitting a lord of Riverspring. Preparations are made for your journey to King's Landing where you have an audience with the queen and hope to find clues to the whereabouts of your missing brother.

CHAPTER 3

BETWEEN A HUNTER AND HIS PREY

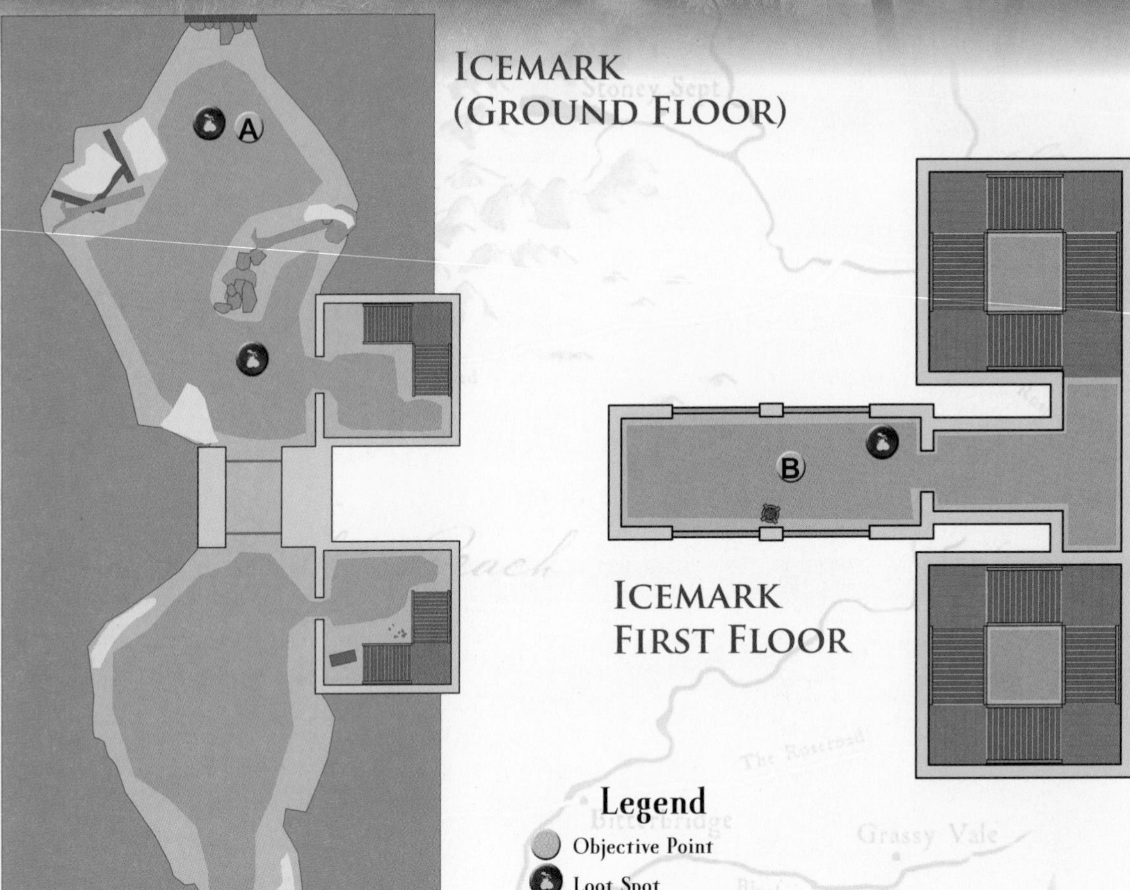

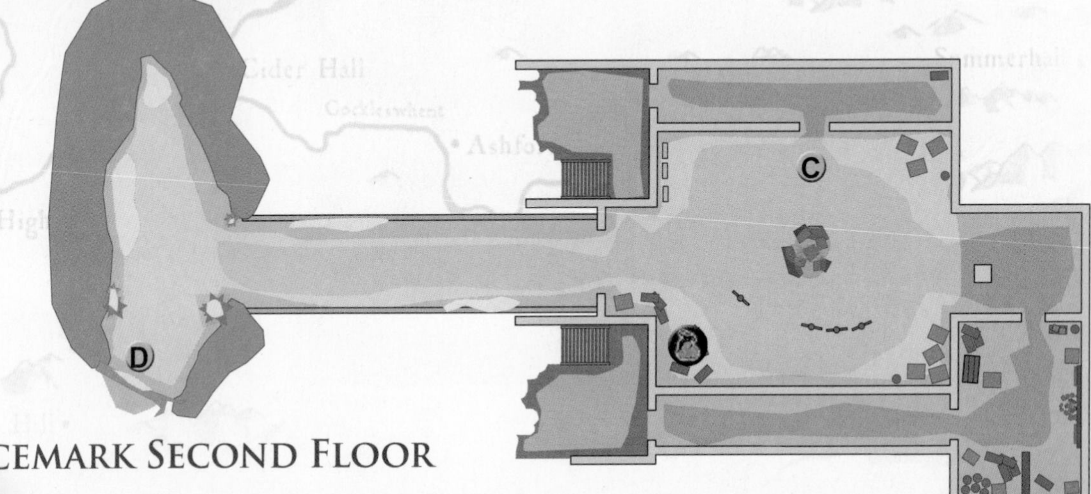

Objectives

1. Return to the balcony to find out what happened to Poddy
2. Track down Poddy
3. Get rid of Poddy
4. Return to Castle Black to give your report to Lord Commander Mormont
5. Meet Jon Arryn's emissary, Ser Godric Donnerly

Quest Checklist

- Gorn's Armor (special item, objective 1)
- Gorn's Axe (special item, objective 1)
- "Treasure Hunt" (side quest, objective 2)
- Lord Commander Mormont (NPC, objective 4)
- Experience Points: 2,000 (upon quest completion)

1. Return to the Balcony to Find Out What Happened to Poddy

Objective Point A

When last you played Mors, you had defeated Gorn as a seemingly endless horde of wildings assaulted you. Unconsciousness overtook you even as you thought you spied Night's Watch brothers arriving to your rescue. As you regain consciousness, Qhorin Halfhand, the leader of your Shadow Tower brothers, fills you in on recent events. They arrived just in time to save you, but there is no sign of Poddy, the young recruit you left on the balcony to cover you during the battle with Gorn's wildlings.

Objective Point B

You thank Qhorin and then must retrace your steps back up to the balcony where you last saw Poddy. Sweep the battlefield for loot, and check Gorn's corpse for two special items: Gorn's Armor and Gorn's Axe (two-handed weapon).

Up on the balcony, look for the bow lying on the floor. Poddy must have dropped his bow and abandoned his post, and since there is no blood around the area, he wasn't attacked by Gorn's wildlings here. He may have fled, so you'll have to track Poddy down.

Switch to Mors's dog and sniff around the area. Once you catch hold of Poddy's scent, you'll see whiffs of yellow mist (the scent trail) leading from his bow back up the stairs. Follow the trail to the outside courtyard with the bonfire.

Objective Point C

In the courtyard, scent trails will start mixing. Yellow represents the main smell you are tracking. White stands for any other quest smells that may exist in the area. Blue scents are exploration smells that lead to hidden items. Stay on the yellow trail if you want to find Poddy.

TIP

Whenever you meet up with a blue scent trail, it means a hidden item is close by. Take a quick detour to add more loot to your inventory.

Objective Point D

Follow Poddy's scent trail out the western exit and down the slope. Dog picks up Poddy's footprint on the edge of the Gift. When he calls Mors to investigate, you see that Poddy's footprints are the only ones in the area—there are no wildling prints—which means he fled on his own and is a deserter.

THE GIFT

Legend

- Objective Point
- Secret Treasure (Dog)
- Side Quest
- Enemy

2. TRACK DOWN PODDY

Objective Point A

You enter the Gift in search of Poddy. The snow-covered forest is a maze, so you'll need to rely on your dog's tracking ability to follow Poddy's scent trail and navigate the twists and turns.

Objective Point B

A boy paces in front of you as you pass the first bridge. He says his family has a campfire nearby and that he hasn't seen Poddy. You advise him to return to his family because of the dangers lurking in the forest.

Objective Point C

After speaking with the boy, you come to an intersection. Take the left path, and a short distance later, you'll see the boy's family's campsite. The boy's father, Ondrew, says that they've seen Poddy pass through here. He asks one of the family to guide you to the spot where they spied Poddy.

Objective Point D

Alas, the family isn't anything more than a band of thieves, and they lead you into an ambush. They ask you to hand over all your valuables; you refuse. No matter what you say, combat ensues.

> **TIP**
>
> If you don't speak to the men next to the campfire and you stay off the main path through the forest, you can avoid the ambush. However, even if you don't speak with the men but use the main path on your hunt for Poddy or on your return, you'll still get ambushed.

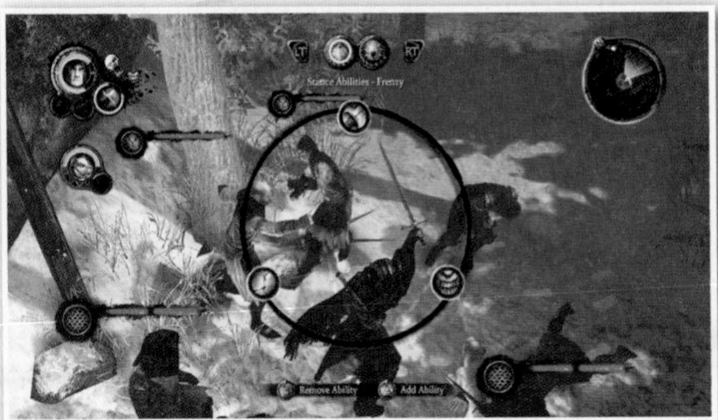

Three of the thugs wear no armor; two wear medium armor. Target the ones with no armor first. Order your dog to assault one of the thugs wearing medium armor to keep him off your back. Cut through the enemies without armor as quickly as possible to reduce the number of attacks against you; abilities that hit multiple foes are powerful at the start since you're surrounded.

When they all lie on the ground, the leader Cley will beg for his life. He tells you that their band has hidden two piles of coins. You can ignore his babbling and kill him, or let him talk before putting him out of his misery. If you let him talk, he gives you the side quest "Treasure Hunt."

Side Quest: Treasure Hunt

Both parts of the "Treasure Hunt" side quest are hidden in the Gift. You might want to set time aside on your main quest to complete this side quest and earn some good coin to upgrade your equipment. The first treasure stash is hidden through some brush, and the second is hidden on the hill with the hollow tree (points marked on the map). Dog must sniff these out, so switch to tracking mode and smell out the blue trails as they lead to each stash. For more details on the treasure stashes, see the "Side Quest" chapter.

Objective Point E

Pick up Poddy's scent again and follow it to the map's southeast section. You'll reach a point where the scent trail goes under a fallen tree. Dog can crawl under this obstacle, but Mors is stuck on the other side. You will have to rely on Dog from now on.

You cannot bring Mors past this point! Dog has to hunt Poddy the remainder of the way alone.

3. Get rid of Poddy

Objective Point F

Sneak through the brush with Dog and creep up on Poddy. You see him attacking a woman, and you have no choice but to attack without Mors. With Dog in assassination mode, go for Poddy's throat and don't give up until he lies dead on the ground. The woman escapes, and Mors finally finds a way around the fallen tree to join up with his dog over Poddy's dead body.

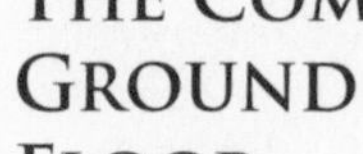

The Common Hall Ground Floor

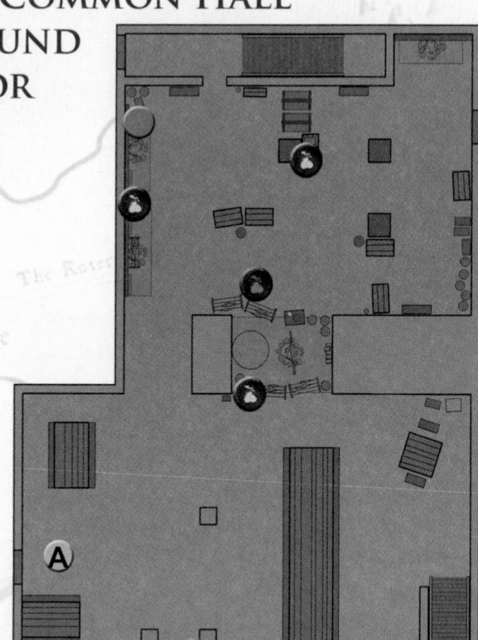

The Common Hall (Castle Black) Second Floor

The Common Hall First Floor

Legend

- Objective Point
- Loot Spot
- Secret Treasure (Alester)
- Codex Entry
- Side Quest
- NPC
- Merchant

4. Return to Castle Black to Give Your Report to Lord Commander Mormont

Objective Point A

After dispatching Poddy, retrace your steps through the Gift and return to Castle Black. Enter the Common Hall in the center of the fortress to find Jeor Mormont. Visit all the merchants in and around the Common Hall to sell unwanted items and upgrade your gear.

Objective Point B

Jeor Mormont waits for you on the top floor of the Common Hall. You discuss the events at Icemark, and you tell him of Poddy's desertion. The Lord Commander also hands you a letter from Jon Arryn, the King's Hand, which has been specially delivered to Castle Black for you. It asks you to protect a young woman and reveals her place of hiding in a riddle that only you can answer. You and Jon were friends in the past, and you use that knowledge to figure out where the young woman is hiding: Mole's Town.

Book Watch: Jon Arryn

In the *A Game of Thrones* novel, Jon Arryn dies early in the story's events. Arryn's passing has a major effect on the game—it is Jon Arryn's letter that compels Mors to accept the quest to protect the mysterious woman Jeyne. Jon's death also had a major effect on the events in the novel, as his friend Eddard Stark then became the King's Hand. We can infer that Mors Westford and Eddard Stark likely knew each other at one point during the great war 15 years ago.

5. Meet Jon Arryn's Emissary, Ser Godric Donnerly

Objective Point C

Mormont asks you to see Ser Godric Donnerly, the man in Jon Arryn's service who personally delivered the letter. He waits for you on the ground floor. Before you leave the top floor, check the table behind Mormont for the King's Hand Codex entry.

Downstairs, speak with Ser Godric. He talks a little about his mission to the north, and in the middle of the conversation, you can get into a heated debate with his lieutenant Jared about an altercation that occurred during the Baratheon Rebellion. You agree to accompany Ser Godric to Mole's Town to find this woman. Unfortunately, the Lord Commander interrupts with grim tidings: A raven has just flown in from King's Landing with a message that Jon Arryn, the King's Hand, is dead. The world has become a darker place.

Chapter 4

The Lion's Will

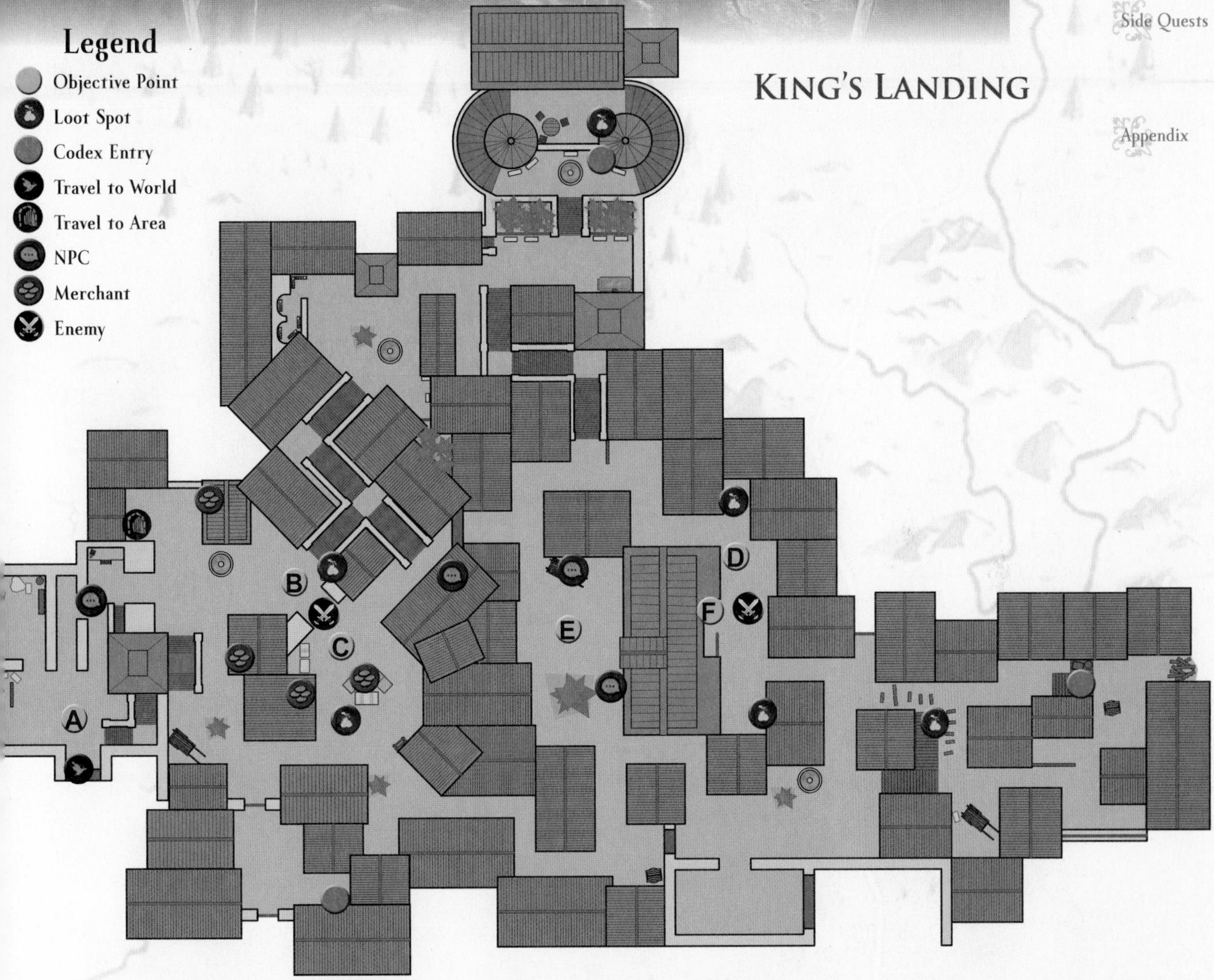

King's Landing

Legend

- Objective Point
- Loot Spot
- Codex Entry
- Travel to World
- Travel to Area
- NPC
- Merchant
- Enemy

A
B
C
D
E
F

Moat Cailin

Objectives

1. Go to the Sarwyck Manse to learn more about the fate of your brother, Gawen
2. Find a way into the Sarwyck Manse to begin your investigation
3. Search the Sarwyck Manse for clues on what happened to Gawen
4. Ask Falena what she knows of your brother
5. Meet in the Red Keep to follow Gawen's tracks
6. Escape from the Red Keep's dungeons
7. Use the gift of sight given to you by R'hllor to locate a secret passage
8. Explore the labyrinth of Maegor's Holdfast to meet Varys
9. Plead your case to Queen Cersei
10. Meet in the throne room's antechamber to await the queen's pleasure

Quest Checklist

- Old Ren (NPC, objective 1)
- King's Landing Tanner (merchant, objective 1)
- King's Landing Armor Merchant (merchant, objective 1)
- King's Landing Blacksmith (merchant, objective 1)
- King's Landing Potions Merchant (merchant, objective 1)
- Letter from Gawen (quest item, objective 3)
- Letter from Falena (quest item, objective 3)
- Sarwyck Giltwaters (special item, objective 4)
- Personal Belongings (special items, objective 6)
- Key to the Red Keep's Cells (quest item, objective 6)
- Experience Points: 1,260 (upon quest completion)

1. Go to the Sarwyck Manse to Learn More About the Fate of Your Brother, Gawen

Objective Point A

You arrive at King's Landing looking for clues regarding your brother Gawen's disappearance. The beggar Old Ren stands in the doorway directly in front of you. He tells you that there are rumors that your brother is back in town. You flip him a coin after the conversation, thinking it's the last you'll see of him, but it's not.

Objective Point B

When you pass under the arch leading toward the market square, Old Ren appears again. He guides a group of thugs called the Reapers to you to collect a hefty reward. The Gold Cloaks, the city's guards, have a reward out for the capture of Gawen Sarwyck, reputed kinslayer. The leader of the Reapers, Axe, believes he can get you to tell him where your brother is hiding out. You can try to bribe or talk your way out of a fight, or you can draw your weapon and take them on.

There are four of the Reapers: two in no armor, one in light armor, and Axe in medium armor. Stun or immobilize as many as possible as you pick away at the Reapers without armor first. As the odds even out, cut down the one in light armor and leave Axe for last. When he falls, the Gold Cloaks arrive; Axe escapes in the confusion, and you're left to explain why a battle just erupted in the streets.

Objective Point C

Proceed to the market square. Visit each of the merchants and check out his wares: armor, weapons, and potion supplies. You don't have much money yet, so mark what you'd like for the future and return the next time you have the coin and the minutes to spare.

Objective Point D

Continue toward the Sarwyck Manse. You'll eventually see two green-garbed cutpurses waiting on either side of the street. It's an ambush; as soon as you cross in front of them, two other cutpurses join them and they attack. Three wear no armor; one has light armor. Switch to cutting weapons and have at them. They can prove a challenge, but if you can stun or immobilize multiple foes so they can't surround you, the odds improve and you can pick them off one by one with your better abilities.

Tip

Remember where you defeated green-garbed cutpurses. After your conversation with Valarr, return to that spot to find the secret entrance into Sarwyck Manse.

Objective Point E

A crowd gathers outside Sarwyck Manse. Valarr and his men are searching for Gawen and drag all the Sarwyck Manse servants outside to question them. No one knows where Gawen is, but that doesn't stop Valarr from brutalizing the servants.

You confront Valarr and he takes pleasure in torturing you about Gawen and the fact that the queen personally requested him to hunt down your brother. Valarr admits that Gawen could be considered the legitimate heir to the Riverspring throne, but once he's lost his head, he won't bother Valarr again. You threaten to take back Riverspring despite Valarr's claims to the contrary. To spite your search, Valarr orders the Manse sealed until further notice. You'll have to find a secret way in.

2. Find a Way into the Sarwyck Manse to Begin Your Investigation

Objective Point F

Speak to Hubb in front of Sarwyck Manse and convince him to show you the secret way into your family home. Return to where you fought the green-garbed cutpurses and enter the red rose garden. Look to the right and you'll spot a trapdoor that leads into the cellar of Sarwyck Manse.

Sarwyck Manse

A

B

C

D

Legend

- Objective Point
- Loot Spot
- Codex Entry
- Primary Quest
- Enemy

3. Search the Sarwyck Manse for Clues on What Happened to Gawen

Objective Point A

You enter the Manse in a quiet and dark basement. No one is around. Feel free to search the areas for valuables left by the staff or Sarwyck family.

Objective Point B

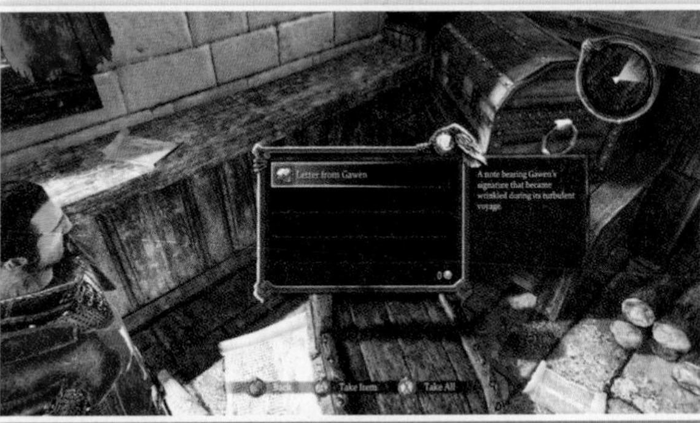

Head upstairs and follow the corridor ahead. Check the first room on the left until you find the Letter from Gawen on the table. It tells of Gawen's efforts to clear his name and attempt an audience with King Robert Baratheon. He never made it.

Objective Point C

Continue following the corridor as it winds around to the southeast. Check the last room for the Letter from Falena. It lies hidden behind the Sarwyck shield on the wall. The letter is from a whore in Madam Chataya's service who had a relationship with Gawen. You don't have any other clues to follow up on, so it's off to Chataya's to speak with Falena.

Objective Point D

Unfortunately, Gold Cloaks patrol the Manse. You have no choice but to fight them in the hall as you exit. One of the Gold Cloaks wears heavy armor, so you'll have to leave him for last as you take down the other lighter armored foes first. Once you're down to the heavy-armored Gold Cloak, switch to a blunt weapon to deal extra damage and finish him off before he finishes you off.

King's Landing

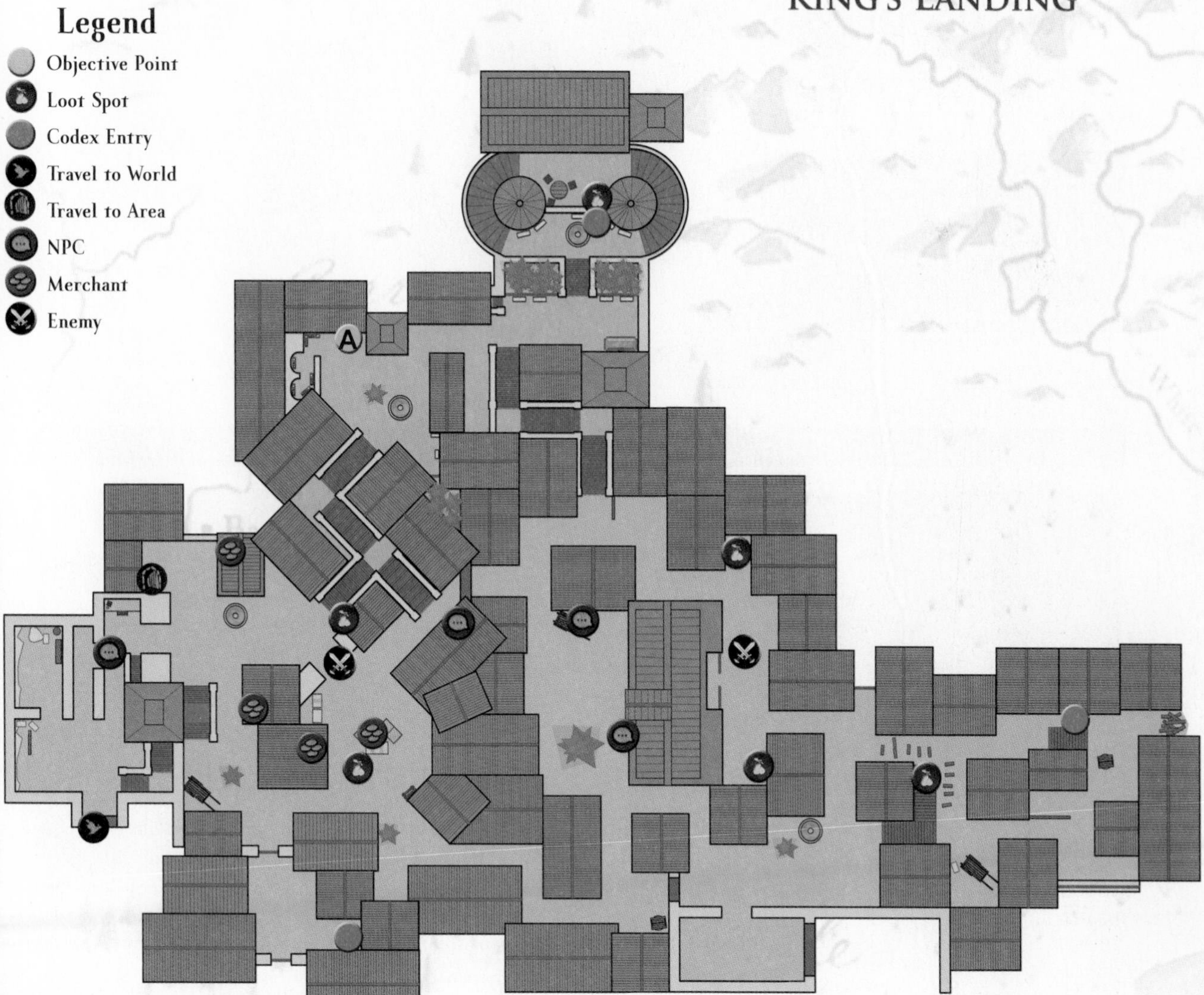

Legend

- Objective Point
- Loot Spot
- Codex Entry
- Travel to World
- Travel to Area
- NPC
- Merchant
- Enemy

A

4. Ask Falena What She Knows of Your Brother

Objective Point A

Leave the Sarwyck Manse and return to King's Landing. Look for the closest stairs and head to the upper levels of King's Landing. Madame Chataya's establishment is in a cul-de-sac with the red rose gardens and red lights out front.

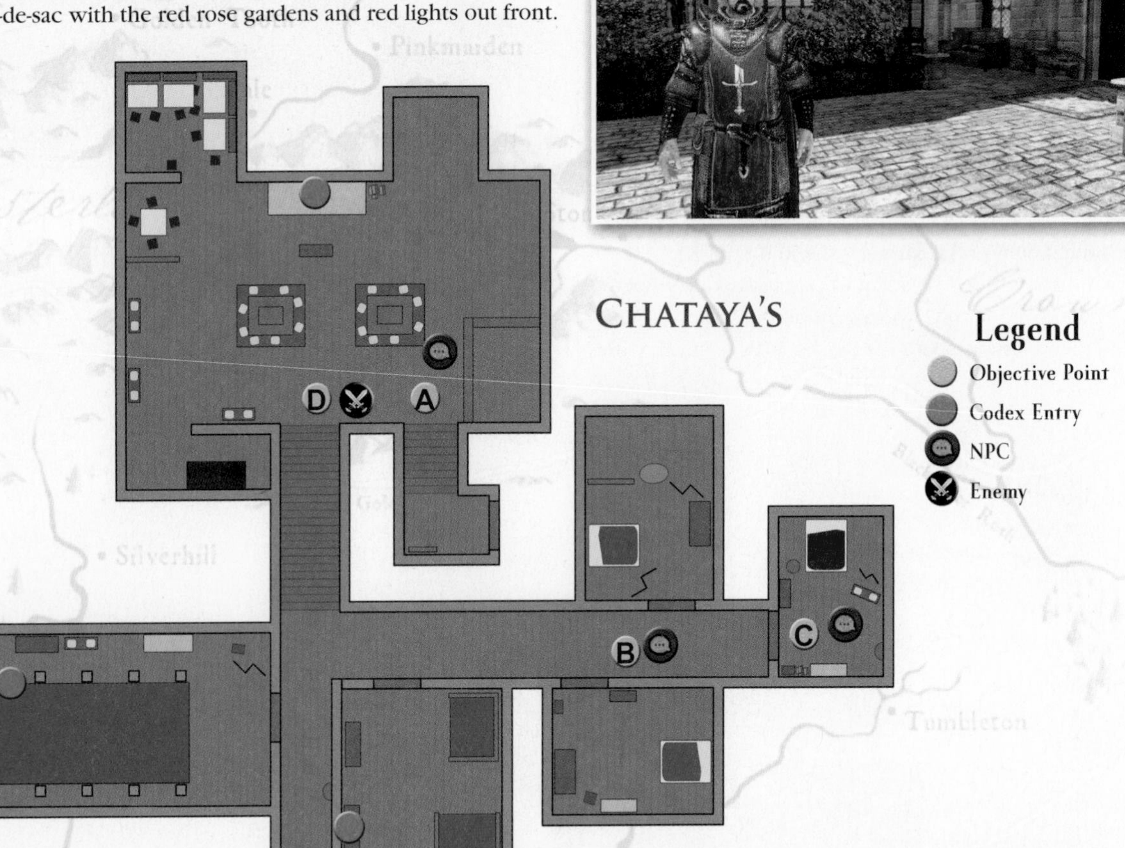

Objective Point A

Speak with Chataya in front of the house. You are old acquaintances, so she tells you where to find Falena without much persuasion. The girl is located upstairs at the end of the corridor on the left.

Objective Point B

A stranger greets you in the corridor upstairs before you can reach Falena's room. He introduces himself as Varys, and you know him as the Spider, a master spy for King Targaryen who has been given a new job with the current ruling family. You also know him to be a eunuch, so he's not in a brothel for the whores; he's looking to run into you. He warns you that Valarr is a formidable foe and that you may need Varys's help against him at a future date.

Book Watch: Varys

Varys is a key character in *A Game of Thrones* novel too. He plays the role of King Robert's master spy and master manipulator in the behind-the-scenes decisions shaping the kingdom. Just as Alester is torn on Varys's ambitions and loyalties—should he trust him or not?—Eddard Stark is put in the same position with dire events transpiring around him.

Objective Point C

After your conversation with Varys, seek out Falena in her room. She informs you that she hasn't seen Gawen in days. You find out that Gawen made it to King's Landing and was headed for the Red Keep when Falena saw him last. Falena also gives you Gawen's old cloak (Sarwyck Giltwaters), which she has been hanging on for him but feels it's better off in your hands. It's probably an upgrade in your cloak slot, so equip it after your conversation ends with Falena.

5. Meet in the Red Keep to Follow Gawen's Tracks

Objective Point D

Return back downstairs. Unfortunately, your past actions have caught up with you. Gold Cloaks have arrived for you after finding their dead comrades at Sarwyck Manse. Apparently, someone spotted you leaving the Manse and the guard followed you to Chataya's. The Gold Cloaks threaten to cause mayhem to the place if you don't come quietly, so you turn over your weapons without a fight. They lock you up in the Red Keep's dungeon, awaiting your trial to clear your name.

Maegor's Holdfast Dungeons

Legend

- Objective Point
- Codex Entry
- Secret Passage
- Loot Spot
- NPC
- Enemy

Maegor's Holdfast Upper Basement

Maegor's Holdfast Lower Basement

H G E F L M J K

Legend

- Objective Point
- Codex Entry
- Secret Passage
- Loot Spot
- NPC
- Enemy

6. Escape from the Red Keep's Dungeons

Objective Point A

You are stripped of your gear and thrown into a cell in Maegor's Holdfast, the dungeons of the Red Keep. You have been stuck in the cell for a while and your trial hasn't come; you're beginning to think you're going to be left down here to rot when your first visitor arrives: Varys. He explains that it will be several more weeks before your trial, and Valarr will have wed your sister by then. Your only chance is to escape the dungeon and convince the queen of your resourcefulness. Queen Cersei may be impressed and see a use for a man like you on the Riverspring throne.

Objective Point B

Lord Varys provides a key to your cell for your escape. He can't guide you out himself—if he were seen, it would be the end of his career as master spy—but he will meet you at the end of the dungeons and give you final instructions before you slip into the Red Keep's throne room and meet the queen. Follow the corridor outside your cell until you come to the room on your left with a guard asleep at his post (drugged by Varys). Take the guard's weapons off the table; now you have something at least to use in combat.

As you proceed farther into the room, two guards in light armor enter. They attack on sight, and you'll have to take both of them down with the guard's weapons and no armor. You aren't as tough as you normally are, so rely on stun, knock-down, and immobilize effects to minimize the hits against you.

Objective Point C

After you defeat the two guards, search the room from which they came. You'll find your personal belongings on the table and the Key to the Red Keep's Cells. Once you've equipped your gear, return to the previous room with the sleeping guard and use your new keys to open the locked door that gives you access to the corridor to the north.

CAUTION

Don't forget to reequip all your armor and weapons! You don't want to battle the rest of the Maegor's Keep guards naked or weaponless.

7. Use the Gift of Sight Given to You by R'hllor to Locate a Secret Passage

Objective Point D

The corridor appears to be a dead end, but it's not. In the last cell on the right, use your gift of sight powers to discover a secret passage. Access the new wall opening to reach the darker labyrinth of Maegor's Holdfast.

8. Explore the Labyrinth of Maegor's Holdfast to Meet Varys

Objective Point E

Eventually you'll reach a winding staircase. The way is barred if you go up, so descend until you see an opening into the upper basement. Your route begins to twist and turn in the Maegor's Holdfast corridors as you move up and down between the dungeons, upper basement, and lower basement levels. Go slowly and make sure you always know how to get back to familiar territory.

Objective Point F

Continue to follow the passages until you reach the corridor with two levers. Pull the first on the left wall to open a door in the next corridor. Pull the second lever in the small room to the right at the corridor's end. This lever opens the locked gate in front of you.

NOTE

During your weaving around the labyrinth, guards will constantly pursue you. As you pass by cracks in the wall, you can hear them talking and see them chasing after you. Don't panic. They can't catch you yet, but you will meet up with them soon.

Objective Point G

Two guards are beating a man in the next corridor. Sneak around the corner and surprise them with your best attack before they get a chance to figure out what's happening. Now that you have your full gear returned, the battle should go smoothly. The man they were beating turns out to one of Varys's "Little Birds," his spies who listen to the kingdom's goings-on and report back to Varys. The Little Bird will guide you to the end of Maegor's Holdfast.

NOTE

The Little Bird will fight by your side in the upcoming battles, but he's not a member of your party. You can't control him directly.

Objective Point H

Follow the Little Bird until he stops in front of a blank wall. Use your gift of sight to open another secret passage in the wall. It leads to another staircase that winds down to the lower basement.

Objective Point I

Circle down the stairs and continue on. Search for the lever in the northwest section of the maze that opens a new passage into a wine cellar. There's a large hole in the wall to your left, and you'll see several guards patrolling the adjacent chamber. If you have a ranged attack, aim at one of the guards to get in some extra damage while you initiate combat. Battle at the opening to prevent the guards from swarming into your room and surrounding you.

TIP

Pick up the Wildfire Codex entry in the wine casket along the back wall.

Objective Point J

Enter the room the guards were just in. Before you exit, search the book on the stand by the exit stairs for another Codex entry.

Objective Point K

More guards will assail you at the top of the stairs. If you have a ranged weapon, let the Little Bird attack the guards in melee while you pelt them from the safety of the stairs. If you want to punish them with melee, go into slow-motion mode when you top the stairs so you have time to set up your attack before the guards are on you.

Objective Point L

Return to the upper basement and follow the twists and turns until you run into another band of guards. Similar to your other battles with the guards, you can use the corner and stairs as cover if you need a few extra seconds to prepare or want to let the Little Bird get in some extra whacks while you defend.

Objective Point M

The Little Bird takes his leave from your company at the last staircase. He can't be seen near the Red Keep's throne room. You'll have to go it alone until you meet up with Varys.

Objective Point N

Walk up the stairs and open the secret door at the top. It opens into a room with three guards. Stay in the darkness and don't enter the room, and the guards won't immediately notice you. If you have a ranged weapon, hit the closest guard with your most damaging attack and retreat back down the stairs. Fighting on the stairs will keep the guards from surrounding you, and you won't pull the second set of guards in the nearby room into the battle. If you have only melee weapons, charge into the room, hammer the closest guard with your initial attacks, and then retreat to the stairs. After all the guards lie dead at your feet, collect any loot from the corpses and then enter the room.

TIP

If you have flammable oil on you and need more damage to slay the guards, use Flaming Weapon to set your weapons alight and your enemies afire.

Objective Point O

More guards are in the adjacent room opposite the stairs. If you battle inside the room, they will charge into the fray near the end of your fight with the first set of guards; if you pull the battle outside the room to the stairs beyond the secret passage, you can finish the first battle and then surprise this second set of guards.

Objective Point P

Once you beat all the guards in the area, Varys opens the door to the Red Keep's throne room on the southern wall. He explains that this secret passage leads directly to the Throne Room's antechamber, and he reminds you that his involvement in this little affair must be kept secret.

Throne Room of the Red Keep First Floor

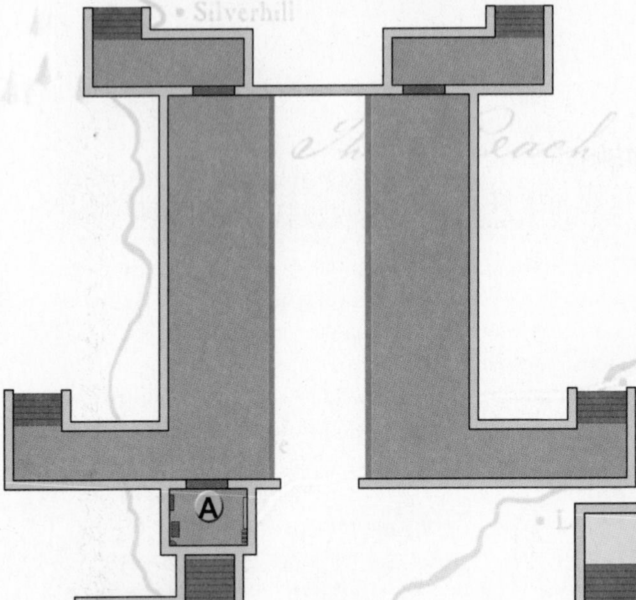

A

Throne Room of the Red Keep Ground Floor

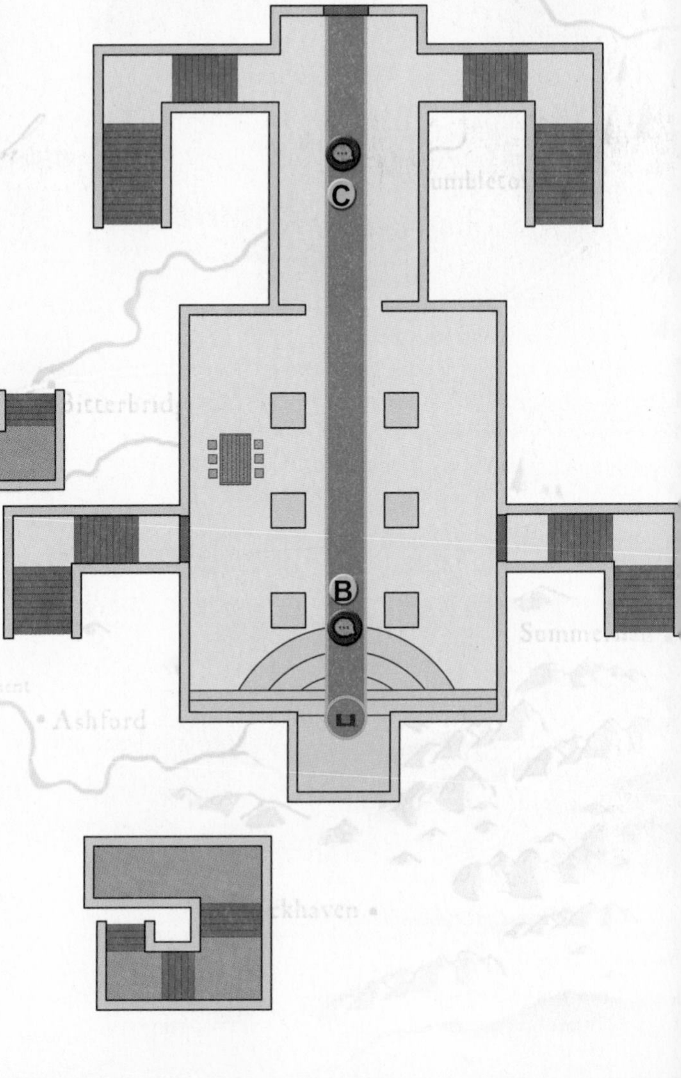

C

B

Legend

Objective Point

NPC

9. Plead Your Case to Queen Cersei

Objective Point A

Take the stairs up to the Red Keep's throne room. There's no more fighting the rest of the way; you will have to rely on your expertise with words to get you through the next encounter.

Objective Point B

When you enter the Throne Room, the Gold Cloaks will be on you immediately. They demand to know how you escaped their notice and get angry when Queen Cersei steps in.

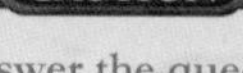

If you refuse to answer the queen, Cersei won't be happy and it's game over. You need to tell her what she wants to hear and accept to work with Valarr.

You should swear allegiance to her and ask that she consider your industrious talents and give you a chance to earn her favor. Cersei agrees that you should serve her needs to win your kingdom, but with a twist—your next mission teams you up with Valarr. She will judge how well you both do and award the winner with Riverspring.

Book Watch: Cersei Lannister

The Queen of Westeros is the most powerful political figure of all the ruling lords and ladies. She makes most decisions for King Robert, who has grown weary of rule and would rather enjoy a good meal and a large tankard of ale. Alester meets with Queen Cersei in the Red Keep to bargain for his future and his kingdom. There's a certain irony that Alester asks Queen Cersei to cancel the marriage between his sister Elyana and his half brother Valarr, as Cersei is secretly involved in an incestuous affair herself in the book.

10. Meet in the Throne Room's Ante-Chamber to Await the Queen's Pleasure

Objective Point C

Cersei asks you to await her in the antechamber while she fulfills other duties. As you leave the throne room, you meet up with Valarr again. Your half brother is surprised that you escaped your dungeon cell, and he's about to be shocked that the two of you are teaming up to hunt down enemies of the throne.

CHAPTER 5

BEAUTY AND THE BEAST

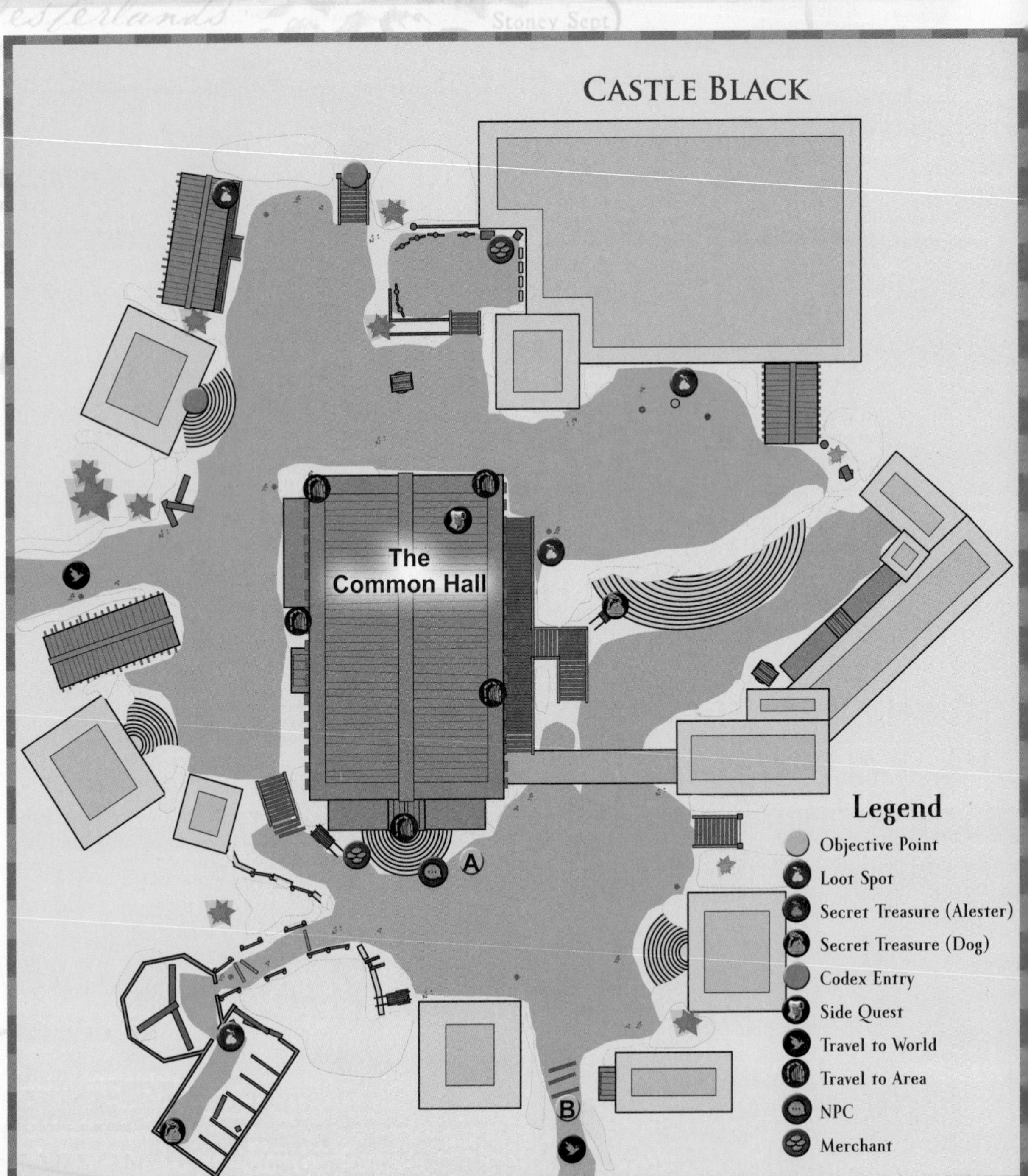

Objectives

1. Accompany Ser Godric to Mole's Town to find the woman Jon Arryn wants protected
2. Hear the report from Ser Godric's men
3. Take your inquiry into the village to find the young woman
4. Take Ser Godric to the brothel to find the woman he's looking for
5. Find the young woman staying in the basement
6. Track the woman down while the scent is still fresh
7. Treason! Strike down Godric before reinforcements arrive
8. Escape this trap as soon as you can
9. Take Jeyne to Castle Black
10. See the Lord Commander at once

Quest Checklist

- Sybelle (NPC, objective 4)
- The Mother statuette (side quest item, objective 5)
- Neck Ring of the First Men (special item, objective 6)
- Jeyne Greystone (NPC, objective 6)
- Patrek (companion, objective 9)
- Experience Points: 1,650 (upon quest completion)

1. Accompany Ser Godric to Mole's Town to Find the Woman Jon Arryn Wants Protected

Objective Point A

You are back at Castle Black, and the Lord Commander has just informed you that your friend and the King's Hand, Jon Arryn, is dead. Ser Godric insists that he will continue his final mission to honor his lord, and you agree to accompany him to Mole's Town, where the young girl in Arryn's letter is hidden. You also dispatch three Night's Watch brethren, led by Theomar, as reinforcements in the Gift to make sure the peace is held while you travel through the forest.

Objective Point B

Make any last-minute preparations by visiting the merchants in and around the Common Hall, and then set off for the outskirts of Castle Black. Call up the world map at either of the exit points and head to the new area that's opened up in the Gift, Mole's Town.

2. Hear the Report from Ser Godric's Men

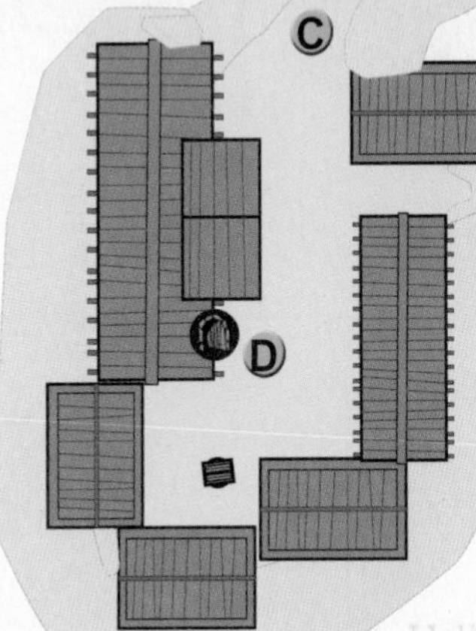

Objective Point A

Ser Godric's camp is in the forest outside of Mole's Town. Follow the path to the southeast to rendezvous with the first set of Godric's men.

Objective Point B

The men inform Ser Godric that the area is secure, and patrols scour the area to make sure no one passes without their notice. They also let you know that Jared, Godric's mean-spirited lieutenant, took some men and headed south to interrogate villagers for information on the young woman you seek.

Objective Point C

Continue south and wind along the eastern edge of the forest until you reach Jared and his men. They're threatening a villager when you arrive, and you order him to release the man. Ser Godric gives Jared a tongue-lashing and sends him away.

3. Take Your Inquiry into the Village to Find the Young Woman

Objective Point D

Continue into the small collection of buildings that serves as the upper level of Mole's Town. As you explain to Godric, most of the town exists belowground in a series of tunnels and rooms to escape the cold. It's there that you'll find the young woman mentioned in Jon Arryn's letter.

Tunnels of Mole's Town Upper Level

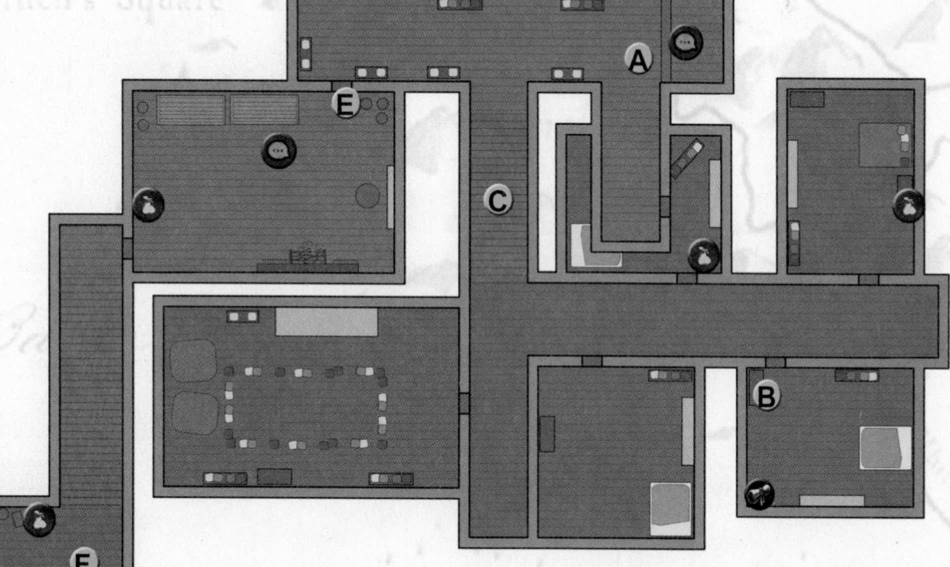

Legend

- Objective Point
- Loot Spot
- Secret Treasure (Dog)
- Primary Quest
- Travel to Area
- NPC
- Merchant

4. Take Ser Godric to the Brothel to Find the Woman He's Looking For

Objective Point A

You take Ser Godric inside and speak with the madam of the brothel, Sybelle. At first she's reluctant to give up her secrets, but through either threats or reason, you convince her that it's in the best interest of the young woman that you locate her immediately. Sybelle says the young woman, Jeyne Greystone, hides in one of the downstairs rooms.

5. Find the Young Woman Staying in the Basement

Objective Point B

Take the stairs down below and turn left. Follow the passage until you reach Jeyne's room (check the map for the scroll icon if you get turned around). She's not in her room. However, check the corner for a trinket with Jeyne's perfume still fresh on it. You can use the perfume scent to track Jeyne.

TIP

Pick up the Mother statuette in Jeyne's room. This is one of the components for "The Faith of Our Ancestors" side quest.

6. Track the Woman Down While the Scent Is Still Fresh

Objective Point C

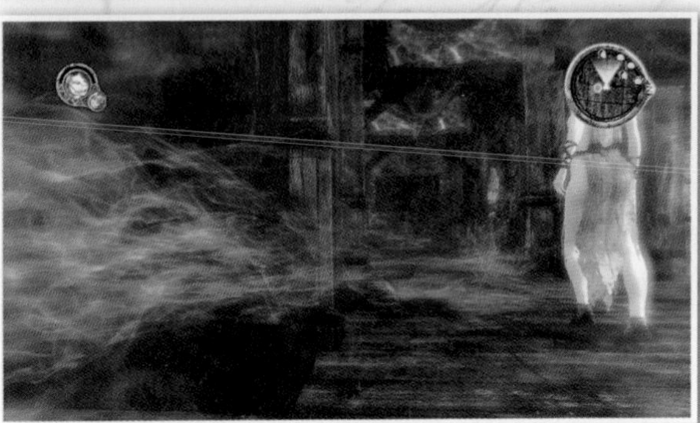

Switch to dog mode and track Jeyne's yellow scent floating in the air. It leads out into the hallways and west. Follow the scent back up the stairs to the common room on the first floor.

Objective Point D

In the common room, you can chat up Patrek and Walder if you like. They will each tell you their tales of how they ended up taking the black. It's a nice diversion if you want to take the time from your main quest, and you earn the King Beyond the Wall Codex entry if you listen to your brothers' stories of woe.

Objective Point E

The scent trail weaves through the kitchen; however, the cook doesn't like dogs wandering into his work space. If you break the red threat circle around the cook, he kicks you out. You can either wait until he moves to the fire in the back of the room and sneak past him, or switch back to Mors and let him have a little chat with the cook. Take the door on the kitchen's far side to continue with the hunt.

Objective Point F

Walk down the short corridor and turn left. Go down the stairs and into the small kitchen storeroom. There's a trapdoor in the corner that leads to the next area. However, if you sniff the air for treasure, you'll discover some hidden loot in the other corner.

Tunnels of Mole's Town Lower Level

Legend

- Objective Point
- Loot Spot
- Secret Treasure (Dog)
- NPC
- Enemy

Objective Point A

Turn left and follow the scent down the tunnel until you reach the next intersection. Turn left again and continue to track the yellow trail.

Objective Point B

Stop when you see a large crowd with an aggressive threat circle that takes up the whole tunnel. Dog can't slip through here undetected; the men don't like dogs and will kick you back each time you try. Instead, switch back to Mors, walk through the men to the far side, and then switch back to dog mode when you're out of the hostility zone.

Objective Point C

Cut through a series of rooms as the trail winds south. It can get confusing as you move between the rooms, so note which door you entered and make sure you don't double back by accident and exit through the entrance door.

Objective Point D

Take a moment to follow a treasure scent in the next big intersection. You'll be rewarded with the Neck Ring of the First Men (+1 Luck) for your troubles.

Objective Point E

When you see the two townsfolk talking about a frightened girl, look for the trail to disappear under the door on the left. Open the door, cut through the room, and exit into the corridor on the far side.

Objective Point F

You've finally found Jeyne when you reach the wooden door next to the tattered cloth on the nearby wall. Open the door and speak with the young woman inside.

As you talk with Jeyne, you realize that she was the woman Poddy attacked in the Gift. Because your dog saved her, she's willing to trust you. However, Jeyne doesn't trust Ser Godric. She met with the real Ser Godric before she came north, and she fingers him as an imposter.

7. Treason! Strike down Godric before reinforcements arrive

Ser Godric attacks as soon as his disguise is up. Wearing heavy armor and wielding an impressive two-handed sword, Godric is one tough opponent. In the small room, you won't have much space to escape his weapon; you'll have to go toe-to-toe with him and should rely on blunt weapons as much as possible. Use your dog's abilities to distract him during crucial parts of the battle, and if you stocked up on any health flasks before you left Castle Black, you might want to chug one or two during this fight. Fortunately, you only have to cut him down to half his health to make him yield.

When you beat Godric, he backs off and lets his lackeys take you on. You can't stop him from escaping, so concentrate on staying alive against Godric's men. The battle picks up where you left off with Godric, which means you'll be at reduced health and energy as Godric's men arrive. Switch to perforating weapons and take down one of the men as your dog engages the other. A third enemy in heavy armor joins the fight late; use similar tactics to your fight with Godric to slay him.

8. Escape this trap as soon as you can

Objective Point G

After the battle, Jeyne thanks you for saving her life. You explain that it's in her best interest to return to Castle Black, and the two of you make a quick exit topside through the nearby door before more of Godric's men find you in the room.

Mole's Town

G
F
E
D
C
B
A

Legend

- Objective Point
- Loot Spot
- Secret Treasure (Dog)
- Travel to Area
- Enemy

9. Take Jeyne to Castle Black

Objective Point A

Godric's men find you outside the entrance to Mole's Town. Patrek also gets caught up in the action, as Godric's men attack him when he leaves the common room. (Walder passed out from too much drink, so he's safe inside.) Together you must battle Godric's men as they pile on you near the entrance. Patrek's Devastation ability can pummel several enemies at once, while you and your dog can isolate and destroy single foes in seconds. If Patrek starts to get overwhelmed, break out his Upheaval attack to knock down the toughest attacker.

Companion Role Call: Patrek

Stats:

- Strength: 8
- Agility: 3
- Luck: 4
- Endurance: 6
- Intelligence: 6

Class: Hedge Knight

Stance: Domination

Abilities: Death from Above, Devastation, Upheaval

Weapon of Choice: Rib-Crusher (2H mace)

Description: Patrek joins your party after he gets attacked by Godric's men outside Mole's Town. Throughout the return trip through the forest between Mole's Town and Castle Black, you can control Patrek during the battles. As a Hedge Knight, he can hit hard. Against single opponents, knock your foe down with Upheaval and follow up with a crushing Death from Above attack. Against groups of two or more, use Devastation to deal a moderate strike to all those in front of you. Patrek is a faithful companion who will get you home at all costs.

Objective Point B

You can choose to fight each group of enemies you stumble across in the Mole's Town forest, or you can use stealth and assassinate foes one by one with Dog. It's advantageous to sneak up on foes and kill them with Dog as long as you can. The farther you get into the forest without the alarm going up, the better. Retrace the steps you took earlier to reach Mole's Town. When you arrive at the first intersection, wait for the first enemy to pass and rip out his throat with a canine sneak attack.

Caution

If you choose to fight your way through all of Godric's men, it could be suicide. Enemies can come from any direction and can easily overwhelm you.

Objective Point C

As Dog, patrol up the path slowly and search for the next enemy ahead in the darkness. Stop when you spot an enemy and watch his route as he walks along the paths. Position yourself in a good ambush spot, and when your foe walks by and shows his back to you, pounce on him and go for the throat.

TIP

You can spot enemies from afar by looking for their red health bars in the gloom.

Objective Point D

When you reach the outskirts of the enemy's main camp, things get tricky. Several guards crisscross on patrol, and they will spot any group walking the paths. Only Dog can sneak through the defenses and pick off guards one by one.

Take out the guard on the left first. Sneak down the path and pass the wagon on your left. Stay close to the edge, away from the advancing guard on the path to your right, and look for a hole in the wall past the wagon. Duck through the hole and climb up the hill to get behind the guard. When you're ready, charge the guard and kill him before he alerts anyone else. Return to your starting point at the camp outskirts without being seen.

Next, eliminate the middle guard. Wait until he walks up the path toward you, and when he turns his back, pounce on him. Be careful that the guard up on the hill to your right doesn't spot your assassination attempt. After the middle guard falls, you have a clear path to the back of the hill. Move in, slip up the hill, and take out the last guard from behind.

CAUTION

There is one guard behind the stone wall at the back of the camp. It's possible to avoid him if you don't want an extra fight, or charge in with Mors and Patrek to overwhelm him quickly.

Objective Point E

Press on to the northwest corner of the main encampment. One of Godric's men guards the door in the wall that leads to north section of the forest. Since he's looking out with his back to the wall, it's impossible for Dog to get him; better to charge with Mors and Patrek and gut him where he stands. If you're quick enough, you can kill the guard, open the door, and dash inside before any other guards join the fight.

Objective Point F

You meet up with three brothers you assigned to the Gift before you left Castle Black. Theomar says they saw Godric race through earlier, and since then the three of them have been dodging Godric's men in the area. You ask their assistance in exiting the forest.

TIP

If you use Dog to spy on Theomar and his two brothers before your whole party arrives, you can learn of their plans and attack the traitors before they lead you into the ambush.

Alas, the three brothers' intentions are not honorable. They lead you a short distance into the forest and then pull their weapons on you. Godric offered them a hefty sum of coin to ambush you, and the three brothers took him up on the offer. It's a Night's Watch on Night's Watch fight, and they're all armed with decent weapons and medium armor. Switch to perforating weapons and hack away. If you, Patrek, and Dog all team up on a single foe, you will cut them down quicker than they can defeat you. Some of Godric's men will participate as the ambush moves on, so it's important to kill Theomar and the other brothers before the odds get too great.

TIP

You can learn of the treachery if you use Dog to listen to the conversation between Theomar and Godric's men. There is a small passage right of the door. If you go through the bushes with Dog, you can spy on them. If you do, Godric's men will not arrive as backup during the fight ; you will fight them after you defeat the turned brothers.

Objective Point G

Scour the fallen bodies for loot before leaving the battlefield. Find the northern bridge, exit the forest, and return to Castle Black with more questions than answers lingering in your mind.

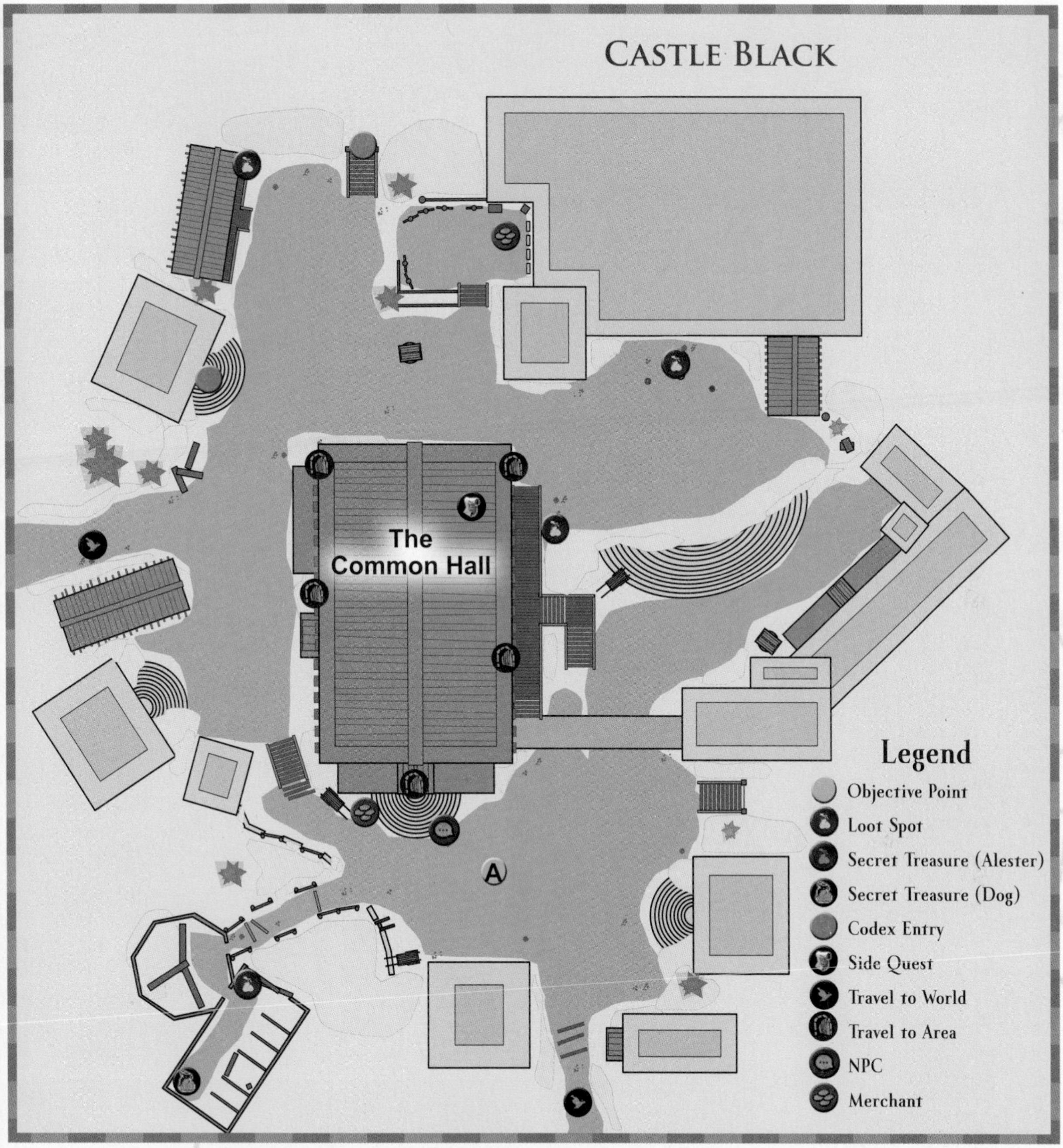

Castle Black

The Common Hall

A

Legend

- Objective Point
- Loot Spot
- Secret Treasure (Alester)
- Secret Treasure (Dog)
- Codex Entry
- Side Quest
- Travel to World
- Travel to Area
- NPC
- Merchant

10. See the Lord Commander at Once

Objective Point A

Back at Castle Black, you explain to Lord Commander Mormont Ser Godric's betrayal and the unsettling notion that some of the Night's Watch might be compromised, bribed by Godric to work against the brotherhood. At the end of your conversation, Mormont sums up the dire straits: "The impostor continues to roam our lands, and we cannot even trust our own men..."

Tip

To get some extra experience, you can trigger a mass fight if you exterminate Godric's men rather than recruit them into the Night's Watch during your conversation with Lord Commander Mormont.

CHAPTER 6

THE CROWN'S DOGS

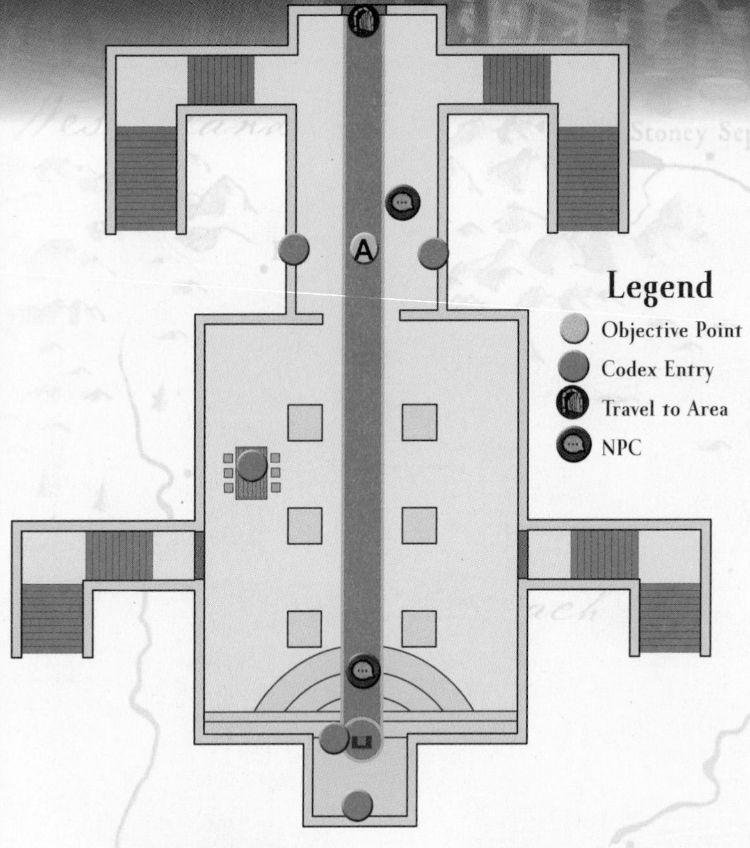

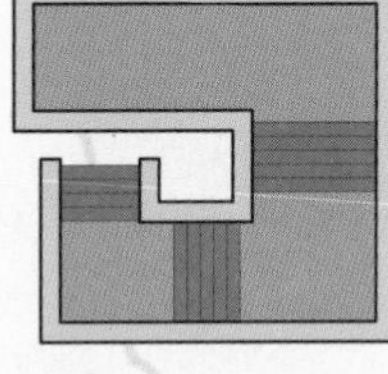

THRONE ROOM OF THE RED KEEP GROUND FLOOR

QUEST CHECKLIST

- **Valarr Hill (companion, objective 1)**
- **Yohn (NPC, objective 2)**
- **Weymar Cirley (NPC, objective 4)**
- **Hen's Keys (quest item, objective 6)**
- **Avalanche (special item, objective 6)**
- **Hen's Documents (quest item, objective 8)**
- **Uthor Donnerly (NPC, objective 10)**
- **"Silence in the Ranks" (side quest, objective 10)**
- **Arwood Harlton (NPC, objective 10)**
- **Experience Points: 1,500 (upon quest completion)**

OBJECTIVES

1. Go and inquire about the queen's decision
2. Head with Valarr to the King's Landing marketplace
3. Kill Master Jaremy's potters OR Question Master Jaremy about Harry
4. Get Harry to find out where the Mother Hen is hiding OR Return to Master Jaremy's workshop to interrogate the wounded
5. Attack the Hen House and find the Mother Hen
6. Chase the Mother Hen and kill him
7. Execute Harry the Mother Hen's protégé
8. Search the Hen House for information on the Mother Hen's activities
9. Return to the queen to give her your report
10. Bring the Greystone girl back to the queen dead or alive

1. Go and Inquire about the Queen's Decision

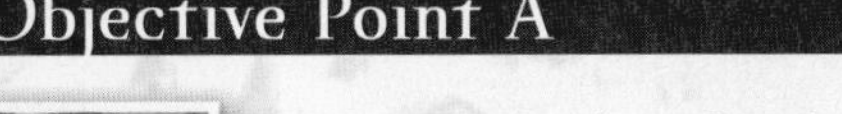

Objective Point A

Queen Cersei has offered you a deal: Your Riverspring title and lands will be returned to you if you agree to work for her and eliminate enemies of the Crown. You await the queen in the antechamber while she speaks with Valarr. Look for the House Lannister Codex entry in the painting on the wall in front of you, and then wait by the red carpet for Cersei and Valarr to exit the throne room. The queen tasks you with finding the criminal called the Mother Hen and retrieving important documents in the Hen's possession.

Legend

- Objective Point
- Loot Spot
- Codex Entry
- Travel to World
- Travel to Area
- NPC
- Merchant
- Enemy

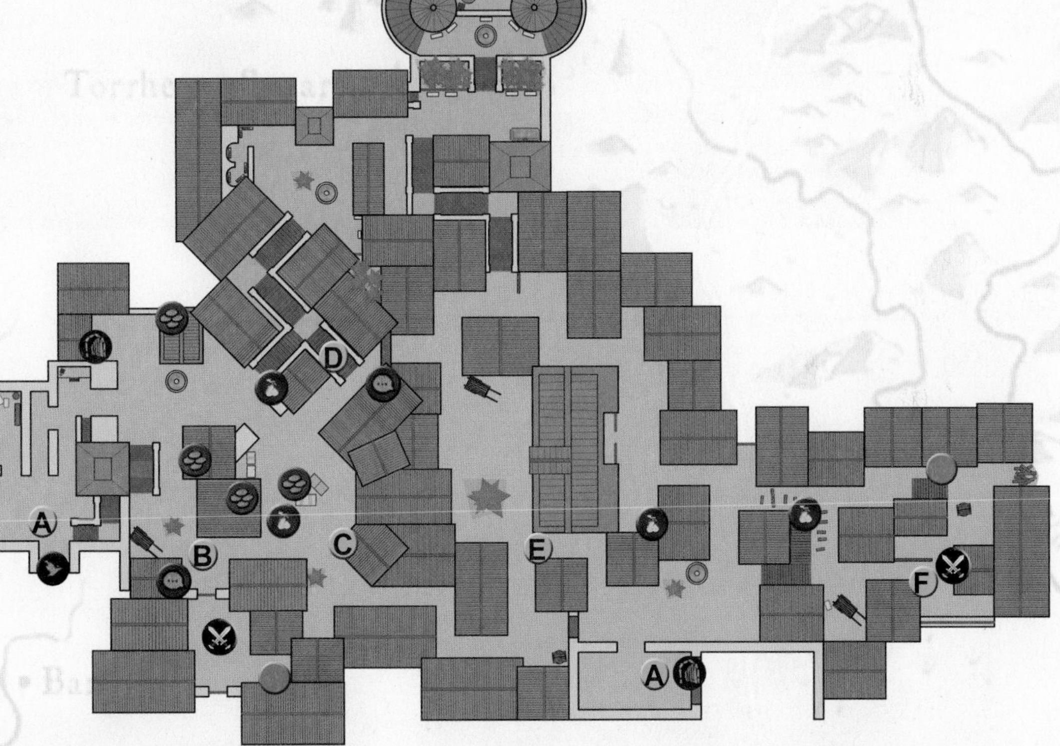

2. Head with Valarr to the King's Landing Marketplace

Objective Point A

Your search for the Mother Hen begins outside the Red Keep in King's Landing. Valarr's spies have a lead on the Hen's location; meet up with Valarr's personal guards, the Bloodseekers, in the marketplace to follow up on that lead.

> **Tip**
>
> You want to stop by the merchants in the marketplace to grab new items. If you haven't already, now is a good time to visit the potion merchant to stock up on flammable oil and Wildfire flasks.

Companion Role Call: Valarr Hill

Stats:

- **Strength: 10**
- **Agility: 8**
- **Luck: 6**
- **Endurance: 7**
- **Intelligence: 7**

Class: Hedge Knight

Stance: Domination

Abilities: Death from Above, Earthquaker, Massacre, Pierce, Upheaval

Weapons of Choice: Valarr's Sword (2H)

Description: As his stance implies, Valarr tries to dominate people with his overwhelming might. His standard attack, Pierce, causes light damage and Bleeding against a single opponent, and Massacre deals light damage against multiple foes in melee. To shake things up, use Earthquaker and stun all nearby opponents. The combo of Upheaval and Death from Above will knock an opponent to the ground and deliver a massive blow to the prone foe. You might not like Valarr's personality, but there's a lot to like about his skill set.

3. Kill Master Jaremy's Potters or Question Master Jaremy about Harry

Objective Point B

You'll find Valarr's Bloodseekers on the edge of the marketplace next to the gate into the potter shop. They've tracked a young boy named Harry Waters here; the Hen's men seem to have taken a keen interest in guarding Harry. When Valarr orders his men to kill the potter apprentices in the yard, you can choose to go along with the violence or intervene to stop the massacre.

NOTE

There are multiple ways to get the Hen House location from the potters. You can use force or persuasion or both, and when Harry makes a run for it, you can either follow him back to the Hen House or interrogate Weymar Cirley for the information.

If you choose to kill the apprentices, they attack as soon as you enter the yard. It's a big group, so don't try to do everything yourself; you have Valarr's big sword and the rest of his team to help you out. Regardless of your main stance, stay back and look for targets of opportunity to quickly slay the wounded.

If you choose to intervene, you'll have a chance to talk with Old Jaremy, the master potter, and avoid a fight with the apprentices. At the end of the conversation with Old Jaremy or your battle with the apprentices, the Hen's guards interrupt your search for Harry and attack. As with the first battle, stay out of the heart of the conflict and pick off wounded enemies or those who charge after you.

4. Get Harry to Find Out Where the Mother Hen Is Hiding OR Return to Master Jaremy's Workshop to Interrogate the Wounded

Whatever your choices at the potter shop, the final result is the same—Harry makes a run for it at the end of the conflict. As he bolts from the shop and heads back into the marketplace, run after him. If you lose sight of him for even an instant, the chase ends and you lose him. No matter the obstacles—thrown barrels, crowds in the way, the twists and turns of the King's Landing streets—keep on his tail if you want to learn the secret of the Hen House's location.

Objective Point C

Keep on Harry's heels as best as you can. When he cuts around the marketplace carts, dodge the first set of barrels he throws in your way. Stay on his tail, but when he knocks down the second set of barrels, cut off to your left around the carts and catch up with him again as he turns left down the side street.

Objective Point D

Follow Harry up the steps and dodge the crowd of people in your way. You'll chase Harry through the upper levels of King's Landing and down toward the Flea Bottom District. Crowds will constantly get in your way. Watch carefully how Harry moves through the crowd, and take the same path. If you bump into a person and stop, you lose Harry.

Objective Point E

Just when you think you've got Harry, he ducks behind a locked gate and seems lost. He's not! Continue running around the building and you'll catch up to him on the far side as the streets continue into the seedier part of town.

Objective Point F

If you've managed to stay on Harry the whole time, he leads you to the Hen House in Flea Bottom. The Hen's guards at the door immediately attack you. Valarr's Massacre attack comes in handy if you fight in the close quarters of the alley, and a stun effect like Paralyzing Powder can lock down the whole enemy group while you pound on them.

NOTE

If you failed to catch Harry, return to the potter shop and interrogate the wounded for the Hen House location.

THE HEN HOUSE UPPER FLOOR

THE HEN HOUSE GROUND FLOOR

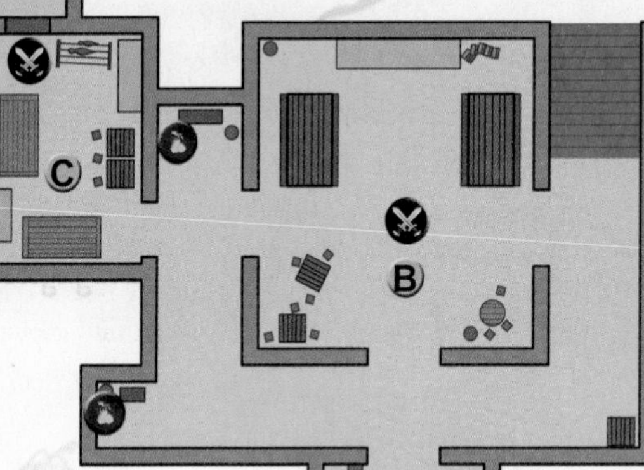

Legend

- Objective Point
- Loot Spot
- Codex Entry
- Primary Quest
- NPC
- Enemy

5. Attack the Hen House and Find the Mother Hen

Objective Point A

Enter the Hen House and search for the Mother Hen. He won't be hard to find; head straight through the arch and into the central room with a large body of blue-garbed soldiers.

Objective Point B

It turns out that the Mother Hen is the real Ser Godric, lieutenant of the King's Hand, Jon Arryn. The queen has dubbed him an enemy of the Crown, so regardless of the man's seeming nobility, you have no choice but to execute him to stay in the queen's good graces.

Of course, he won't go down without a fight. As the Mother Hen strategically retreats to the cellar, his men converge from all sides. This is your biggest battle yet, and it will take strong tactics to survive. Switch back and forth between Alester and Valarr to make maximum use of their abilities. Alester's stun and immobilize effects can help slow down enemy attacks, as can Valarr's Upheaval against one of the more heavily armored enemies. If you need to reset your positions, use Valarr's Earthquaker ability and coordinate your attacks while the guards are stunned.

6. Chase the Mother Hen and Kill Him

Objective Point C

While Valarr sends his Bloodseekers to engage the Hen's men upstairs, the two of you go after the Mother Hen and Harry; they have disappeared into the cellar. Follow the corridor to the west and ambush the pair of enemies guarding the cellar door. Slay the light-armored foe first, then concentrate your efforts on the enemy with heavy armor.

Objective Point D

Descend into the cellar. Watch out when you spot the first long corridor. Though it seems there is only one soldier guarding the corridor, there are many doors along the walls, and guards will pour out of them. Use a ranged attack if possible to lure the single enemy toward you; then, when enemies attack from their rooms, they will appear in front of you rather than surrounding you. When the dust settles and enemies have stopped twitching, continue on.

Objective Point E

Stop after you turn around the final corner. If you look ahead, you'll see Hen's men standing in the cellar's last room. You can duck into a small storeroom on your left for some additional loot, and when you're ready to take on the Mother Hen, enter the last room.

CAUTION

Save your game before the final confrontation against the Mother Hen. His wildfire attacks make it an extremely difficult battle, and you may need several attempts to best him in combat.

Objective Point F

With five enemies against the two of you, the battle would already prove difficult; it's almost impossible when you throw in the Mother Hen's wildfire attacks...unless you know how to deal with them.

Left unchecked, the Hen will destroy you with wildfire: Each wildfire attack deals massive damage and may kill you in a single dose. The key to the battle is relying on Valarr.

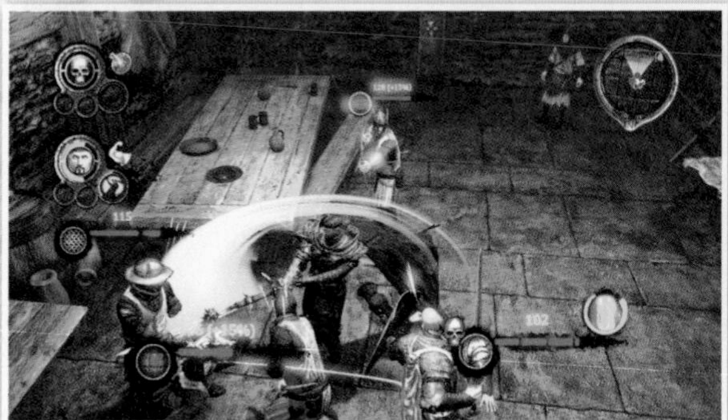

Valarr and Alester should coordinate attacks on the normal foes and slowly kill them off one by one. Let Alester concentrate on the normal foes. Valarr can aid with an occasional big attack here and there, but he really has to conserve energy for the Mother Hen.

TIP

Valarr's Earthquaker and Upheaval are the key abilities against the Mother Hen.

When it comes to the Mother Hen, Valarr must be vigilant and watch his every move. As soon as you see Mother Hen begin to cast Wildfire (he pulls his head back and drinks a potion to activate Wildfire), immediately interrupt him. You can use Valarr's Upheaval if you're standing next to him, or use Earthquaker if Mother Hen is nearby but others are in the way. You must prevent him from dousing Valarr or Alester with wildfire. Even better, you may catch him on fire with his own attack and make your job that much easier.

TIP

If Mother Hen douses you with wildfire, run into as many enemies as you can, especially Mother Hen! Wildfire spreads and can consume more than one target.

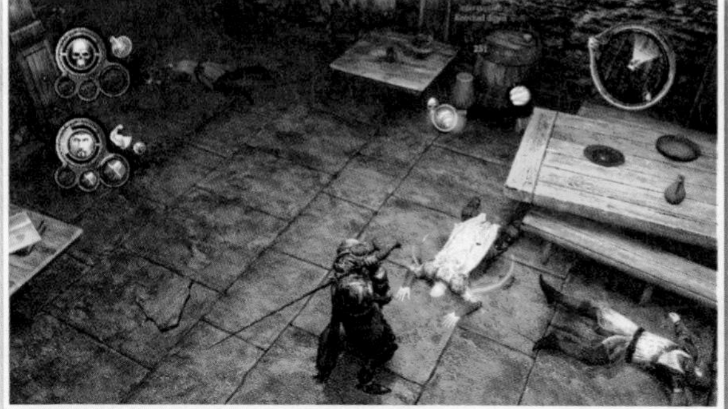

If you can avoid wildfire and work together well, Valarr and Alester will eventually take down Mother Hen and his men. Godric gives his final speech, and you see him for the honorable man he is even as Valarr finishes him off.

7. Execute Harry the Mother Hen's Protégé

Objective Point G

With the Mother Hen's death, Harry has nowhere else to hide. You can end the boy's life quickly or let Valarr do it. Either way, the boy dies because the queen has decreed it. Before you leave to return upstairs, grab the Hen's Keys from Godric's corpse, as well as Avalanche, his sword, and a small flask that will be useful for holding potions in the future.

8. Search the Hen House for Information on the Mother Hen's Activities

Objective Point H

The documents you're searching for are upstairs. Walk past the corpses of the Hen's slain men and follow the red-carpeted hallway to the end.

Objective Point I

Use the Hen's Keys on the locked chest in the final room. You uncover the Hen's Documents that the queen so desperately wants. From reading the letters, you discover that Godric sent a young woman (Jeyne Greystone) to Castle Black to escape Valarr's grasp. He sends Yohn after Jeyne, asking him to infiltrate the Night's Watch by posing as the dead Ser Godric.

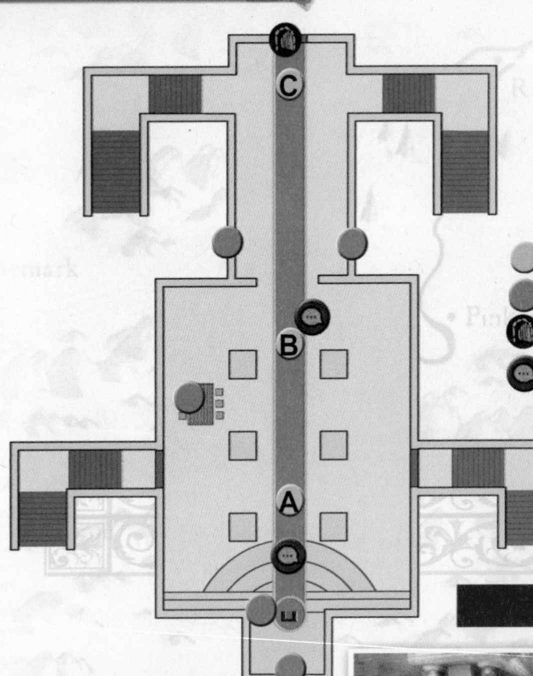

THRONE ROOM OF THE RED KEEP GROUND FLOOR

Legend

- Objective Point
- Codex Entry
- Travel to Area
- NPC

9. RETURN TO THE QUEEN TO GIVE HER YOUR REPORT

Objective Point A

Return to the Red Keep. Queen Cersei grants you and Valarr an audience. She's disappointed by some of your antics—namely, leaving a string of dead bodies across King's Landing—but she's happy that you flushed her enemies out into the open and killed the Mother Hen. Despite all that, she has more work for you to do together. She wants Jeyne Greystone delivered to her by whatever means. Finally, you've come full circle, and you now know how Alester's and Mors's paths connect.

10. BRING THE GREYSTONE GIRL BACK TO THE QUEEN DEAD OR ALIVE

Objective Point B

Uthor Donnerly is a young, outspoken knight who was under Jon Arryn's service and now dares to criticize the queen in her own throne room. He believes that she is a murderer and a traitor plotting against her husband and king. Initiating conversation with him starts the "Silence in the Ranks" side quest.

Side Quest: Silence in the Ranks

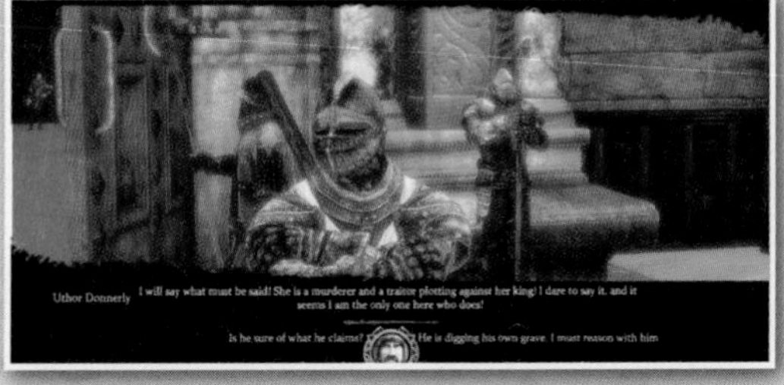

Uthor Donnerly in the Red Keep's Throne Room begins the "Silence in the Ranks" side quest. He's a very unhappy knight who wants to see the downfall of Queen Cersei. You have many options while talking to him: Will you bring his treasonous words to the queen? Can you resolve the situation with blood on the marble floors? For more details on interacting with Uthor Donnerly and completing the quest, see the "Side Quests" chapter.

Objective Point C

As you leave the throne room, Lord Arwood Harlton of Castlewood asks for a minute of your time. He was a friend of your father's and claims to have news of your missing brother. Before you set out on your mission to find Jeyne Greystone, Harlton urges you to seek him out in King's Landing where the two of you can talk in private about things better left unsaid in the heart of the Red Keep.

Chapter 7

Stray Dog

Quest Checklist

- Addam Flowers (NPC, objective 1)
- "The Black Bloodhound" (side quest, objective 1)
- "New Blood" (side quest, objective 1)
- Recruiter's Cloak (special item, objective 1)
- Raff Mouldy (NPC, objective 3)
- Willow (NPC, objective 4)
- Sybelle (NPC, objective 4)
- Key to the Master Bedroom (quest item, objective 4)
- Baratheon Guard Shield (special item, objective 5)
- Parade Sword (special item, objective 7)
- Finely Crafted Dagger (special item, objective 9)
- Experience Points: 1,440 (upon quest completion)

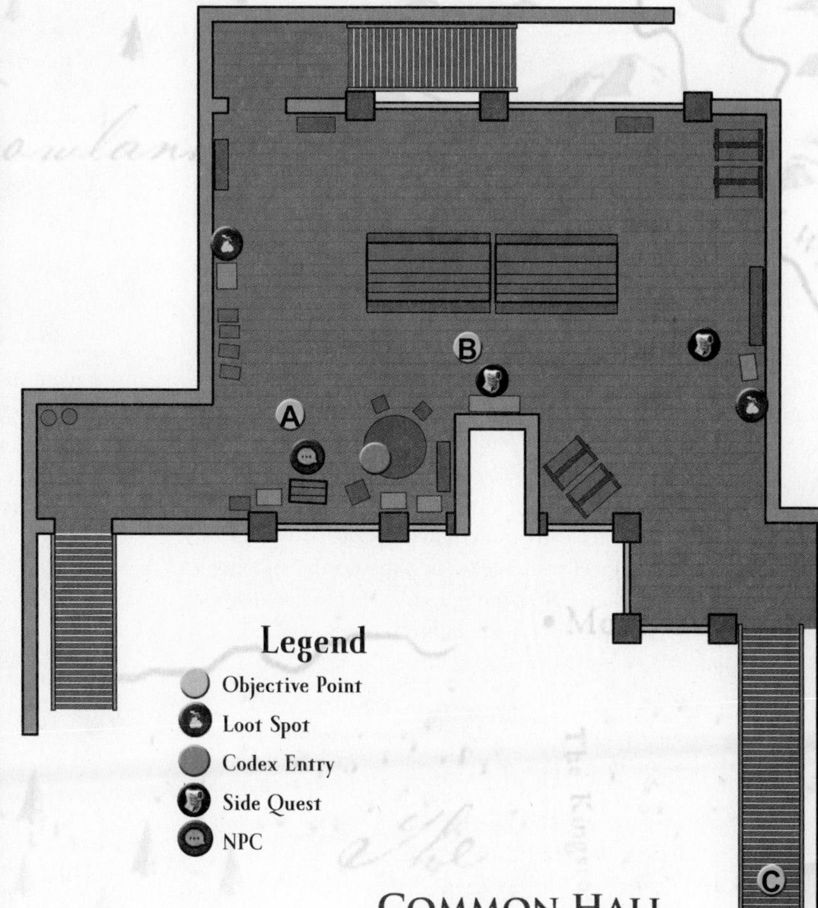

Objectives

1. Go back to Mole's Town and track down the impostor passing himself off as Godric Donnerly
2. Let Lothor lead you to the man who is bribing some of the Night's Watch
3. Follow the scents to learn more about this sorry business
4. Interrogate the corrupt brothers currently enjoying their newfound fortune at the whorehouse in Mole's Town
5. Cross through the smugglers' tunnels under Mole's Town to return to Yohn's camp
6. Scout the area around Yohn's camp without entering the center
7. Get rid of Yohn and his men once and for all
8. Speak with Jeyne when you're ready to leave the north for good
9. Search the cottage for your family

1. Go back to Mole's Town and track down the impostor passing himself off as Godric Donnerly

Objective Point A

You return to Castle Black and meet up with the Lord Commander in the upper level of the Common Hall. He has decided that a fellow brother, Addam Flowers, will lead an investigation into flushing out any traitors in the Night's Watch. Mormont also names you a recruiter of the Night's Watch, which will allow you to remain Jeyne Greystone's protector and travel with her outside the northern domain of the Night's Watch. First, though, you need to take Patrek and hunt down the Ser Godric impostor somewhere in the Gift.

TIP

Equip the Recruiter's Cloak after your conversation with Mormont.

Objective Point B

If you want to begin "The Black Bloodhound" side quest, speak with Addam Flowers on the second floor next to Lord Commander Mormont. If you plan on working on the "The Faith of Our Ancestors" side quest, turn in your Mother statuette to Walder, who is standing near Flowers.

Side Quest: The Black Bloodhound

If you want to take part in the inquiry to identify the corrupt brothers, speak with Addam Flowers after your initial conversation with Lord Commander Mormont. All the brothers you want to question are currently in the Common Hall. Make sure you complete this side quest during this chapter of the main quest or you miss your opportunity. For more details on the various interrogations and completing the quest, see the "Side Quests" chapter.

Side Quest: New Blood

When Lord Commander Mormont deputizes you as a recruiter of the Night's Watch, he also bestows the "New Blood" side quest on you. On your journey, your task is to locate as many men as possible who are prepared to take the black. The underground tunnels of Mole's Town are a great place to start, and you can continue to recruit even when you venture south. For more details on the best recruitment areas and completing the quest, see the "Side Quests" chapter.

Objective Point C

Leave the Common Hall and exit Castle Black when you're ready to head back out to Mole's Town. Don't forget to upgrade gear and restock potions.

Tip

Patrek joins your party again for your trip back to Mole's Town and the Gift.

Mole's Town

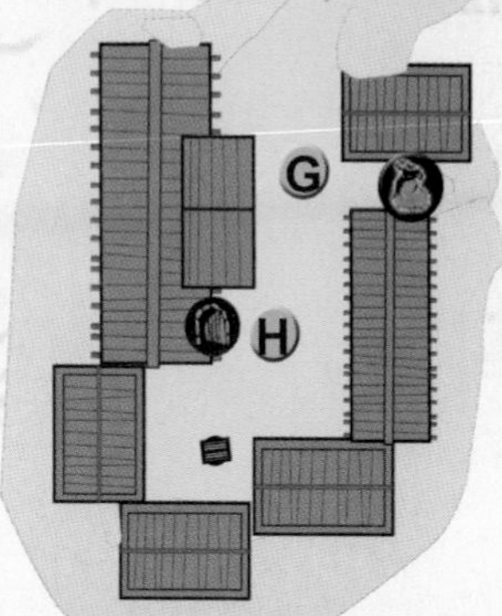

Legend

- Objective Point
- Loot Spot
- Secret Treasure (Dog)
- Travel to Area
- NPC
- Enemy

2. Let Lothor Lead You to the Man Who is Bribing Some of the Night's Watch

Objective Point A

You see two thugs beating up one of your brothers a short distance into Mole's Town. For you, Patrek, and Dog, these two will barely make you break out in a sweat. After you dispatch them, the brother, Lothor, explains that he refused to accept the bribe to betray the Night's Watch and join the impostor's men, and he would have died for that decision if you hadn't arrived. Before he returns to Castle Black, he offers to show you where the men who bribed him are hiding.

Objective Point B

Follow Lothor. He will lead you straight to Jared, the impostor's lieutenant, who has been charged with getting as many of the Night's Watch to betray their vows and hunt down Jeyne.

Objective Point C

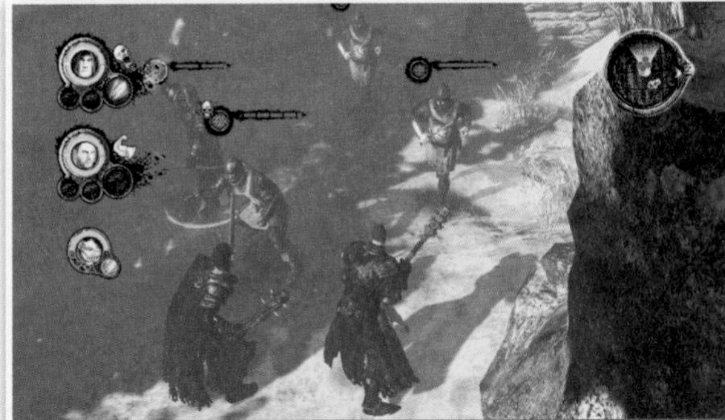

You confront Jared when you reach the secluded spot where they've been bribing some of the Night's Watch. After some banter back and forth, weapons are drawn and it's combat time. Jared can rally his men with some of his abilities, so make sure that Mors or Patrek smack Jared with an interrupt attack when he tries to bolster the enemy troops. Send Dog to immobilize one of the enemies while Patrek takes on another. You can easily handle two yourself, with health to spare to help out with the others.

3. Follow the Scents to Learn More About This Sorry Business

Objective Point D

Dog can track three scents from the bribing spot. Lock on to the first scent and follow its yellow trail through the forest. The greenish trails are the other scents, and if you spot a blue trail, you might want to detour momentarily to seek out some hidden treasure.

Objective Point E

The first scent trail leads to the dead body of one of the Night's Watch. He was likely killed for his coins. The scent trail continues, leading north from the corpse.

Objective Point F

The end of the first trail leads to Raff Mouldy, a trader with a very questionable past. There's no doubt that he murdered your brother for the money, so you confront him on it.

Knowing that he's been caught, Mouldy draws his weapons and a fight breaks out. Whenever he tries to perform an action, have Mors, Patrek, and Dog take turns interrupting it. With all three chipping in damage, Mouldy will fall quickly.

Objective Point G

Return back to Jared's corpse and hunt for the person leaving the second scent. It will lead you south toward Mole's Town. Just before you reach the main door, the scent veers off to the left. You discover a hidden treasure in the alley. Mors claims the coins, which the turncoat must have buried in the stump for safekeeping.

Objective Point H

The second and third scent trails converge and lead to the main door to Mole's Town. The betrayers have entered Mole's Town, likely wanting to spend their new coin on the vices within.

Legend

- Objective Point
- Loot Spot
- Side Quest
- NPC
- Merchant
- Enemy

A

B

C

Tunnels of Mole's Town Upper Level

4. Interrogate the Corrupt Brothers Currently Enjoying Their Newfound Fortune at the Whorehouse in Mole's Town

Objective Point A

You're back in Mole's Town, so speak with Sybelle behind the desk at the entrance. After some conversation, she tells you where the corrupt brothers are and hands you the Key to the Master Bedroom, which opens the locked door downstairs.

Tip

If you speak with Willow next to the main door, she will provide a lead on a man who you can recruit for your "New Blood" side quest.

Objective Point B

Head downstairs and open the door into the master bedroom. You have a choice here: attack the corrupt brothers or show them mercy. If you choose "I need to find out where the impostor is hiding," they will give you information in exchange for their lives, and you learn the password to open the smugglers' door in the tunnel below. You send the corrupt brothers back to Castle Black to await punishment from Mormont. You now know the impostor's name is Yohn, and you will have to navigate the tunnels beneath Mole's Town to follow Yohn's trail and catch him in the Gift.

Tip

For extra experience, you can choose to put the corrupt brothers to the sword when you confront them in the master bedroom.

Objective Point C

Out in the hallway, you meet up with two more of the Night's Watch, Myles and Wat. They were sent by Mormont to help you on your mission against the impostor Yohn. You, Patrek, and Dog will do the heavy fighting; Myles and Wat are assigned to protect Jeyne during the last part of your vengeance venture.

Note

Though Myles and Wat join your party, you cannot control them directly.

Objective Point D

Return back upstairs and find the stairs behind the kitchen. They lead down to the trapdoor that grants access to the tunnels beneath Mole's Town. When you're ready, enter the tunnels and prepare for some heavy fighting in tight confines.

Tunnels of Mole's Town Lower Level

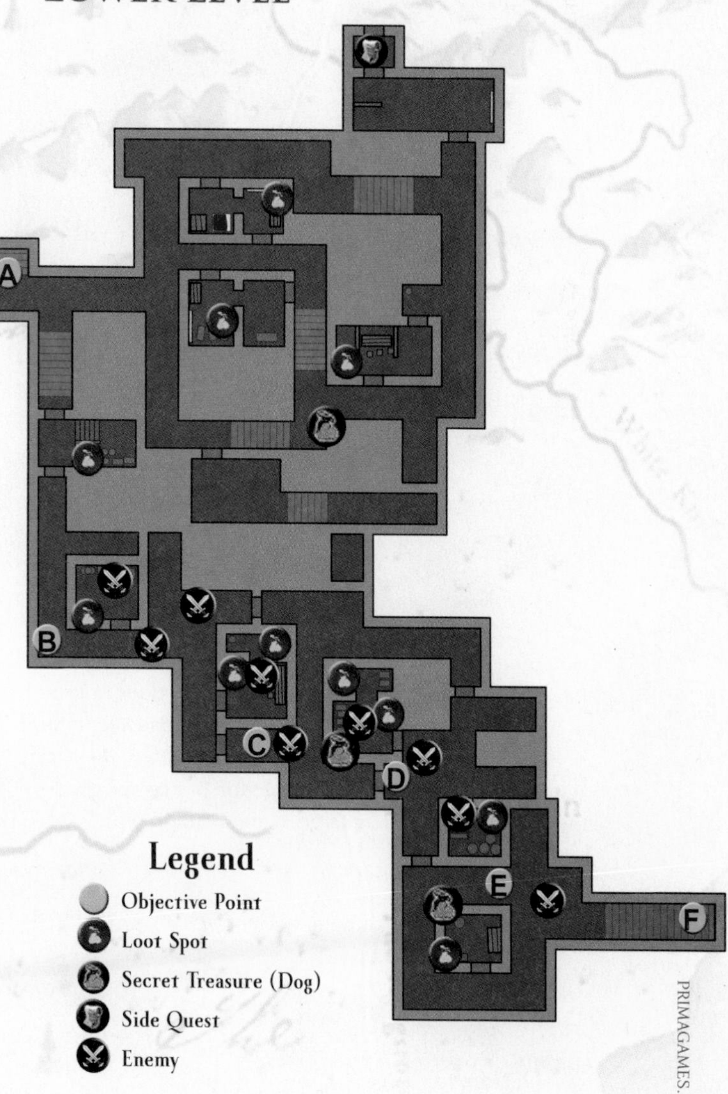

5. Cross Through the Smugglers' Tunnels under Mole's Town to Return to Yohn's Camp

Objective Point A

Descend to the lower level and give the proper password ("The feast will begin soon") at the smugglers' door. If you want, you can kick the door in and knock out the smuggler behind it.

Objective Point B

Continue south until you reach the first of Yohn's men guarding the tunnels beyond the password door. At this point, if you see a lone guard, you should send Dog in on a sneak attack to keep the guard from sounding the alarm. With bigger groups, it's impossible for Dog to sneak up on them, so you'll have to charge in and battle it out.

There's a closed door on the left wall that leads to a storage room. It's possible to eliminate the guard in the hallway, open the door, and sneak attack the second guard in the storage room. If you can't surprise him, you still have him trapped in the storage room where it's easy to gang up on him.

Objective Point C

Continue east and look for the first large enemy group past the next door. If you have ranged weapons, unload on the enemies before they can advance. If not, use your stuns and knockdowns to keep enemies from piling on you. Use Dog to immobilize or interrupt enemies that try to team up on Mors. You may have to quaff a healing potion in this battle if it starts to go against you.

Objective Point D

To the east lies a second large enemy group. Rely on similar tactics to the last fight. There are several small side rooms along this tunnel. Beware of enemies lurking inside those rooms, and duck into any of the rooms for cover if you need some extra defense or a few extra seconds to regain energy or sip a healing potion.

TIP

The Baratheon Guard Shield lies discarded in the small storeroom in the northwest section of this area.

Objective Point E

One last battle stands in your way of the tunnel exit. As with the two previous fights, maximize your stuns, knockdowns, and extra-damage abilities on key targets. You have a little more room to maneuver in this battle, especially near the exit stairs.

Objective Point F

After you've scoured the bodies for loot, find the stairs leading up to the trapdoor. Open the trapdoor out into the Gift and continue your hunt for Yohn.

Legend

- Objective Point
- Secret Treasure (Dog)
- Enemy

A B C D E

THE GIFT

6. Scout the Area Around Yohn's Camp Without Entering the Center

Objective Point A

You track Yohn down to his camp. From up on the hill overlooking the campsite, you and Patrek discuss an attack strategy. You have two choices: You can rush in and begin the battle immediately, or you can opt to sneak around and take out the perimeter guards first. If you don't choose the sneaky route and eliminate the outer guards, you're in for a very difficult battle against Yohn.

Caution

Before beginning the camp fight, slay Yohn's perimeter guards first or the enemy can easily overwhelm you.

Objective Point B

Stay clear of the campfire and sneak around the paths that surround the camp. There are three sets of sentries. Use Dog to silently take out the first one from behind. You also notice that this an excellent vantage point for an archer, which will prove advantageous for the fight against Yohn.

Objective Point C

Repeat your tactics on the second sentry. If you approach from the main path, his back is to you. Rip his throat out without alerting the others.

Objective Point D

The last sentries are a pair. You can use Dog to locate them, but once you get close, switch to Mors and charge in. Once you slay the last two sentries, the campsite no longer has reinforcements. Return to Patrek on the first hill.

7. Get Rid of Yohn and His Men Once and for All

Objective Point E

If you found the archer position, order Wat to the overlook for extra support. Let Patrek know you're ready and confront Yohn and his handful of remaining men. Before you come to blows, Yohn reveals he's working for Ser Valarr Hill.

It's a much easier fight if you take out all the sentries first. Keep your party close to Yohn and rotate powerful attacks against him. If you throw a variety of stuns and damaging effects on him, Yohn won't strike back hard and his men will die in short order without their leader's powerful presence.

While searching the bodies after the battle, you find Jeyne's missing valuables, including a ring engraved with a crowned stag, the royal sigil. Jeyne eventually confesses that she's King Robert Baratheon's mistress, and you figure that's a likely reason why these men are out to kill her.

TIP

Remove the Parade Sword from Yohn's corpse and equip it if the blade's an upgrade.

Book Watch: King Robert Baratheon

After the battle with Yohn, Jeyne Greystone reveals that she had an affair with the king. She met Robert Baratheon on one of his hunting expeditions. Jeyne describes him just as we find Robert Baratheon in the novel *A Game of Thrones*: jovial and tempestuous, always eating and shouting, and yet, he has a deep sorrow inside. Jeyne wisely speculates that he's unhappy with his marriage to the queen and started their fling as a way to escape from his kingly duties. That same impulsive behavior gets him into trouble in the book.

8. Speak with Jeyne When You're Ready to Leave the North for Good

You bid Patrek, Wat, and Myles good-bye as they return to Castle Black. As you head south, it will only be you, Jeyne, and your hound.

After a long march, you camp in the Riverlands for the night. You talk with Jeyne for a while, and you can share stories about your pasts if you choose. You tell her that you're heading to Westford Cottage, a secluded home that only a few know about. Your wife and daughter hid there when you took the black, and you figure it's as safe a place as any while you're on the run with Jeyne. You also desperately want to see your family after 15 years.

9. Search the Cottage for Your Family

Westford Cottage

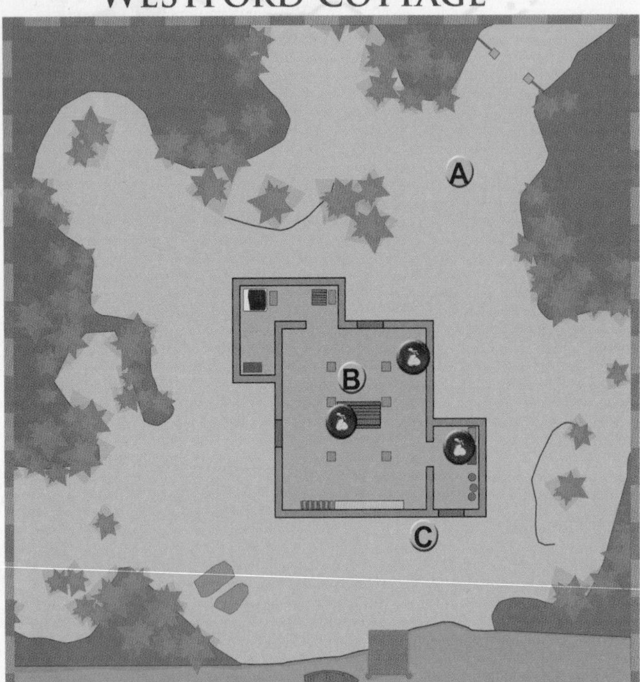

Legend

Objective Point

Loot Spot

Objective Point A

You arrive at your old home after such a long, long time. As you wander about the grounds and inside the cottage, black-and-white flashbacks from your last moments with your wife flood your memory. Walk through the cottage to see the entire sad tale of when you left your family for the Night's Watch.

Objective Point B

Pick up the Finely Crafted Dagger on the table inside the cottage. Continue to walk around and watch the flashback scenes. When you read the parchment from your father, it unlocks the Westford Legacy and House Westford Codex entries.

Objective Point C

When you leave through the back door, you push Jeyne aside as she tries to stop you from seeing what's in the backyard: the grave markers for your wife, Cerenna, and your daughter, Tya. Despite all you gave up, they never survived. All these years you've been dreaming of meeting back up with them, and now it's all for naught.

You don't have long to mourn. You realize that when you accidentally shoved Jeyne out of the way, she fell and grasped her belly. You discover that's she with child—the bastard child of King Robert Baratheon—and new enemies have found you. Dog barks and warns you of an imminent attack.

CHAPTER 8, PART 1

A NEW HOPE

Legend
- Objective Point
- Loot Spot
- Codex Entry
- Travel to World
- Travel to Area
- NPC
- Merchant

KING'S LANDING

A B C

OBJECTIVES

1. Meet Lord Harlton outside his residence in King's Landing
2. Your brother's disappearance seems to be connected to a disturbing crime that took place in the sewers of King's Landing
3. Now that you are in the tunnels, quietly make your way to where Harlton was supposed to meet Gawen and search for clues
4. The Reapers appear to be related to the murder. Find their den by following the signs they use to mark the way
5. Search the town and assemble a Gold Cloaks' uniform or purchase the items from shops
6. Use the uniform you've obtained to infiltrate the City Watch Tower
7. Speak to the guards to gather information and access the dungeons without arousing suspicion
8. Find Gawen's body
9. Interrogate the murderer held prisoner in the basement
10. Access the officers' quarters to search the City Watch commander's office
11. Help Orys escape, or leave him to rot
12. Go back to Lord Harlton's residence and tell him what you've discovered
13. Join Rupert in the arena hidden in the Sewers of King's Landing
14. Get ready in the preparation room downstairs, then tell the guard when you want to start the fight
15. Defeat the arena champion and return to Rupert
16. Meet Lord Harlton outside his residence in King's Landing to study the book that Maester Rupert gave you

1. Meet Lord Harlton Outside His Residence in King's Landing

Quest Checklist

- Arwood Harlton (NPC, objectives 1, 12, 16)
- Desmond Hardyng (companion, objective 2)
- Key to the Sewer Drain (quest item, objective 3)
- Gawen's Broken Locket (quest item, objective 3)
- Reapers' Master Key (quest item, objective 4)
- Gold Cloak Coat of Mail (quest item, objective 5)
- Gold Cloak Kettle Hat (quest item, objective 5)
- Chataya (NPC, objective 5)
- City Watch Cloak (quest item, objective 5)
- Gold Cloak Leather Boots (quest item, objective 5)
- Gold Cloak Leather Gloves (quest item, objective 5)
- Raymun (NPC, objective 7)
- Caron (NPC, objective 7)
- Humphrey (NPC, objective 8)
- Key to Orys' Cell (quest item, objective 8)
- Orys (NPC, objective 9)
- A Mission Order (quest item, objective 10)
- "Self-Made Girl" (side quest, objective 12)
- Rupert (NPC, objectives 13, 15)
- "Blood on the Sand" (side quest, objective 16)
- Experience Points: 1,250 (upon quest completion)

Objective Point A

Lord Harlton has information regarding your brother's disappearance. Now that you've arrived in King's Landing, it's time to seek him out. Head through the city to the northern section and speak with the lord of Castlewood.

Objective Point B

Lord Harlton's estate is a majestic place with gardens on either side of a stone arch. Walk up the stairs inside the arch and speak with the green Castlewood guards in the courtyard. They'll give you a hard time but will eventually let you in to see their master.

Harlton briefs you on Gawen's recent activities. A friend of his had helped Gawen find refuge in the sewers beneath King's Landing, but then something terrible happened. Harlton fears that your brother has been murdered. He lends you Ser Desmond Hardyng to help on your quest to find clues to the truth behind Gawen's disappearance.

2. Your Brother's Disappearance Seems to Be Connected to a Disturbing Crime That Took Place in the Sewers of King's Landing

Objective Point C

You set off with Ser Desmond for the sewers. He knows an entrance to the sewers near the marketplace. Before you descend into the dangerous tunnels, you may want to visit the merchants in the marketplace and spend your coin on upgrades or potions in preparation for the journey.

Companion Role Call: Desmond Hardyng

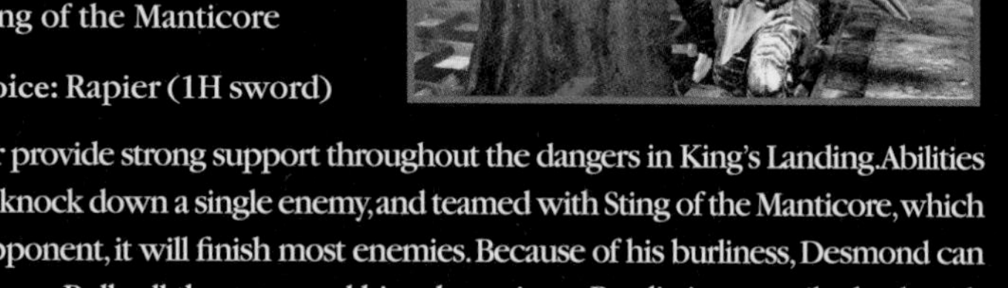

Stats:

- **Strength: 6**
- **Agility: 8**
- **Luck: 6**
- **Endurance: 7**
- **Intelligence: 8**

Class: Water Dancer

Stance: Intensity

Abilities: Bully, Calm as Still Water, Fierce as a Wolverine, Retaliation, Smooth as Summer Silk, Sting of the Manticore

Weapons of Choice: Rapier (1H sword)

Description: Ser Desmond and his rapier provide strong support throughout the dangers in King's Landing. Abilities like Calm as Still Water can interrupt and knock down a single enemy, and teamed with Sting of the Manticore, which deals big damage to a knocked down opponent, it will finish most enemies. Because of his burliness, Desmond can frequently charge into the center of a group, Bully all those around him, then trigger Retaliation to strike back with precision. Even if you want Alester to take the lead, Desmond can hack away with the best of them.

Sewers of King's Landing

Legend

- Objective Point
- Loot Spot
- Secret Treasure (Alester)
- Codex Entry
- Travel to Area
- NPC
- Enemy

3. Now That You Are in the Tunnels, Quietly Make Your Way to Where Harlton Was Supposed to Meet Gawen and Search for Clues

Objective Point A

Desmond guides you to the sewers and informs you that your route will have to go through the arena, a pit where patrons bet on warriors who battle it out, sometimes to the death. He warns you to be on your guard throughout the sewer tunnels: all manner of scum float through here.

Objective Point B

Enter the arena area. Feel free to explore all the doors and corridors that connect to it. Some lead to the lower levels where combatants prepare for battle; others lead up to the surface. You can collect some additional loot through exploration.

Objective Point C

When you're ready to proceed deeper into the sewers, take the door in the arena's southwest corner. Pass through the tattered curtain in the corridor and turn left at the next intersection.

Objective Point D

You approach a mugging in progress. It's too late to save the poor man, but you can make the muggers pay for their cruelty. Send Desmond in to Bully them while you hang back and cut down the wounded.

Watch out for a second group that may appear from behind you. Eliminate the first group, then have Desmond Bully the second group and defend with Retaliation as you deliver killing blows with your better abilities. After you kill off all the enemies, retrieve the Key to the Sewer Drain from the dead man who was mugged.

Objective Point E

Continue on and use the keys you just received to enter the storeroom to the south. Two members of the Reaper clan discuss their latest mercenary deed, and when you finally confront them, they attack.

One Reaper wears heavy armor, and the other wears medium armor. Match up with whichever enemy you think you can handle, and let Desmond take on the other. Remember to switch your weapon to either perforating or blunt to deal extra damage against your foe.

One Reaper survives the fight: Porky. Ask him to give you Gawen's Broken Locket, your first clue that your brother was indeed here in the sewers. Porky also tells you how to find the Reaper den where his bosses reside. Follow the Reaper symbols painted on the walls, and they lead you to the den. At the end of the conversation, you can choose to kill or release Porky, and you need to grab the Reapers' Master Key from the other dead Reaper.

4. The Reapers Appear to Be Related to the Murder. Find Their Den by Following the Signs They Use to Mark the Way

Objective Point F

Continue south and use the Reapers' Master Key to penetrate deeper into the sewers. Follow the skull and scythe symbols painted on the walls to locate the Reapers' den.

Objective Point G

Head east and carefully peek around corners and open doors. The Reapers infest these corridors, and you'll have to fight through guards to reach the den. If you take the groups out one by one and don't run around and draw attention to yourself, you should be fine.

Objective Point H

Take the opportunity to ambush enemy groups with a sneak attack if you have a ranged weapon. If not, charging around a corner at an enemy group can close you to melee range quickly before they can ready ranged weapons of their own.

Objective Point I

Flip the lever in the small room to the north. This allows you to continue on to the Reapers' den.

Objective Point J

You have one last fight before the Reapers' den. A group of guards defend the chamber in front of the stairs leading up to the den. Send Desmond into their midst to corral them with Bully; then hit them with an ability that affects multiple foes or stun any enemy that breaks away from the pack. You'll have them all down on the ground in less than a minute if you attack wounded enemies before the healthier ones.

Objective Point K

You've reached the Reapers' infamous hideout. Enter through the large oak door with the skull and scythe symbol on it to confront the Reaper leaders.

Objective Point L

Attack the guards inside the door with the same tactics you've been using. There are also guards in the hallway beyond. Once you've killed them all, you can finally find Axe, the Reaper lieutenant, behind the last door to the south.

Objective Point M

Axe and his cronies, the same Reapers who tried to mug you when you first arrived in King's Landing, are running affairs while their leader, Orys, is missing in action. Axe doesn't take kindly to you barging into their den, so it's brawl time.

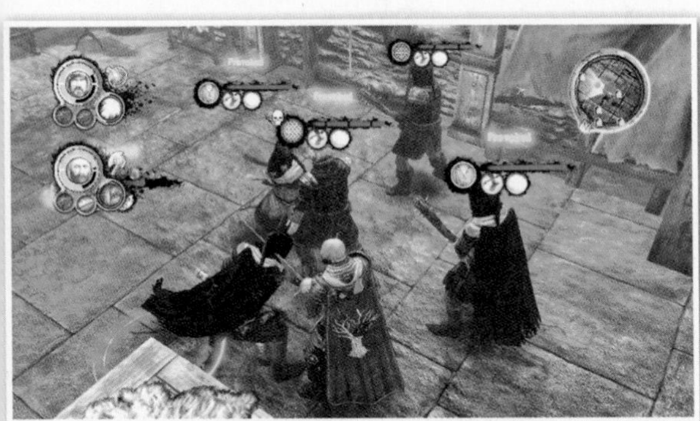

You should have your teamwork down by now: Desmond draws foes toward him with Bully and defends well with Retaliate, and you slay enemies one by one with your best damage-dealing attacks. There are a lot of foes, but most aren't well armored. Pick off the lightly armored foes and leave Axe for last.

Remove Ability
Add Ability
Desmond

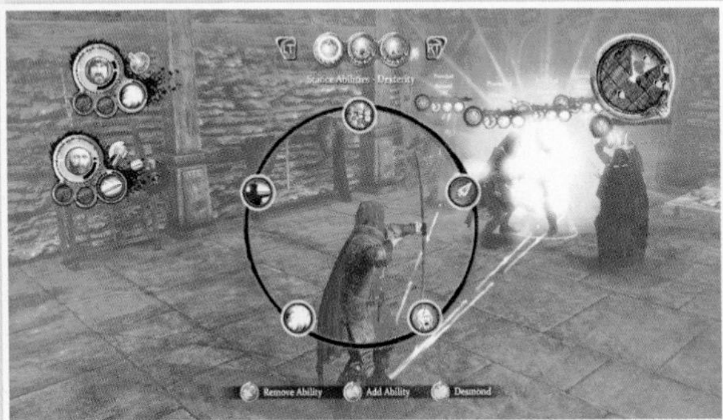

When you take Axe down, he concedes. He doesn't know much about Gawen's disappearance, but his boss, Orys, might. Axe explains that Orys was captured by the Gold Cloaks and brought to the City Watch Tower. If you want to learn more about how the Reapers obtained Gawen's necklace, you'll have to infiltrate the Watch Tower. You can then choose to kill Axe or release him.

> **TIP**
>
> If you choose to spare him, Axe will show up later in the adventure and fight by your side. However, if you kill him, you will be able to loot Axe's body for his powerful one-handed axe.

Objective Point N

Axe
Enough... You win. I have to admit you're a good fighter.

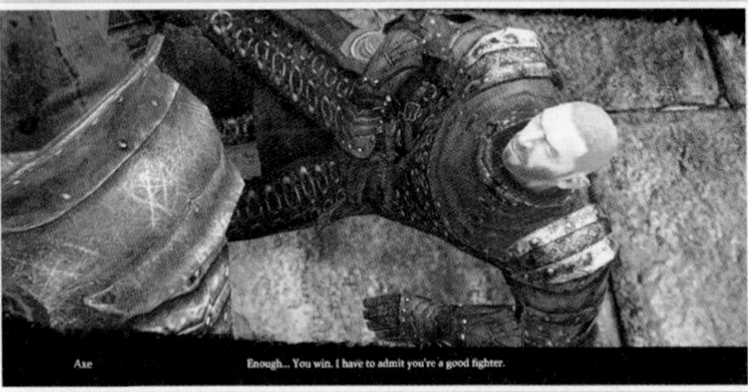

Exit back to King's Landing through the den's back door. Desmond agrees that the City Watch Tower holds your answers, but first you'll have to pose as a Gold Cloak and obtain a full uniform: breastplate, helm, boots, gloves, and cloak.

King's Landing

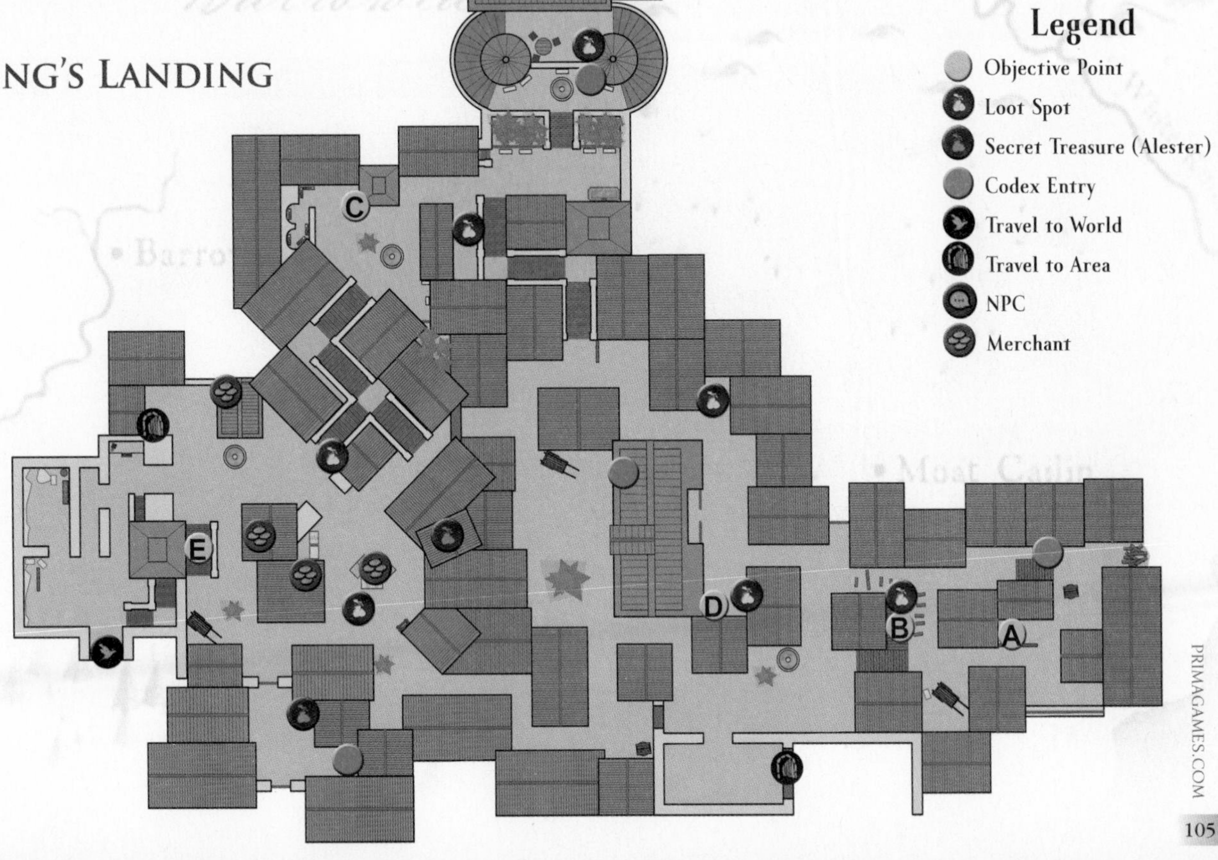

Legend
Objective Point
Loot Spot
Secret Treasure (Alester)
Codex Entry
Travel to World
Travel to Area
NPC
Merchant
A
B
C
D
E

5. Search the Town and Assemble a Gold Cloaks' Uniform or Purchase the Items from Shops

Objective Point A

If you're flush with cash, you can simply go to the market and buy what you need to assemble a Gold Cloak uniform. It's expensive, though, so you can skip paying the merchants if you want to save coin for future upgrades or don't have the money to buy the items.

Tip

You don't have to buy the Gold Cloak armor items. You can find them all in King's Landing with Ser Desmond's help.

Objective Point B

When you pass the inn with Desmond, he mentions how he used to come here for drinks with his buddies. That's your clue to search the area. Turn the corner and look out on the landing behind the building.

Sure enough, you discover a city guard passed out on the landing. While he sleeps off the wine, you can grab his breastplate and helm. Cross off two of the five items on your Gold Cloak list and move on.

Objective Point C

Return to Chataya's for some more help. The madam stands outside this time, and after you explain your needs, she is able to procure a cloak from one of the Gold Cloaks inside having a good time with her girls.

Objective Point D

When you pass near the gardens that hold the secret entrance to the Sarwyck Manse, Desmond says that city guards sometimes take naps in this peaceful area. Look around the corner and you'll spot a Gold Cloak resting in the shade.

Unfortunately, when you try to grab his items, the guard awakes. You have to fight him. It's not much of a challenge—one guard against the two of you—so cut him down quickly and take his gloves and boots.

6. Use the Uniform You've Obtained to Infiltrate the City Watch Tower

Objective Point E

Don your Gold Cloak outfit and walk over to the City Watch Tower. If you don't have the full uniform on, the guard at the top of the steps will not let you in. Once you have all five armor pieces equipped, you can enter the tower.

City Watch Tower Upper Basement

City Watch Tower Ground Floor

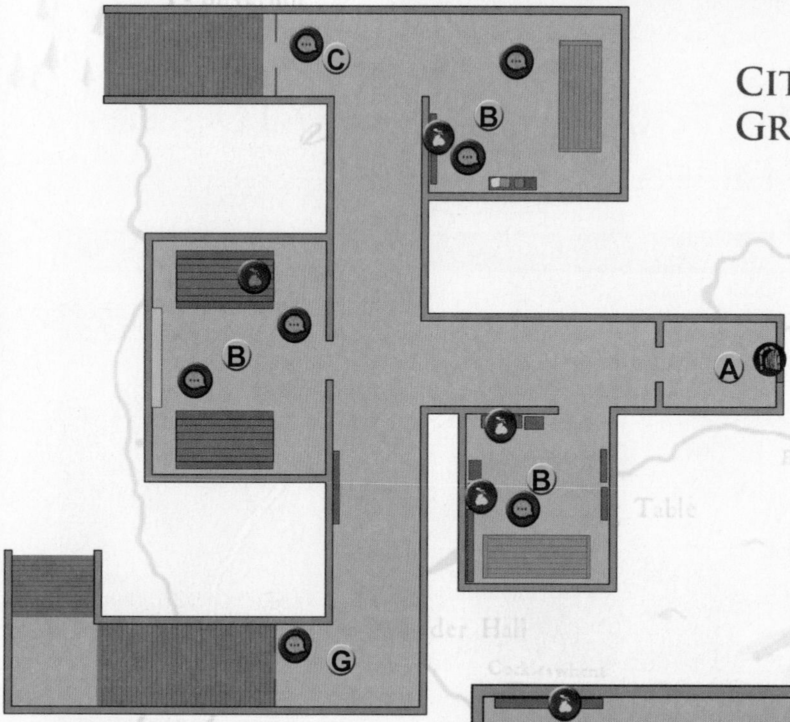

City Watch Tower First Floor

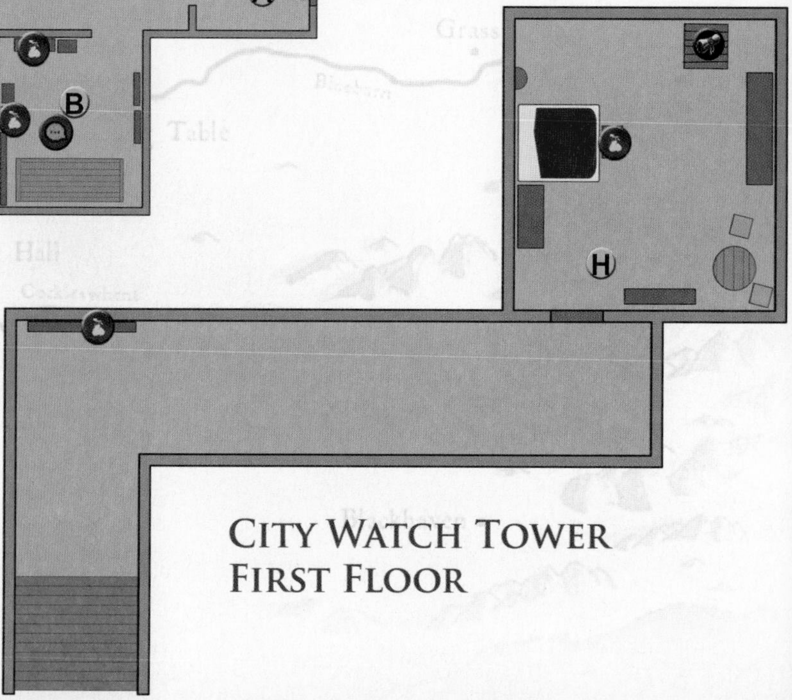

Legend

- Objective Point
- Loot Spot
- Secret Treasure (Alester)
- Primary Quest
- Travel to World
- Travel to Area
- NPC

7. Speak to the Guards to Gather Information and Access the Dungeons without Arousing Suspicion

Objective Point A

Enter the City Watch Tower. While in uniform, you can roam freely throughout the main floor. Talk to as many guards as you can before making your decisions on how best to pursue your mission in the tower.

Objective Point B

Interview the guards and you'll learn this: The guards are wagering on how long the final prisoner will survive in the tower dungeon; Commander Janos Slynt is in charge of the tower, but he's left for the Red Keep; and the guards are all afraid of Ser Harrold.

Objective Point C

Speak with Caron when you want to see the corpse and the prisoner down in the dungeon. If you tell Caron that you want to wager on the prisoner and that you want to see him first before you make the bet, he'll let you downstairs.

8. Find Gawen's Body

Objective Point D

You can speak with Humphrey, who guards the cells in the basement area. The conversation doesn't really impact your objective ; Humphrey will let you pass to see the body in both cases.

Objective Point E

Inspect the dead body in the side room. It appears to be your brother Gawen: He wears the Sarwyck crest on his clothes, and there's a letter on the body from Falena.

While you torture yourself over the corpse and how you should have done more for your brother, Humphrey checks on you. He wants to know if you're through, and you ask to see the prisoner. He refuses on the grounds that you might kill the prisoner and he'll lose the wager he bet on him. You can choose to bribe Humphrey, threaten him with your "connections" to Ser Harrold, or simply attack him to get through to see the prisoner.

9. Interrogate the Murderer Held Prisoner in the Basement

Objective Point F

Go see the prisoner, Orys, locked in his cell. You explain that you're not really a Gold Cloak and it's in his best interest to talk to you. Orys says it was Janos Slynt who paid him to kill those men in the sewers, and then the Commander of the City Watch betrayed Orys and locked him away. He also recognized a letter from Valarr to Slynt in the Commander's office upstairs; if you could get that, it would prove Valarr's involvement in the whole seedy affair. Before you leave, you have the opportunity to attack Orys, or you can wait to attack him later or set him free.

Tip

If you spare Orys's life and get him out of the City Watch Tower, he will fight for you later in your adventure.

10. Access the Officers' Quarters to Search the City Watch Commander's Office

Objective Point G

Return to the ground floor and speak with Raymun, who guards the stairs up to the first floor. If you pretend to be on a mission, tell him that Janos Slynt sent you, and remind him that Slynt isn't in the tower at the moment and hates to be disappointed, he'll give in and let you upstairs.

Objective Point H

Return to Orys down in the cells. Make your choice whether he lives or dies.

TIP

Don't forget to pick up Commander Janos Slynt's official seal in this room with the Vision of R'hllor vision if you want to free Orys.

11. Help Orys Escape, or Leave Him to Rot

Objective Point I

If you kill Orys, you can simply walk out of the tower and no one will be the wiser. If you leave with Orys, Caron will stop you when you return to the ground fl oor. If you have the seal and tell Caron that Orys is being transferred, you can leave without a fight. If you try to lie to him in any other manner or attack him outright, you will have to battle through every guard in the tower to escape.

Objective Point J

If you choose to fight it out, prepare for a very long battle against several groups of Gold Cloaks. To make matters worse, Orys has only a dagger, so the enemies have better armor by far than your small group. Orys will need a lot of supportive damage if he leads the charge. It's generally better for you to take on the Gold Cloaks and let Orys chip away with damage from the perimeter.

Companion Role Call: Orys

Stats:	**Strength: 8**	**Endurance: 6**
	Agility: 10	**Intelligence: 8**
	Luck: 8	

Class: Sellsword

Stance: Assassination

Abilities: Deterring Strike, Pommel Strike, Precision Strike, Savage Strike

Weapons of Choice: Misericorde (1H dagger)

Description: Because Orys isn't wearing armor and relies on the Assassination stance, Alester should draw most of the attention in the City Watch Tower battle. Orys can support well with Precision Strike, which Bleeds an opponent; Savage Strike, which interrupts and deals massive damage if your opponent is stunned; and Pommel Strike, which also interrupts and has a chance to disarm your opponent. If too many guards swarm Orys, use Deterring Strike to send all enemies in range at Alester and off Orys, but only if Alester can handle those numbers and not be overrun himself.

CAUTION

The City Watch Tower battle is one of the most difficult fights in the game!

King's Landing

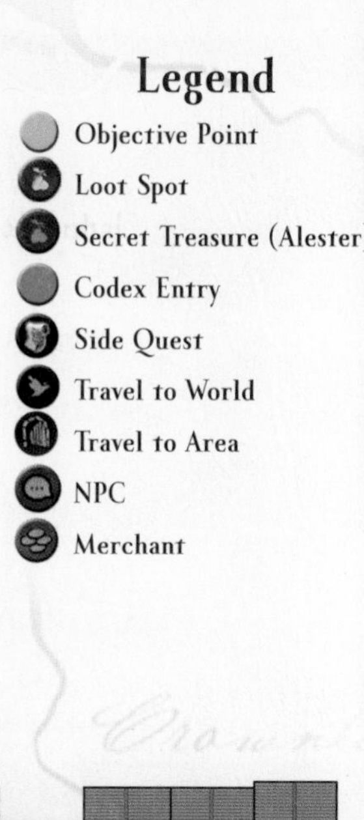

12. Go back to Lord Harlton's residence and tell him what you've discovered

Objective Point A

Whether alone or with Orys by your side, you finally escape the City Watch Tower and exit back out into King's Landing. Say farewell to Orys if you saved him, and set off for Lord Harlton's estate. You don't have to wear your Gold Cloak armor any longer; however, it may be an upgrade to your previous equipment, in which case you may want to keep it on.

Side Quest: Self-Made Girl

Speak with Hubb near the fountain at the entrance to the city after you exit the City Watch Tower to pick up this side quest. A friend of Hubb's, Bethany, is in trouble, and he asks for your help to save her. You can start this quest now or pick it up anytime for the next several chapters, so decide when you'd like to take a break from the main quest. For more details on how to earn the Maiden statuette and complete the quest, see the "Side Quests" chapter.

Objective Point B

Speak with Harlton back at the estate. You tell him that you have discovered that Valarr had a hand in murdering Gawen, and Harlton links the series of murders in King's Landing to the bastard child. It seems the queen is ordering that bastard children be executed, including Harry Waters, who you executed earlier. Harlton has a lead on a book that discusses the lineage of the Seven Kingdoms, which Jon Arryn thought valuable before his death and Harlton also thinks is worth looking into. You volunteer to go with Ser Desmond to the arena again and talk to Harlton's man about this lineage book.

Objective Point C

Head back to the trapdoor that leads into the sewers. If you want to upgrade some equipment or restock potions, now is a good time to detour to the marketplace before visiting the arena.

Sewers of King's Landing

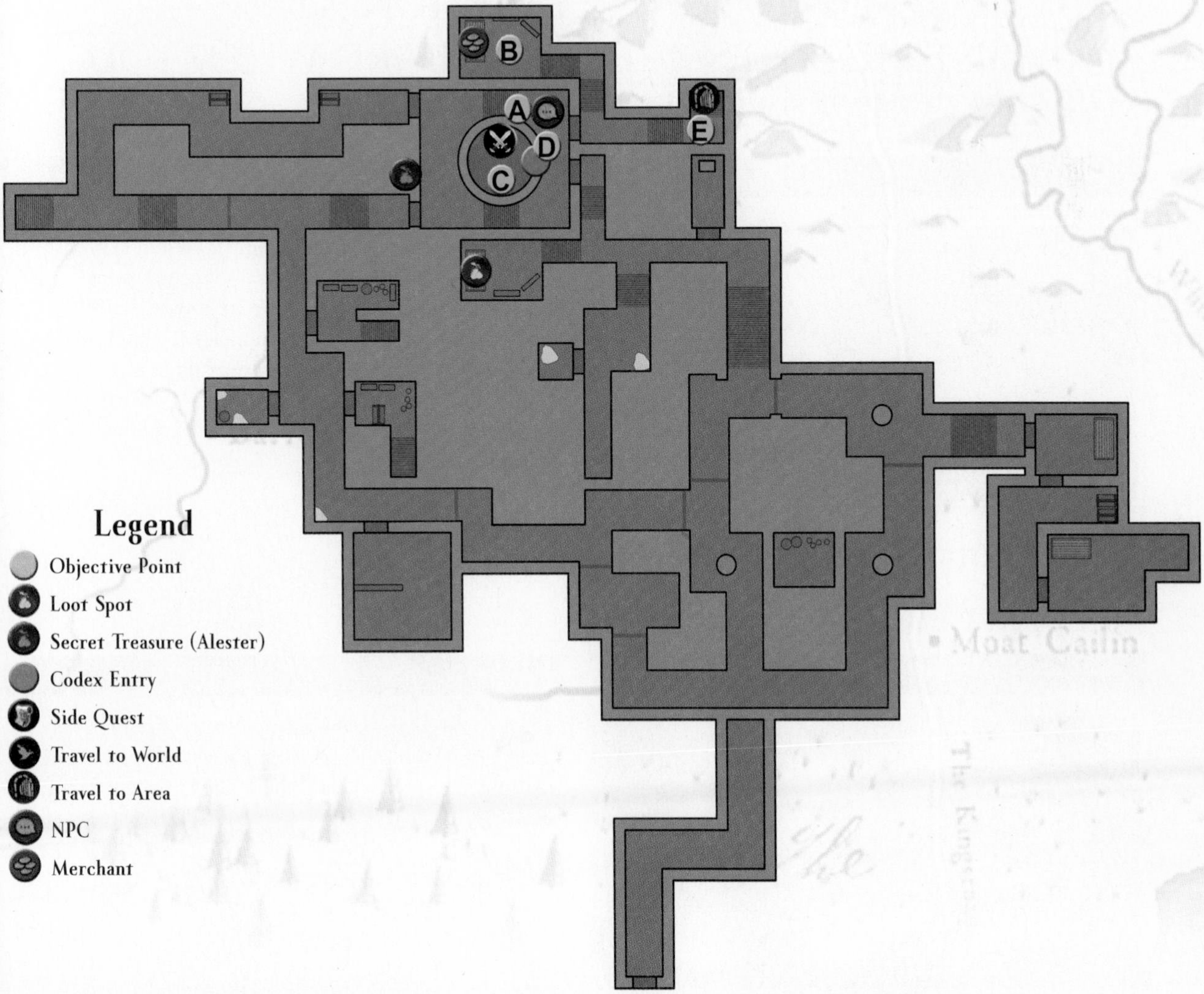

Legend

- Objective Point
- Loot Spot
- Secret Treasure (Alester)
- Codex Entry
- Side Quest
- Travel to World
- Travel to Area
- NPC
- Merchant

13. Join Rupert in the Arena Hidden in the Sewers of King's Landing

Objective Point A

Find Rupert in the back corner of the arena's upper level. He'll give you the book and his notes...if you help him out of a jam. He's got himself into considerable debt betting on the arena battles, and he's headed for indentured servitude unless you step in and offer to clear his debts by fighting in the arena.

Ossifer, the arena pit boss, arrives to finalize the deal. You can choose one of three names for your arena battle: keep your own name, choose a name that inspires fear (the Red Demon), or choose a name in honor of R'hllor (Azor Ahai). After Ossifer enters you into the arena tournament, you can prepare for the fight ahead.

14. Get Ready in the Preparation Room Downstairs, Then Tell the Guard When You Want to Start the Fight

Objective Point B

Go downstairs to the ready chamber. Desmond preps you with some information on your opponent: you can learn his weakness (he's vulnerable to Bleeding), and you can learn his strength (he has a Fear attack that prevents you from using your abilities; if you learn about this, you can try and avoid the attack in the arena). Or you can choose to rely on your instincts (you don't get any bonus heading into the arena).

15. Defeat the Arena Champion and Return to Rupert

Objective Point C

Speak to the guard at the gate and enter the arena. The champion, Errok, emerges to the crowd's cheers. Ossifer explains the rules of engagement, and it's a duel to the death.

Rely on your stun and knockdown effects to keep Errok off of you. He has a big melee attack, so you don't want to stand toe-to-toe with him. Try to use an interrupt as he winds up his fear attack; if he manages to get off the fear ability, circle around the arena until it wears off. While the fear effect lasts, you cannot use any special abilities. If you continue the hit-and-run tactics and apply damage here and there, you can beat the big giant.

Objective Point D

Return upstairs to Rupert. He gives you the book, and because of the spectacular show you put on, Ossifer invites you back to the arena any time. You might take him up on that if you accept the "Blood on the Sand" side quest.

Objective Point E

Use the trapdoor exit to which Desmond gives you the keys. You now have an entrance/exit to the sewers right next to the Harlton estate.

King's Landing

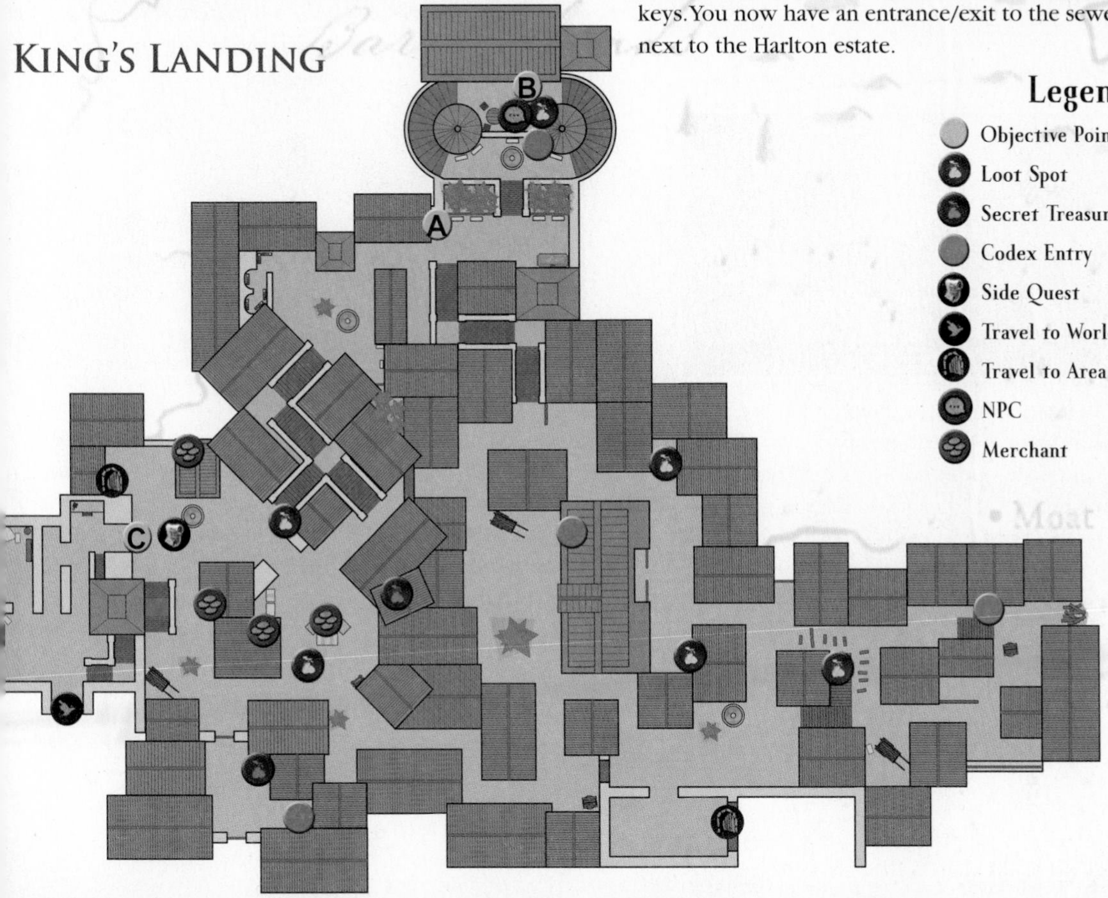

Legend

- Objective Point
- Loot Spot
- Secret Treasure (Alester)
- Codex Entry
- Side Quest
- Travel to World
- Travel to Area
- NPC
- Merchant

16. Meet Lord Harlton outside his residence in King's Landing to study the book that Maester Rupert gave you

Objective Point A

Once you're topside, you can return to Lord Harlton, or you may want to venture around the city first. At this point, you receive the "Blood on the Sand" side quest and can return to the arena to battle multiple combatants and earn a lot of coin.

TIP

The "Blood on the Sand" side quest has the most lucrative money rewards of all your quests. If you want extra coins to spend, take the time to do this quest.

Side Quest: Blood on the Sand

After your first victory in the arena, and after you leave the sewers, you can return for the "Blood on the Sand" side quest. You have the chance to battle five times and wager on yourself or your opponent to earn coin. You can make a lot of money on this quest, so it's highly recommended that you participate as soon as you have the extra time on your hands. For more details on the arena fights and completing the quest, see the "Side Quests" chapter.

Objective Point B

After puzzling through the book together with Lord Harlton, you figure out that the queen's children are illegitimate and the bastards who have been killed recently are the true descendants of King Robert Baratheon. Harlton confides in you that he's been secretly trying to overthrow the current regime, with your father as one of his co-conspirators, and return rule back to the Targaryens. Harlton also informs you that your father kept a list detailing all of Valarr's abuses of power and that it must be hidden back at Riverspring.

Objective Point C

Leave for Riverspring when you are ready. As you near the exit, Marianne Harlton, Arwood's niece, catches up with you. Through the conversation, you learn that Marianne and Arwood are the last two remaining Harltons and that the Harlton family has suffered greatly because they supported the old regime, the Targaryens. Finally, Marianne bids you farewell and you return to your home city.

Chapter 8, Part 2

Legacy

Objectives

1. Return to Riverspring to find the documents you need
2. Maester Harwyn might know something about your father's documents
3. Gawen is unworthy of the title of lord! Return to your office and make good on your threat!
4. The object of your search is likely to be concealed in the secret passage leading from your father's office. Find a way to access it
5. Search the underground tunnels to find the documents
6. Go to Castlewood and hand the precious documents to Lord Harlton
7. Tell Lord Harlton what you have discovered

1. Return to Riverspring to Find the Documents You Need

Quest Checklist

- Elyana Sarwyck (NPC, objective 1)
- "Rings and Chains" (side quest, objective 1)
- Harwyn (NPC, objective 2)
- Bunch of Keys to Riverspring Castle (quest item, objective 4)
- The Enigma of the Keys (quest item, objective 4)
- Raynald Sarwyck's Collar (special item, objective 4)
- The Father's Key (quest item, objective 4)
- The Warrior's Key (quest item, objective 4)
- The Stranger's Key (quest item, objective 4)
- The Maiden's Key (quest item, objective 4)
- The Mother's Key (quest item, objective 4)
- The Smith's Key (quest item, objective 4)
- The Crone's Key (quest item, objective 4)
- Minutes of the Shadow Council (quest item, objective 5)
- "Avenge Riverspring" (side quest, objective 5)
- Victor (NPC, objective 6)
- Arwood Harlton (NPC, objective 6)
- Experience Points: 1,500 (upon quest completion)

Objective Point A

You arrive in Riverspring looking for your father's secret documents that will denounce Valarr and his claim to your throne. Head straight for Riverspring Castle. Victor the ferryman intercepts you and thanks you for saving his life during the riots. He offers to ferry you anytime; he's located on the docks for when the time comes for a boat ride.

TIP

Now is also a good time to see how your past actions have affected Riverspring. Some people you saved may be waiting for you in the city. The faction you helped the most during the riots will add a new merchant : the noble shop is in the port, the villager shop is in the marketplace, and the guard shop is in the castle courtyard.

Objective Point B

Enter the main castle gates to find your sister Elyana. She might have information on your father's practices and these mysterious documents. Go through the courtyard and then enter the castle proper.

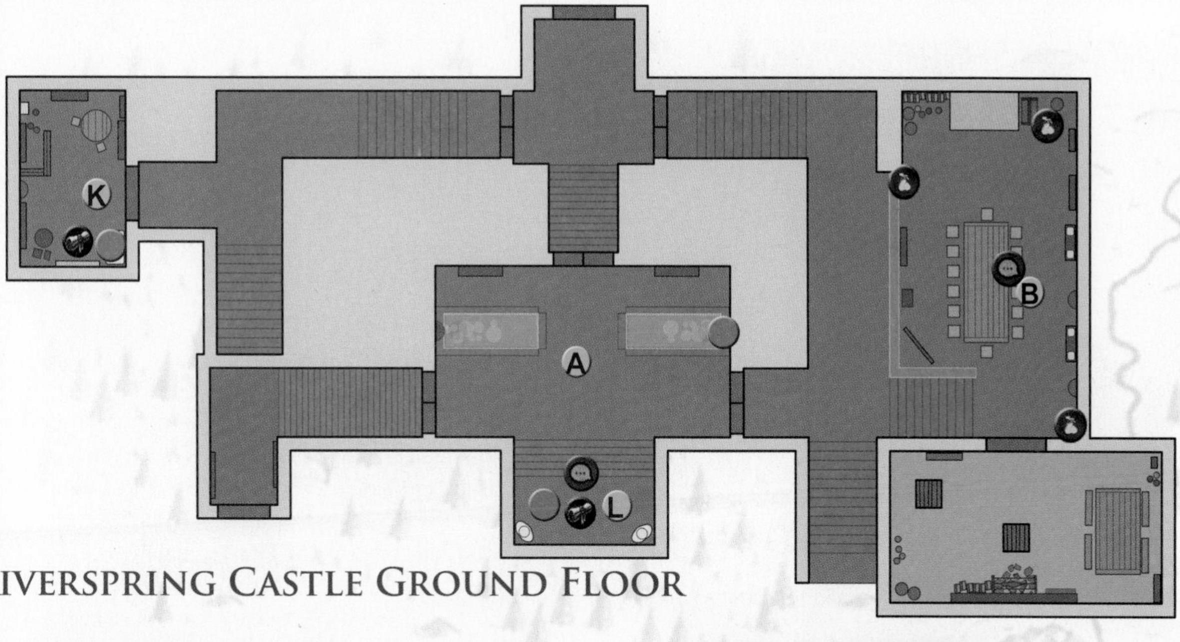

Riverspring Castle Ground Floor

Riverspring Castle First Floor

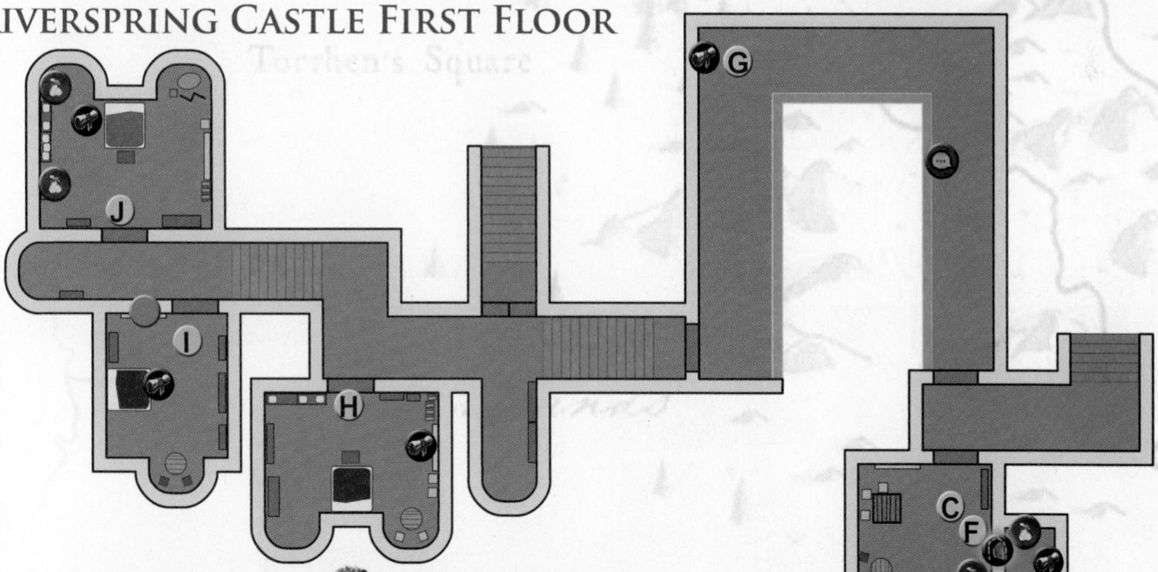

Book Watch: Riverspring

Although Riverspring isn't a notable city in the novel, its location puts it squarely in the midst of the major events transforming Westeros. It lies in the Riverlands almost directly between two major cities: west of the capital King's Landing and east of the Lannister's Casterly Rock. Just north of the Goldroad, we see that Riverspring is a busy place in the game, and the Sarwycks are behind-the-scenes lords who have influenced politics for many generations.

Legend

- Objective Point
- Loot Spot
- Codex Entry
- Secret Passage
- Primary Quest
- NPC

Objective Point A

Meet Elyana in the Riverspring throne room. She's happy to see you, but you shatter that joy when you explain that your brother Gawen is dead, and by Valarr's orders. Elyana doesn't know where your father may have hidden the secret documents, but she advises talking to Harwyn about the whole affair.

CAUTION

You must complete the "Rings and Chains" side quest in this chapter before you meet Victor on the docks to leave for Castlewood.

Side Quest: Rings and Chains

After you speak with Elyana in the throne room, you get a sense that something is wrong. If you want to get involved with the "Rings and Chains" side quest, see Elyana in the courtyard. She has made a deal with the Roxton family to gain money to help pay Riverspring's debts, but she can't repay them yet, and they're pressing the matter. For more details on the political intrigue and completing the quest, see the "Side Quests" chapter.

2. Maester Harwyn Might Know Something About Your Father's Documents

Objective Point B

You find Harwyn in the dining room. When you tell him of Valarr's treachery, he relates the tale of your father's last day and his argument that led to disinheriting Gawen.

3. Gawen Is Unworthy of the Title of Lord! Return to Your Office and Make Good on Your Threat!

Objective Point C

For a few minutes, you take over as Raynald Sarwyck during his final encounter with Gawen. Walk up the stairs out of the dining room and climb to the office on the first floor. You interrupt Gawen going through the office papers; he says that he knows about the brotherhood between Raynald and Arwood and that he just wants to help. Frustrated with Gawen's previous failures, you disinherit your youngest son and banish him from the castle.

4. The object of your search is likely to be concealed in the secret passage leading from your father's office. Find a way to access it

Objective Point D

Harwyn finishes telling you the sad tale and leaves you to your search. Scour your father's office thoroughly. There are a few red herrings that fail to lead to clues, but don't give up hope.

Note

You receive the Tytos Lannister's Shield here if you did not give out food from the castle stockpile during the riots. If you gave food to the starving townsfolk, the shield has been sold to replenish the food stores.

Objective Point E

Look in the back corner, and you'll spy a stone square that's different from the wall face. You'll see the familiar wavy heat lines that signal a secret item, and if you use the Vision of R'hllor, you can access a secret door behind the desk. The secret door requires seven special keys to open it. Read the Enigma of the Keys letter, which provides a riddle to locating each of the seven keys.

Tip

From here you have two different ways to open the secret door. You can either collect all seven keys in the castle or retrieve your father's master key. As Harwyn hints to you, the master key is around your father's neck ; look for it in the tunnels under Riverspring in your father's crypt.

Objective Point F

The first key is in the office. Look for another wavy pattern in the air next to the candle holder on the eastern wall. Use the Vision of R'hllor to open a secret passage into a small alcove. Inside you'll find the Father's Key and Raynald Sarwyck's Collar special item.

Objective Point G

Leave the office and head out to the hallway that runs along the balcony overlooking the ground floor. Stand in front of the statue of a warrior in the northwest corner. Use the Vision of R'hllor to uncover the Warrior's Key.

Objective Point H

Search the first bedroom in the western section of the first floor. Use the Vision of R'hllor in the center of the room to expose the Stranger's Key hidden in the side cabinet.

Objective Point I

Use the Vision of R'hllor in the second bedroom in the western section of the first floor. You'll find the Maiden's Key hidden in front of the bed.

Objective Point J

Proceed north and use the Vision of R'hllor in the third bedroom. The Mother's Key appears in a fruit platter on a small side table to the bed's left. You can easily miss it if you don't search carefully.

Objective Point K

Travel downstairs and seek out Harwyn. If you use the Vision of R'hllor in Harwyn's room, the Smith Key appears in the room's fireplace.

Objective Point L

The final key, the Crone's Key, is located in the Riverspring throne. Use your Vision of R'hllor power to uncover it. Return to the secret door behind the desk in your father's office. With all seven keys, the door now opens and you have access to the tunnels under Riverspring.

Tunnels Under Riverspring Secret Chamber

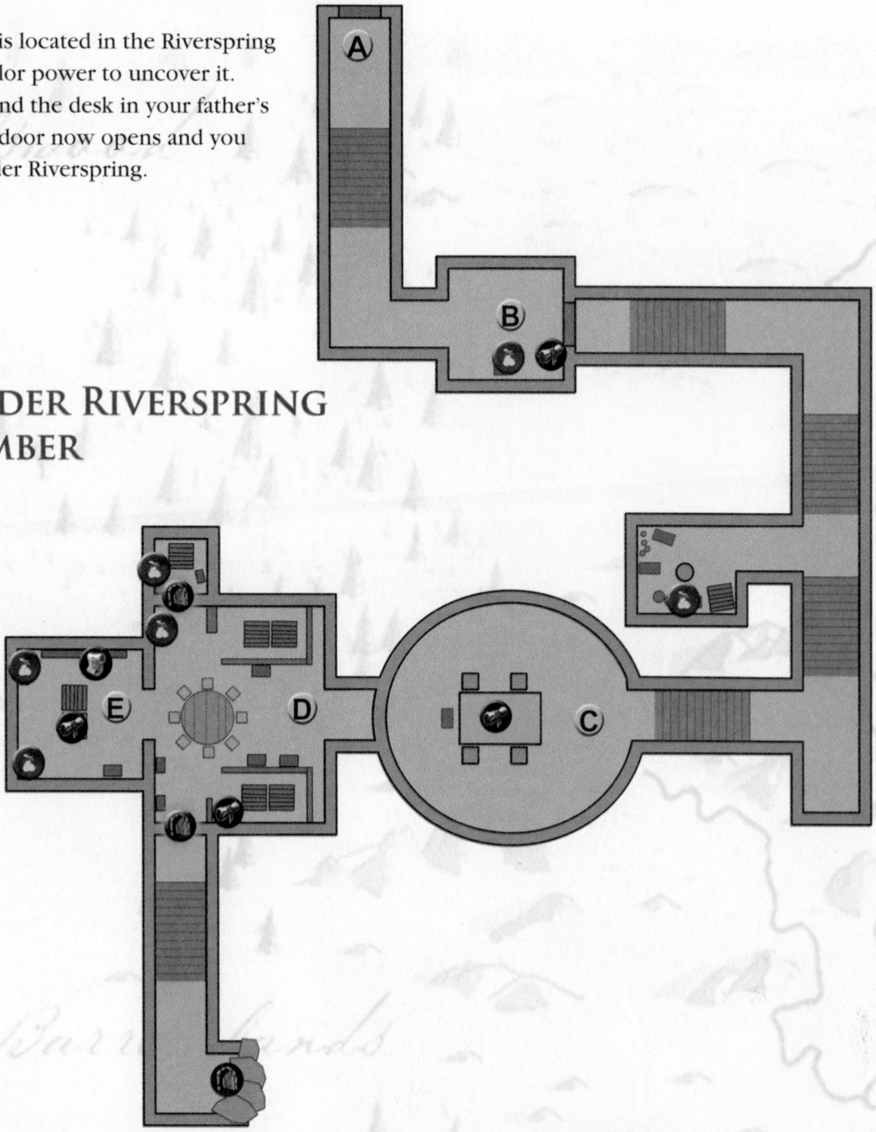

A
B
C
D
E

Legend

- Objective Point
- Loot Spot
- Secret Passage
- Side Quest
- Primary Quest

5. Search the Underground Tunnels to Find the Documents

Objective Point A

Enter the tunnels and begin your search for the secret documents. There are no enemies inside the tunnels—only puzzles to keep you at bay—so sheathe your sword and sharpen your wit.

Objective Point B

Continue until you reach the large chamber with locked doors. There's a plaque to the right of the doors that holds three questions about the Sarwyck sword. Answer them all and you open the door.

The first question asks about the color of the Sarwyck sword. Choose "Whitewashed" to pass the first challenge and release the first mechanism.

The second question asks about the state of the Sarwyck sword. Choose "Broken" to pass the second challenge and release the second mechanism.

The third question asks where the Sarwyck sword is kept. Choose "On his sigil" to pass the third challenge and open the door.

Objective Point C

You come to another seemingly dead-end room, but this one has a series of seven stone turnstiles around the room's edge and a single lever near the center. Your goal is to set each of the stone turnstiles with the correct symbol facing outward, pull the lever, and open the secret passage in the floor. The hints for which symbol is correct for each stone turnstile are out in the hallway leading up to the chamber. If a symbol appears once, it's used on the first turnstile; if it appears twice, it's used on the second turnstile, and so on.

Search the hallway for the symbol that appears once, and set the first stone turnstile with the three-headed dragon symbol.

Search the hallway for the symbol that appears twice, and set the second stone turnstile with the fire symbol.

Search the hallway for the symbol that appears three times, and set the third stone turnstile with the blood symbol.

Search the hallway for the symbol that appears four times, and set the fourth stone turnstile with the keyhole symbol.

Search the hallway for the symbol that appears four times, and set the fourth stone turnstile with the Iron Throne symbol.

Search the hallway for the symbol that appears six times, and set the sixth stone turnstile with the crow symbol.

Search the hallway for the symbol that appears seven times, and set the seventh stone turnstile with the seven-pointed star symbol.

Now pull the lever. A section of the floor recedes and reveals stairs leading into the secret chamber of the Brotherhood.

Objective Point D

Descend to the chamber and scout around. Pick up the Minutes of the Shadow Council, an official document of Harlton's Brotherhood, from the scroll rack on the wall.

Use the Vision of R'hllor to reveal a secret passage in the north wall. Search it for some extra loot.

Objective Point E

You finally discover the secret documents in the last chamber. The encrypted writings are impossible to understand, but if you bring it back to Harlton, he has a translator who will begin work on it at once.

6. Go to Castlewood and Hand the Precious Documents to Lord Harlton

Return to Riverspring and meet up with Victor at the docks. He will ferry you to Castlewood.

Side Quest: Avenge Riverspring

In the Brotherhood's secret chamber, you find additional documents that implicate a member of the Brotherhood named the Collector in a scheme to make money off Riverspring's misfortunes. If you want to punish the man for his transgression against your city, you can visit his manse in King's Landing and exact revenge. For more details on the Collector and completing the quest, see the "Side Quests" chapter.

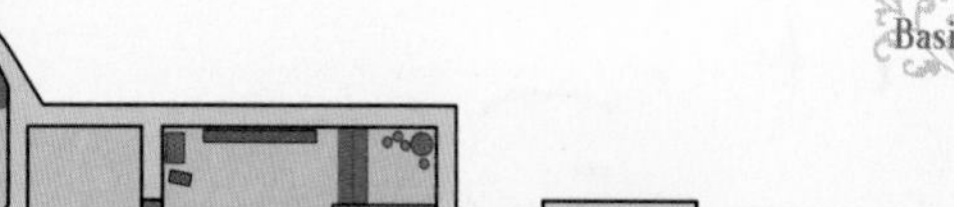

Castlewood Ground Floor

Legend

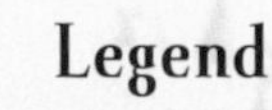

Objective Point
NPC

7. Tell Lord Harlton What You Have Discovered

Objective Point A

After Victor drops you off in Castlewood, seek out the entrance to the main gate. Enter and look for Lord Harlton in the throne room.

Objective Point B

Deliver the secret documents to Harlton. After he sends the documents off for translation, he explains that Jeyne Greystone is the key to the Brotherhood's plans: Targaryen blood runs in her veins, and her child will be a direct descendant in the Targaryen royal line. The child can be king.

CHAPTER 9

PROMISE

WESTFORD COTTAGE

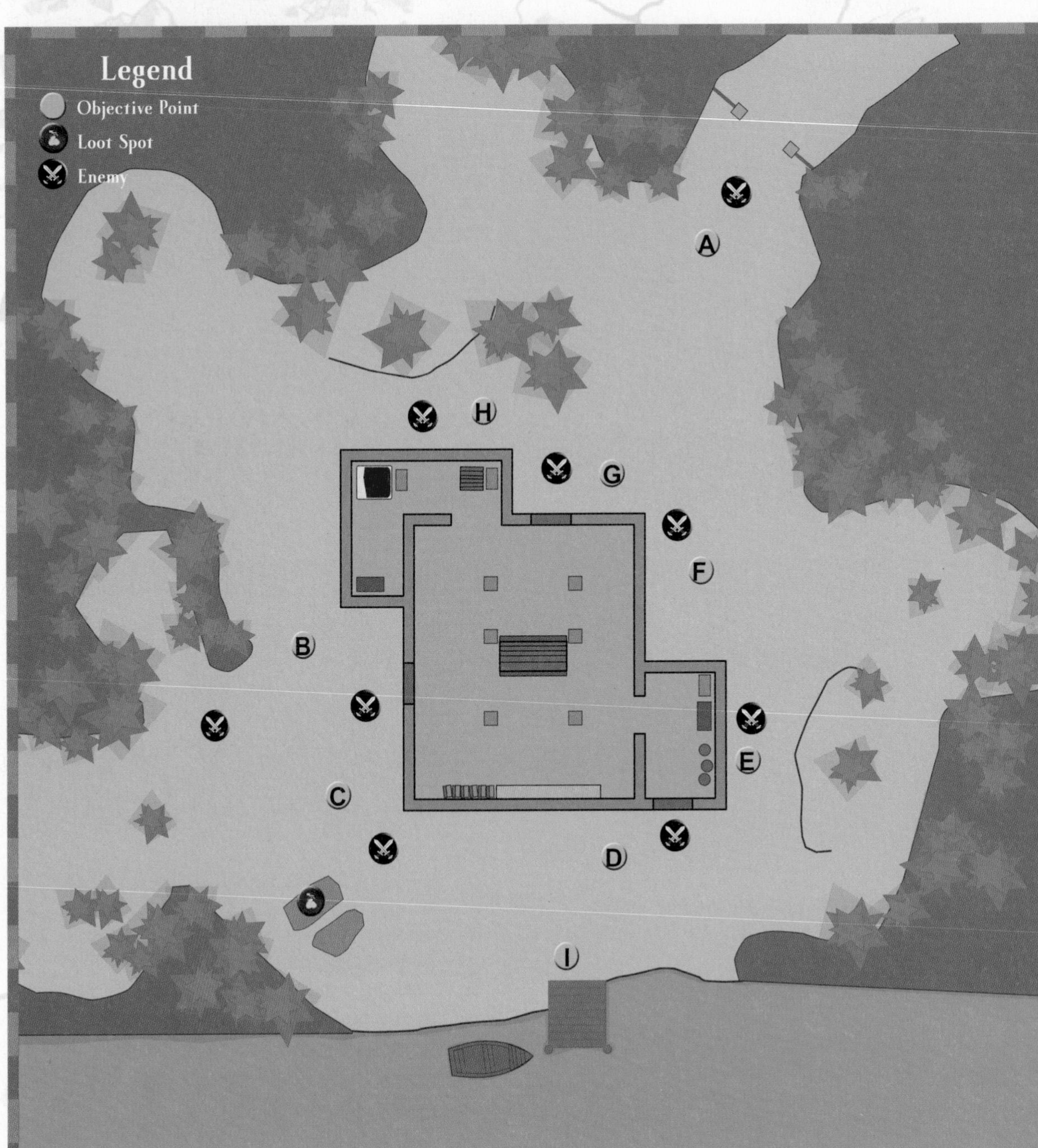

Objectives

1. Defend the western gate from the vanguard
2. Find and kill the reinforcements
3. Defend the rear gate from the vanguard
4. Find and kill the reinforcements
5. Defend the main gate from the vanguard
6. Find and kill the reinforcements
7. Kill Deziel, Valarr's lieutenant, who leads the assault
8. Go find Ethan, head of your temporary allies
9. Your group will be staying here for the night. Use this time to better acquaint yourself with your new companions
10. Introduce yourself to Arwood Harlton, Lord of Castlewood
11. Go find Jeyne in Maester Martin's chambers
12. Meet Lord Harlton for dinner
13. Confront Lord Harlton's guard
14. Your dog has regained consciousness. Use him to try and free your temporary ally

Quest Checklist

- **Endrew (companion, objectives 1, 9)**
- **Rhoynish Pride (special item, objective 7)**
- **Ethan (NPC, objectives 8, 9)**
- **Jeyne Greystone (NPC, objectives 9, 11)**
- **Arwood Harlton (NPC, objectives 10, 12)**
- **Experience Points: 1,350 (upon quest completion)**

1. Defend the Western Gate from the Vanguard

Objective Point A

Valarr's men have caught up with you and surround Westford Cottage. Endrew, one of Lord Harlton's men who has infiltrated Valarr's Bloodseekers, saves you from a few enemies and then hurries you inside the cottage to plan your defense. Once you establish a plan, you use the main door of the cottage and confront a pair of enemies at the front gates. When they fall, a larger group attacks the western gate.

Objective Point B

Follow Endrew and run to the western gate. It's a race against time as the Bloodseekers attack the cottage and try to force open the door and kill Jeyne. As you engage each group, use abilities that will inflict maximum damage. However, don't waste those abilities; you can't afford to use an ability with a large energy requirement on an enemy that is almost dead already. With Endrew, tag team enemies at the western gate to rip them apart quickly and efficiently.

> **Tip**
>
> Eliminate enemies as quickly as possible! Use your best abilities and match your weapon types to enemy armor to maximize damage. The Bloodseekers will break down the cottage doors and kill Jeyne if you don't hurry.

Companion Role Call: Endrew

Stats:

- **Strength: 7**
- **Agility: 7**
- **Luck: 4**
- **Endurance: 9**
- **Intelligence: 8**

Class: Magnar

Stance: Frenzy

Abilities: Flurry of Blows, Rage, Slash

Weapons of Choice: Turn-Cloak (1H short sword), Braavosi Stiletto (1H dagger)

Description: Endrew has some quality staple attacks at his disposal, which you'll need in the battle at Westford Cottage. Flurry of Blows is his best: It hammers an opponent with three straight attacks of increasing damage. Slash deals light damage but causes your opponent to Bleed. Rage distributes light damage to all nearby enemies. Because of the volume of enemies around the cottage, circumstances will force Endrew to sometimes fight by himself, which is all right with your newfound ally.

2. Find and Kill the Reinforcements

Objective Point C

Reinforcements will arrive after you defeat each main Bloodseeker group. Battle them the same way you did the main group: Attack with Endrew in unison and shred enemies quickly and efficiently. If you see any enemy pounding away at a cottage door, make him your priority. If a single enemy gets inside the cottage, you lose.

TIP

Listen for hints from Jeyne inside the cottage. She will tell you which door the Bloodseekers will attack next.

3. Defend the Rear Gate from the Vanguard

Objective Point D

Hustle to the rear gate. Intercept incoming enemies and fight by Endrew's side. At this point in the battle, you may need to use a recover action to regain energy. Do so only if you have the current fight in hand and no one is at the cottage doors.

4. Find and Kill the Reinforcements

Objective Point E

More enemies converge on the cottage. You have no choice but to keep going; there is no rest until the end. If you're low on health, drink a healing potion to bolster your effectiveness.

5. Defend the Main Gate from the Vanguard

Objective Point F

Circle around the cottage to the main gate again and take on the next enemy group. One Bloodseeker in heavy armor joins the fray; switch to blunt weapons to engage him. Remember to use Dog to immobilize (or traumatize) any enemies you can't deal with immediately.

6. Find and Kill the Reinforcements

Objective Point G

One last set of reinforcements arrives. Dispatch them before heading off to take on the Bloodseeker leader, Deziel.

7. Kill Deziel, Valarr's Lieutenant, Who Leads the Assault

Objective Point H

Deziel will hang back and puncture you with crossbow bolts if you let him. While Endrew deals with Deziel's men, you should focus on the leader and stun or knock him down to minimize his attacks against your party. If you can't reach him immediately and have to cut through a few Bloodseekers first, send Dog to immobilize and otherwise distract him. With enough damage and superior tactics, you and Endrew will survive the long battle and save Jeyne.

8. Go Find Ethan, Head of Your Temporary Allies

Objective Point I

After the battle, you can pick up Deziel's Rhoynish Pride crossbow, all the other loot lying on the corpses littering the cottage fields and you wife's pendant on her tomb. Jeyne needs to see a maester to check on her baby, so speak with Ethan when you're ready to leave Westford Cottage. Your new allies will guide you to a safe haven in the woods, before eventually taking you to Castlewood.

A Camp in the Woods

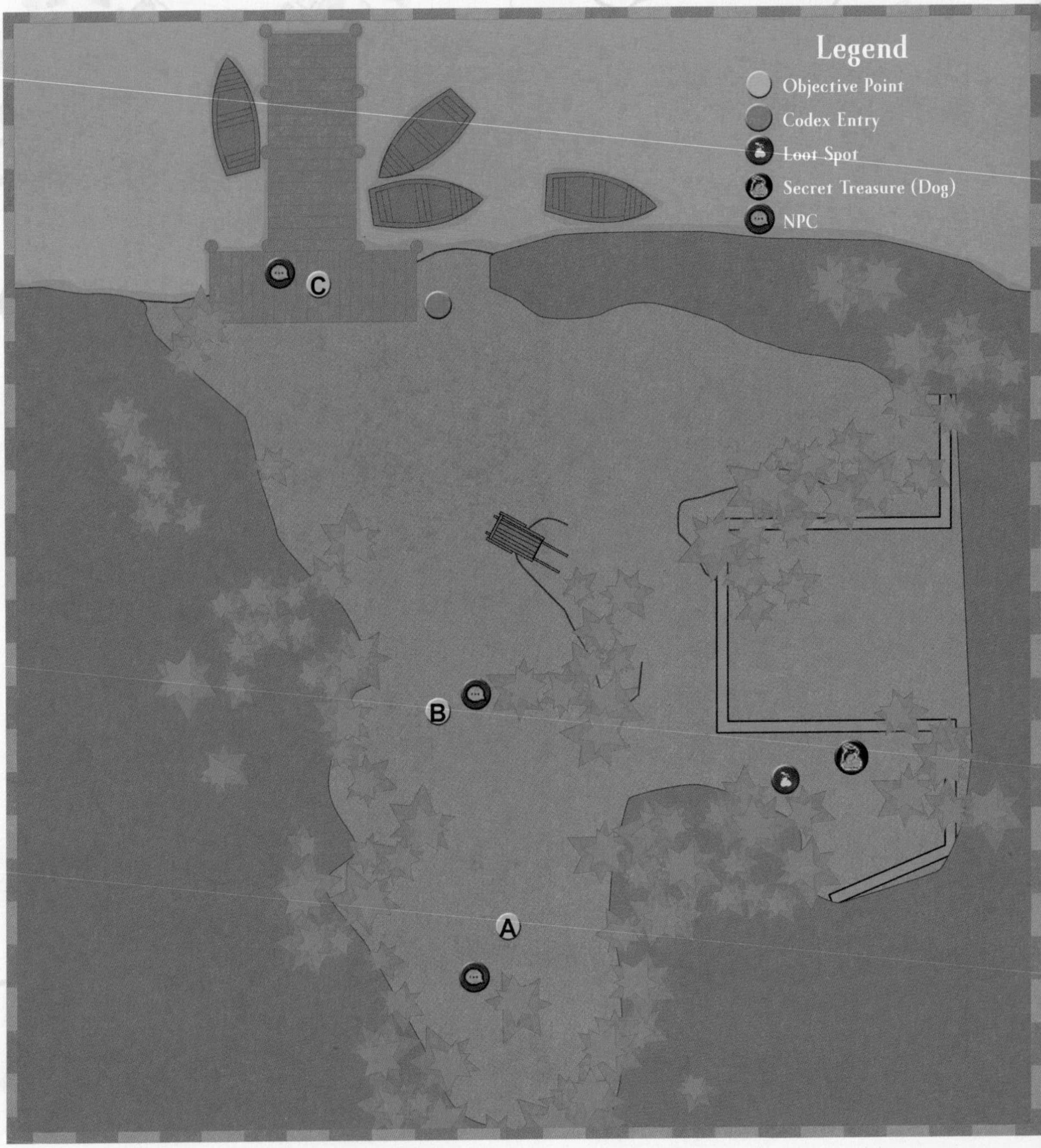

Legend
Objective Point
Codex Entry
Loot Spot
Secret Treasure (Dog)
NPC

C

B

A

9. Your Group Will Be Staying Here for the Night. Use This Time to Better Acquaint Yourself with Your New Companions

Objective Point A

Once you are settled into the sheltered campsite, speak with Jeyne. She is feeling better, but will still see a maester when you arrive in Castlewood. She also confesses that King Robert Baratheon is the child's father, and though she is of Targaryen descent, she believes her family vile and cruel and doesn't want her son to grow up in the Targaryen shadow.

Objective Point B

Next, speak with Endrew. You know he's a spy, so you keep your guard up. He assuages your fears about being allies, and he elaborates on Valarr's nasty reputation.

Objective Point C

You find Ethan out on the dock. He'll chitchat with you, and you learn that Lord Harlton has a particular keen interest in Jeyne, which further raises your suspicions. You can also explore this small zone to find a few loots, such as one hidden dog loot in the ruined tower area. When you are ready to leave camp, return to Jeyne and let her know it's time to go.

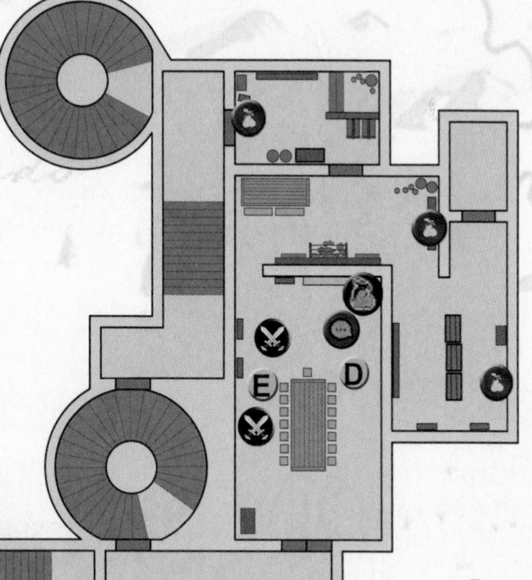

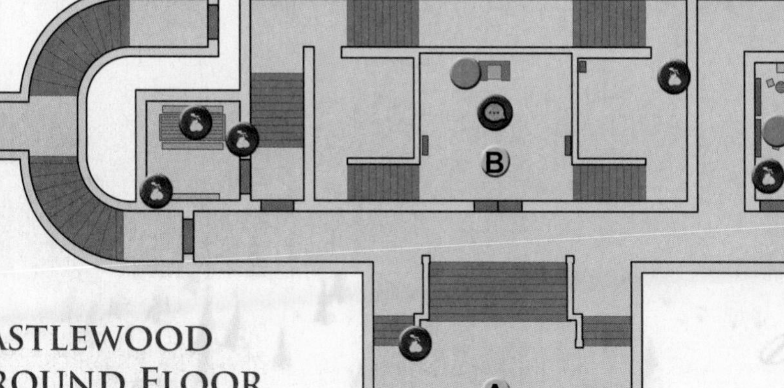

Castlewood Ground Floor

Legend

- Objective Point
- Loot Spot
- Secret Treasure (Dog)
- Codex Entry
- NPC
- Enemy

10. Introduce yourself to Arwood Harlton, Lord of Castlewood

Objective Point A

You arrive at Castlewood, stronghold of House Harlton. Follow Endrew through the beautiful courtyard to the castle's main gate.

Objective Point B

Proceed straight ahead into the throne room. Lord Harlton will greet you with his chief lieutenants. He welcomes you and offers his maester to assist Jeyne and her baby. If you want to escort Jeyne to the maester, you can; simply return to the throne room after you drop her off.

Harlton quizzes you on your past, and you speak about the war 15 years ago. He praises you as a worthy soldier and invites you to discuss more politics over dinner.

11. Go find Jeyne in Maester Martin's chambers

Objective Point C

Go see how Jeyne is doing with Maester Martin. All is well. Once you've finished exploring around the castle, speak with Jeyne and tell her that Lord Harlton has prepared a dinner for you both.

12. Meet Lord Harlton for Dinner

Objective Point D

Attend the dinner with Lord Harlton to see what his plans are for you and Jeyne. He reveals that he's been planning this moment for a long time. Harlton knew about Jeyne's Targaryen bloodline and was the one who arranged to have the king meet her in a "chance encounter" so that he could join Targaryen and Baratheon as one with Jeyne's child. He wants to raise that child as the heir apparent for the Iron Throne.

Jeyne wants no part of Harlton's sch PAGE 156: Change tip to read: Defeat six of Harlton's guards and you'll earn "The Butcher Comes to Dinner!" achievement. You can also earn the story trait, "Habit," here that provides a 2% increase to Mors' damage resistance to critical hits. eme. She just wants to live somewhere quiet with her child and not have to worry about the mad political games for the throne. You want to help Jeyne, but Harlton has poisoned you. Even as you yell for her to flee, the poison weakens your every move.

Book Watch: The Targaryen Bloodline

Jeyne Greystone mirrors a main character from the *A Game of Thrones* novel: Daenerys Targaryen. Like Jeyne, fair-haired Daenerys is also a daughter of King Aerys II, the last Targaryen king to rule the Seven Kingdoms, and is on the run from the Crown. Daenerys's troubles take her across the sea to the free city of Pentos, where she eventually marries a powerful lord of the Dothraki people, Khal Drogo.

13. Confront Lord Harlton's Guard

Objective Point E

Harlton summons his guards, and you have a huge battle on your hands. The poison makes those hands tremble, and you have very little time before the poison takes effect. Fight as long as you can, but no matter what you do—even if you defeat all the guards—you fall to the poison and Harlton captures Jeyne.

Tip

Defeat six of Harlton's guards and you'll earn "The Butcher Comes to Dinner!" achievement. You can also earn the story trait, "Habit," here that provides a 2% increase to Mors' damage resistance to critical hits.

Castlewood Dungeons

Legend

- Objective Point
- Secret Treasure (Dog)
- Enemy

Objective Point A

When you regain consciousness, you're in the dungeons. Two torturers have bloodied and bruised your body. On day one, the torturers will ask you a series of simple questions. If you tell the truth, you will be left relatively unharmed. If you defy them, they will badly injure you (see sidebar for permanent injuries). If you try to lie to them and fail, they will badly injure you. If you refuse to answer at first, but then tell the truth on the second set of day one questions, they will lightly injure you but leave no permanent marks.

Permanent Injuries

If you don't cooperate with the torturers, they will badly injure you and leave permanent marks. You receive a broken nose (permanent change) the first time they badly injure you. You receive scars on your torso the second time the torturers badly injure you. You receive burns on your back the third time they badly injure you. If you survive the torturing, these marks permanently disfigure you for the rest of the adventure.

The pain keeps you from contacting Dog, but you can communicate with the prisoner in the cell next to you. He tells you to keep stringing the torturers on with interesting tidbits so they keep you alive.

On day two, the torturers return, and if you tell the truth, they don't harm you. If you defy them, they badly injure you. If you lie successfully to the torturers, they lightly injure you but leave no marks. If you fail in your lies to the torturers, they badly injure you. After they leave, the prisoner says he will try and find a way to free himself and then you.

On day three, Harlton arrives to question you. If you tell him the truth (and if you told the torturers the truth on day two), they execute you after receiving the information. If you defy him, the torturers badly injure you. If you lie successfully, you go unpunished, but if you get caught in your lies, they badly injure you.

So long as you don't tell the truth too much, you will survive another day. You know they will eventually kill you, so you have to play the one trick you have left: Dog. Link with your faithful canine and guide him to your location.

14. Your Dog Has Regained Consciousness. Use Him to Try and Free Your Temporary Ally

Objective Point B

Dog awakes in a cell just as two guards pass by out front. Wait for the guards to disappear around the corner before figuring a way out of your cell.

Look for a small hole in the side wall. You can slip through this hole into the adjacent cell, which is open. Follow the guards who just passed by, but don't get close enough for them to spot you.

Objective Point C

Wait until the guards pass the lone guard standing in the passage. Slowly creep in and sneak attack the guard from behind. One good throat rip will do him in.

Objective Point D

At the next intersection, two guards talk to each other with their backs to you. Quickly slip behind the guards and take the corridor to the left.

Objective Point E

Before you meet up with the next set of guards, duck through the hole in the wall to your right. This brings you into a side room with a guard standing with his back to you. Assassinate the guard before he knows what hit him.

Objective Point F

Dodge the guards on patrol in the next corridor section. The best place to hide is an open cell; they won't detour to check the cells if you hide in the back shadows.

Objective Point G

Crawl through another hole and then watch the guards in the next cell area. When they stop to talk with a prisoner, run across the open chamber and into the vacant cell to the right of the guards.

Objective Point H

You are now adjacent to Mors's cell. You can't free him directly; you have to free the other prisoner first.

Objective Point I

Cut through one last hole in the wall next to Mors's cell. You are now next to the other prisoner's cell.

Objective Point J

When you emerge from the hole, you appear behind the guard watching over the other prisoner. Run up behind him and go for the throat!

Objective Point K

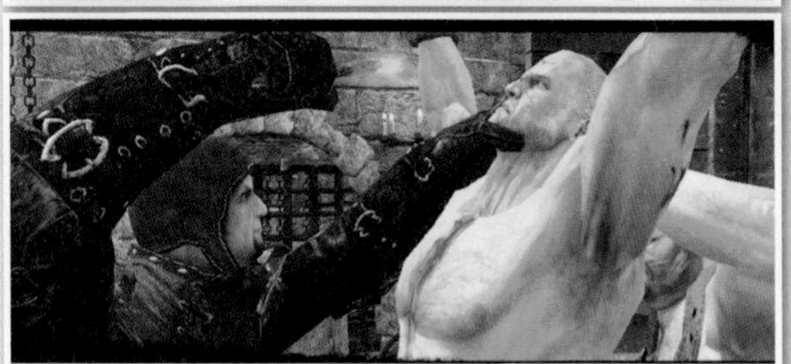

You've slipped through the guards as fast as you can, and now you've given the other prisoner the means to free himself. The downed guard falls next to the prisoner, and he uses the guard's keys to open his cell. Even as the prisoner approaches Mors's cell, you see the torturers have a very unpleasant surprise for your master, and he'll never be the same again.

CHAPTER 10

CROSSROADS

A

B

C

F

H

CASTLEWOOD FIRST FLOOR

Legend

- Objective Point
- Loot Spot
- Secret Treasure (Dog)
- Codex Entry
- Side Quest
- Primary Quest
- NPC
- Enemy

CASTLEWOOD GROUND FLOOR

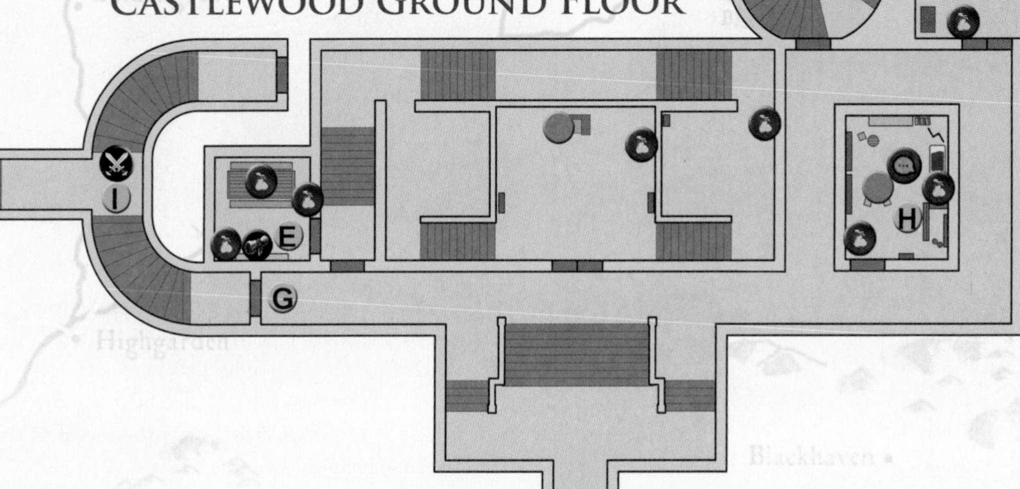

Objectives

1. Open the book Lady Marianne sent to your bedchamber
2. Marianne is waiting for you. Go to the cellar when you are ready
3. Trust Marianne or Gawen
4. Fight through the castle guards or find a way to heal Gawen and retrieve a helm he can wear so that he can move about the castle unnoticed
5. Find a way into the dungeons to find the prisoner your brother told you about
6. Get the keys from Alesander
7. Find out where the prisoner Gawen told you about is being kept
8. Avenge the blood of the Sarwycks!
9. Bring back Mors' dog
10. Snatch Jeyne away from Castlewood's guards

Quest Checklist

- **A Letter from Marianne (quest item, objective 1)**
- **Marianne Harlton (NPC, objective 2)**
- **Gawen Sarwyck (NPC, objectives 3, 4)**
- **Ointments (quest item, objective 4)**
- **A Guard's Helm (quest item, objective 4)**
- **"The Maggot in the Apple" (side quest, objective 5)**
- **Shorei (NPC, objectives 5, 6)**
- **Milk of the Poppy (quest item, objective 6)**
- **Key to Castlewood Dungeon (quest item, objective 6)**
- **Turn-Cloak (special item, objective 9)**
- **Key to Castlewood's High Tower (quest item, objective 11)**
- **Experience Points: 1,580 (upon quest completion)**

1. Open the Book Lady Marianne Sent to Your Bedchamber

Objective Point A

One of the Castlewood servant ladies, Shorei, enters your bedchamber with some news. It's been weeks since you've been able to speak with Lord Harlton, and you're getting antsy sitting around waiting. Shorei delivers a letter from Marianne Harlton asking you to attend a secret meeting in the cellar.

Objective Point B

Head to the main stairwell and descend to the ground floor. You can either visit Marianne directly or explore Castlewood. You may want to venture outside to the courtyard and check to see what the merchants have to offer.

2. Marianne is waiting for you. Go to the cellar when you are ready.

Objective Point C

Speak with Marianne in the cellar. You converse about Lord Harlton's plans and the risks involved. She seems to agree with your reservations about Lord Harlton's single-minded pursuits, but don't be fooled—she's fully committed to her uncle and is just gauging how loyal you are to the cause.

3. Trust Marianne or Gawen

Before you make a final decision on how you will support the Harltons, a man in a guard's uniform slips behind Marianne and puts a knife to her throat. He claims to be your brother Gawen, who has just escaped from the Harlton dungeon.

Caution

If you choose to side with Marianne over Gawen, you will have to fight your way through the entire castle.

You have a big choice to make now: trust Marianne or trust Gawen. If you trust Marianne, she ultimately betrays you and sets the entire castle guard on you. Depending on your lust for blood, you may want the extra experience from fighting a castle full of guards. The safer, and more honorable, choice is siding with your brother, Gawen. The Harltons have had him locked in their dungeons, and it was Lord Harlton who staged Gawen's death in the first place. You knock out Marianne and leave her in a large chest, out of sight from prying eyes.

If Marianne has betrayed you, the battle is on, and you'll have to fight through the guards to eventually reach the dungeons below. If you sided with Gawen, he's in no shape to travel yet after all that he's been through in the dungeons. First, you have to find him some healing ointments to ease the pain, and next you'll have to find a helmet to complete his guard disguise so that he can travel about the castle without arousing suspicion.

4. Fight Through the Castle Guards or Find a Way to Heal Gawen and Retrieve a Helm He Can Wear So That He Can Move About the Castle Unnoticed

Objective Point D

Seek out Maester Martin down the hall. If you chat him up about his knowledge on the healing arts, he will give you Ointments; return to Gawen to aid in the healing process.

Objective Point E

Next, travel to the castle's western section and find the guards talking about their exploits with the castle serving ladies. One brutish guard, Alesander, boasts about his conquest over Shorei last night. Ignore them for now and pick up the helm on the chair next to the fireplace.

Objective Point F

Return to your brother and give him both items; he'll be ready to travel incognito now. Feeling better, he tells you what has happened to him over the past few months. He learned of your father's dealings with the Harlton's secret brotherhood and that Harlton's master plan was to find a woman named Jeyne Greystone and use her child to bring Targaryens back into power.

Your father wanted no part in forcing an innocent mother and child into the game of thrones, so he wrote a letter to Jon Arryn and warned him (thus setting Mors's story line into motion). In response, Harlton had your father poisoned. Eventually, Harlton captured Gawen and spread the rumors that it was the son who poisoned the father. Gawen was able to escape only because of the heroic actions of another prisoner (Mors), so you both decide to free that prisoner before leaving Castlewood.

Side Quest: The Maggot in the Apple

Before entering the dungeons, you may want to complete "The Maggot in the Apple" side quest to help reduce the threats against you as you escape. Alester remembers that the best of Harlton's fighters train out in the courtyard; it's the perfect opportunity to get rid of them without attracting unnecessary attention. Venture outside to the courtyard and wound the men training to soften up the defenses. For more details on the sneak attack and completing the quest, see the "Side Quests" chapter.

5. Find a Way into the Dungeons to Find the Prisoner Your Brother Told You About

Objective Point G

Proceed to the door leading down to the dungeons. You discover that it's locked, but Gawen knows that Alesander has the key from his many times being tortured. You recall the conversation that just took place with the guards and figure Shorei can help you get the key.

Tip

You can also ask Alesander to follow you in order to meet Shorei. He will slowly walk to the cellar where you met Marianne. When you reach your destination, you can fight Alesander and his friends and then take the key from his dead body.

6. Get the Keys from Alesander

Objective Point H

Speak with Shorei in the dining area. You can convince her to poison the guards, since she serves them their drinks. Go talk to Maester Martin and get him talking about his profession so that he doesn't suspect anything. At the end of the conversation, Martin will hand you Milk of the Poppy. Bring it back to Shorei and let her take care of the rest.

Shorei serves the poison drinks to the men. They're all dead by the time you arrive in the guard room where you found the helm for Gawen. Grab the Key to Castlewood Dungeon off Alesander's corpse and unlock the door to the dungeons.

Objective Point I

The guards in charge of dungeon access have strict orders not to let anyone in. You can't change their minds. The only way in is through them, so trigger the fight and let them have it. The guard with heavy armor is the most difficult foe; concentrate your blows on the other two, bring them down, and then team up on the final heavy-armor guard.

Note

Gawen accompanies you and fights in the battles, but you cannot control him.

Castlewood Dungeons

Legend

- Objective Point
- Loot Spot
- Secret Treasure (Dog)
- Secret Passage
- Enemy

7. Find Out Where the Prisoner Gawen Told You About Is Being Kept

Objective Point A

Enter the dungeon area and begin your search for Mors. When you reach the bars, turn right and then left to access the corridor with your first set of enemy guards.

Objective Point B

Cut through the enemy guards in the corridors. You have plenty of room down this long corridor, so rather than charge them, use a ranged weapon to deal long-range damage first. When the enemy comes to you, switch to the appropriate melee weapon to match their armor types and hack away. After the guards' death, continue down the corridor and enter the door at the end to find Mors.

Objective Point C

You finally free Mors from his torturers and let him exact his revenge. You catch up on each other's tales and see how your different paths have led you to this chance meeting. Before you can make up your mind on the next course of action, Endrew sneaks into the torture chamber and assassinates Gawen. Shocked, you have barely enough time to draw your weapons before Endrew and his men are on you.

TIP

Change the tip to read: Mors doesn't have to fight empty handed! If you had his second weapons slot equipped before entering the torture sequence, you can switch to these weapons during the fight.

8. Avenge the Blood of the Sarwycks!

If you have a mass stun ability, use that as Endrew and his men surround you. Back up and move Mors and Alester together so that you can vanquish targets quickly with coordinated attacks. You know Endrew's abilities from your previous battles together at Westford Cottage; nothing he throws at you should be a surprise.

Concentrate attacks on the weaker-armored foes and work your way up to Endrew. If you have a ranged attack, back up into the corridor leading into the torture chamber and pick off enemies from afar. So long as you give Mors a good weapon or two, and you work together in the battle, it won't be long before Endrew joins his dead comrades on the cold dungeon stone. Retrieve Endrew's weapon, Turn-Cloak, from his corpse before you leave the area.

9. Bring Back Mors' Dog

Objective Point D

Now you need to recover Dog. Retrace your steps north and head west through the quiet corridors. You won't face any resistance until you encounter a pair of guards abusing Dog. Compared to the battle against Endrew, this one's a picnic. You can even surprise the two guards with a ranged attack and then charge in and clean up.

Castlewood Upper Basement

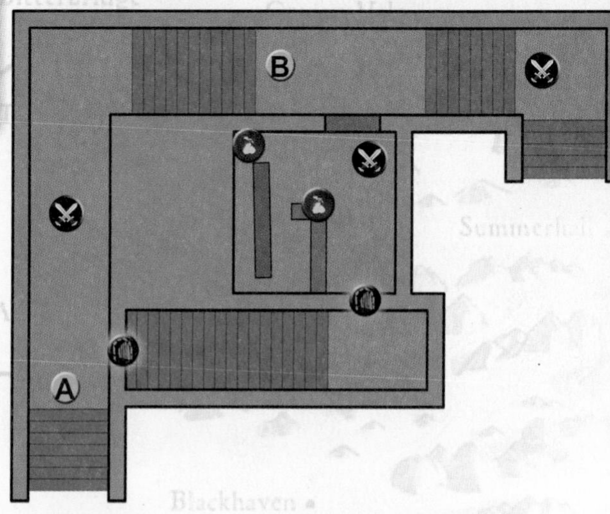

Legend
- Objective Point
- Loot Spot
- Secret Passage
- Enemy

10. Snatch Jeyne Away from Castlewood's Guards

Objective Point A

One of the guards has Jeyne's scent on him, so use Dog to follow the scent trail back to your missing companion. Follow the swirling yellow trail through the corridors until it reaches the door leading to the staircase up to the Upper Basement.

Note

You will have less resistance here if you completed "The Maggot in the Apple" side quest. You instantly kill the guards if the side quest was completed.

As with most of your battles to the top of the castle, use a ranged attack first (if you have one) while you have the element of surprise and soften up your enemies. When they charge at you, command Dog to immobilize one target while Alester and Mors beat on a single foe. In larger groups, have each character take on one foe. If you get into trouble, use a stun or knockdown ability and regroup. If you get into serious trouble, drink a healing potion or tap into Alester's R'hllor powers to ignite opponents.

Objective Point B

Continue along the corridor until you reach another set of stairs. Engage the enemies here in a similar fashion: hit them with a ranged attack first, then work as a coordinated group of three to bring them down.

Legend

- Objective Point
- Loot Spot
- Enemy

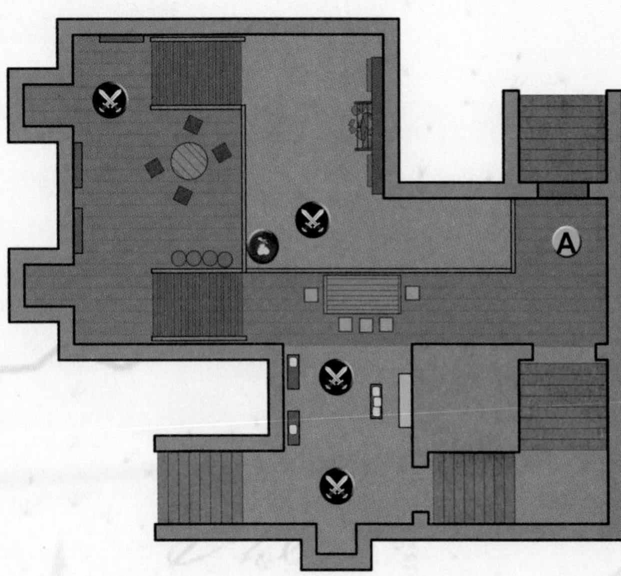

Castlewood Ground Floor

Objective Point A

Take the stairs up to the ground floor. Follow Jeyne's scent trail, which leads through a series of guard encounters. Pull each enemy group toward you with a ranged attack, or challenge them without running too far past them. You don't want to alert any other enemy groups to your position; it's better to kill all the enemies in their immediate area.

CASTLEWOOD FIRST FLOOR

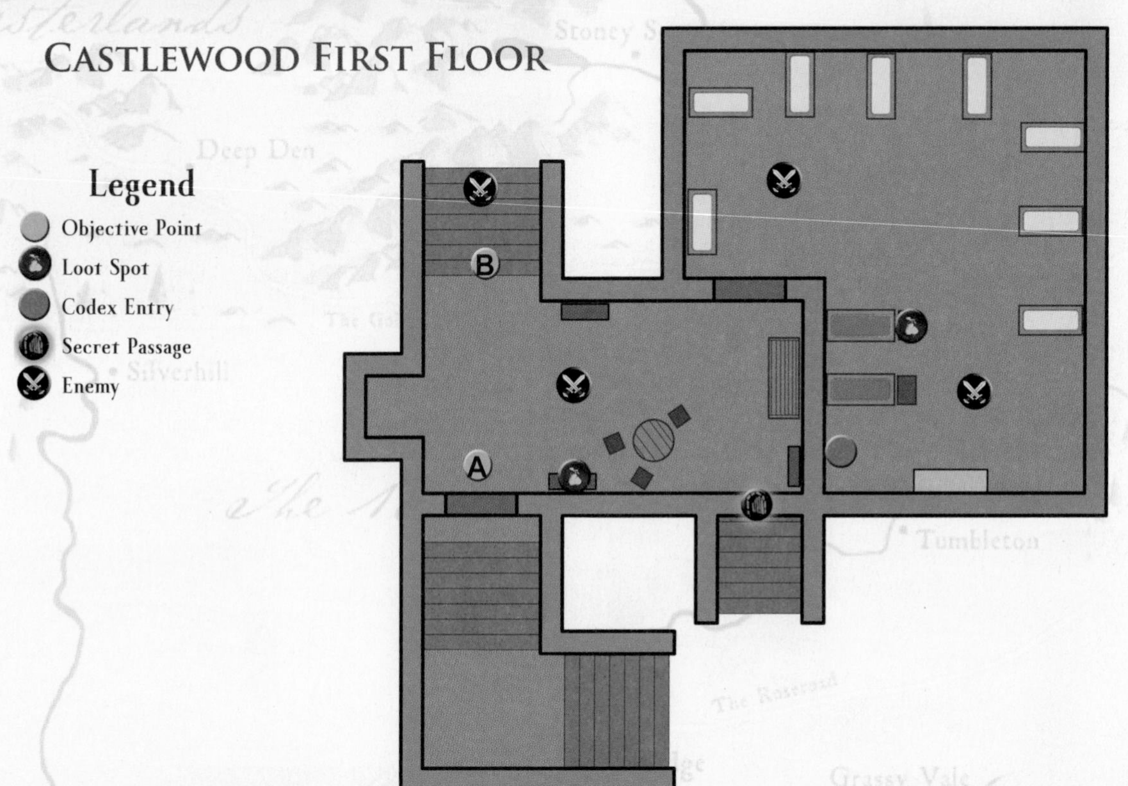

Objective Point A

Continue up the stairs to the first floor. Quietly sneak into the first room and let Dog sneak attack the first guard from behind. Once you rip out his throat, you can concentrate Mors's and Alester's attacks on the guards near the stairs.

Objective Point B

Snipe the guards on the stairs with a ranged attack and then set Alester and Mors on one opponent while Dog distracts the other. They won't stand a chance against your superior tactics and skills.

Tip

You gain the story trait "Ladykiller" if you kill Marianne. The trait gives you a +2% bonus to critical damage.

Castlewood Second Floor

Objective Point A

As you enter the second floor, there are two enemy groups close together. Attack the group on the right even as you send Dog to distract the group across the room.

Use your more damaging attacks on the first group to kill them quickly so that the two groups don't have time to gang up on you. At the end of the battle, retrieve the Key to Castlewood's High Tower from one of the dead guards.

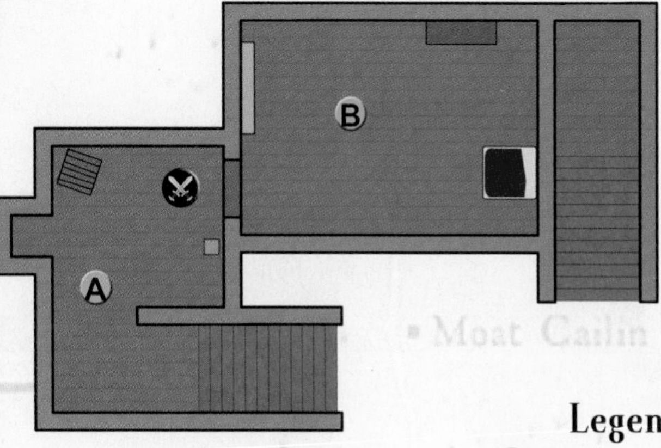

Castlewood Third Floor

Legend

- Objective Point
- Loot Spot
- Codex Entry
- Secret Passage
- Enemy

Objective Point A

Attack the two guards on the third-floor landing. You can catch them by surprise with a free attack or two, which should weaken them so they fall quickly. If you put up a decent fight, immobilize one with Dog while you gang up on the other one; then have all three take down the final guard.

Objective Point B

You burst into the tower room to find Marianne confronting Jeyne. She escaped your bonds from earlier and now she threatens Jeyne. You grab Marianne, but before you can make your escape, Lord Harlton arrives with too many men to overcome. You're trapped!

You can choose to release Marianne or slit her throat. Either way, Lord Harlton won't let you go. He's prepared to kill you when Jeyne steps in the way and acts as a human shield. Harlton won't risk hurting Jeyne and the child, so he orders his men to hold. In that moment of hesitation, Alester and Mors dive out the tower window and make a daring escape.

Chapter 11

Breaking Point

Quest Checklist

- Ryman Sarwyck (NPC, objective 1)
- Harwyn (NPC, objectives 1, 3)
- "Safer Streets" (side quest, objective 2)
- Elyana Sarwyck (NPC, objective 2)
- Guardian Helm (special item, objective 4)
- Wex (NPC, objective 5)
- Valarr (NPC, objective 5)
- Experience Points: 1,640 (upon quest completion)

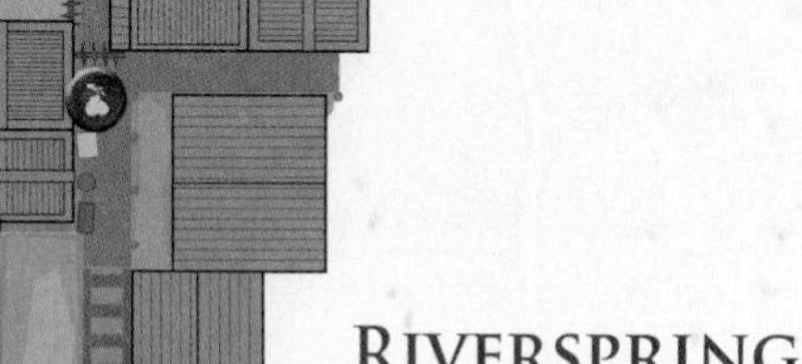

Objectives

1. Valarr is in town, and he plans to wed your sister later today. Find Maester Harwyn at the docks and finalize your plan.
2. Ask your sister, Elyana, for support
3. Go back to Harwyn and await Ryman's arrival
4. Clear a path to the castle
5. You have gotten past Valarr's defenses. It is time to confront him.
6. Triumph against Valarr in a trial by combat

1. VALARR IS IN TOWN, AND HE PLANS TO WED YOUR SISTER LATER TODAY. FIND MAESTER HARWYN AT THE DOCKS AND FINALIZE YOUR PLAN.

Objective Point A

After fleeing Castlewood, you cross through the swamps to reach Riverspring. Mors confronts Alester on what happened to his family. Alester confesses that he was unable to protect them and that it must have been brigands who slaughtered Mors's wife and daughter while Alester was attending to other matters of the kingdom.

TIP

From here, you can leave Riverspring before stopping the wedding if you want to continue your side quests. Proceed to King's Landing with Mors if you like and you may find new recruits for the Night's Watch there.

Once you return to Riverspring, Ryman Sarwyck meets up with you a few paces down the main street. He updates you on the current situation: Valarr and his Bloodseekers have taken over the town, and affairs have deteriorated into misery and chaos. Anyone who defies Valarr is put to the sword.

NOTE

Alester and Mors fight together in your party throughout this quest.

As you speak with Ryman, Bloodseekers stumble upon you. They have strict orders from Valarr to kill Alester on sight. A battle erupts in the streets. With Ryman's help, rip through the Bloodseekers without mercy. Alternate stuns and potent damage-dealing abilities between Mors and Alester to keep off balance at all times.

Objective Point B

Ryman advises you to find Harwyn on the docks and ask him to aid in the plan to recapture Riverspring. Set off for Harwyn in the north while Ryman searches the city for more soldiers loyal to your cause. All is eerily quiet as you find Harwyn alone on the docks. He explains that Valarr is to wed Elyana before the day ends, so time is of the essence. You ask Harwyn to arrange a secret meeting with Elyana outside the castle so you can involve her in your plans.

Side Quest: Safer Streets

Harwyn asks you to clean up the streets in Riverspring before you confront Valarr. Comb the city for Bloodseeker activity and quell the deeds by slaying the perpetrators. You can complete this side quest only while in Riverspring and before you trigger the events in the castle. For more details on all the Bloodseeker encounters and completing the quest, see the "Side Quests" chapter.

TIP

Complete the "Safer Streets" side quest and you will face fewer enemies at the gates when you attempt to enter the castle.

2. Ask your sister, Elyana, for support

Objective Point C

Speak with Elyana in front of the waterwheel. If you are nice to her while asking for her help, she will side with you later in the courtyard and convince Wex to back down. If you're dismissive with Elyana, she will not appear in the courtyard and you'll have to fight Wex's men to enter the castle.

3. Go back to Harwyn and await Ryman's arrival

Objective Point D

Return to Harwyn and wait for Ryman to arrive. The Bloodseekers beat him to you, and a group of Valarr's men challenge you. Before the first sword unsheathes, Ryman and his men show up. You can either let them run and warn Valarr of your arrival (which won't change events) or silence them with a quick battle.

If you choose to silence the Bloodseekers, break out your weapons and attack. There are many bodies on the tight dock landings. Switch to melee weapons and stun often so that your side gets in more attacks. Even though the enemies are heavily armored, your numbers should prevail.

4. Clear a path to the castle

Objective Point E

Caution

If you did not complete the "Safer Streets" side quest earlier, you will have to deal with roaming Bloodseeker patrols as you head to the castle.

Confront the Bloodseekers at the main castle gate. It's a smaller battle if you eliminated all the Bloodseekers during the "Safer Streets" side quest; if not, you'll need to rely heavily on Ryman and his men to keep the odds even.

Courtyard of Riverspring Castle

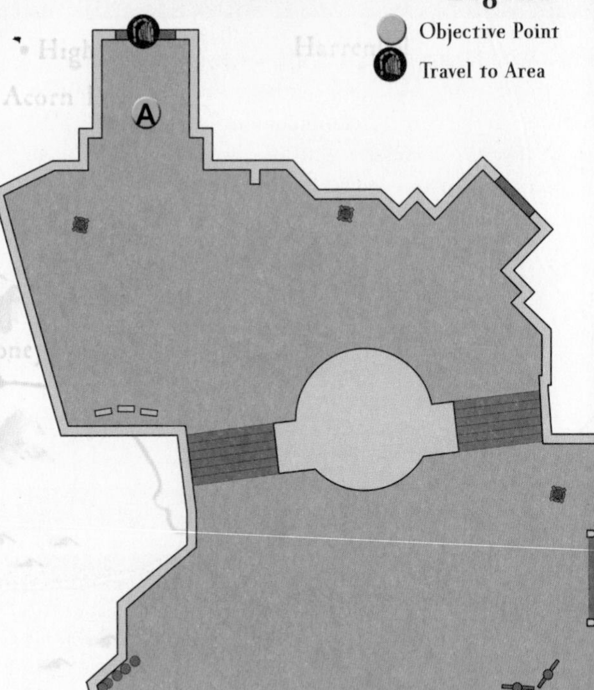

Switch to blunt weapons against most of your enemies, including the Bloodseeker leader at the gate. Cut down the weaker enemies first, then converge with numbers on the stronger, more heavily armored foes. You may not have Dog's immobilizing tactics, but Mors's stun and damage-dealing abilities still complement Alester's combat maneuvers well. After a fierce battle, the gate will eventually be yours. Retrieve the Guardian Helm from the fallen Bloodseeker leader and enter the courtyard.

Objective Point A

When you enter the courtyard, Wex calls down to you from the castle's upper wall. If you parted with Elyana unhappily at the waterwheel, you will have to fight Wex's men to enter the castle. If you allied with Elyana, she will command Wex to stop and get him to think about the consequences of killing a Sarwyck without consulting Valarr. At this point, you can skip the fight or fight anyway to enter the castle.

Riverspring Castle

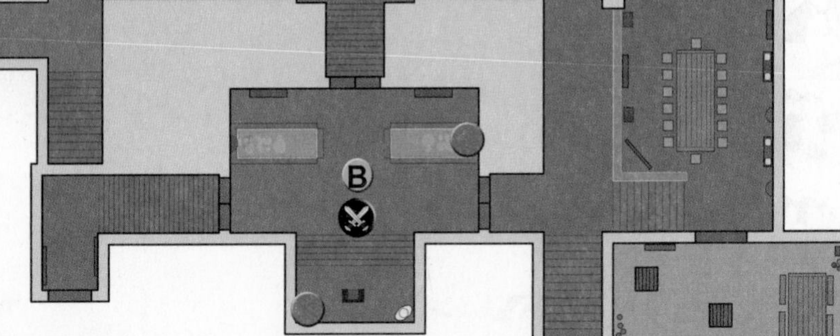

Legend
- Objective Point
- Codex Entry
- Enemy

5. You Have Gotten Past Valarr's Defenses. It Is Time to Confront Him

Objective Point A

Interrupt Valarr in the throne room and condemn his treatment of the Riverspring people. He tries to lie his way out of the situation and orders you to surrender or he'll turn his men loose on the city. Mors calls for a duel to the death to settle matters, and Valarr accepts.

6. Triumph Against Valarr in a Trial by Combat

Objective Point B

Valarr will try to get under your skin before the fight begins and weaken your resolve. To avoid a combat penalty, choose the dialogue option "I need to concentrate on the fight" at the end of Valarr's taunts.

Begin the fight with a strong attack, preferably one that will stun and keep Valarr off balance. He hits very hard with his big two-handed sword; the more strikes you avoid from him, the better.

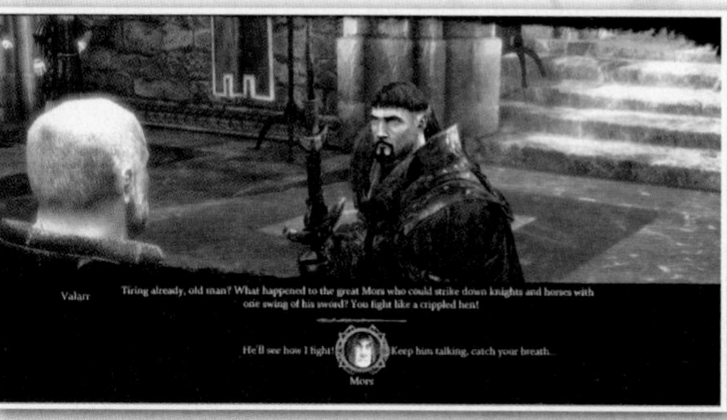

When you knock him down one-quarter of his health, you break out of combat and Valarr taunts you again. This time keep him talking, and you can catch your breath and recover more energy for the next portion of the battle.

When you see Valarr wind up for a bit attack, interrupt him immediately. When you have the opportunity, hit him with a damage-over-time ability like Bleeding to chip away at his health total while you trade blows. When you knock him down to half health, you break out of combat again.

Mors Westford What? What do you know about my family?

As much as you try to keep your composure, Valarr gets to you at the fight's end. He taunts you about the death of your family; he seems to have specifics on how they died. You furiously go after him for the final portion of the battle.

Give it everything you've got now. Use up all your energy and unleash your best attacks on Valarr. You have to drop his remaining health total before he finishes off yours. If you continue to keep him off balance with stuns and knockdowns, you should avoid the majority of his huge attacks and outdamage him.

Unfortunately for Mors, Valarr doesn't fight fair. Even as you beat him in combat and throw him to the ground, he draws upon black magic and conjures up a shadow behind you. Alester tries to warn you, but it's too late—the shadow stabs you through the back. Before you die, Valarr whispers in your ear that it was he who slaughtered your family.

There's an uproar from the crowd at the treachery. The lords and ladies in attendance see Valarr for the evil coward that he is. They denounce him as potential ruler, so he has them all executed. Only Ryman manages to escape in the bloody chaos.

The Bloodseekers bring Alester and Elyana before Valarr, who asks Alester where Jeyne Greystone is hidden. He threatens Elyana if Alester doesn't reply. Alester tells him that Harlton has Jeyne in Castlewood, and Valarr thanks him by lopping Elyana's head off. In a fit of rage and despair, Alester screams as Valarr orders his men into Riverspring to kill as many as they need to make them acknowledge they have a new regent.

Chapter 12: Fight Fire with Fire

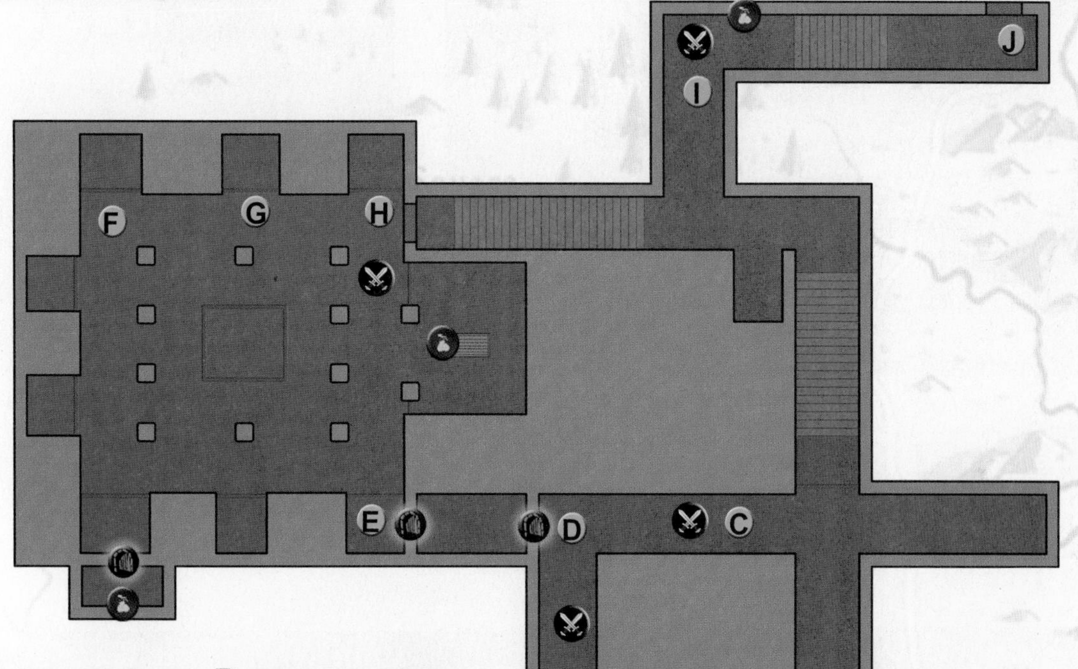

Tunnels of Riverspring

Legend

- Objective Point
- Loot Spot
- Secret Passage
- Enemy

Objectives

1. Use the secret passages under Riverspring to reach the dungeons where the guards are being held.
2. Find the keys to the dungeons and free the guards that Valarr had locked in there.
3. Free Greydon and his men. The cells hold other prisoners, some of whom you put in there yourself. They could be of use to you.
4. Infiltrate Valarr's army and study their defenses, and find a way to open the gates for Ryman and his men.
5. Maester Harwyn is alive! Before launching the attack, you must ensure his safety.
6. It is time to take back your castle. Find a way to open the gates for your men.
7. Take back your castle and slaughter the Bloodseekers that infest it.
8. Find Greydon and his men to clear the city.
9. Now that the Bloodseekers have scattered, strike their officers down. Eliminate Wex.
10. Now that the castle is yours, find Harwyn to come up with a plan of action.
11. Go and pay your respects to Mors' body in the castle courtyard.

Quest Checklist

- **Percelion Sarwyck's Bow (special item, objective 1)**
- **Symbol of Defiance (special item, objective 2)**
- **Key to Riverspring's Cells (quest item, objective 2)**
- **Wex (NPC, objectives 4, 5)**
- **Harwyn (NPC, objectives 5, 9)**
- **Blurd (NPC, objective 6)**
- **Ravella (NPC, objective 6)**
- **The Crone (special item, objective 6)**
- **Greydon (NPC, objective 8)**
- **Splasher (special item, objective 9)**
- **Experience Points: 1,000 (upon quest completion)**

1. Use the Secret Passages Under Riverspring to Reach the Dungeons Where the Guards Are Being Held.

Objective Point A

Rather than kill you quickly, Valarr decides to seal you in a sarcophagus deep below in the Riverspring tunnels amid the tombs of your forefathers. You would be dead if not for the resourceful Ryman, who, after having escaped the massacre in the throne room, slips down into the tunnels to free you. Ryman tells you that the remainder of his men are locked in the dungeons, and you make a plan to rescue them.

Objective Point B

Enemies patrol the tombs, so be careful as you advance. You'll likely attract attention at the first intersection. As with most of your fights side by side with Ryman, let the elder warrior engage and keep the majority of enemies focused on him while you assist with stuns and damage. If you take the first enemy patrol by surprise, they should go down easily.

TIP

Pick up Percelion Sarwyck's Bow at the end of the first eastern tunnel.

Objective Point C

Engage the next set of guards in front of the secret passage wall. Take care of them before you proceed to the far end of the corridor and investigate.

Objective Point D

Look for the shimmering in the air at the corridor's end. It appears to be a normal wall; however, if you use the Vision of R'hllor here, you reveal a secret passage that leads from the tomb area to the prisoner area. Pull the lever behind the secret passage to open the second door and enter the prison.

Objective Point E

A large enemy group guards the prisoners on the far end of the prison. Initiate combat with a ranged attack and send Ryman charging into their midst. Pick off as many as you can at range, then switch to your melee weapon and match it against the appropriate armor type for maximum damage. The prisoner area is big; if enemies start to swarm you, stun them and find a more advantageous location to renew your assault. With some hard work, you can kill all the guards and look for the keys to open the prison cells.

TIP

If you sent Tyrek to prison during the Riverspring riots, you can take the Symbol of Defiance off the poor loyalist tortured to death in the side room.

2. Find the Keys to the Dungeons and Free the Guards That Valarr Had Locked in There.

Objective Point F

Recover the keys from the table in the northwest corner and release the Riverspring soldiers. They will join up with you for the assault later against the castle.

TIP

Look for a secret door and a treasure room in the prison's southwest corner.

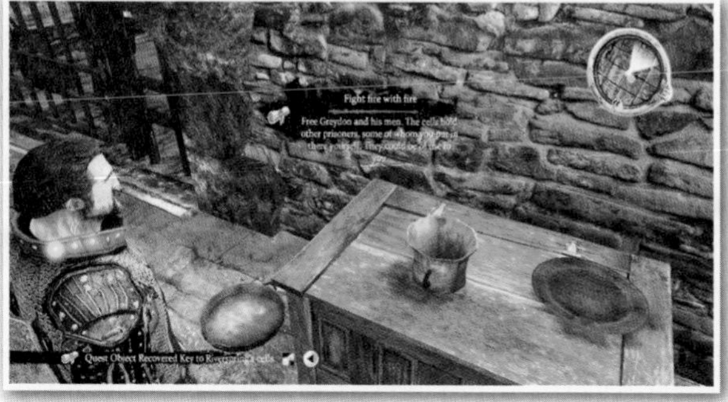

3. Free Greydon and his men. The cells hold other prisoners, some of whom you put in there yourself. They could be of use to you.

Objective Point G

If you threw anyone in the dungeons previously during the riots, you have a choice of releasing them now. They will all fight for you, though some take more convincing than others. However, be wary that any released prisoners won't be available for the « New Blood » recruitment quest later (except Mellara). So leave them rotting in their jail if you want to get the recruitment achievement.

4. Infiltrate Valarr's army and study their defenses, and find a way to open the gates for Ryman and his men.

Objective Point H

While Ryman and his men ready for an assault on the castle, you change into the armor and helmet of a guard so that you can infiltrate the castle defenses, gauge the enemy's strength, and eventually open the gates for Ryman and his men. They leave you now, and you're on your own again.

TIP

You can avoid combat with the guards here by selecting the dialogue option, "This soldier is clearly not respecting the rules." Also, change the second sentence in the Objective Point I text to read: You can try talking your way through, but unless you say the right thing about respecting the rules, the guards aren't falling for your bluff.

Objective Point I

One final group patrols the tunnels between the prison and the door to Riverspring Castle. You can try talking your way through, but the guards aren't falling for your bluff. When combat ensues, stun them immediately so they don't overwhelm you, then target the weaker one with medium armor and kill him first. Stun or knock down one of the two remaining guards, switch to a blunt weapon, and deal lethal damage to the second enemy as quickly as possible. If you can kill the second one before the final guard hacks away at you, the battle should go your way.

Objective Point J

Find the castle door and exit the tunnels. You've left the dangerous enemies of the tunnels behind for even more dangerous foes holding the castle.

RIVERSPRING CASTLE GROUND FLOOR

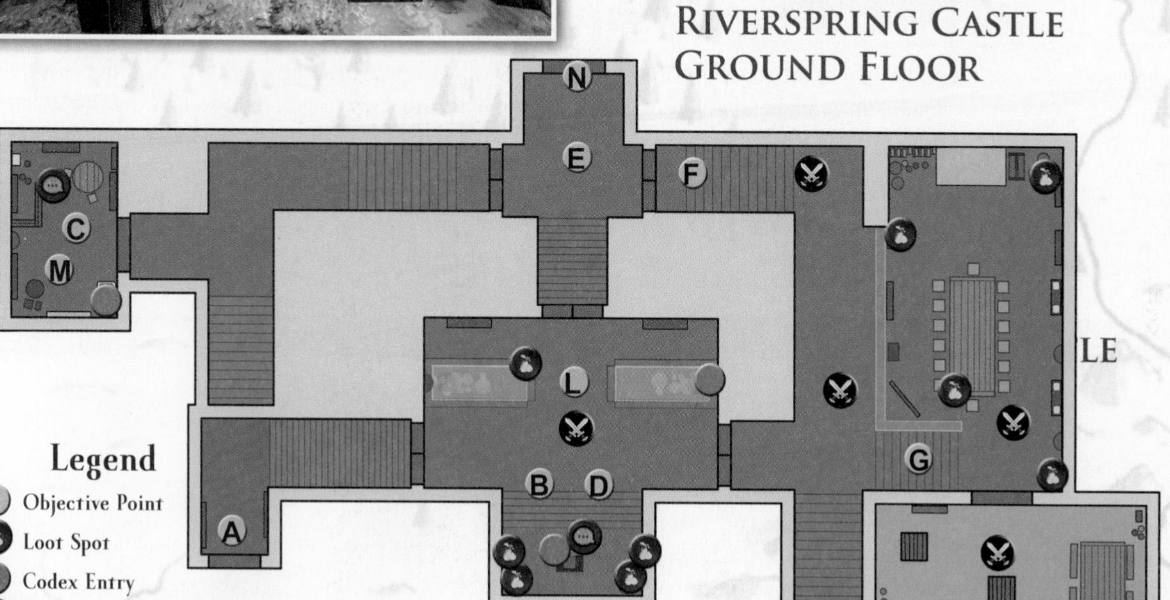

Legend

- Objective Point
- Loot Spot
- Codex Entry
- NPC
- Enemy

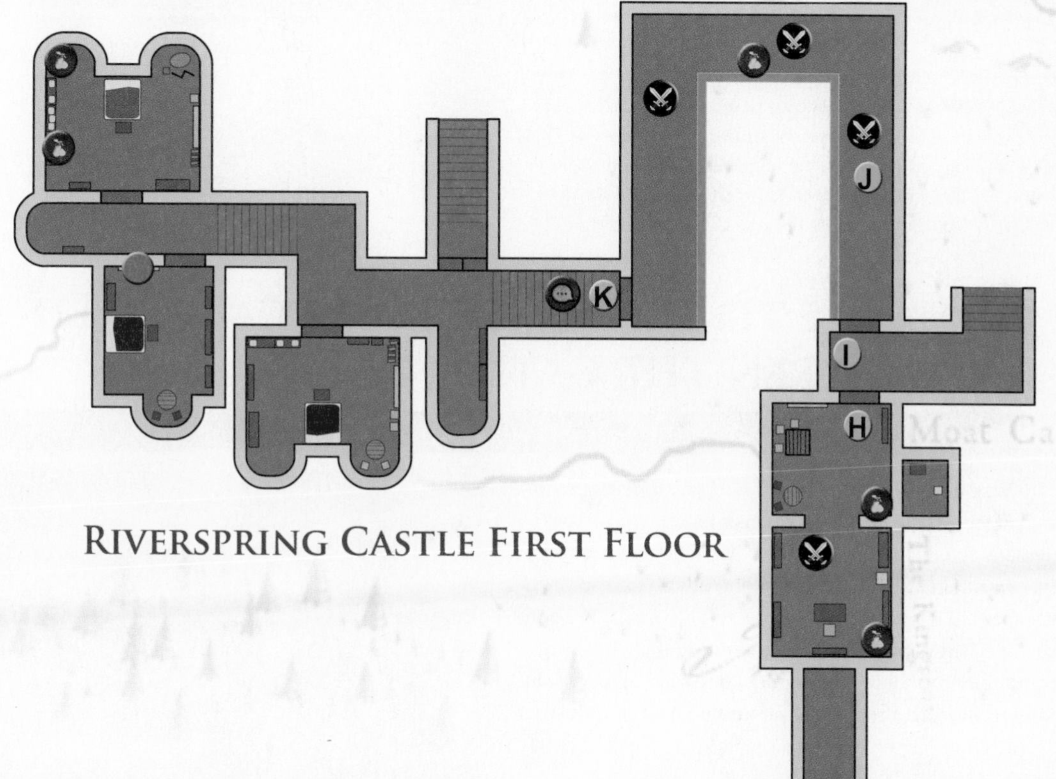

RIVERSPRING CASTLE FIRST FLOOR

Objective Point A

You enter the castle's ground floor at the stairs that lead up to the throne room. Ready yourself and go speak with Wex at the top of the stairs.

Objective Point B

Talk with Wex in the throne room. He won't recognize you in the new armor and helm, and you find out that Maester Harwyn is alive and treating the wounded in his room.

5. Maester Harwyn is alive! Before launching the attack, you must ensure his safety.

Objective Point C

Go see Harwyn in his room. You secretly reveal that you've infiltrated the guards and ask him for a status report. He explains that one of Wex's chief soldiers is severely wounded, and he has been tasked with saving him. If you convince Harwyn to save the man, Wex will be grateful later and he will give you the means to opening the main doors. Harwyn will also be saved. If you don't save the wounded man, you will have to kill Jorah up in Alester's room and loot the seal from Jorah's body to get the main doors open. You can also retrieve Gawen's locket there, which will provide you with a stat bonus..

Tip

You can try to save some of your people in the castle. A noble woman is dancing on the dining table for some Bloodseekers ; you can free her by paying them. Some servants are also being mollested in your mother's room; you can help them by attacking the two Bloodseekers there.

6. It is time to take back your castle. Find a way to open the gates for your men.

Objective Point D

Return to Wex in the throne room. If you saved his man, he will be in a good mood and you can ask for a favor or two. First, demand Ravella for your reward. He will give her to you, and you can safeguard her. In return, she gives you the Crone statuette for "The Faith of Our Ancestors" side quest. Second, ask Wex for permission to go into town now that the castle is secure and fully plundered. He agrees, and you can take that command to Blurd at the main door and he'll let you through.

As soon as you open the main doors, Ryman and his men storm through. Overwhelm the three enemies at the door and set up your position to attack the rest of the castle.

7. Take Back Your Castle and Slaughter the Bloodseekers That Infest It.

Objective Point E

Before you siege the castle, you have a choice at the main doors: take the left wing (the greater challenge) or take the right wing (the lesser challenge). Since you and Ryman are a much more formidable fighting group than the normal soldiers, opt for the left wing and let your other soldiers take on fewer enemies in the right wing.

When the doors to the left wing open, attack the guard on the stairs with a ranged weapon and draw him to you. With you and Ryman working together, he won't be a threat for long.

Objective Point F

Advance up the stairs to the balcony overlooking the dining area. Engage the nearby enemies without alerting the ones down below. If you move into the dining area while fighting these foes, you'll have trouble—both enemy groups converging on you will be a very difficult task even for your advanced skills.

Objective Point G

Proceed to the stairs leading down into the dining area, and attack the next set of guards. Look out for the enemy with a ranged weapon who will pelt you from the other side of the long table. Retreat to the stairs and use them as cover if the enemies begin to flank you.

After you kill the dining room enemies, open the door to the right of the stairs into the kitchen and take out the two remaining foes who missed out on the last fight.

Objective Point H

Climb the stairs and open the door into your father's office. More enemies roam the large room. Ensure they don't ever leave.

Advance a little farther down the balcony and draw the next enemy group toward you. There are more enemies on the other side of the balcony, so be careful not to draw their attention too. Finish off these foes before circling the balcony to the far side.

Objective Point I

Now open the door opposite the office. This leads out onto the main balcony overlooking the ground floor. A series of enemy groups guards the balcony. Take out the first group from the cover of the landing or the door's threshold.

Objective Point J

If you have a ranged weapon, it's possible to shoot across the open expanse and strike the enemies on the far side. Otherwise, charge around to their side and let Ryman take their blows while you pick them off one by one.

8. Find Greydon and His Men to Clear the City.

Objective Point K

You'll locate Greydon in the stairwell on the balcony's other side. He says the battles in the other wing were brutal, and only he and one other man survived. They will join you as you assault the throne room, but there are only four of you to take on Wex and his men.

9. Now That the Bloodseekers Have Scattered, Strike Their Officers Down. Eliminate Wex.

Objective Point L

Challenge Wex and his remaining men in the throne room. It's a large battle, so save your stuns and knockdowns for Wex or for when enemies begin to gang up on you. Take out the enemies in light armor first, then move on to the heavier-armored foes and Wex. Try to interrupt Wex's attacks and keep him contained until two of you can double-team him. After the battle, you can pull Splasher off Wex's corpse.

10. Now that the castle is yours, find Harwyn to come up with a plan of action.

Objective Point M

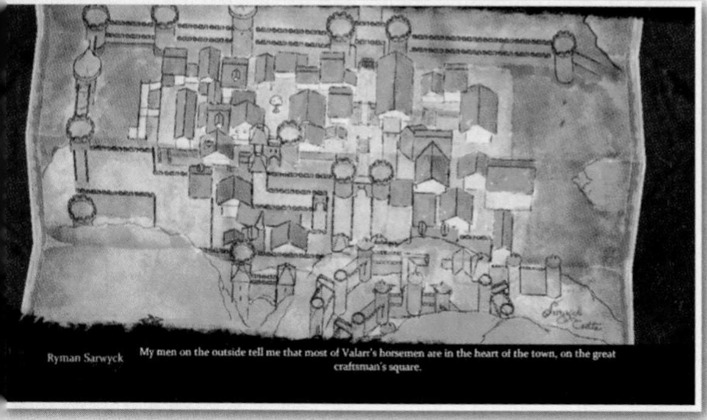

Gather all your men and plan out the attack against the Bloodseekers in Riverspring. You have three major choices to make during the attack: where to place your bowmen, where to place your pikemen, and where to place the armed villagers. Ideally, you'll place bowmen with Ryman, pikemen with Greydon, and armed villagers with Jon. This will achieve the greatest success in the battle. Most other combinations will succeed (see Caution), but with great losses, including the death of Ryman if he's with the armed villagers or the death of Greydon if he's with the bowmen.

Caution

The game ends if you send the armed villagers with Ryman, the bowmen with Greydon, and the pikemen with Jon. Don't do this!

11. Go and pay your respects to Mors' body in the castle courtyard.

Objective Point N

The battles are over for now. Go visit your friend Mors in the courtyard. You didn't have time before, but now you can give him R'hllor's kiss as a final send-off to the after-life. You leave the dead, feeling a great sorrow settling over you. Suddenly, unbelievably, Mors revives and sits straight up!

CHAPTER 13

BOUND

OBJECTIVES

1. You must find a boat to enter Castlewood from Riverspring.
2. Jeyne is being held somewhere in the castle. Find her and free her.
3. You must defeat Ethan of the Reach and his men to free Jeyne.
4. Find a way to flee quickly.
5. Fight your way through Harlton's army to flee Castlewood.
6. When you are ready to take vengeance on Valarr, return to your chambers in Riverspring Castle.

QUEST CHECKLIST

- **Victor (NPC, objective 1)**
- **Key to Castlewood Cellar (quest item, objective 2)**
- **Stormbreaker (special item, objective 2)**
- **Harlton's Bunch of Keys (quest item, objective 2)**
- **Guardless Broadsword (special item, objective 3)**
- **"Not So Wild" (side quest, objective 6)**
- **"Ritual and Litanies" (side quest, objective 6)**
- **Experience Points: 2,485 (upon quest completion)**

RIVERSPRING

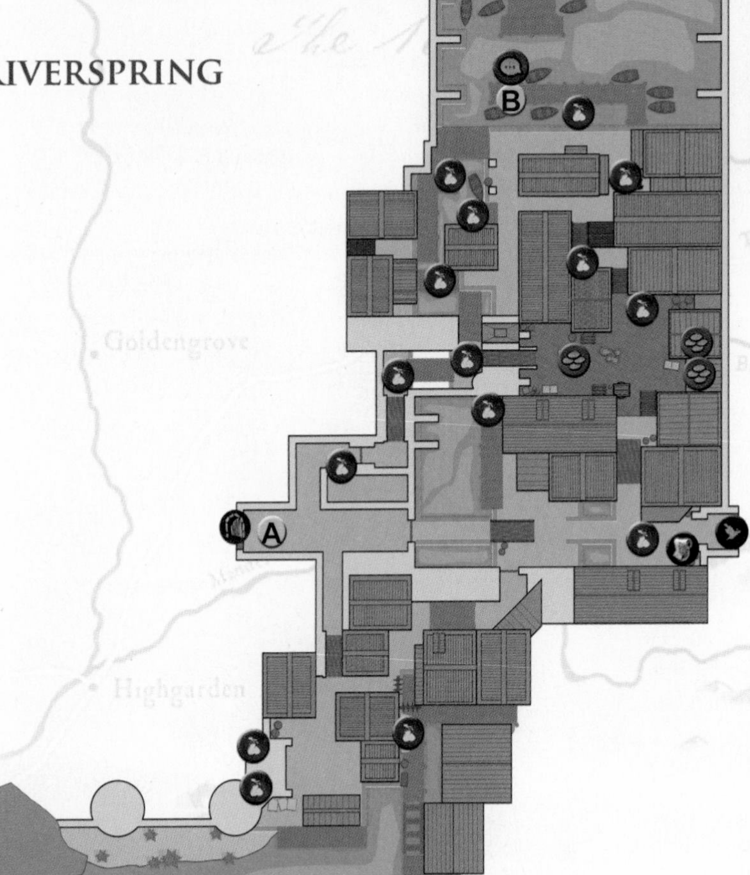

Legend

- Objective Point
- Loot Spot
- Side Quest
- Travel to World
- Travel to Area
- NPC
- Merchant

1. You must find a boat to enter Castlewood from Riverspring.

Objective Point A

Alester catches Mors up on events after his miraculous resurrection. Valarr and his small army are headed to Castlewood to kill Jeyne, so it's up to the two of you to sneak into Castlewood, find Jeyne, and safeguard her and the child out of Harlton's and Valarr's clutches.

Tip

You can search the streets of Riverspring and the castle jail for many potential Night's Watch recruits to help fulfill Mors's "New Blood" side quest.

Objective Point B

After you have walked Riverspring for potential Night's Watch recruits and visited any merchants you want, rendezvous with Victor on the docks. He agrees to ferry you to Castlewood. You hope that the soldiers guarding the castle will be too preoccupied with Valarr's army at their gates to notice one small boat slipping into the side gate that Alester noticed during your previous escape from Castlewood.

Legend

- Objective Point
- Loot Spot
- Secret Treasure (Alester)
- Secret Treasure (Dog)
- Codex Entry
- Enemy
- Travel to Area
- Secret Passage

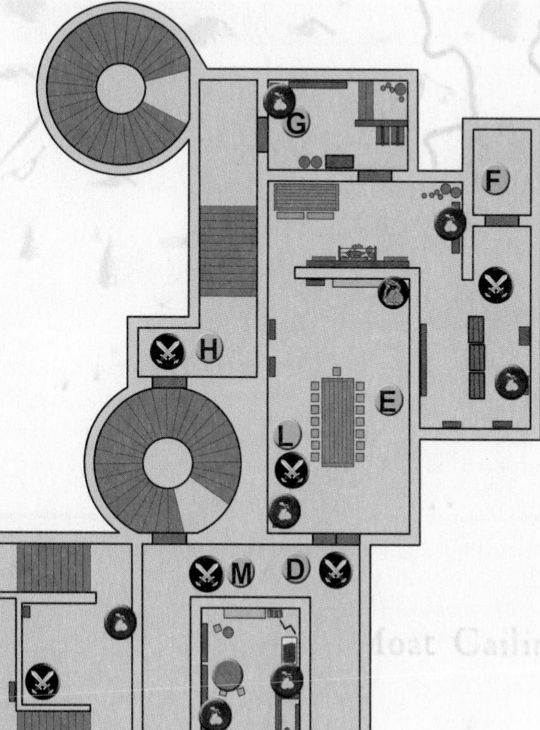

Castlewood Ground Floor

CASTLEWOOD FIRST FLOOR

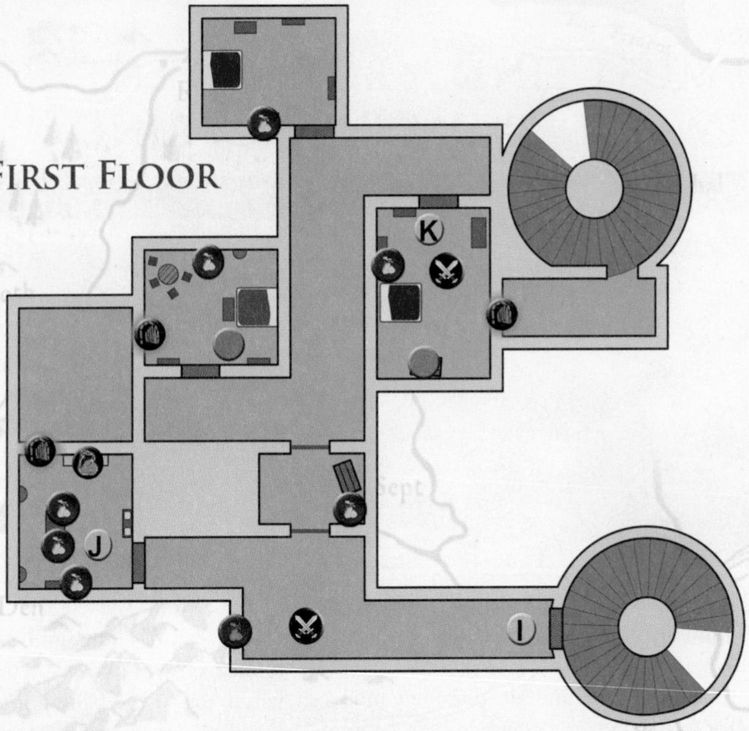

Legend

- Objective Point
- Loot Spot
- Secret Treasure (Alester)
- Secret Treasure (Dog)
- Codex Entry
- Enemy
- Travel to Area
- Secret Passage

K

J

I

2. JEYNE IS BEING HELD SOMEWHERE IN THE CASTLE. FIND HER AND FREE HER.

Objective Point A

Victor drops you off at the unguarded side entrance and you infiltrate the castle unseen. Climb the steps and meet up with Dog on the next landing. Since Mors's dog just came from sitting next to Jeyne, he can trace a scent trail back to her.

TIP

You will face fewer foes if you sneak through the castle. Let Dog guide you, hide from any guards you see, and attack only when necessary. Don't forget to go back to the guard room where Alesander was : a new powerful weapon can be found there.

Objective Point B

When you reach the entrance foyer, wait in the shadows and watch the lone guard pace back and forth from the main door to the throne room. Time a canine sneak attack for when the guard marches toward the main door and has his back to you. Rip out his throat before anyone else has a chance to notice, revert back to Mors, and then take the entire party across the foyer and through the door on the opposite side.

Objective Point C

You'll see a large group of guards at the end of the next hallway. You don't have to fight them! The scent trail turns left and into the side hallways. Wait for the guard in that hallway to continue his patrol to the opposite corner, where he talks with another guard for a few seconds; then the second guard joins the large enemy group that you first saw.

Objective Point D

The lone guard is far away enough from the large enemy group that Dog can assassinate him without alerting the other nearby enemies. Quickly run the whole party down the side hallway, past the dead guard, and through the next door.

Objective Point E

You are now in the dining hall. Watch for the patrolling guard on the hall's far side; when he disappears into the storeroom to the north, creep up to the doorway separating the main dining room from a side dining room.

Objective Point F

Switch to Dog and scamper into the side alcove in the northeast corner of the second dining area. The guard will walk past the opening of this alcove and present his back to you as he loops back on his route. Strike when the guard is most vulnerable and make sure your teeth are faster than his sword.

Objective Point G

Snatch the Key to Castlewood Cellar off the dead guard and continue into the storeroom. Pass through the next room and open the door leading into the stairway that leads to the main stairwell. Wait in the doorway until the guard mounts the steps and stands in front of the door on the landing.

Objective Point H

Sneak up on him with Dog and eliminate him without raising the alarm. Open the door into the stairwell and take the stairs to the first floor.

Objective Point I

Unfortunately, despite your stealth, when you open the door onto the first floor, one of the guards spots you from down the long hallway, runs to alert the others, and locks a gate behind him. The only way through is to find the hidden key to the gate. You can still try to kill him with Dog since the door has a hole.

TIP

You can also kill the guard with Dog by going through the locked gate, or you can use the Vision of R'hllor in Harlton's office to reveal a secret passage and sneak into Jeyne's room through the concealed room. Both earn you an achievement.

Objective Point J

You can't get through the locked gate yet, but you can enter Harlton's nearby office. Search the room for various items of interest in plain view: a Missive from Beyond the Narrow Sea Codex entry, the Stormbreaker two-handed sword, and a letter from Raynald Sarwyck addressing his concerns about the Brotherhood's troublesome course of action. The item you need, however, is hidden. Switch to Dog and have him sniff out the blue treasure scent that leads to the fireplace. Revert to Mors and grab Harlton's Bunch of Keys from the fireplace ashes. You can also go past this gate with a secret passage in Harlton's office. Use the Vision of R'hllor next to the fireplace to find it.

Objective Point K

Open the locked gate with Harlton's keys and race down the corridor when you hear Jeyne's cries. Turn the corner and burst through the door to confront Jeyne's aggressors. Harlton's man Ethan holds Jeyne hostage and won't release her.

3. You must defeat Ethan of the Reach and his men to free Jeyne.

The battle against Ethan and his men occurs in a small bedchamber. You don't have much room to maneuver, and the close confines can work against you or for you, depending on your tactics. The guards have the numbers, so they have the immediate advantage of landing many attacks from which you can't escape. However, because of the tight quarters, your area-of-effect attacks and stuns will affect almost everyone at once. Alternate potent abilities between Mors and Alester to keep the enemies from gaining offensive momentum, and send Dog to immobilize the most problematic target (likely Ethan).

TIP

Pick up the Guardless Broadsword from Ethan's corpse after the conversation with Lord Harlton in the corridor.

After you defeat Ethan and his men, you attempt to escort Jeyne quickly out of the castle. She's going to give birth any minute, so time is running out. Alas, time is also not on your side—at the very moment you decide to leave, Lord Harlton and a small army check on the disturbances and meet you in the hallway. There's no convincing the madman of his errors, so you're forced to retreat back to the room with Harlton's guards banging on the door and out for blood.

4. Find a Way to Flee Quickly.

With Mors holding the door, Alester should search the room. You need to find a secret passage leading out of the room, so use Vision of R'hllor near a shimmering in the air next to the torch on the empty wall. A panel will slide up and reveal a small area connecting the bedchamber to the main stairwell. Take the stairs back down to the ground floor and prepare to battle your way out of the castle.

5. Fight Your Way Through Harlton's Army to Flee Castlewood.

Objective Point L

As you move through the empty rooms and hallways that you cleared when you came up to save Jeyne, labor pains cause Jeyne to collapse. The baby is coming any minute. Jeyne needs a breather, so it's up to the two of you and Dog to protect her as an enemy patrol finds you. Rely on your standard tactics with Mors, Dog, and Alester. A few well-timed stuns and knockdowns, along with dealing a healthy amount of damage to your enemies, should take care of the threat.

Objective Point M

Open the dining room doors to spot two enemy patrols: one straight ahead and one down the hall to your right. Concentrate on a single patrol and eliminate them before moving on to the second one. If the second patrol closes too quickly, send Dog to immobilize one of the enemies and slow the group down. A few major attacks and critical blows later, both enemy patrols will fall.

Objective Point N

Harlton and his men surround you and force your party into the throne room. He plans to force Jeyne to submit to his will and orders Desmond Hardyng and his men to kill everyone but the woman.

You begin in a bad position in the throne room: Desmond and other melee brawlers surround you on the ground floor, while archers fire away at you from the balconies flanking the main chamber. Order Dog to immobilize one of the archers to cut down on incoming attacks, while Mors and Alester pair up on one foe after the other. Cut down the lesser-armored foes first.

If you have a ranged weapon, fire back at the archers with a powerful attack or two. Eliminating the archers gives you more time to deal with Desmond and his crew.

Keep up the damage on Desmond and interrupt when he winds up for a big attack. As the other enemies die, you can add more attacks to overwhelm him.

Even after you slay Desmond, it's not over. Harlton sends his final enemies after you in a second wave. If you're low on health, retreat to a balcony for extra cover. Kill the archer on that side and focus on each enemy who comes up the stairs. When only the opposite side archer remains, race over and finish the job.

You defeat Harlton and his men. The Lord of Castlewood stares around, unbelieving, at the carnage you've left in his throne room. Then it gets worse. A shadow passes through the wall behind Harlton. It slays his men and then moves in to kill Harlton. You quickly escape the throne room as Harlton's screams echo off the stone walls.

Objective Point O

You try to get Jeyne out, but in the end, she falls to the floor in the foyer and delivers the baby. Soon after, Valarr's army breaches the castle. With time running out, Mors hands the baby off to Alester, who races ahead to Victor. Mors half drags Jeyne toward the exit...when Valarr enters the foyer.

Valarr doesn't know Jeyne has delivered her baby. Realizing she won't make it and happy that her son will be safe if Valarr thinks he's killed mother and son, Jeyne valiantly pushes Mors down the corridor and seals it shut with a portcullis. Looking back through the portcullis, helpless, Mors watches as Valarr slays Jeyne. He then flees the castle to escape Valarr, and the three men and a baby row back to Riverspring.

Riverspring Courtyard

A

B

Legend

- Objective Point
- Loot Spot
- Travel to Area

6. When You Are Ready to Take Vengeance on Valarr, Return to Your Chambers in Riverspring Castle.

Objective Point A

It goes from bad to worse when you return to Riverspring. You receive news that the king is dead, and the streets of King's Landing have erupted in violence as the Lannisters set upon members of House Stark.

You agree, though, that you must hunt down Valarr in King's Landing. You give the child to Maester Harwyn temporarily; he will meet you in King's Landing after you've made the dangerous journey and all seems safe.

Side Quest: Not So Wild

After you speak to Harwyn in the Riverspring Courtyard, a raven arrives for you from Castle Black. Qhorin Halfhand needs your help back at the Wall to help track down some wildlings who are holed up in Mole's Town. For more details on the mission against the wildlings and completing the quest, see the "Side Quests" chapter.

Side Quest: Rituals and Litanies

If you return to Castle Black, you can also discover this second side quest in your old home. Patrek has been accused of murdering some brothers of the Night's Watch, and it's up to Mors to clear his friend's name. For more details on saving Patrek and completing the quest, see the "Side Quests" chapter.

Objective Point B

Enter the castle and find your room. Inside, Alester and Mors each make a case for why vengeance should be carried out on Valarr.

CAUTION

At this point in the story, you must choose to play either Mors or Alester. This choice determines who the main character will be in the climax, and which path of destiny you may see in the epilogue.

When you are ready for the final end to the story, and you've made all your preparations for the difficult journey ahead, choose either Mors's destiny or Alester's destiny to continue. Once you select your character, you cannot go back. You will then play that character to the end and make the choices that will ultimately shape his final destiny.

CHAPTER 14:

LIGHT AND SHADOW

QUEST CHECKLIST

- Falena (NPC, objective 2)
- Harwyn (NPC, objective 3)
- Clement Buckler (NPC, objective 4)
- Valyrian Steel Claymore (special item, objective 4)
- Varys (NPC, objectives 5, 7)
- Roland (NPC, objective 5)
- Silver Key (quest item, objective 9)
- Master Pyromancer's Ring (special item, objective 9)
- Experience Points: 1,250 (upon quest completion)

KING'S LANDING

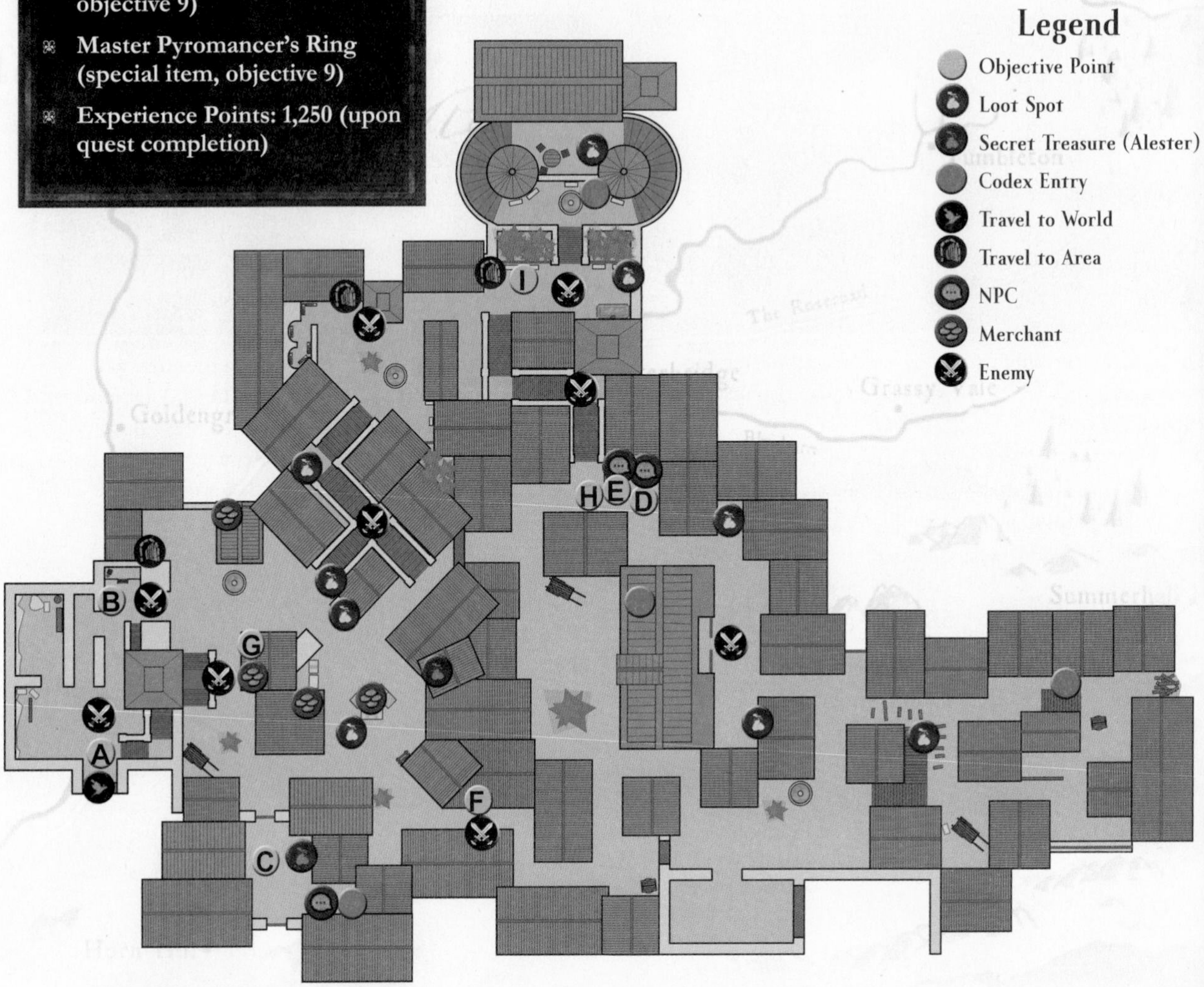

Legend

- Objective Point
- Loot Spot
- Secret Treasure (Alester)
- Codex Entry
- Travel to World
- Travel to Area
- NPC
- Merchant
- Enemy

A B C D E F G H I

Objectives

1. Find Harwyn at the agreed-upon location, behind Jaremy's pottery shop.
2. Pick up Harwyn's trail in King's Landing OR Speak with Falena to find out that Varys has taken Harwyn somewhere in the rich quarter of King's Landing.
3. Go meet Harwyn.
4. Without a weapon made of Valyrian steel, you will be powerless against Valarr's shadows. You must find one in the town before confronting him.
5. Now you have something to use when confronting Valarr. Go back to Varys to proceed with your plan.
6. There is a passage linking the sewers of King's Landing with Maegor's Holdfast, through which you can infiltrate the Red Keep. Go to the sewers to find it.
7. Look for the secret passage near the violet lantern left by Varys, which will lead you to the royal palace.
8. The throne room isn't much further. Pick your way through the maze of the Maegor's Holdfast.
9. Dispose of Valarr's last henchmen, Petyr and Stevron the pyromancers.
10. Nothing more stands in your way. Go to the throne room where your fight with Valarr awaits.
11. It's time for vengeance. Fight Valarr and kill him.

1. Find Harwyn at the Agreed-Upon Location, Behind Jaremy's Pottery Shop.

Objective Point A

As soon as you arrive in King's Landing, you're greeted by the city guard at the gate. The Red Cloak leader questions you while his Gold Cloak brethren take positions around you. No matter if you give your true names or not, the Red Cloak leader won't be fooled, and you have a choice: pay the bribe to have the guards look the other way as you enter the city or fight them.

If you choose to fight them, expect heavy resistance. The Red Cloak is tougher than the standard Gold Cloak, and there are more of them than you. Alternate stuns between Alester and Mors, and sic Dog on a third foe to temporarily incapacitate him. Switch to perforating weapons for most of the Gold Cloaks, and use blunt weapons against the Red Cloak.

NOTE

Orys, Axe, or both will show up in front of the marketplace to join your party if you spared their lives earlier. If you didn't aid either of the two Reapers, they will not appear and there will be no fight against the city guards.

If you saved either of the Reapers earlier in your King's Landing adventures (or both), you will find them confronted by the city guard in front of the marketplace. If you only spared Axe, he and a henchman will be there. If you saved only Orys, he and a henchman will be there. If you helped both Axe and Orys earlier, the two of them will fight with you against the city guards and join your party. In this case, you outnumber the city guards, so they should perish without too much pain on your parts.

Objective Point B

2. Pick up Harwyn's trail in King's Landing or Speak with Falena to find out that Varys has taken Harwyn somewhere in the rich quarter of King's Landing.

Objective Point C

When you finally get to the agreed-upon meeting place at the potter shop, Harwyn isn't there. You have a choice to track him down: Dog can follow his scent trail, or you can speak with Falena, who stands waiting in the side alley next to the shop.

Speaking with Falena is the easier path. If you are nice to her, she will tell you that Varys intercepted Harwyn and brought him to a new location in King's Landing. The new location is marked on your map, which makes finding Harwyn and Varys simple. If you don't speak with Falena or are dismissive in your talks, she won't reveal much of anything and you'll have to track down Harwyn through his scent.

3. Go meet Harwyn.

Objective Point D

The city guards patrol the streets. You can sneak around and avoid getting spotted to reach your destinations, or you can take the patrols one at a time. As you kill patrols, it will be easier to navigate the city without fear of unwanted combat.

Book Watch: Starks vs. Lannisters

At this point in our story, Alester's and Mors's quest for vengeance against Valarr interweaves closely with the major events from the novel. We hear about King Robert's death, and when Alester and Mors arrive in King's Landing, they see the bloodshed in the streets firsthand, as Stark guards have been cut down by the city watch loyal to Queen Cersei and the Lannisters. Later, while Eddard Stark gives his final confession to the lords and ladies of the Crown outside, you will find your way inside to an unguarded Red Keep throne room.

Objective Point E

Varys tells you that he had to bring Harwyn here for safety reasons and that he has spread rumors around that you will deliver Jeyne's baby to the queen in the throne room. He hopes that Valarr will try to intercept you there, and you can then exact your vengeance on the murderer. First, though, you need to acquire a weapon made from Valyrian steel; it's the only material capable of harming the shadows that serve Valarr.

4. Without a weapon made of Valyrian steel, you will be powerless against Valarr's shadows. You must find one in the town before confronting him.

Objective Point F

Varys knows of one person in King's Landing who owns a Valyrian steel weapon: your old friend Clement Buckler. Meet up with Clement and ask him nicely for the sword; he won't give it to you, but it was worth a try.

Instead, you'll have to fight him for it. Clement has a mean, two-handed swing that damages everyone around him. He can quickly kill multiple foes in melee. If you have a ranged weapon, back up and strike him repeatedly from safety while the Reapers or Dog keep him occupied. Alternately, Mors or Alester can go toe-to-toe with Clement and deliver as much damage as possible before his energy expires; then stun Clement, back out, and switch positions with your teammate. When you bring Clement's health to zero, he will submit and hand you his special weapon.

5. Now you have something to use when confronting Valarr. Go back to Varys to proceed with your plan.

Objective Point G

Return to Varys when you have Clement's Valyrian Steel Claymore. If your Stance relies on wielding a two-handed weapon and you like it as a sword, you're all set and can proceed. If not, Varys explains how to reforge the weapon into something more useful. Seek out the blacksmith Roland in the marketplace. You can reforge the Valyrian Steel Claymore into a more appropriate one-handed weapon, a bow, a crossbow, or a different type of two-handed weapon.

Objective Point H

Return to Varys again. You debate the best course of action and ultimately decide to trust him to bring Jeyne's son to you in the throne room after you've dealt with Valarr. Varys informs you of a secret route through the sewers and into Maegor's Holdfast, where you can take the same path you took earlier to the secret door into the throne room.

6. There is a passage linking the sewers of King's Landing with Maegor's Holdfast, through which you can infiltrate the Red Keep. Go to the sewers to find it.

Objective Point I

You've opened several entrances into the sewers by now. The closest entrance is likely near Lord Harlton's old estate, but you can take any of the sewer access points around the city. Just be careful of the city watch on patrol as you head to the sewers.

Sewers of King's Landing

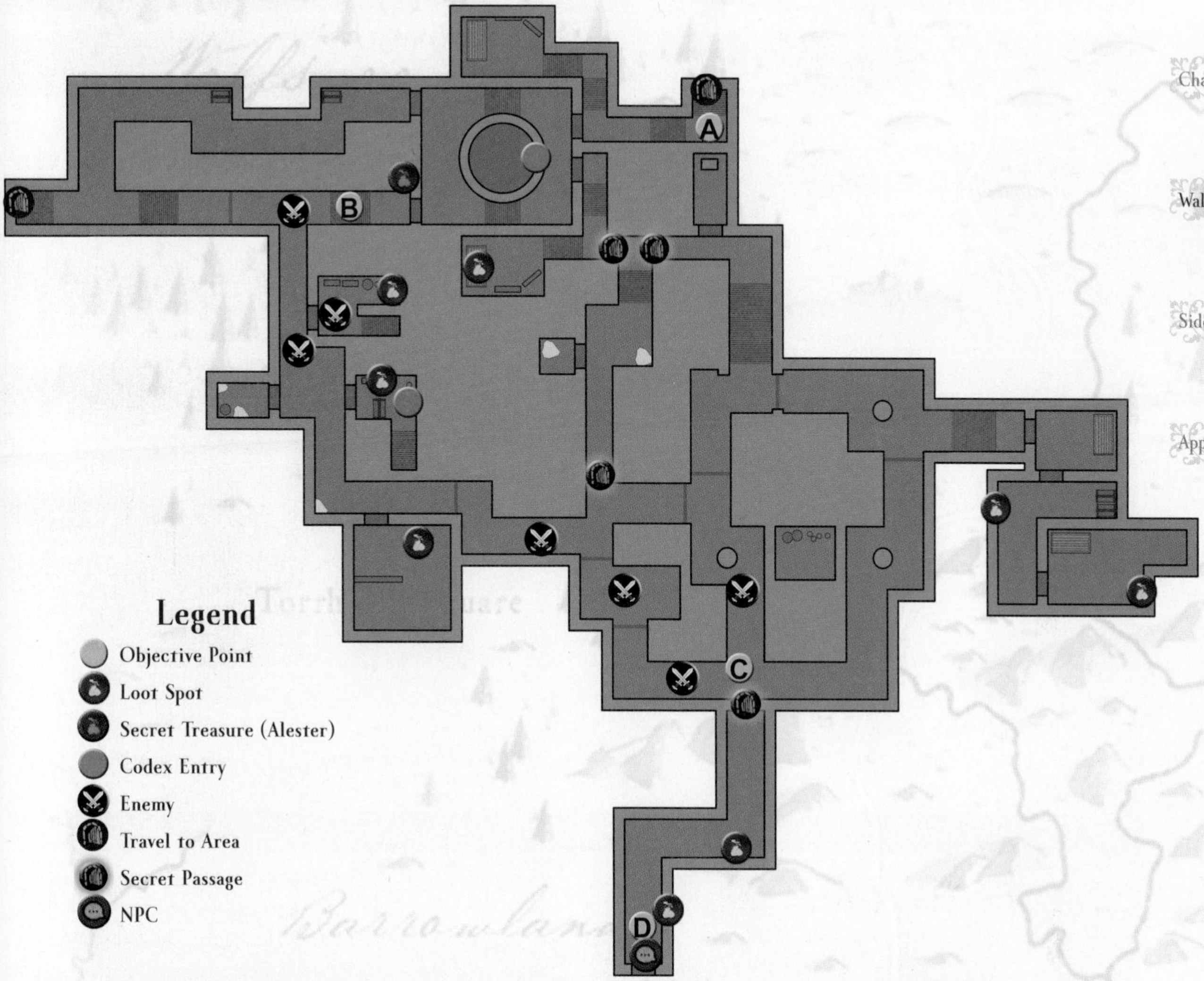

A
B
C
D

Legend

- Objective Point
- Loot Spot
- Secret Treasure (Alester)
- Codex Entry
- Enemy
- Travel to Area
- Secret Passage
- NPC

7. Look for the secret passage near the violet lantern left by Varys, which will lead you to the royal palace.

Objective Point A

Varys has marked the location of the secret passage into Maegor's Holdfast with a violet lantern. The secret passage is hidden in the southern section of the sewers.

Objective Point B

Anticipating your movements in King's Landing, Valarr has left Bloodseekers to guard the sewers. Move slowly through the tunnels and peek around each corner to spot the enemies before they spot you. Each enemy group shouldn't be too difficult, especially if you have both Orys and Axe to aid in the battles.

Objective Point C

As you get close, the intersection that holds the secret door is clearly marked with a purple light. Watch for an enemy patrol that crosses the intersection. Sneak up on them and attack in force before looking for the secret passage.

Use the Vision of R'hllor directly under the violet lantern. You'll reveal a hidden mechanism on the torch to the lantern's right. Pull the torch lever and open the secret door.

Objective Point D

Enter the secret area and find Varys at the end before you enter Maegor's Holdfast. If you have Orys and/or Axe in your party, they say farewell here. They won't travel with you on the final part of your journey. After they leave, Varys guides you into Maegor's Holdfast.

Maegor's Holdfast Upper Basement

Maegor's Holdfast Lower Basement

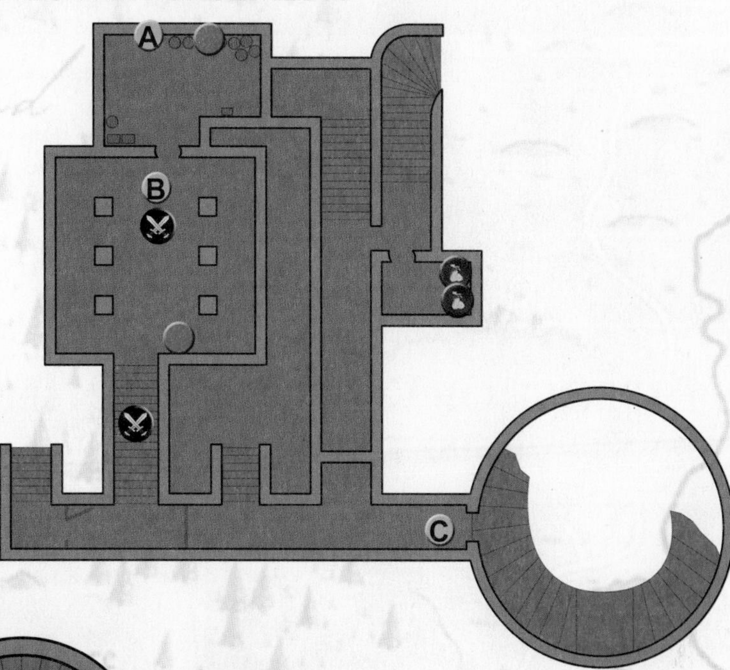

Maegor's Holdfast Dungeons

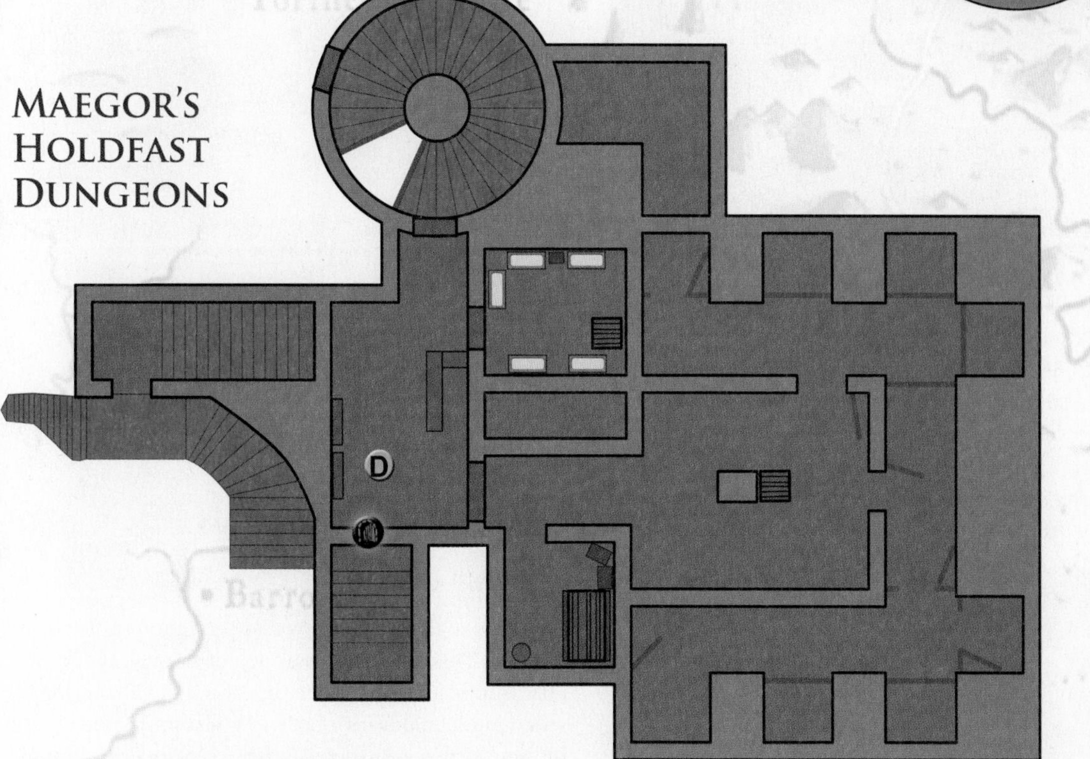

8. The throne room isn't much further. Pick your way through the maze of the Maegor's Holdfast.

Objective Point A

You begin on the lower basement level of Maegor's Holdfast. Varys has guided you as far as he can and will now go retrieve Jeyne's baby and meet you in the throne room. Retrace the familiar rooms and tunnels you took earlier in Maegor's Holdfast to reach the throne room.

9. Dispose of Valarr's last henchmen, Petyr and Stevron the pyromancers.

Objective Point B

You won't get far before pyromancers of the Alchemists' Guild intercept you. Valarr has placed these potent last guards to ensure you never reach the throne room. The first of two encounters with the pyromancers takes place in the large chamber next to the wine cellar. One pyromancer can set you on fire; he is the priority target. Interrupt his actions, even if it means cycling through Mors's, Alester's, and Dog's abilities to keep him from launching a damaging attack.

After you kill the pyromancer, turn your attention to the other guards. When enemies clump together, rely on your abilities against multiple foes to maximize damage. If you get into trouble against the ranged attackers, retreat through the collapsed wall and let them come to you in closer quarters. It's a long battle, but one that you can win with perseverance.

Objective Point C

Continue to the second pyromancer fight near the main stairwell. This time you'll have to cut through the normal guards to reach the pyromancer, and it's in a much smaller space in the middle of a hallway. Use a stun to move past the standard guards to reach the pyromancer. Continue damaging the guards while one party member keeps the pyromancer incapacitated. If you can avoid the pyromancer's big flame attacks, you'll win the battle. Afterward, pick up the Master Pyromancer's Ring from his corpse, along with the Silver Key that unlocks the door ahead.

10. Nothing more stands in your way. Go to the throne room where your fight with Valarr awaits.

Objective Point D

Head up to the secret door that Varys met you at during your last encounter in Maegor's Holdfast. Use the Vision of R'hllor to expose the secret door and enter into the Red Keep throne room.

Throne Room of the Red Keep

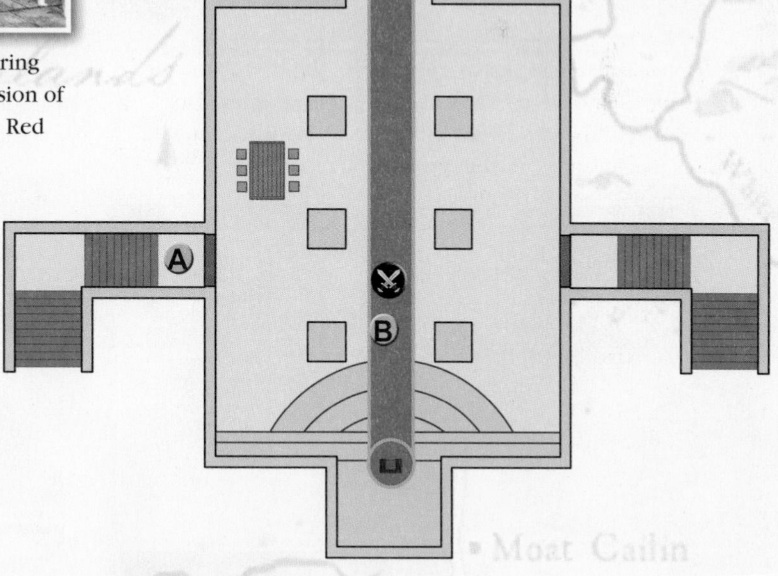

11. It's time for vengeance. Fight Valarr and kill him.

Objective Point A

Head up the stairs and enter the throne room. From the balcony, watch Valarr enter and walk up the red carpet. After he taunts you from below, find the stairs down to the ground floor and initiate the final fight against Valarr.

Objective Point B

Open by stunning or knocking down Valarr with one of your abilities. Dog's Throat Lunge is a great opener for Valarr, who doesn't fight with a shield. Lay into him with as much damage as you can until he recovers.

When you bring Valarr down to half his health total, he cheats. Valarr backs away from you, cuts his hand, and summons forth a shadow with dark magic. You now have to fight Valarr and one shadow.

Tip

If you don't have a Valyrian steel weapon, or if the person wielding the Valyrian steel falls in combat, ignore the shadows and concentrate on Valarr. If you deal enough damage to kill him before the shadows destroy you, you can still win the battle.

Whoever is armed with the Valyrian steel should now concentrate on the shadow. The special weapon deals 10 times normal damage against shadows, which offsets the shadow's ability to regenerate health very quickly. A normal weapon against a shadow will do very little; the Valyrian steel can kill it with some effort. If you don't have Valyrian steel, use an attack with mass damage like Wildfire, which can still kill it; however, it's best to aim for Valarr and hope you can slay him before the enemies overwhelm you.

When you kill off the shadow, return to ganging up on Valarr to increase his wounds. When you drop him below one-quarter of his health, he summons a second shadow.

It's imperative that you've slain the first shadow by this point or they will start slaughtering you.

Even though you've stacked up the wounds on Valarr, he isn't easy to kill. He regenerates health back up to full when the second shadow arrives. Repeat the same tactics as with the first shadow: the person with the Valyrian steel kills the shadow, then returns to team up on Valarr.

With the second shadow dissipated, combine all your attacks on Valarr and continue rotating with stuns and knockdowns. Eventually, all your attacks add up and you deliver the killing blow to Valarr.

Valarr stumbles back and lands on the Iron Throne. You finally put him out of his misery, but not before he spits out the secret Alester has dreaded since he met up with Mors: It was Valarr and Alester who murdered Mors's wife and daughter.

CHAPTER 15:
OLD SCAR

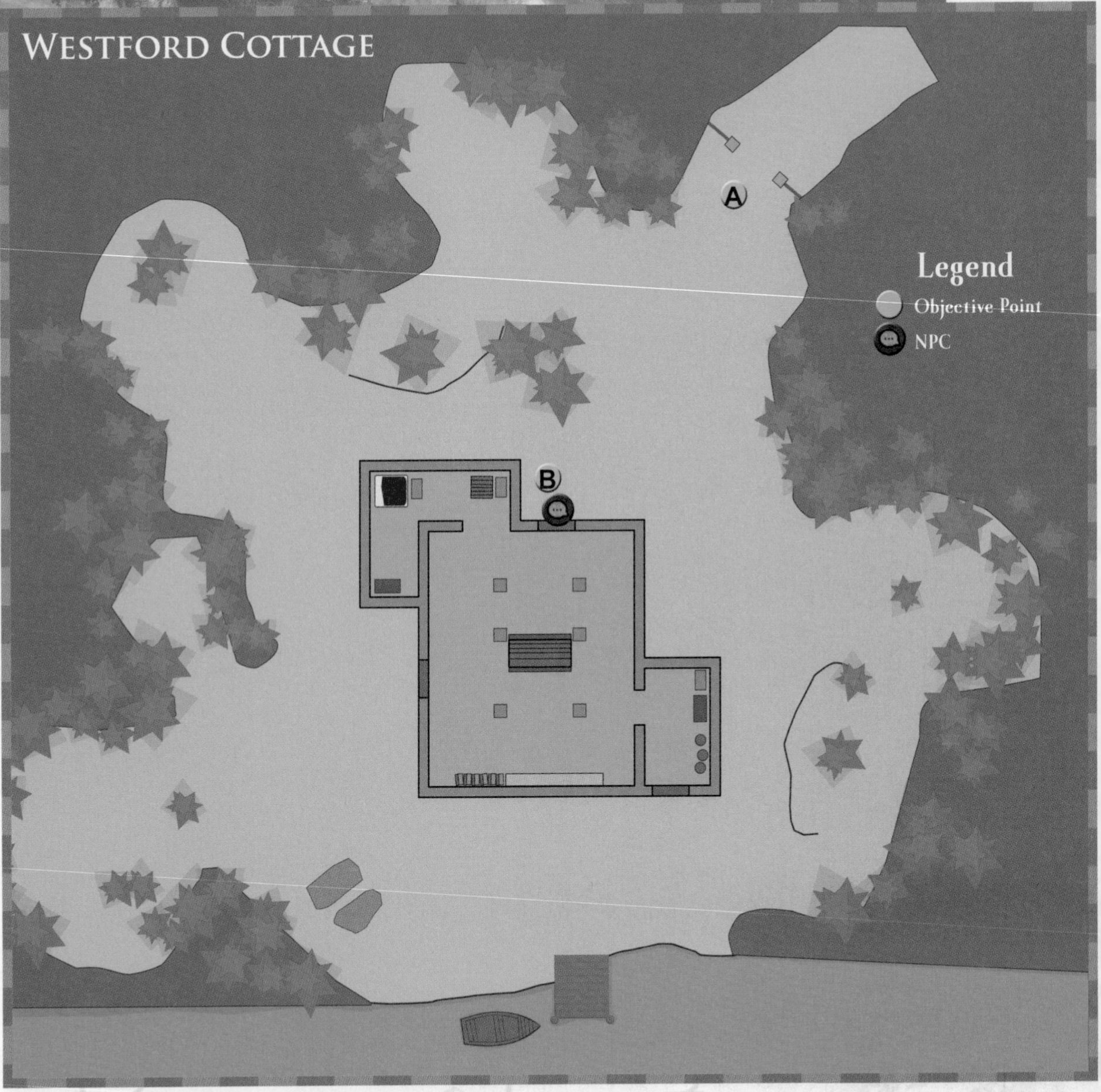

WESTFORD COTTAGE

A
B

Legend
Objective Point
NPC

OBJECTIVES

1. Your orders are clear. Like it or not, House Westford must pay for having disobeyed their liege lord.
2. Do your duty.

QUEST CHECKLIST

- Cerenna Westford (NPC, objective 1)

1. Your Orders Are Clear. Like It or Not, House Westford Must Pay for Having Disobeyed Their Liege Lord.

Objective Point A

In a flashback sequence, you arrive as Alester at the Westford Cottage alongside your half brother, Valarr. Mors has left for the Night's Watch, and he has entrusted you to protect his family. Alas, you cannot. Lord Tywin Lannister has discovered Mors's family cottage and ordered you and Valarr to execute Mors's wife and child as an example for disobeying a direct command during the war.

Approach Cerenna Westford near the cottage. She's shocked to see you—and with a stranger by your side. Eventually she deduces that you're here to kill her. She begs for mercy, or at the very least for you to kill her but to let her daughter go.

2. Do Your Duty.

Objective Point B

Valarr sadistically volunteers to torture and kill Mors's daughter, Tya. You are left with Cerenna and have two choices: kill her or not. It would seem the moral choice is to not kill her; however, that works out worse. If you kill her, you slit her throat quickly and it's over. If you choose to let her live, Cerenna has to listen to her daughter's screams as she bangs futilely on the locked cottage door. When the screams finally stop, she attacks you in despair and you end up stabbing her anyway.

Valarr exits the cottage enthused with the brutality. Despising him for the loathsome bully that he really is, you want to kill him, but he's blood. In a fit of rage and grief, you slash Valarr's face instead, leaving him a constant reminder of this day and a burning hatred that will come back to haunt you 15 years later.

FINAL CHAPTER:

ICE AND FIRE

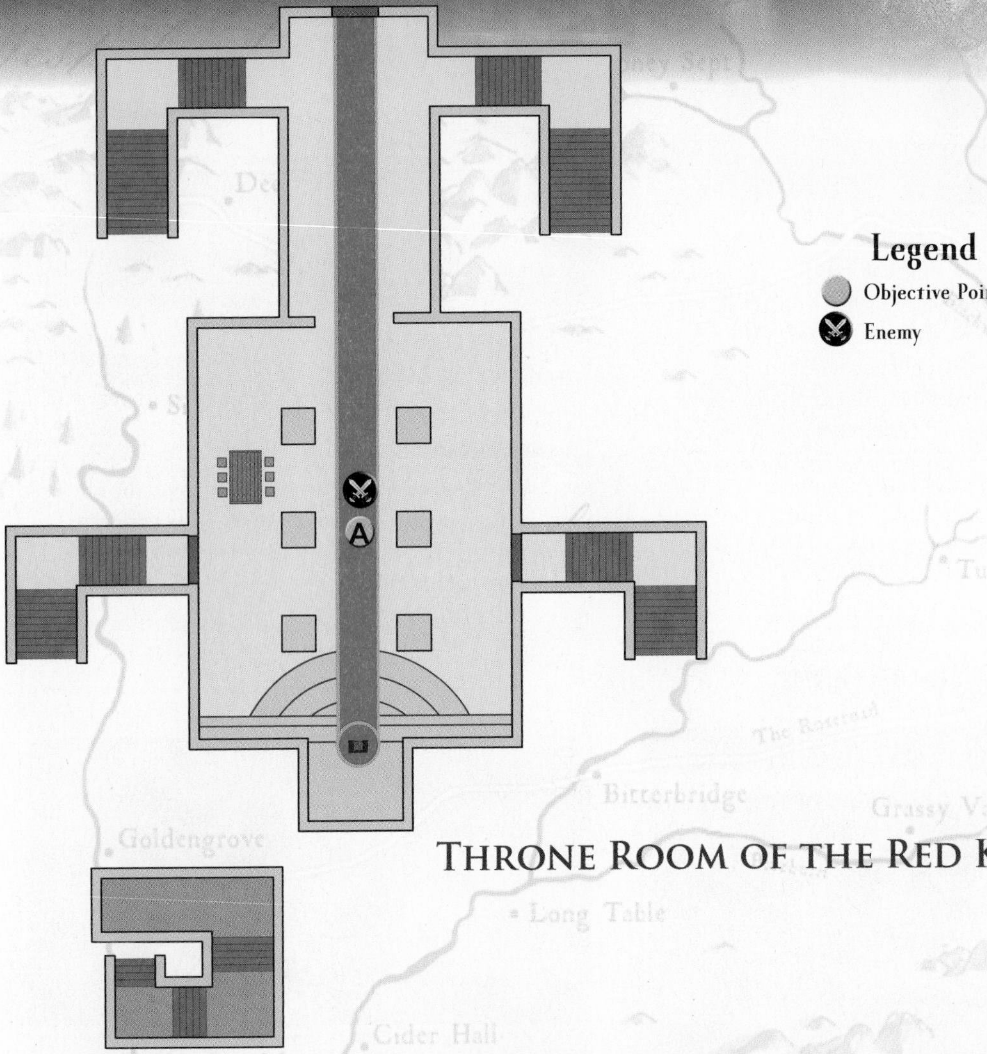

Legend

Objective Point

Enemy

THRONE ROOM OF THE RED KEEP

OBJECTIVES

1. Triumph over Mors in a duel or triumph over Alester in a duel.
2. Strike down the group of Gold Cloaks that interrupted your duel.
3. There is nothing left that can prevent this fight. Your friend must die...

QUEST CHECKLIST

- Experience Points: 500 (upon quest completion)

Basics

Characters

Walkthrough

Side Quests

Appendix

1. Triumph over Mors in a Duel or Triumph over Alester in a Duel.

Objective Point A

After you hear the tale of what really happened that fateful day at Westford Cottage, Mors condemns Alester. No matter what is said, too much pain has occurred to forgive. The two of you will duel to the death.

> **Note**
>
> You will control whoever you picked back in Riverspring when Varys asked you to choose Alester's or Mors's destiny. To survive, you must kill the one you called friend and companion on this long quest.

If you are playing Mors, begin by commanding Dog to open with his best attack, preferably one that will stun or knock down Alester. Follow up with a powerful attack of your own that takes advantage of his incapacitated state. Pay attention to your abilities that Bleed or deal extra damage based on the situation; if you use these efficiently, you'll deal more damage to Alester over the course of the battle. Conserve energy too. It's a long battle, and though you want to get off your big attacks, you don't want to be drained of energy at a crucial point in the fight when you desperately need a stun or an interrupt ability.

While Dog's ability recharges, use a stun or knockdown ability to keep Alester off balance. Attacks like Shield Strike, Earthquaker, and Cutthroat give you precious seconds to recharge energy and avoid damage.

When you knock Alester down to half of his health, the Gold Cloaks who were pounding on the door to the throne room come crashing in. They interrupt your battle, and you're forced to deal with them before you can continue your duel to the death.

If you are playing Alester, you won't have Dog, so stun Mors immediately and follow with a powerful attack that takes advantage of his incapacitated state. Pay attention to your abilities that poison or deal extra damage based on the situation; if you use these efficiently, you'll deal more damage to Mors over the course of the battle. Conserve energy too. It's a long battle, and though you want to get off your big attacks, you don't want to be drained of energy at a crucial point in the fight when you desperately need a stun or an interrupt ability.

Use a stun or knockdown ability to keep Mors off balance. Attacks like Calm as Still Water, Strong as a Bear, Blinding Dust, and Paralyzing Powder give you precious seconds to recharge energy and avoid damage. Look for combos in your stance that exploit Mors's vulnerable state, such as Dexterity's Head Shot, which interrupts and knocks down Mors, and Focus, which regenerates energy quickly; it's possible to set up a cycle of continuous Head Shots that will keep Mors down on the ground for the majority of the fight.

When you knock Mors down to half of his health, the Gold Cloaks who were pounding on the door to the throne room come crashing in. They interrupt your battle, and you're forced to deal with them before you can continue your duel to the death.

2. Strike down the group of Gold Cloaks that interrupted your duel.

After the Gold Cloaks break into the throne room, they surround you. In one last battle together, you agree to fight as a team against the queen's men. There are many tough enemies in this final large group battle. It will take a coordination of talents to escape alive.

Use the pillar around the room to your advantage. If you need to hide temporarily from enemy archers, duck behind a pillar, or if several enemies try to swarm you, move around a pillar to break them apart.

Mors or Alester should stun immediately so that you can get out of the middle of all the attacking weapons. Send Dog to immobilize a nearby enemy, preferably one who isn't stunned or begins to chase after you. Work together on dealing damage to cut down enemies one by one.

Powerful abilities can keep the enemies at bay, and a flask full of Wildfire will destroy a foe in seconds. This fight will tax your reserves, so carefully weigh when to use abilities and when to conserve. You will need to recover at least once during the fight; just make sure that both Alester and Mors don't have to recover at the same time. In the end, your superior group tactics and proven battle experience will beat the Gold Cloaks.

3. There is nothing left that can prevent this fight. Your friend must die...

With the queen's guards dead, you return to your duel. Continue with similar tactics as earlier to keep your opponent on the defensive. If you're playing Mors, when you drop Alester to half his health, he uses his powers of R'hllor to ignite his weapon; he will set you on fire and cause additional damage over time, so you'll have to quicken your damage output. If you're playing Alester, when you drop Mors to half his health, he will get a free charge on you, unexpectedly damaging you and suddenly placing you both face-to-face in melee.

At one-quarter health, Alester calls upon greater R'hllor fire powers to destroy you as Mors. In similar fashion, Mors roars when he's down to one-quarter of his health and bolsters a fierce counterattack against you in the final moments of the battle.

It will be a bloodbath, but in the end you will have to beat your companion to survive. When you land the final blow to drop his health to zero, you are victorious and trigger your friend's death scene.

After some parting words, you finish off your friend with one last executioner's stroke. One destiny ends while the other continues to a fork in the road.

Varys shows up with Jeyne's child as promised. The fork in your destiny appears when you have to make one final choice. For Mors, he must choose to take care of the child for Jeyne's sake, or live and die at his post on the Wall. For Alester, he must choose to hand the child over to Queen Cersei as ransom for his kingdom or defy the queen and keep the boy's whereabouts a secret.

NOTE

Your decision regarding Jeyne's child determines one of four endings, two epilogues per hero. Turn to the next chapter to see Alester's and Mors's fates.

EPILOGUES

NOTE

Based on your dialogue choice with Varys in the Red Keep's throne room, you will earn one of two epilogues for each hero.

ALESTER'S EPILOGUE 1: "I WILL OFFER HIM TO THE QUEEN IN RETURN FOR RIVERSPRING."

If you play through the game's end as Alester and choose the dialogue option "I will offer him to the queen in return for Riverspring," when Varys brings Jeyne's child to the throne room, you unlock Alester's first epilogue. Queen Cersei enters the throne room looking for the child she was promised and you deliver him to her.

You exchange the child's life for your kingdom. Except, it's not what you had imagined. The kingdom is failing, and your conscience eats away at you. So many lives have been lost. Was the cost worth it?

In your despair, you return to your room. You stand in front of the fire, the fire of your god R'hllor, with those thoughts lying heavy on your shoulders and a noose hanging behind you waiting for your neck.

ALESTER'S EPILOGUE 2: "THIS CHILD WILL LIVE, IN MEMORY OF MORS."

If you play through the game's end as Alester and choose the dialogue option "This child will live, in memory of Mors," when Varys brings Jeyne's child to the throne room, you unlock Alester's second epilogue. Queen Cersei enters the throne room looking for the child she was promised.

You have other plans. You refuse to tell Cersei where the child is, and you've taken every measure possible to ensure she never finds the boy who could one day command the Crown.

Even as Cersei's guards close in for the kill, you defiantly cry out, "Better to die than to be tainted!" The guards slay you, but you are no longer the queen's pawn—you are the noble leader of Riverspring.

MORS'S EPILOGUE 1: "I WILL CARE FOR HIM, FOR JEYNE'S SAKE..."

If you play through the game's end as Mors and choose the dialogue option "I will care for him, for Jeyne's sake," when Varys brings Jeyne's child to the throne room, you unlock Mors's first epilogue. As promised, you take the boy back to your family's cottage, far away from the troubles in King's Landing.

You are taking care of Jeyne's son as if he were your own, though you have your doubts on how someone who knows only violence and death could ever make a good father.

Just then Dog hears something. You grab your sword and slowly walk out to meet the threat, whether it be the Night's Watch hunting you down for desertion or assassins out to kill the boy who is a threat to the throne back in King's Landing. The life you've chosen will be one always on the run, protecting Jeyne's son until he is old enough to protect himself.

Mors's Epilogue 2: "I Will Live and Die at My Post...at the Wall."

If you play through the game's end as Mors and choose the dialogue option "I will live and die at my post...at the Wall," when Varys brings Jeyne's child to the throne room, you unlock Mors's second epilogue. You return to Castle Black just as Lord Commander Mormont orders another execution.

The deserter is Patrek, and the guilt from forsaking Jeyne's child combined with seeing your former companion moments from death plunges you into despair. You scare Mormont's youngest crop of recruits by telling them that they're just marking time until death comes for them... soon.

You grab the executioner axe and lop off Patrek's head. You have honored your commitment to the Night's Watch by returning to the Wall, but maybe you've dishonored your soul in the process.

SIDE QUESTS

SIDE QUEST 1: THE FAITH OF OUR ANCESTORS

SIDE QUEST 1

For: Mors

Location: Common Hall in Castle Black

Quest Giver: Walder

Availability: Chapter 1 to Chapter 13

Experience Points: 900

Special Rewards: 62 silver stags, Ashes of the Seven (Alester) or Glory of the Seven (Mors)

Objectives:

1. If you find another statuette, take it to Walder at Castle Black, and he'll restore it.

1. If you find another statuette, take it to Walder at Castle Black, and he'll restore it.

Objective Point A

Find Walder on the top floor of the Common Hall in Castle Black. He has restored the Father statuette for you, which has been a family heirloom for many generations. If you find other statuettes spread across Westeros, you can return to Walder at Castle Black and he'll restore those for you as well. Collect all seven and you earn a magical trinket for either Alester or Mors. If you choose to burn the statuettes for Alester, you gain the Ashes of the Seven, a symbol of Alester's devotion to R'hllor that grants +30% energy recovery. If you choose to honor Mors's ancestors, you gain the Glory of the Seven, which represents Mors's sense of duty and unfailing devotion to his family, and grants +120 health and -25% energy costs on abilities.

You can locate the seven statuettes in the following places around the world:

- **The Crone statuette: Ravella gives this to you after rescuing her in Chapter 12. You can also loot it from her corpse in Chapter 13 if you don't rescue her.**
- **The Father statuette: You find this statuette in a dresser inside Westford Cottage after reading Mors's father's letter (Chapter 7).**
- **The Maiden statuette: Bethany gives this statuette to you at the end of the "Self-Made Girl" side quest if you send her back to Chataya.**
- **The Mother statuette: You can find this statuette inside Jeyne's room in the Mole's Town brothel (Chapter 5).**
- **The Smith statuette: Purchase this statuette from the Riverspring Armor Merchant for 1 gold and 20 silver.**

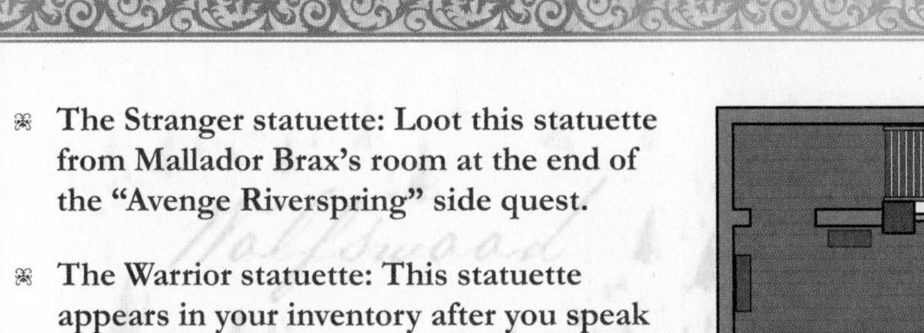

- The Stranger statuette: Loot this statuette from Mallador Brax's room at the end of the "Avenge Riverspring" side quest.
- The Warrior statuette: This statuette appears in your inventory after you speak to Walder.

COMMON HALL, SECOND FLOOR

SIDE QUEST 2: THEIR WATCH IS ENDING

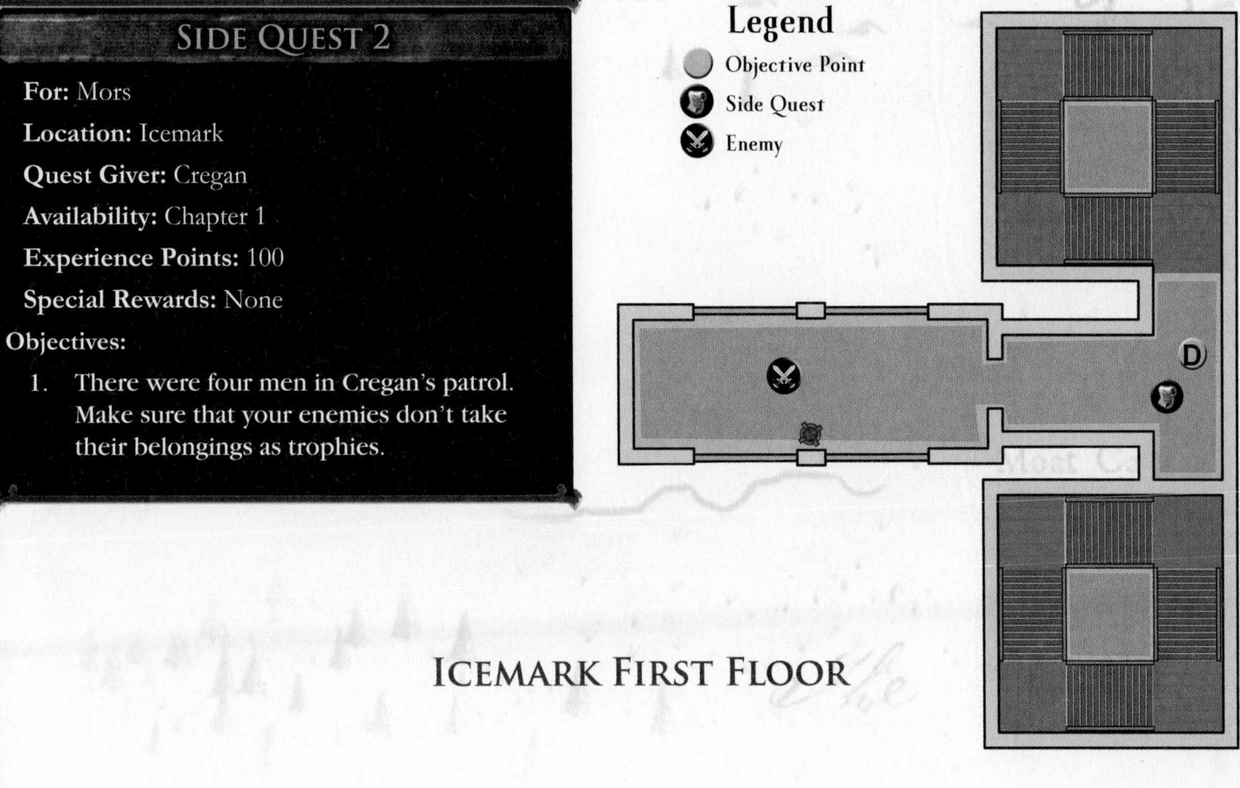

SIDE QUEST 2

For: Mors

Location: Icemark

Quest Giver: Cregan

Availability: Chapter 1

Experience Points: 100

Special Rewards: None

Objectives:

1. There were four men in Cregan's patrol. Make sure that your enemies don't take their belongings as trophies.

ICEMARK FIRST FLOOR

ICEMARK GROUND FLOOR

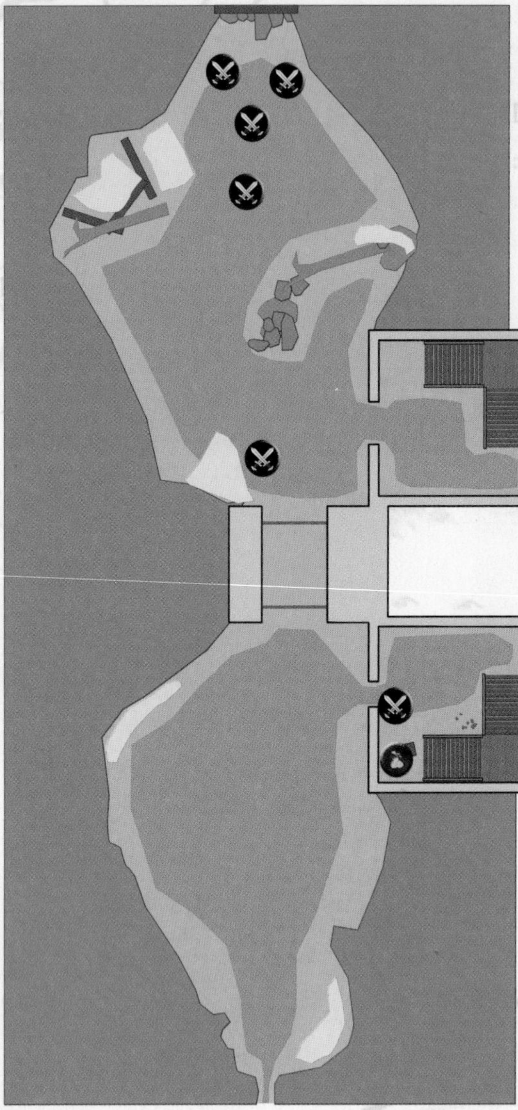

Legend

- Objective Point
- Loot Spot
- Codex Entry
- Side Quest
- Enemy
- NPC

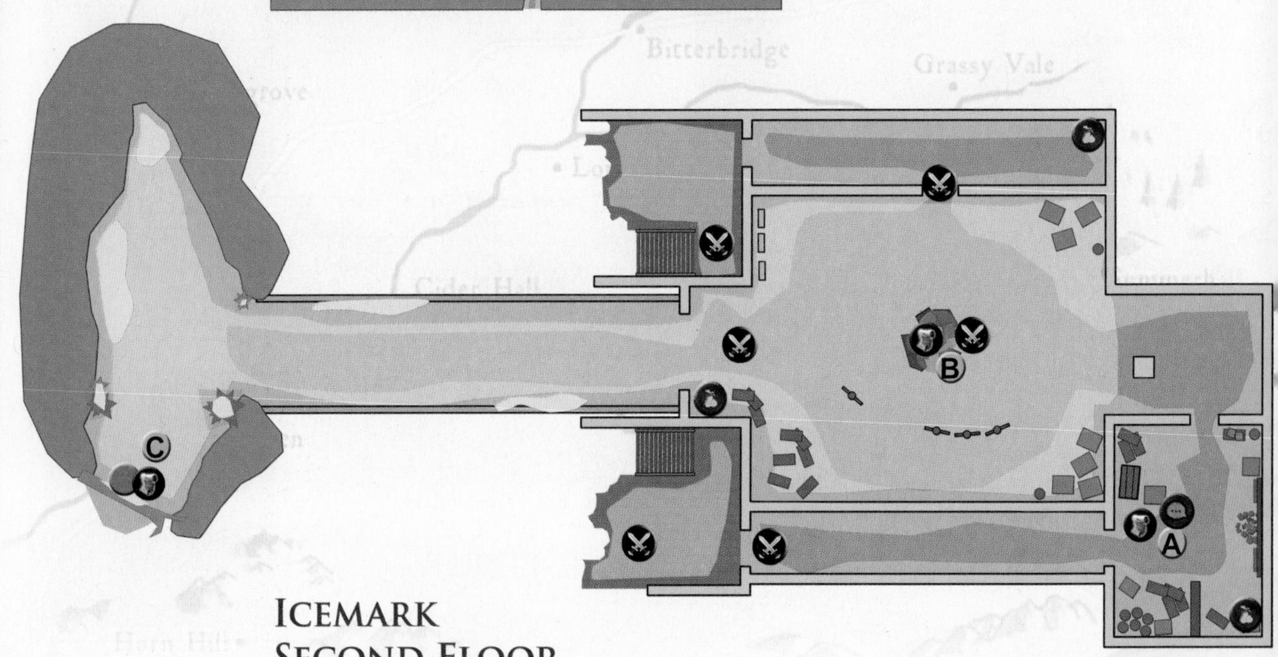

ICEMARK SECOND FLOOR

1. There were four men in Cregan's patrol. Make sure that your enemies don't take their belongings as trophies.

Objective Point A

Cregan gives you this side quest with his dying breath in Icemark. You can remove the A Ranger's Personal Belongings item from Cregan's corpse. It's up to you to retrieve the other three Night's Watch brothers' belongings before the wildlings get to them and use them as trophies.

Objective Point B

The second set of belongings is on the poor brother burned alive in the bonfire that the wildlings have started outside in the courtyard. Defeat the wildlings around the fire and retrieve his belongings.

Objective Point C

The third set of belongings lies with the fallen brother in the snow, west of the courtyard. There are no enemies nearby, so it's easy to retrieve the belongings.

Objective Point D

The fourth set of belongings is on the dead ranger on the stairwell. Battle through the wildlings guarding the stairs to retrieve the last belongings and show a final token of respect for your brothers.

Side Quest 3: Treasure Hunt

Side Quest 3

For: Mors

Location: Common The Gift

Quest Giver: Ondrew

Availability: Chapter 3

Experience Points: 200

Special Rewards: 50 silver stags

Objectives:

1. It looks like some money has been hidden in the forest. It was buried in two separate places, one on a ledge next to a hollow tree trunk, the other half lying in the bushes. This money could be very useful...
2. Get the first half of the stash.
3. Get the second half of the stash.

THE GIFT

Legend

- Objective Point
- Secret Treasure (Dog)
- Side Quest
- Enemy

1. It looks like some money has been hidden in the forest. It was buried in two separate places, one on a ledge next to a hollow tree trunk, the other half lying in the bushes. This money could be very useful...

Objective Point A

After the band of thugs waylay you in the Gift, you can receive this side quest if you force Ondrew to tell you after the battle. Before you put him out of his misery, Ondrew confesses that they buried two separate treasure stashes in the forest, one in the bushes and one next to a hollow tree trunk.

2. Get the first half of the stash.

Objective Point B

Control Dog and sniff around the area, looking for the blue treasure scents. You can follow the one to a bushy area that looks just like any other, except you can push through the undergrowth and locate the secret treasure in a tree stump on the small hill.

3. Get the second half of the stash.

Objective Point C

The second treasure stash is a bit tricker. Sniff around with Dog and look for a fallen tree trunk that runs up the side of a hill.

Dog can run through the hollow trunk and gain the top of the hill. Sniff out the treasure in the trunk next to the twisted tree and then uncover your loot reward with Mors.

Side Quest 4: Silence in the Ranks

Side Quest 4

For: Alester

Location: Throne Room of the Red Keep

Quest Giver: Ser Uthor Donnerly

Availability: Chapter 6

Experience Points: 200

Special Rewards: Ring of the Lioness (Bargaining Chance +8%, Critical Hit Chance +2%)

Objectives:

1. Report Ser Uthor's statements to Queen Cersei and put a stop to his slander.

Throne Room of the Red Keep Ground Floor

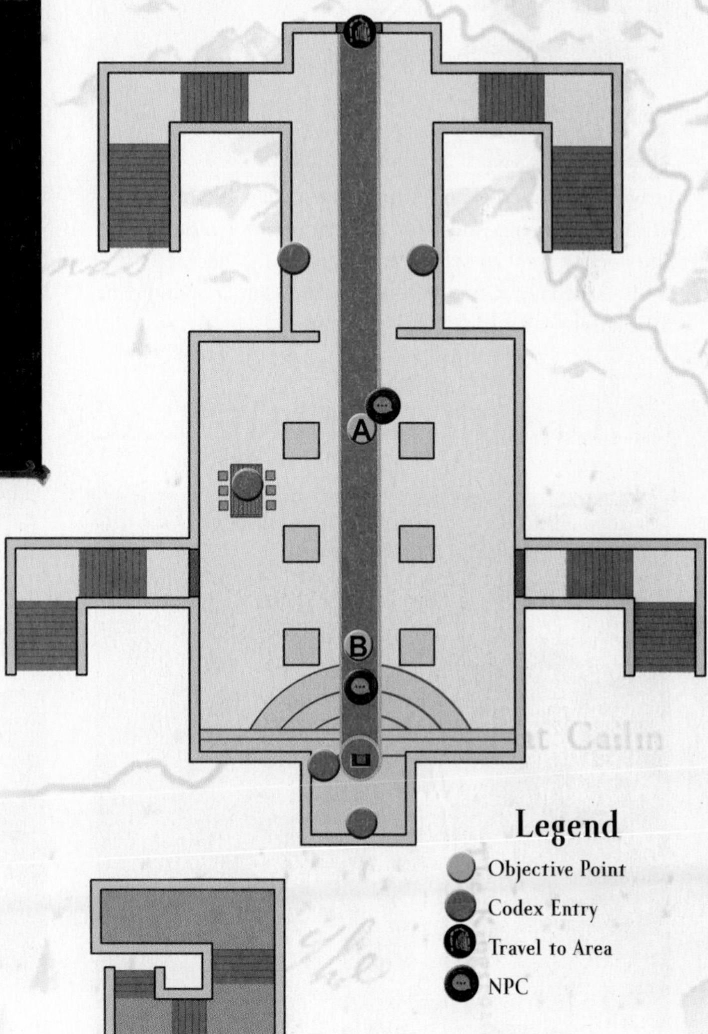

1. Report Ser Uthor's statements to Queen Cersei and put a stop to his slander.

Objective Point A

The best way to finish this quest is to threaten Uthor first. When the queen sends you back to Uthor, chose to explain the situation to him and there will be no fight. The queen will be extremely pleased with you action.

Otherwise, after you speak with Queen Cersei in the Red Keep's throne room, look for Ser Uthor Donnerly on the right side of the red carpet as you exit. He believes the queen has murdered his former master, Jon Arryn, and won't keep quiet about his distaste for the queen

Objective Point B

Leave Ser Donnerly and return to the queen. Report Uthor's statements and listen to what the queen has to say. She doesn't want to make a scene and won't be happy if you kill the knight, but she does agree to let you handle the matter.

Return to Ser Donnerly. He doesn't want to listen to what you have to say, and he has a quick temper, so you may end up battling him anyway. Even if you can't convince him to keep quiet and it comes to blows, you will complete the quest despite the queen's disappointment.

Side Quest 5: The Black Bloodhound

Side Quest 5

For: Mors

Location: Common Hall at Castle Black

Quest Giver: Lord Commander Mormont

Availability: Chapter 7

Experience Points: 100

Special Rewards: None

Objectives:

1. Talk to Addam Flowers if you want to take part in the inquiry to identify the corrupt brothers
2. Investigate the men who were with Godric. Addam Flowers has gathered them all in the Common Hall.

1. Talk to Addam Flowers if you want to take part in the inquiry to identify the corrupt brothers.

Objective Point A

Speak with Addam Flowers on the top floor of the Common Hall after you gain the "Stray Dog" primary quest

Common Hall Ground Floor

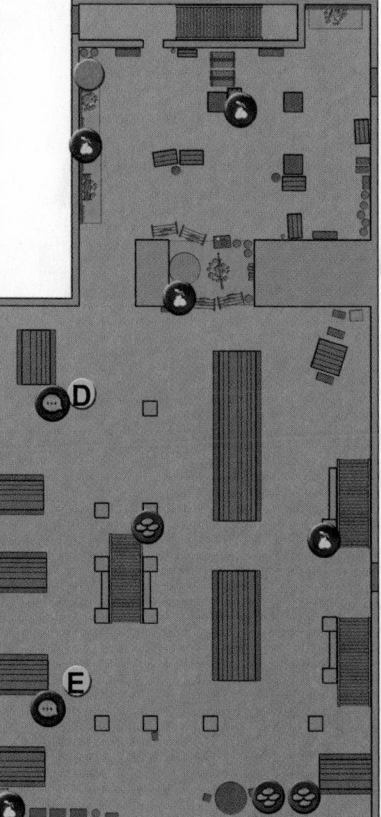

Common Hall First Floor

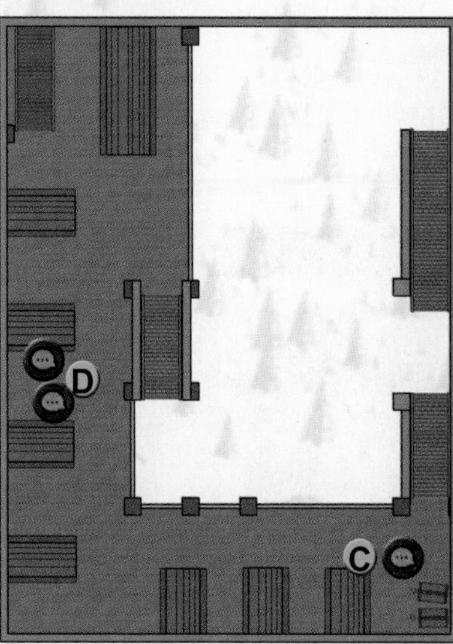

Legend

- Objective Point
- Loot Spot
- Codex Entry
- Side Quest
- NPC
- Merchant

Common Hall Second Floor

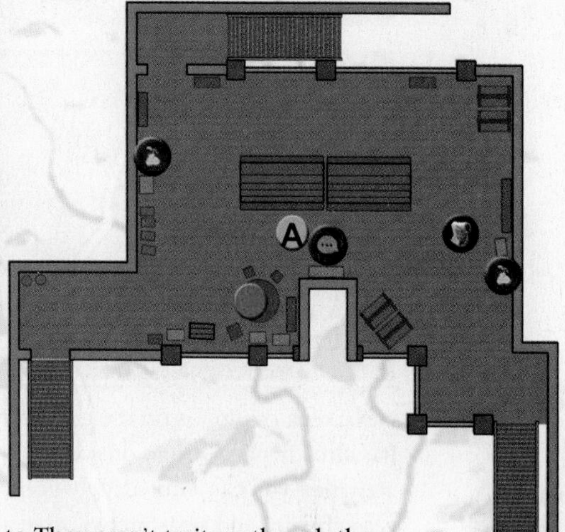

ınd before you leave for Mole's Town. Flowers is a strange :haracter whose paranoia makes him the ideal brother to nonitor potential corruption in the ranks. If you agree to :he side quest, Flowers entrusts you to question five broth-:rs who are suspected of collaborating with the duplici-:ous Ser Godric: Grance, Jonos, Bartram, Arthur, and Trebor (all in the Common Hall).

2. Investigate the men who were with Godric. Addam Flowers has gathered them all in the Common Hall.

Objective Point B

See Arthur and Trebor first on the first floor. Trebor has no self-control, so if you immediately tease him, he lets slip what they've been up to. They aren't traitors, though they have committed murder. They discovered that another brother, Domeric, had sold his services to Godric's men, and when they confronted Domeric, a fight broke out. They killed Domeric and then hid the body during all the recent commotion. You can either agree to forget the incident because they were protecting the Night's Watch or report them to the Lord Commander.

Objective Point C

Bartram claims that he's being set up by the crazy Flowers again. He says he's never spoken to Godric and instead gives you dirt on Jonos, who he spotted uncharacteristically giving credit to several brothers. However, after you speak with Grance and return to Bartram, he admits to speaking with Godric atop the Wall. You've caught Bartram in a lie but you can't prove that he is a traitor. Take the dog and pick up Bartram's scent. Follow the scent to one of the sworn brother who guards the doors during the investigation. The guard will move toward some stuff and start fetching in a bag. Call Mors with the dog and you'll discover that the guard, Gwayne, is Bartram's accomplice. They were planning on deserting with Godric's dirty money. If you try to confront him you will be ending up fighting against him. You can now return to Bartram and confront him about his treachery. You can either decide to fight and kill him or let Mormont decides his fate.

It's best to let Flowers decide what to do with him or else you'll end up battling Bartram when you catch up with Jared in the Gift during the "Stray Dog" quest.

Objective Point D

Next, seek out Jonos on the ground floor. Since Bartram has already filled you in on some of Jonos's suspicious activities, you can immediately confront him on it. Jonos is a schemer, and he is mixed up in all sorts of gambling illegalities in and around Castle Black, but he's also not a traitor. If you let him go and don't report his infractions, Jonos gives you 25 silver stags.

Objective Point E

Finally, speak with Grance on the ground floor. If you intimidate him, he will report on Arthur and Trebor and Bartram. Return to Bartram and confront him on his lie about speaking with Ser Godric. If you return to Grance and rattle him some more, he eventually admits to talking about the Night's Watch in casual conversation with Godric. The old man gave away valuable information, but unintentionally so; you have another dilemma: look the other way or report on Grance.

After talking thoroughly with all the suspects, return to Addam Flowers. You can choose to incriminate any of the brothers, though Bartram is the only one guilty of treason.

Side Quest 6: New Blood

Side Quest 6

For: Mors

Location: Common Hall at Castle Black

Quest Giver: Lord Commander Mormont

Availability: Chapter 7 to Chapter 13

Experience Points: 600

Special Rewards: 62 silver stags, Recruiter's Cloak

Objectives:

1. You are now a recruiter for the Night's Watch. Your task while on your journey is to find as many men as possible who are prepared to take the black.
2. Search the underground tunnels of Mole's Town to find men who could swell the ranks of the Night's Watch.
3. Search the streets of Riverspring and find recruits. You could also see the contents of the stronghold's dungeons.
4. Search the town of King's Landing and for recruits to send back to the Night's Watch. Don't forget to look in the Red Keep.
5. Your recruitment is now over. Go back to Castle Black and give a report to the Lord Commander.

Common Hall Second Floor

A
Legend
Objective Point
Loot Spot
Codex Entry
Side Quest
NPC

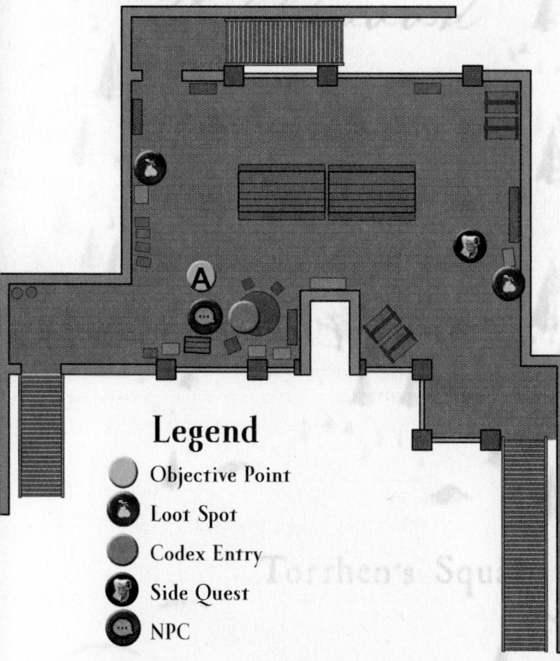

1. You are now a recruiter for the Night's Watch. Your task while on your journey is to find as many men as possible who are prepared to take the black.

Objective Point A

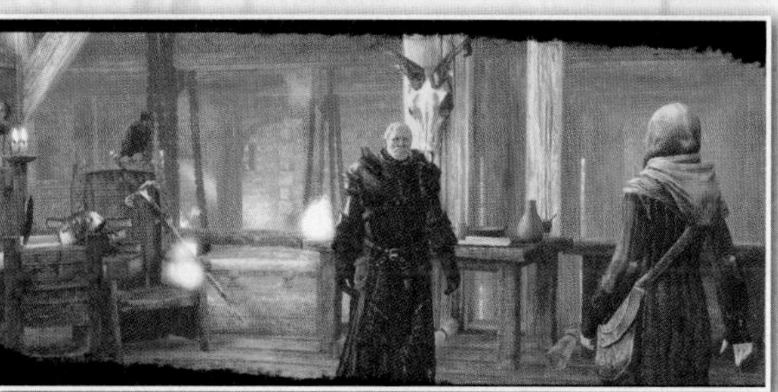

Lord Commander Mormont gives you this recruiting quest when you agree to take Jeyne south from the Wall. There are three primary areas from which to recruit brothers for the Night's Watch: Mole's Town, Riverspring, and King's Landing. You can recruit as Mors from now until the end of Chapter 13. To show that you're an official recruiter, the Lord Commander hands you a letter with his official seal and the Recruiter's Cloak.

Lower Level

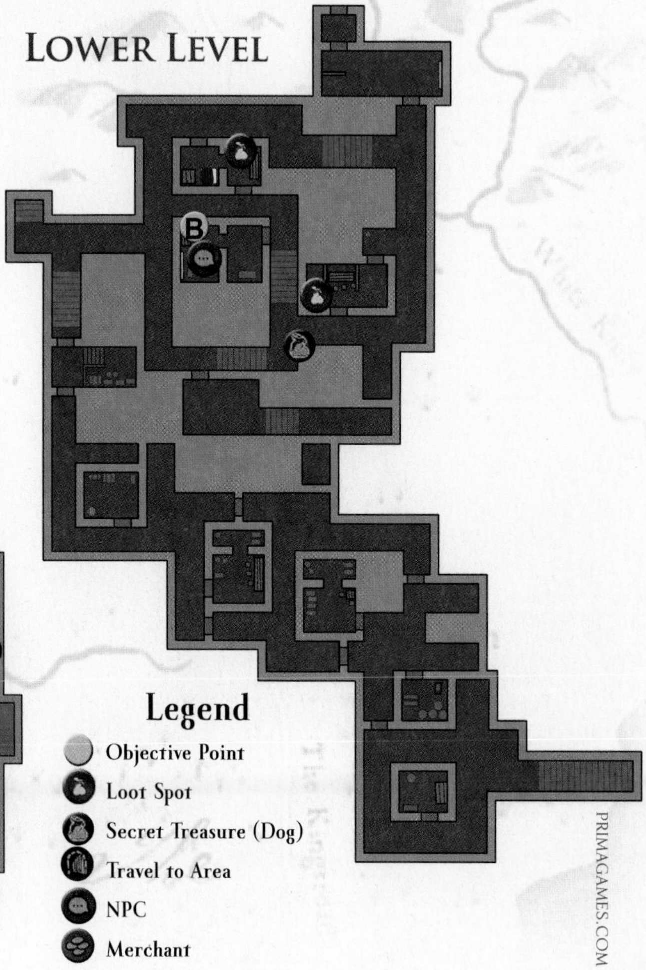
B
Legend
Objective Point
Loot Spot
Secret Treasure (Dog)
Travel to Area
NPC
Merchant

Tunnels of Mole's Town Upper Level

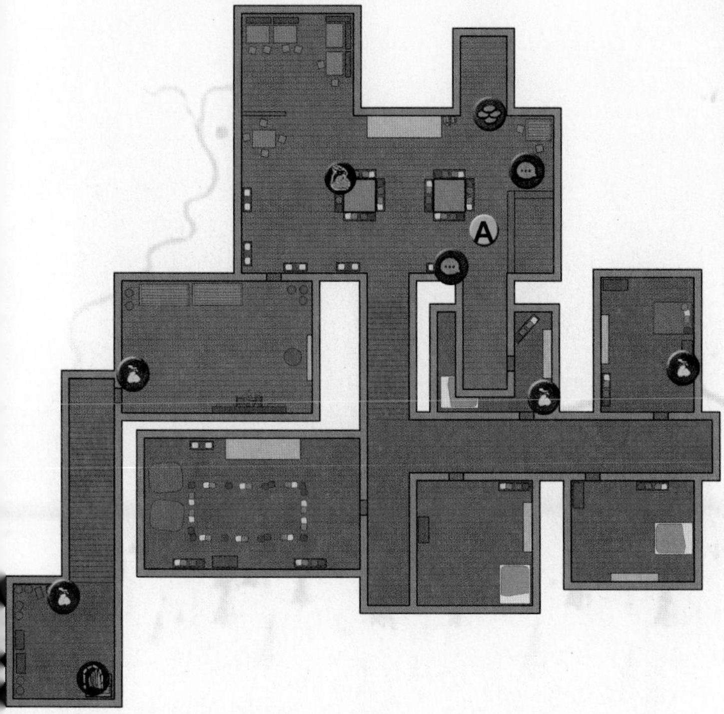
A

2. Search the underground tunnels of Mole's Town to find men who could swell the ranks of the Night's Watch.

Objective Point A

If you're looking for recruits in Mole's Town, begin by speaking with Willow near the entrance. She tells you that a freeloader won't leave her room, and you can agree to speak with this Gulian about relocating to Castle Black. Also, you can speak with Andar next to the bar and discover he's a deserter from the Night's Watch. You can either kill him or force him back to his post and collect another recruit.

Objective Point B

The man is a bard of some sort. You can convince Gulian to write songs that will inspire others if he signs up for the Night's Watch. Keep pushing him and he'll head north and you'll have your first recruit under your belt.

RIVERSPRING

Legend

3. Search the streets of Riverspring and find recruits. You could also see the contents of the stronghold's dungeons.

Objective Point A

When you're ready to search for recruits after Riverspring has been freed from Valarr's control, speak with Jon near the front gate. He informs you that many will join the Night's Watch because of the unfortunate circumstances that have recently befallen Riverspring. Once you speak with Jon, you'll see the NPCs you can recruit on the map.

Objective Point B

Speak with Donnor in the marketplace. He's a swordsman who wants a challenge; if you beat him in a duel, he'll respect your brotherhood and join the Night's Watch.

Objective Point C

Next, seek out the villager to the west. He's swamped in debt, and thugs are out for his pound of flesh if he can't pay. You can try to convince him to join the Night's Watch, but Alester will step in and insist that you deal with these thugs rather than cave in to their demands.

You'll find the thugs just around the corner intimidating another villager. Attack the thugs and beat them to the ground. When you do, you can choose to save the leader's life and send him to the Wall. Return to the villager. You can scare him into thinking that others will come after him soon and his best option is to the join the Night's Watch. You just got two recruits with one visit.

Objective Point D

In the city's southwest section, a female villager will beg you to join the Night's Watch for the sake of adventure. You can dismiss her or give in to her wishes and send her north. The Lord Commander, however, won't be happy with a woman recruit and denies her membership for her own protection.

Objective Point E

Waltyr, a man who has lost everything in the battle for Riverspring, stands forlornly out on the landing in front of the waterwheel. You can convince him that he can find a new family with the Night's Watch where his life will mean something again.

Objective Point F

Don't forget to check the Riverspring dungeon for more recruits. Those who are truly desperate may join the brotherhood rather than rot in their cells.

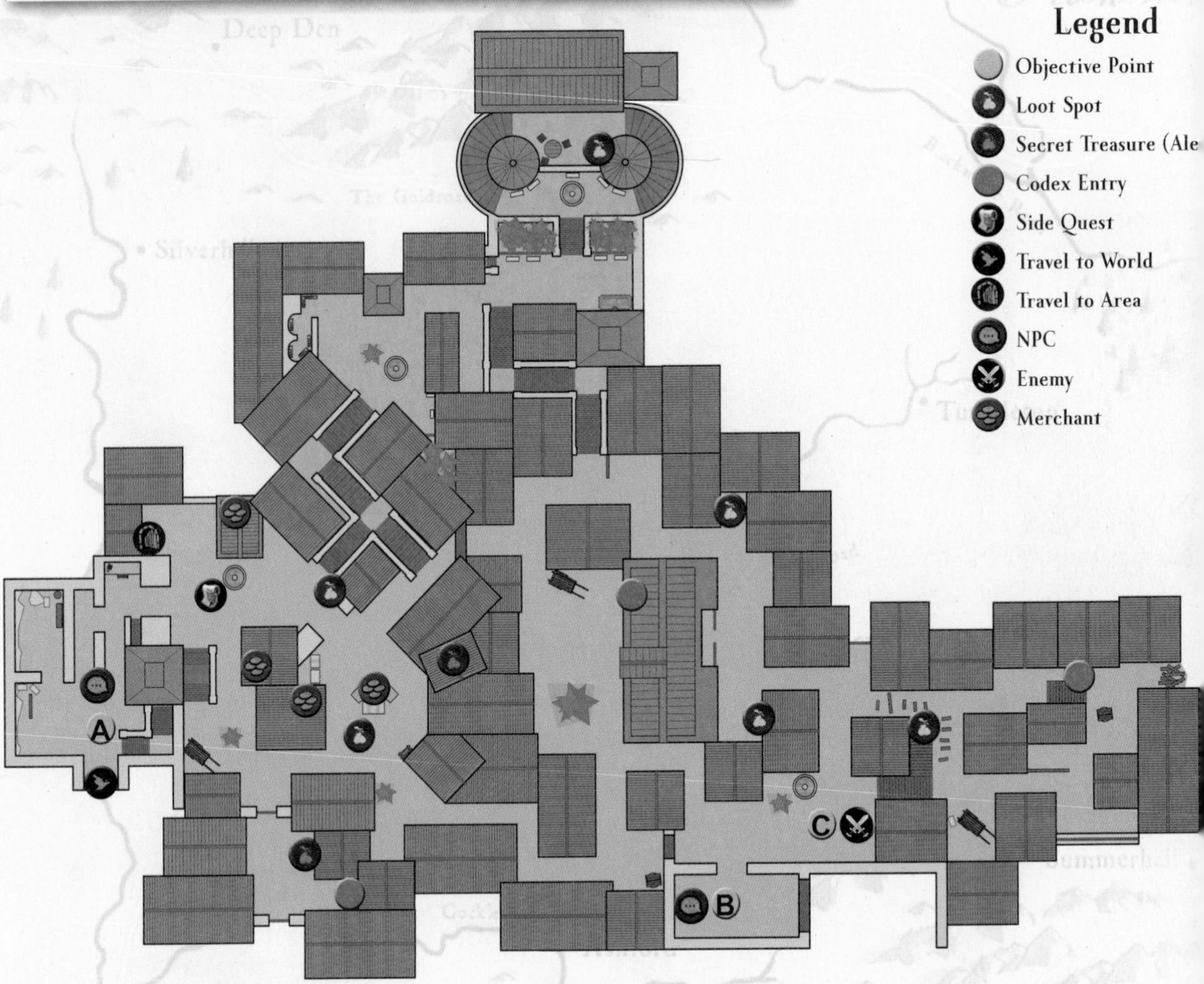

Legend

- Objective Point
- Loot Spot
- Secret Treasure (Ale
- Codex Entry
- Side Quest
- Travel to World
- Travel to Area
- NPC
- Enemy
- Merchant

A

B

C

King's Landing

4. Search the town of King's Landing and for recruits to send back to the Night's Watch. Don't forget to look in the Red Keep.

Objective Point A

When you're ready to search for recruits in King's Landing, speak with Morros near the front gate. He recommends searching the dungeons of the Red Keep and the area around Flea Bottom.

Objective Point B

Talk to the city guard near the Red Keep entrance if you want to enter the dungeons. He guides you inside where you can speak with the Gold Cloak jailkeeper.

The jailkeeper asks you for a bribe to hand over four prisoners for the Night's Watch. You can pay him and the recruits are yours, or you can threaten him to let them out. Threaten him once and he'll drop the price slightly; threaten him a second time and he opens the prison cells and makes you fight the prisoners.

Objective Point C

A mob has gathered around two psychopaths who are involved in some grisly murders. You can tell the angry mob that the Night's Watch is a dreadful place and they'll eventually let you take the two killers for the Wall. If you don't convince the mob that the Night's Watch is a fate worse than death, they will attack the two killers and you have a big battle on your hands. After the battle, you can take the killers (if they survived) as new recruits for the Night's Watch.

5. Your recruitment is now over. Go back to Castle Black and give a report to the Lord Commander.

Upon completion of your recruitment, return to the Lord Commander and give your final report. He will reward you for a job well done as the new recruits are hardened into your future Night's Watch brothers.

> **TIP**
>
> **If Mors sends 10 recruits back to the Wall, you earn the Endless Watch Achievement.**

SIDE QUEST 7: SELF-MADE GIRL

SIDE QUEST 7

For: Alester

Location: King's Landing

Quest Giver: Hubb

Availability: Chapter 8 to Chapter 13

Experience Points: 250

Special Rewards: 93 silver stags, The Maiden

Objectives:

1. Go and see Bethany to find out what her troubles are.
2. Go and find Ser Gyles Langward and explain to him Bethany's predicament.
3. Ask Chataya what she knows about Bethany.
4. Go to Bethany's bedchamber to look for clues.
5. Inform Ser Gyles of your conclusions.
6. Meet up with Ser Gyles on the way to Flea Bottom and talk to Bethany.
7. Go back to Chataya's to make sure that everything is in order OR inform Chataya of Bethany's refusal to return to the brothel.

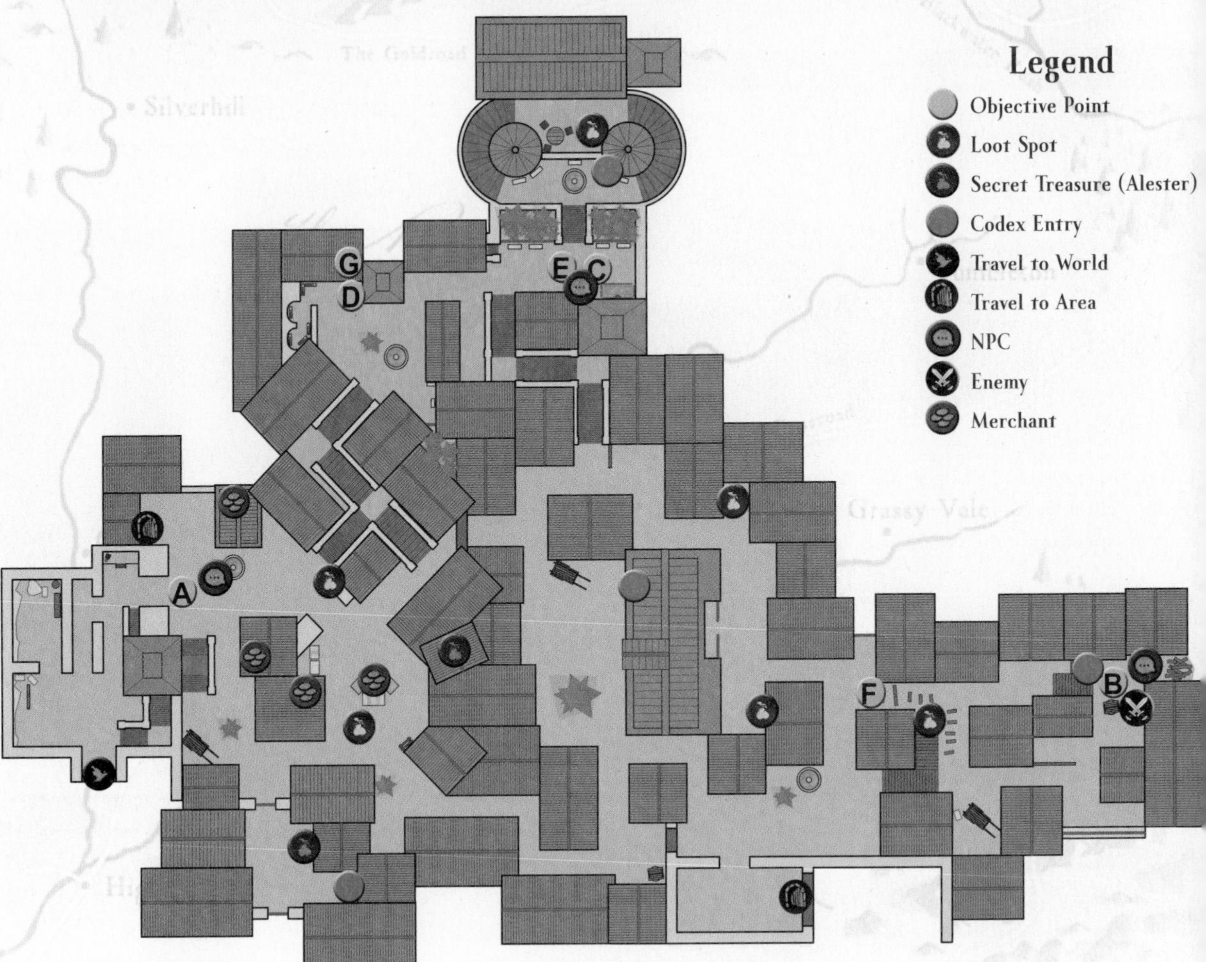

KING'S LANDING

. Go and see Bethany to find out what ıer troubles are

Objective Point A

o pick up this quest, see Hubb near the main entrance to ::ing's Landing. His friend Bethany is in trouble, and only lord can aid her because the trouble stems from the ill ntentions of another noble.

Objective Point B

3ethany lives in the western part of Flea Bottom. When 'ou find her, she is in the middle of a heated conversation vith her "cousin," a burly fellow with a foul tongue. She ells you that she's in love with a nobleman, Ser Gyles of Iouse Langward, but he hasn't called on her for some ime. She fears that Ser Gyles's family has kept him from ıer because of her common lineage. You agree to speak vith Ser Gyles on her behalf.

:. Go and find Ser Gyles Langward and :xplain to him Bethany's predicament.

Objective Point C

When you speak with Ser Gyles in the noble section of King's Landing, you discover that all is not as it seems: Ser Gyles is getting married and Bethany is one of the girls from Chataya's; he had a good time with her, but now that he's betrothed, Gyles can't be seen with Bethany no matter how much he cares about her. If you want to know more about the story, tell Gyles you'll look into the matter further.

3. Ask Chataya what she knows about Bethany.

Objective Point D

Speak with Chataya in the brothel. She fills in more of the story: Bethany was indeed one of her girls, but she left and owed Chataya a lot of money. She would like either the money or the girl back.

4. Go to Bethany's bedchamber to look for clues.

Chataya lets you search Bethany's old room upstairs in the brothel. Check the side table for a Crumpled Letter in Ser Gyles's hand that explains he is not coming back. It seems Bethany has lied about events and that Ser Gyles's tellings are more in line with the truth. Speak with Chataya on your way back out and she'll give you a little more of the sordid tale.

5. Inform Ser Gyles of your conclusions.

Objective Point E

Now head back to Ser Gyles's house and speak with him. It turns out that he, too, owes Chataya money; this might be one of the reasons why he didn't return to visit Bethany. Regardless of whether you get him to take responsibility for his actions, the two of you will set off for Bethany's.

6. Meet up with Ser Gyles on the way to Flea Bottom and talk to Bethany.

Objective Point F

Meet Ser Gyles at the top of the alleyways that lead down into Flea Bottom. It's time to confront Bethany once and for all. It's obvious from the start of the conversation that Bethany doesn't have any love for Gyles and that's she's using the child as an excuse for money. Even so, she is pregnant and is asking for child support. You can choose to side with Bethany or against her. If you side with her, Gyles pays up. If you side with Gyles, Bethany shouts for her cousin and you get ambushed by several men.

7. Go back to Chataya's to make sure that everything is in order OR inform Chataya of Bethany's refusal to return to the brothel.

Objective Point G

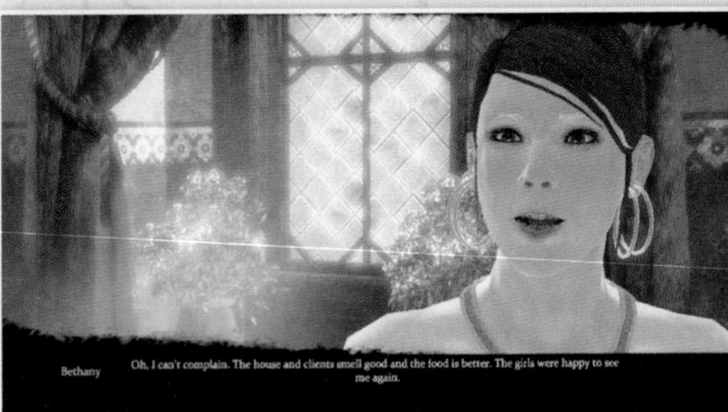

Depending on who you sided with, Bethany may or may not get her money and she may or may not return to Chataya's. If you side with Bethany, she gives you the Maiden statuette as a reward for helping her out. If you sided with Gyles, you can visit Bethany back at the brothe she has reformed a bit and gives you the Maiden statuette to thank you for trying to help her.

Side Quest 8: Blood on the Sand

Side Quest 8

For: Alester

Location: Sewers of King's Landing

Quest Giver: Ossifer

Availability: Chapter 8

Experience Points: 0

Special Rewards: 8 golden dragons

Objectives:

1. If you're interested in the gladiator fights, return to Ossifer in the sewers of King's Landing.
2. Go and speak with the guard down below when you're ready.
3. If you wish to continue fighting, return to Ossifer and speak with him.
4. You have bested Lucifer, the pit's most celebrated warrior! Return to Ossifer to claim your reward. If you have asked Rupert to place a bet for you, don't forget to speak with him as well.

Sewers of King's Landing

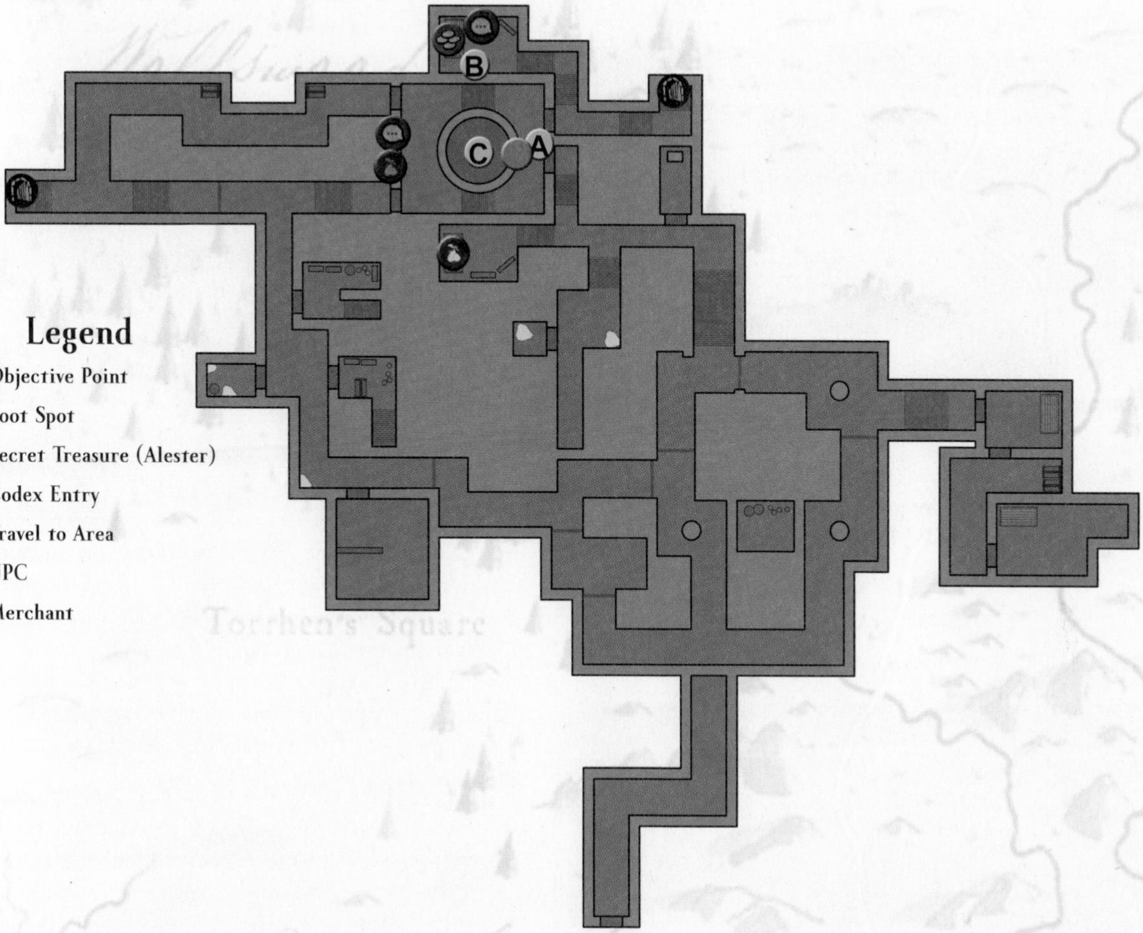

Legend
- Objective Point
- Loot Spot
- Secret Treasure (Alester)
- Codex Entry
- Travel to Area
- NPC
- Merchant

1. If you're interested in the gladiator fights, return to Ossifer in the sewers of King's Landing.

Objective Point A

The best way to earn quick money in the game is through the arena battles offered by Ossifer. If you want to earn a pocketful of gold, return to the sewers before you leave King's Landing in Chapter 8. Before each contest, Ossifer will present you with the name you choose during your earlier battle in the arena (see "Chapter 8, Part 1" in the walkthrough). After the first match, you can bet on yourself or your opponent to win by seeing Rupert.

Each time you win a contest, your odds increase and you earn less money if you bet on yourself. If the odds are better on your opponent, you can bet on him to win and earn more money; however, make sure you can survive a loss (see the "Crowd Favor" sidebar). To learn more about your opponents, chat up the barkeep or speak with your opponents directly if they happen to be standing around the arena.

Crowd Favor

You can earn the crowd's favor by buying them drinks at the bar or by listening to what they want after each contest (spare or kill your opponent). You lose crowd favor by ignoring what they want at the end of a contest. When the crowd loves you, they will ask your opponent to spare your life if you lose a match. When the crowd hates you, they will ask your opponent to kill you if you lose a match, and the game is over.

2. Go and speak with the guard down below when you're ready.

Objective Point B

Go downstairs and speak with the guard next to the arena gate when you're ready to fight. You can also see the Arena Merchant if you need to stock up on some last-minute items before a match.

3. If you wish to continue fighting, return to Ossifer and speak with him.

Objective Point C

You can fight up to six times in the arena. Remember to bet with Rupert after the first match, and always maintain the crowd's favor, even if it means shelling out the money for a round of drinks so that if you do lose, your opponent won't kill you.

Your first contest is very difficult. You fight three brothers at once, and one of them has a poisoned weapon. Look for the Rubec brother with the sword; he's the one with the poison, and he should be your primary target when you direct your early damage. Use your stuns and immobilization abilities as often as possible, at least until you can get the odds down to two-on-one or one-on-one. If you can avoid the poison and keep all three from attacking you at once, you should have enough firepower to beat all three brothers.

After each match, speak with Ossifer for your reward and return to the arena when you want to begin the next battle. Your second contest is against Ser Symon. He's a tough combatant who can heal throughout the fight. Save your interrupt abilities for his heals. If you can prevent him from healing, you should deal enough damage to bring him down. Listen to what the crowd says at the end of the battle to bolster your standing.

> **TIP**
>
> Each arena opponent who you spare is a potential partner in the fourth-round team battle.

You battle Bayard next. His brother is the guard who lets you into the arena, and he offers you 20 silver stags if you spare his brother should you win. Bayard is a competent fighter but can't really hold up to your special abilities and superior damage. Saving Bayard might be at odds with what the crowd wants, so you'll have to weigh the 20 silver stags versus the crowd's favor.

The fourth battle is against Alequo. He will attempt to stun you early and often. Stun him first or keep him out of melee range so that you can chip away at his health total. So long as he doesn't prevent you from using your abilities, you should be able to overcome his quickness.

Now it's time for the team battle. You get to choose from any of the men you bested in the arena and whose life you spared. The two of you will take on a deadly duo from the Iron Islands. Work with your teammate to keep your opponents off balance with stuns or knockdowns and concentrate your damage on one enemy until he's dead. After that, it should be relatively easy to defeat the second enemy with two-on-one teamwork.

4. You have bested Lucifer, the pit's most celebrated warrior! Return to Ossifer to claim your reward. If you have asked Rupert to place a bet for you, don't forget to speak with him as well.

You have achieved as much glory as you can in the arena, and the news has reached the previous champion. Lucifer returns and challenges you to a duel to the death, with the stakes as high as ever. You stand to win the most money off this fight: bets are increased and Ossifer's payout is great.

Lucifer is the fiercest combatant in the arena. He is relentless with his damage attacks, and it will take a long battle to drop his health total. If you have access to flammable oil or Wildfire, now is the time to use it. Wildfire in particular can erode Lucifer's health down to a manageable number. It's also crucial to stun him as much as possible to prevent counterattacks. If you can conserve enough energy to stun often and hit him with a potent attack in between stuns, you'll eventually come out on top.

Collect your considerable fortune from Ossifer. With your victory over Lucifer, the arena is closed. There's no more business here; the fans have gotten the most thrills possible out of the local talent, and Ossifer and Rupert are taking their show on the road. Be happy that you pocketed enough coin for several major upgrades and live to continue with your main quests.

SIDE QUEST 9: RINGS AND CHAINS

SIDE QUEST 9

For: Alester

Location: Courtyard of Riverspring Castle

Quest Giver: Elyana

Availability: Chapter 8

Experience Points: 240

Special Rewards: 93 silver stags

Objectives:

1. Elyana seems to be in trouble. You can find out what the problem is by meeting her in the Courtyard of Riverspring Castle.
2. Inquire about the business that has set the Roxton family against Elyana.
3. Question Elyana.
4. Question the younger Roxtons.
5. Go into town to find Criston.
6. Escort Criston to the castle safely.
7. Go and find Elyana.

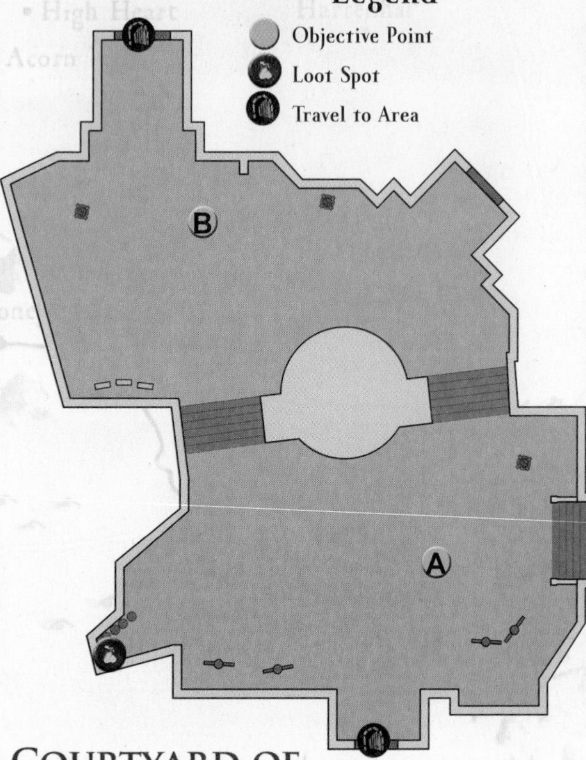

COURTYARD OF RIVERSPRING CASTLE

1. Elyana seems to be in trouble. You can find out what the problem is by meeting her in the Courtyard of Riverspring Castle.

Objective Point A

After your conversation with Elyana in the throne room during the "Legacy" main quest, seek out your sister in the courtyard when you're ready to embark on this side quest.

2. Inquire about the business that has set the Roxton family against Elyana.

You learn that two years ago, Riverspring had borrowed money from an allied kingdom led by the Roxtons when times were tougher, and when Riverspring couldn't immediately repay the debt, Lord Roxton demanded Elyana's hand in marriage.

3. Question Elyana.

You also discover that Elyana was courting another local, Criston, and even though nothing happened, Lord Roxton found out about it. In a jealous rage, he called off the wedding. He then returned to Riverspring with some men and began seizing property that was "owed" him as part of the debt. Elyana dispatched the city guard and had Lord Roxton locked up in the dungeons.

4. Question the younger Roxtons.

Objective Point B

You can also speak with Edwyn and Meredyth Roxton in the courtyard. They are here looking for their missing father, and Meredyth is particularly concerned with the gold the Sarwycks "owe" the family.

RIVERSPRING

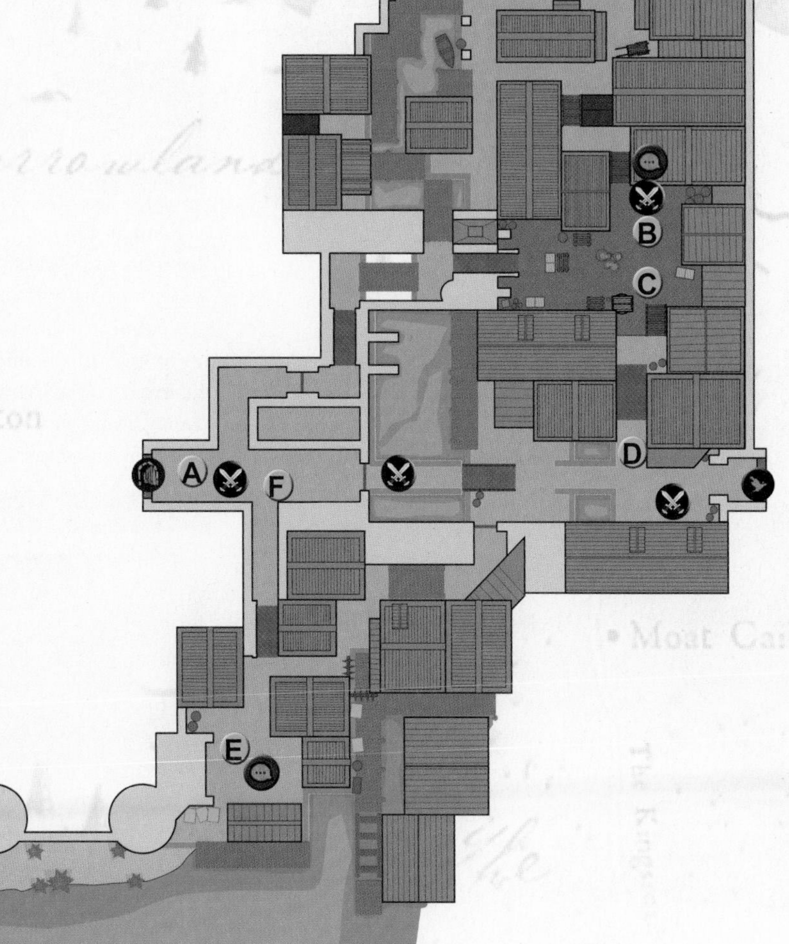

Legend

- Objective Point
- Travel to World
- Travel to Area
- NPC
- Enemy

5. Go into town to find Criston.

Objective Point A

To figure out what's going on, you decide to speak with Criston in town. He can either corroborate Elyana's story or the Roxton's; both parties see things in a slightly different way. Talk to the guard to your left as you enter Riverspring and ask for an escort; it's better to have a few extra guards at your side with the troubles ahead.

Objective Point B

You'll find two Roxton guards pounding on Criston's door in the marketplace. Order them to stand aside so that you can resolve the matter with Criston.

As soon as Criston comes out of his house, the Roxton guards attack and try to kill the man. You and your Riverspring guards are forced to kill the Roxton guards before they can murder Criston.

6. Escort Criston to the castle safely.

Objective Point C

Criston seems to confirm Elyana's story: Nothing too forward happened between them, so Lord Roxton acted rashly and the debt has been repaid honorably in Alester's eyes. You need to escort Criston back to the courtyard and confront the Roxtons. Criston suggests taking the route to the main gate, rather than the route through the docks (which could hide an ambush). You set off toward the main gate as his protectors.

Objective Point D

As soon as you top the steps from the marketplace, Roxton's next set of guards attacks. If Criston dies, Elyana will not be happy, so to avoid the wrath of your sister, protect him at all costs. Stun any foe attacking Criston and try to lure the enemies toward you and the Riverspring guards. If you match your weapon type to the appropriate enemy armor, you should easily deliver enough damage to kill them quickly.

Objective Point E

Your next battle occurs on the bridge. Stand in front of Criston at the top of the stairs, and when the enemies charge, hit them with ranged attacks or stuns as they near. They will try to slip past you to get at Criston, which presents great opportunities to strike from behind or deal major damage without retaliation. Cut them down efficiently so they don't gang up on Criston.

Objective Point F

More enemies guard the main entrance. Deal with the groups as they close on you. Keep your tactics similar to the earlier battle. Your main concern should be Criston: Prioritize any enemy that attacks him and spend your better abilities to get him out of trouble. Enter the castle grounds once all enemies are dead.

7. Go and find Elyana.

Speak with Elyana in the courtyard again. She confesses that she used poor Criston as a pawn to make Lord Roxton jealous and call off the wedding. You decide to release Lord Roxton from his cell and then have several choices regarding the debt and Criston's fate. You can choose to pay the debt, and Lord Roxton drops his claims against Riverspring. If you choose to sacrifice Criston for the Roxtons' honor, Lord Roxton drops his claims against Riverspring.

You can duel Edwyn Roxton, and if you win, the claims are dropped. You can also let Criston duel Edwyn Roxton, in which case Criston dies but the Roxtons are satisfied and don't pursue the matter.

If you accept the quest but don't complete it before leaving Riverspring, the Roxtons will thank you for not interfering and the quest fails. The quest will also fail if you let Criston die while escorting him to the courtyard.

Side Quest 10: Avenge Riverspring

Side Quest 10

For: Alester

Location: Tunnels of Riverspring

Quest Giver: Documents in Secret Brotherhood Chamber

Availability: Chapter 8 to Chapter 13

Experience Points: 320

Special Rewards: 187 silver stags, The Stranger

Objectives:

1. The Collector is draining resources from Riverspring. Pay him a visit in his manse in King's Landing to put things right.
2. Your enemy is hiding around here somewhere. Find him and avenge your people.

King's Landing

Legend
- Objective Point
- Loot Spot
- Secret Treasure (Alester)
- Codex Entry
- Travel to World
- Travel to Area
- NPC
- Merchant

A

B

1. The Collector is draining resources from Riverspring. Pay him a visit in his manse in King's Landing to put things right.

Objective Point A

After you receive this side quest from collecting the secret documents from the tunnels under Riverspring (see "Chapter 8, Part 2" in the walkthrough), head off to King's Landing. You can do this quest anytime you're roaming King's Landing from Chapter 8 through Chapter 13.

Objective Point B

Look for the door to the Collector's manse in the noble section of King's Landing. It's at the end of the long balcony near the central staircase.

The Collector's Manse

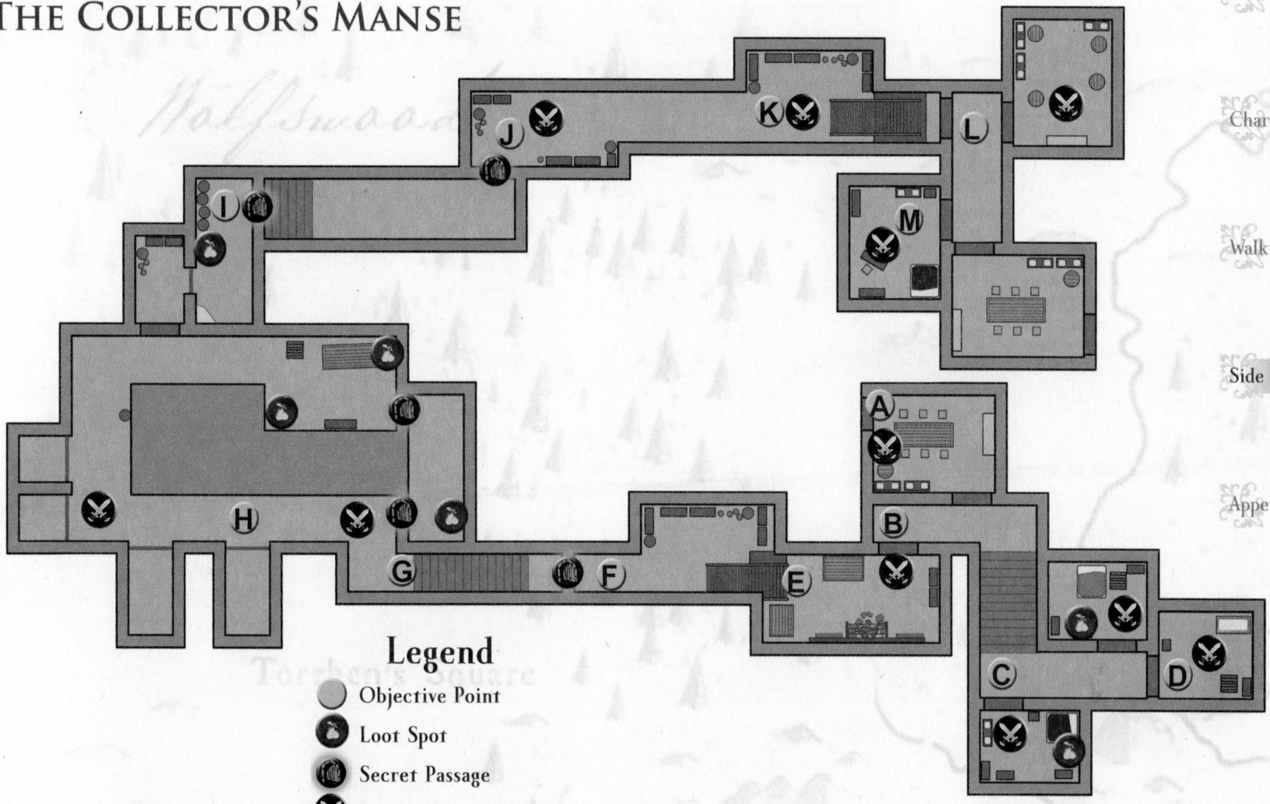

Legend
- Objective Point
- Loot Spot
- Secret Passage
- Enemy

2. Your enemy is hiding around here somewhere. Find him and avenge your people.

Objective Point A

A greeter welcomes you inside the manse. He refuses to admit that Mallador Brax is the Collector, and when you force the issue, he calls the guards on you.

You have to fight a handful of guards in the small room. You can use the central table to your advantage by keeping melee enemies at bay, and if you have a ranged weapon, you can attack them without them reaching you. However, one of the enemies wields a crossbow, so you'll have to deal with him with projectiles of your own or cut him down when you reach that side of the table.

Objective Point B

If you open the door next to the first room, a burly cook with a meat cleaver will charge at you. He has a lot of health but no armor. Stun him a couple of times and slay him with a steady supply of damage. You'll return to the kitchen later, after you've recovered the Key to the Collector's Cellars.

Objective Point C

Take the stairs to the top floor and battle a series of guards in the various rooms. Open each door and fight that group one at a time; you don't want to run around and alert any other guards to your position. Use the doorways as choke points to keep the enemies from charging out and surrounding you. Attacks that damage multiple foes or that spread, such as fire and poison, are very effective in the small rooms.

Objective Point D

When you finally track down the greeter who first met you at the manse, kill him and his buddies and then loot the Key to the Collector's Cellars from the man's corpse. Return back downstairs.

Objective Point E

Use your new key on the grate locking the basement area. Enter the cellar and prepare for lots of resistance.

Tip

There are many secret passages in the cellar. Move along slowly and watch for the familiar heat distortions in the air that mark secret mechanisms.

Objective Point F

It appears to be a normal, relatively empty cellar. However, if you use the Vision of R'hllor on the western wall, it reveals a secret mechanism. Pull the candle holder and the wall slides up to expose a new corridor.

Objective Point G

In the secret corridor area, you'll run into more of the Collector's guards. Dispatch them in similar style to how you handled the earlier enemies. Take each group slowly, one at a time, and don't move forward until you know you've cleared all the enemies in the immediate area.

Objective Point H

You discover that the Collector is a slave trader and a thief. He has close to a dozen prisoners awaiting export to the slave trades. To free them, you must find the Key to the Collector's Slave Cells from the guard up ahead.

Objective Point I

Search for another secret passage at the wall marked with a black skull plate. Use the Vision of R'hllor to reveal the door and continue on.

Objective Point J

Sneak up on the next set of guards. Try to kill one of them before they can counterattack, and stun the second one quickly thereafter. As long as you don't let all of them attack you at once, you should be fine.

Objective Point K

Hunt down the guards to the east. You can retreat back down the corridor toward the slave cells if you have a ranged weapon and want to keep space between you and your targets. Slay the guards as they converge, and remove the Key to the Collector's Slave Cells from the purple-robed enemy. Return and free all the prisoners from the slave cells.

Objective Point L

More guards fill the rooms to the east of the slave cell area. If you confront them, hit them with a damaging attack inside the room. Next, use the doorway as a choke point to hold them back as you continue wounding them until they fall one by one.

Objective Point M

You've finally caught up with the infamous Collector. He taunts you as you enter his office, and then the three enemies converge on you.

Make sure you've switched to a blunt weapon: two of the enemies, including the Collector, wear heavy armor and the third wears light. Stun immediately and take down the enemy in light armor as quickly as you can. Drink a healing potion if your health drops below half; the Collector can deal a huge amount of damage in one shot with his two-handed mace, so you don't want to drop too low on health and put yourself at risk of dying with a single enemy blow. Stack damage on the other guard until he's out of the fight, then throw everything else you have at the Collector until he's down. After a hard-fought struggle through the manse, you have your vengeance and some nice rewards to line your backpack, including the Stranger statuette from the Collector's loot stash.

SIDE QUEST 11: THE MAGGOT IN THE APPLE

SIDE QUEST 11

For: Alester

Location: Castlewood

Quest Giver: Gawen (after healing him)

Availability: Chapter 10

Experience Points: 100

Special Rewards: Fewer enemies during the "Crossroads" quest

Objectives:

1. Men are training with arms in the courtyard. No one would be surprised if they were wounded during their exercise.

1. Men are training with arms in the courtyard. No one would be surprised if they were wounded during their exercise.

Objective Point A

You receive this quest after you heal Gawen in the Castlewood Castle. Walk outside to the courtyard and speak with Domeric. He explains that Ser Ethan is training his men at the opposite end of the courtyard. If you want to spar, head over there.

CASTLEWOOD EXTERIOR

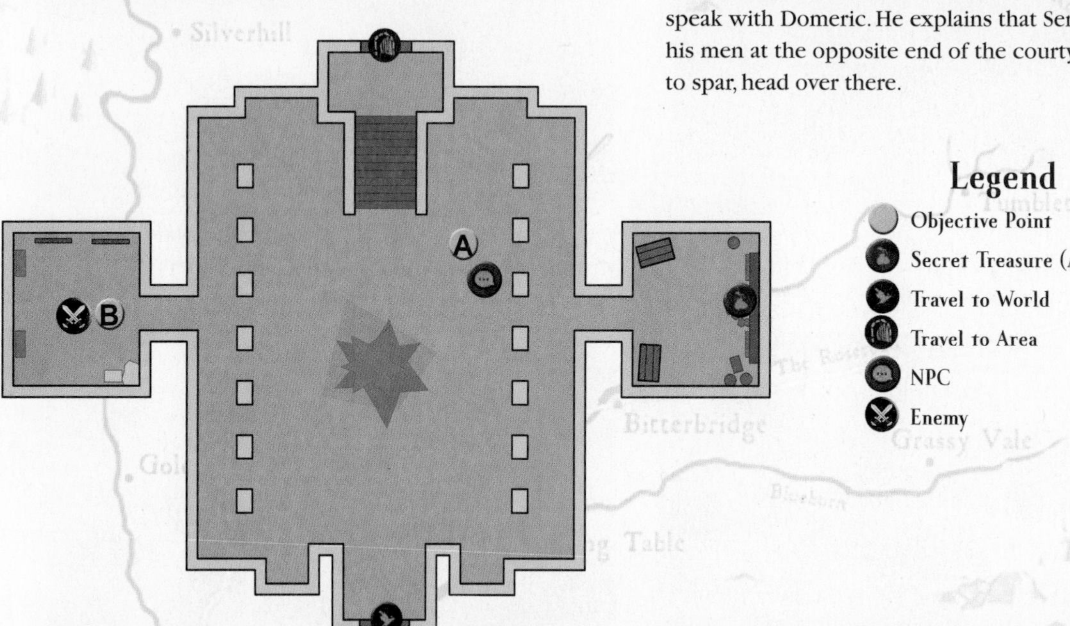

Objective Point B

Ser Ethan taunts you a bit when you arrive in the training area. When you get to the choice about who to spar, choose to take on his men first.

You have three enemies to manage simultaneously. Stun immediately and unload on one of them as quickly as possible to reduce the odds against you. If you need more defense, back up into the archway and create a choke point so it's more difficult for the enemies to flank you. If you can distribute damage quickly and efficiently, you can defeat all three enemies and live to taunt Ser Ethan some more.

Despite Ser Ethan being a tougher foe, the battle against him will probably go smoother than the fight with his men. You have to worry about only one foe, and if you have stuns and knockdowns at your disposal, you can keep his big attacks from landing and chip away with damage. Eventually, the Castlewood knight will bow down to your superiority and you'll have wounded all the guards in the courtyard. This makes life a lot easier for you later when you team up with Gawen inside the castle.

Side Quest 12: Safer Streets

Side Quest 12

For: **Alester**

Location: **Riverspring**

Quest Giver: **Harwyn**

Availability: Chapter 11

Experience Points: 100

Special Rewards: **None**

Objectives:

1. Clean the Riverspring streets of the Bloodseekers.

Riverspring

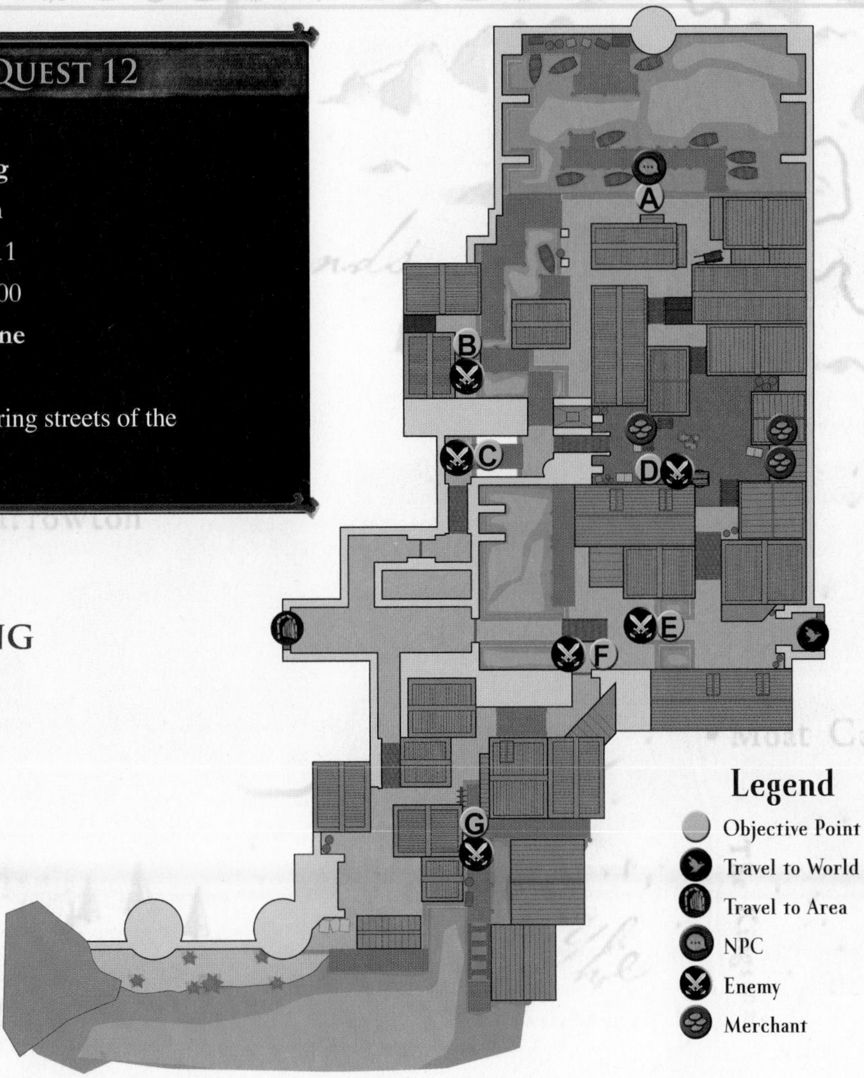

A
B
C
D
E
F
G

Legend

- Objective Point
- Travel to World
- Travel to Area
- NPC
- Enemy
- Merchant

1. Clean the Riverspring streets of the Bloodseekers.

Objective Point A

Harwyn gives you this quest before you embark on your quest to take back Riverspring. He asks you to end all the Bloodseeker activity in the streets. You must shut down the Bloodseekers in all of the areas across the city to complete the quest.

Objective Point B

Begin with the activity in the northwest section nearest the docks. Bloodseekers ravage a girl and you're just in time to stop it before it gets worse. The two of you should decimate the Bloodseekers if you go all out.

Objective Point C

Just south of the girl, more Bloodseekers pound away at a gate and threaten you immediately when you approach. This is a larger battle, so conserve energy and alternate stuns and knockdowns between Alester and Mors. If you want the enemies to go down quicker, team up on single foes one by one.

Objective Point D

Bloodseekers try to intimidate a merchant in the marketplace when you arrive here. You can initiate the battle with a strong ranged attack if you have a suitable weapon; if not, charge in and overwhelm them mercilessly with your powerful abilities.

Be on alert for roving Bloodseeker patrols. You don't want them to run into you while you're battling another enemy group or it could prove very costly. Better to take the patrols out when you see them first.

Objective Point E

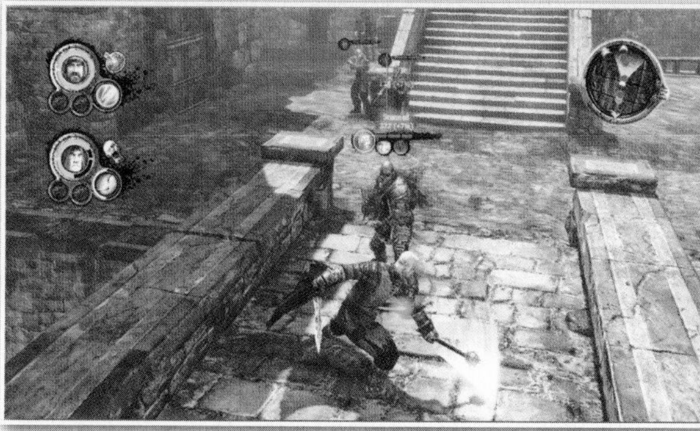

Engage the next set of Bloodseekers on the main bridge. If you stand on the bridge, you can prevent flanking and can control the large enemy group better. Combine your damage on each foe that attacks and continue forward until they all lie dead at your feet.

Objective Point F

Creep up on the two Bloodseekers talking on the side of the main stairwell. If you've dealt with all other Bloodseekers in the immediate area, these two won't prove much of a challenge.

Objective Point G

The last Bloodseeker group terrorizes townsfolk on the southern docks. Stun the foe in heavy armor and eliminate the others first. Combine your attacks on the final enemy and you complete the "Safer Streets" side quest.

Side Quest 13: Not So Wild

Side Quest 13

For: Mors

Location: Riverspring

Quest Giver: Harwyn

Availability: Chapter 13

Experience Points: 985

Special Rewards: Wildling Bracelet

Objectives:

1. Go to Castle Black and help out Qhorin Halfhand.
2. Go to Mole's Town to find the wildlings' tracks.
3. Follow the schemers' tracks to discover what they're up to.
4. The wildlings are waiting for Byam in the woods near Mole's Town. Go and find them there.
5. Pursue the fleeing wildling to follow her to her clan.
6. Crush Magnar Sabraque and destroy his clan OR go up and speak with Magnar Sabraque.
7. Return to Castle Black and report back to Qhorin Halfhand.

Legend

- Objective Point
- Loot Spot
- Codex Entry
- Side Quest
- NPC

1. Go to Castle Black and help out Qhorin Halfhand.

Objective Point A

Meet up with Qhorin Halfhand back at the Common Hall in Castle Black if you want to embark on another quest against the wildlings. Stock up on supplies in the hall, and you can also pick up the "Rituals and Litanies" side quest just outside the main door to the hall.

2. Go to Mole's Town to find the wildlings' tracks.

When you arrive at the outskirts of Mole's Town, you see some wildlings speaking with a suspicious trader. They immediately split up and run for it when they spot you. Dog can follow either trail, but eventually the scents lead to the same path.

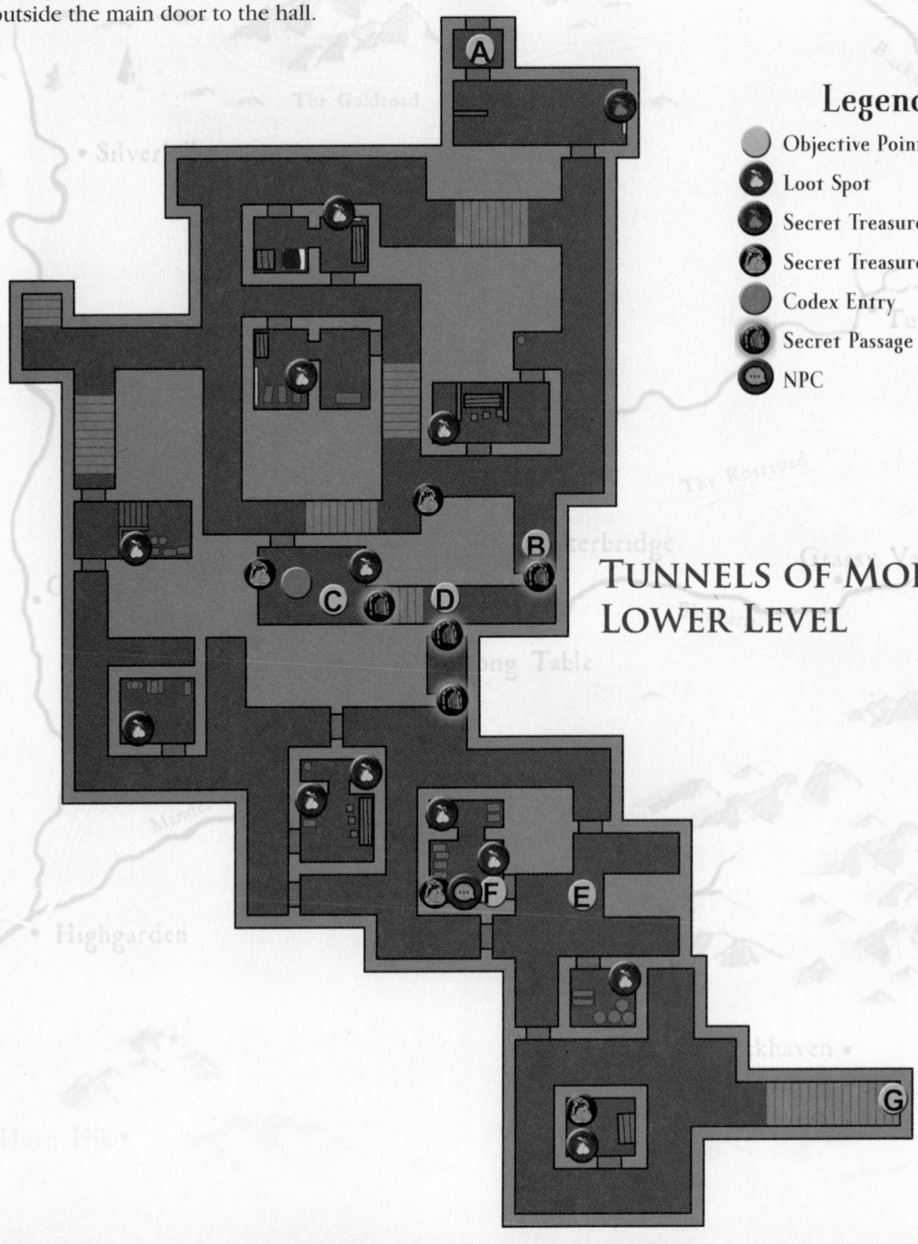

Legend

- Objective Point
- Loot Spot
- Secret Treasure (Alester)
- Secret Treasure (Dog)
- Codex Entry
- Secret Passage
- NPC

A B C D E F G

TUNNELS OF MOLE'S TOWN LOWER LEVEL

3. Follow the schemers' tracks to discover what they're up to.

Objective Point A

Enter the door that the trader took and switch to Dog to follow his scent. You can track him throughout the tunnels under Mole's Town; however, he uses some secret passages that may confuse you if you don't know where to look.

Objective Point B

When the scent trail seemingly dead-ends at the first wall, use the Vision of R'hllor to reveal a secret mechanism in the skull plaque on the wall. Open the door and continue following the trader's scent into the new area.

Objective Point C

The scent trail leads to another hidden room. Pull the lever and open the sliding door to enter the room. Search the side table for the Key to Mole's Town Crime Scene. You can now open any of the locked doors in the tunnels.

Objective Point D

Continue east and look for another secret passage out in the next corridor. This opens up the southeast area of the tunnels, where both the trader and the wildlings fled to when they spotted you.

Objective Point E

Both scent trails intersect in the chamber with the hanging red lights. Follow the yellow scent directly to the trader's room a few feet away.

Objective Point F

Confront the trader inside his room. His name is Byam, and he claims to be helping out foreigners new to the Gift. With enough pressing, however, he admits to aiding wildlings with supplies and you fear that they may be making a new attempt at scaling the Wall. Byam also tells you that the wildlings are waiting at a campfire in the Gift for a delivery from him. Once you have all the information, you can choose to let him go or kill him for being a traitorous trader.

Objective Point G

Switch back to Dog outside Byam's room and follow the other scent that leads to the wildlings. A short way down the tunnel, you reach the trapdoor back up to the Gift.

THE GIFT

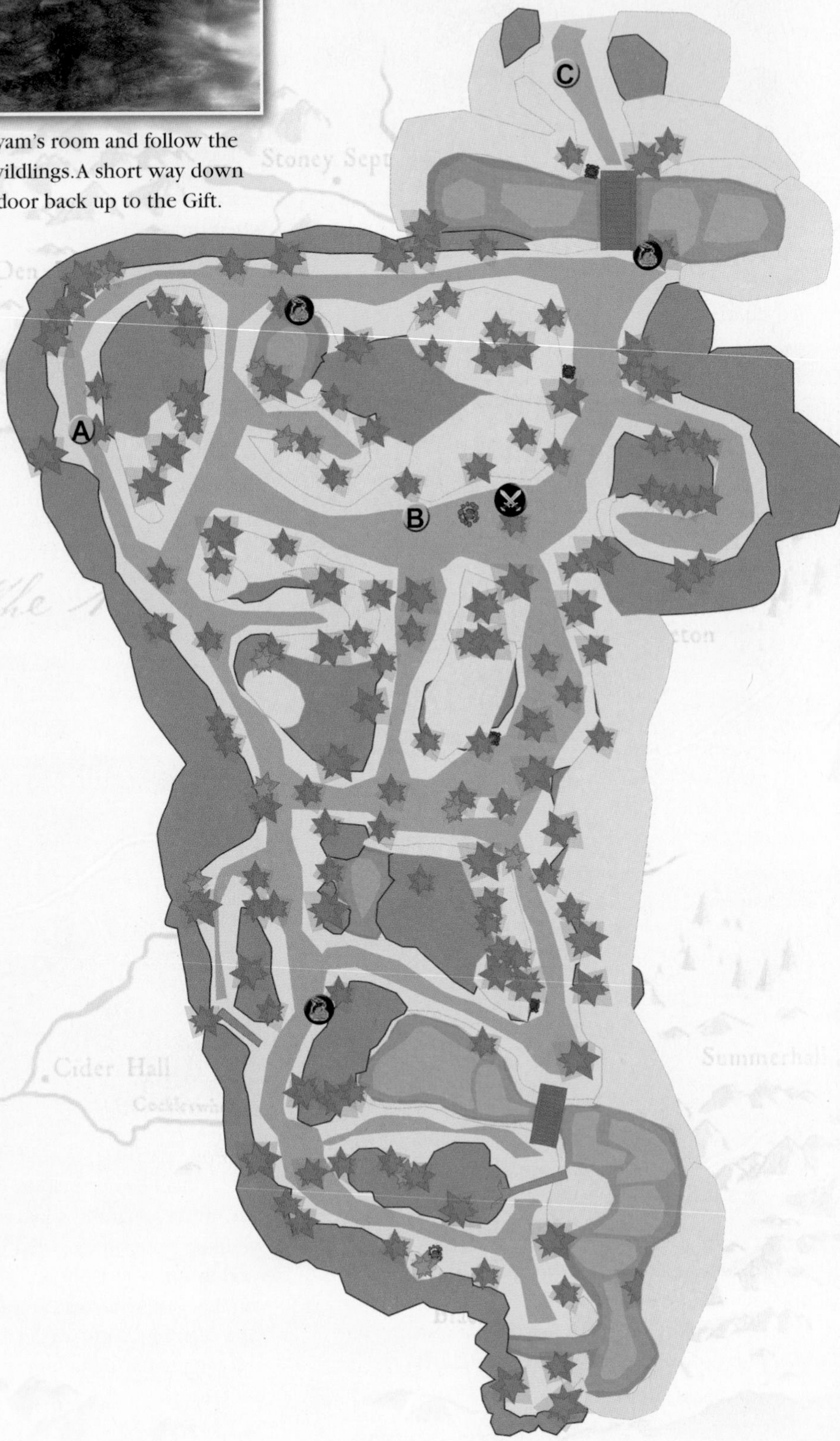

Legend

- Objective Point
- Secret Treasure (Dog)
- Enemy

4. The wildlings are waiting for Byam in the woods near Mole's Town. Go and find them there.

Objective Point A

As soon as you enter the Gift, switch to Dog so you can track the wildlings again. Weave through the forest until you spot the campfire in the distance.

Objective Point B

Confront the wildlings at the campfire. Three stay behind so that one, Thistle, can escape and warn their leader that the Night's Watch is after them.

A small battle erupts at the campfire and you have to put down the three wildlings. Between Alester and Mors tag-teaming foes and Dog immobilizing and pestering stragglers, the wildlings have no chance against you.

5. Pursue the fleeing wildling to follow her to her clan.

Objective Point C

Once Dog has Thistle's scent, it's easy to track her through the rest of the Gift. The path eventually leads to the edge of the forest, and Mors can tell by the direction that she's headed to Icemark.

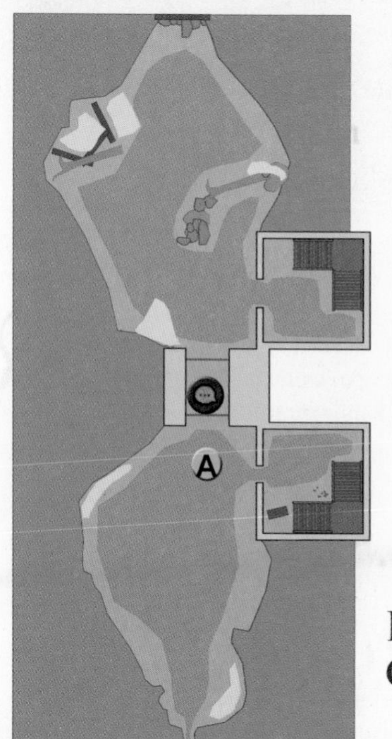

Legend
- Objective Point
- NPC
- Enemy

ICEMARK GROUND FLOOR

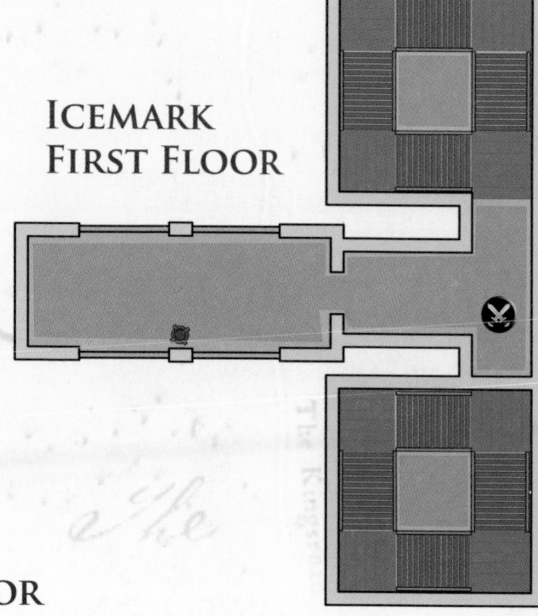

ICEMARK FIRST FLOOR

ICEMARK SECOND FLOOR

B

Legend

- Objective Point
- Secret Treasure (Alester)
- NPC
- Enemy

6. Crush Magnar Sabraque and destroy his clan OR go up and speak with Magnar Sabraque.

Objective Point A

The wildling leader, Sabraque, meets you at the entrance to Icemark. He claims that the wildlings are not in the Gift for plunder but that they are fleeing from the horrors to the north and merely want to keep their families safe. You can either make peace with the wildlings or destroy them.

Objective Point B

If you choose to destroy them, you must battle your way up through Icemark again. Cut a path through the wildling defenders to reach Sabraque's group at the bonfire in the main courtyard. It's a large battle, so conserve your energy and retreat to the inside if enemies begin flanking you. Match your weapon type to armor for maximum damage and kill the less armored foes first. Eventually, you'll have Sabraque left. Avoid his flaming sword hits as much as possible, and combine Mors's, Alester's, and Dog's abilities to keep him down in the snow for long periods of time until you can finish him off.

If you choose to make peace with the wildlings, Sabraque will invite you to a council at the bonfire. Accept and make your way up to the courtyard. You can speak with Sabraque about several topics, including the Others, wargs, and living in exile. At the end of the conversation, Sabraque will hand you the Wildling Bracelet, which increases a few of Dog's abilities.

7. Return to Castle Black and report back to Qhorin Halfhand.

With your mission complete, return to Qhorin Halfhand at Castle Black's Common Hall. You update him on events and he thanks you for another job well done in service of the Night's Watch.

Side Quest 14: Rituals and Litanies

Side Quest 10

For: Mors

Location: Castle Black

Quest Giver: Duncan Paege

Availability: Chapter 13

Experience Points: 850

Special Rewards: Shadow Fiend

Objectives:

1. Patrek's name must be cleared. Go to the scene of the murder to start your investigation.
2. Pick up the scent of Myles's body to follow his trail.
3. Follow Myles's trail to find out what he was doing before he died.
4. Patrek was seen with Myles just before he died. Go ask him about it.
5. Patrek mentioned a quarrel between Wat and Myles, the victim at Castle Black. Wat will probably have more information for you.
6. The murders seem to be linked to an old mission that Wat and Myles were part of. Check the patrol records in Mormont's office to find out more.
7. Addam was the leader of the mission and is the only one of those abducted by the wildlings to have survived. Search his belongings on the ground floor of the common hall to try and find out more.
8. Addam seems to be deeply involved in this sorry business. Find him as soon as possible.
9. Addam Flowers left Castle Black for Mole's Town with the last survivors of the patrol. You must find him as soon as possible.
10. Go and find Addam Flowers in the forest of Mole's Town before he reaches the point of no return.
11. Kill the deranged Addam Flowers.
12. Go and report back to Duncan Paege to clear Patrek's name.

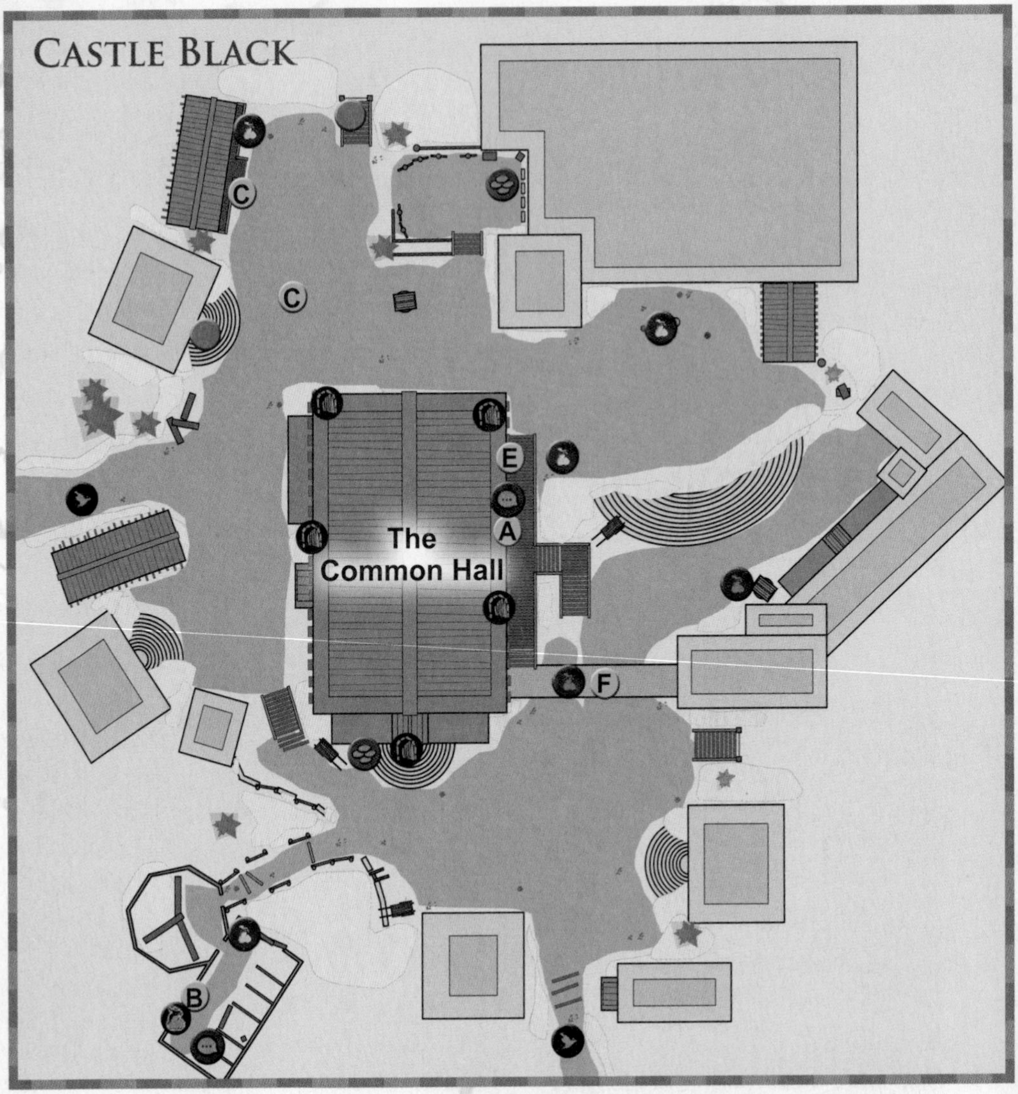

CASTLE BLACK

The Common Hall

A B C C E F

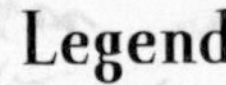

Legend

- Objective Point
- Loot Spot
- Secret Treasure (Alester)
- Secret Treasure (Dog)
- Codex Entry
- Travel to World
- Travel to Area
- NPC
- Merchant

1. Patrek's name must be cleared. Go to the scene of the murder to start your investigation.

Objective Point A

To begin this side quest, speak with Duncan Paege just outside the main door of the Common Hall in Castle Black. Patrek has been accused of a string of murders, but he says he doesn't even know the murdered brothers very well. It's up to you to clear his name.

Objective Point B

Head to the southwest section of Castle Black and investigate the deserted buildings. You'll find Addam Flowers in the back of the farthest building standing over the ritual killing of your brother Myles, who accompanied you during your adventures in the tunnels of Mole's Town. He explains that there is a lot of evidence pointing to Patrek, and you tell him that you're going to look into matters yourself.

2. Pick up the scent of Myles's body to follow his trail.

Objective Point C

Switch to Dog and sniff Myles's scent. Follow it to the northwest section of Castle Black, where you meet up with two brothers talking about the murders.

3. Follow Myles's trail to find out what he was doing before he died.

Objective Point D

One of the brothers hanging outside the building where Myles was last seen says that he saw Patrek and Myles leave the building together. This means that Patrek was lying before when he told you that he didn't know the murdered brothers.

4. Patrek was seen with Myles just before he died. Go ask him about it.

Objective Point E

Return to Patrek and tell him you know he was with Myles just before he died. Patrek eventually breaks his vow of silence for his brother and admits that he promised Myles that he wouldn't reveal the truth: Myles was going to desert the Night's Watch because of the recent troubles, and Patrek was trying to talk him out of it.

5. Patrek mentioned a quarrel between Wat and Myles, the victim at Castle Black. Wat will probably have more information for you.

Objective Point F

It seems that Myles's partner on the Wall, Wat, would know a lot about what happened to Myles. Seek him out on the bridge and ask him some questions. Wat reveals that they were both in an old patrol where horrible things happened north of the Wall. Now, years later, members of that same patrol are being murdered one by one. Unfortunately, his memory of that time is faulty, so he doesn't have any more clues for you.

COMMONS HALL GROUND FLOOR

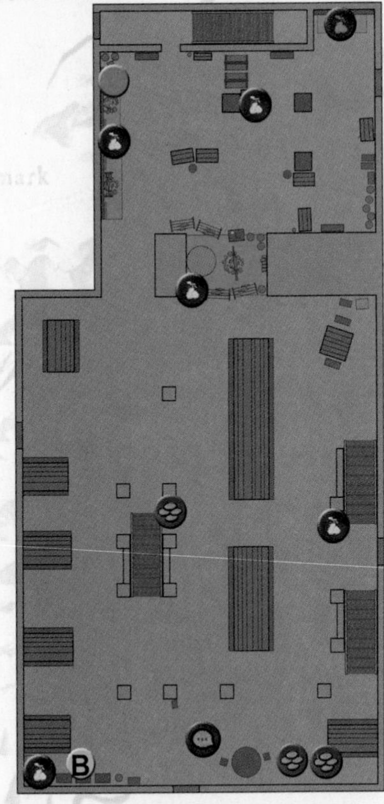

COMMONS HALL FIRST FLOOR

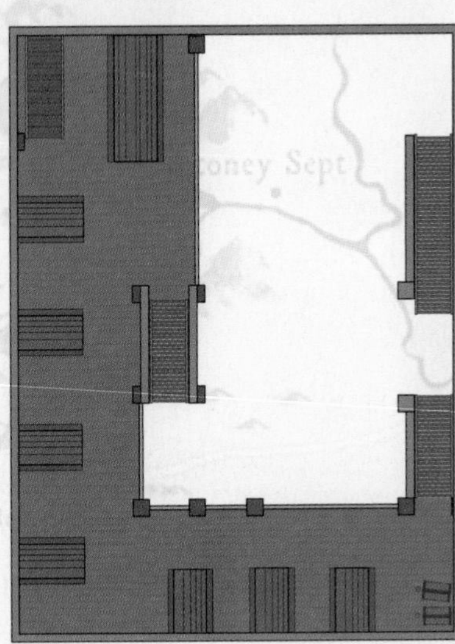

Legend

- Objective Point
- Loot Spot
- Secret Treasure (Alester)
- Codex Entry
- NPC
- Merchant

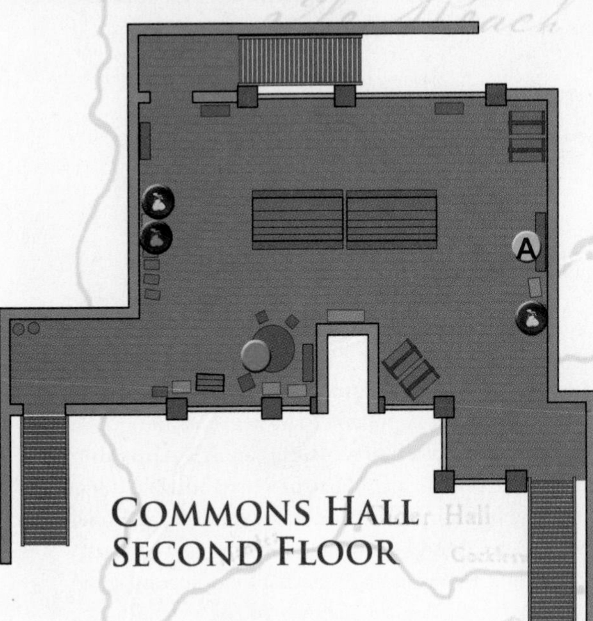

COMMONS HALL SECOND FLOOR

Objective Point A

Enter the Common Hall and search the Lord Commander' office area for papers on the old patrol that Myles and Wat were in. If you search the books, you'll find a report on the patrol that explored the Haunted Forest. You learn tha Addam Flowers led that patrol and that he was abducted by wildlings on that cursed mission.

6. The murders seem to be linked to an old mission that Wat and Myles were part of. Check the patrol records in Mormont's office to find out more.

7. Addam was the leader of the mission and is the only one of those abducted by the wildlings to have survived. Search his belongings on the ground floor of the Common Hall to try and find out more.

Objective Point B

Iead down to the ground floor and search Flowers's ocker. You find an anonymous blackmail letter that threat-:ns to expose Flowers as a wildling spy unless he drops ive golden dragons at the well in Mole's Town.

3. Addam seems to be deeply involved in this sorry business. Find him as soon as ɔossible.

t seems as if Flowers is the true culprit in this sinister urn of events. Once he was blackmailed, he decided to rack down all the old patrol members and kill them off to nake sure no one discovered his secret. Return to Myles's :orpse and you discover that Flowers has left for Mole's Town with the rest of his old patrol. You have to race to top him from committing more atrocities.

9. Addam Flowers left Castle Black for Mole's Town with the last survivors of the patrol. You must find him as soon as possible.

As you leave for Mole's Town, a group of brothers intercepts you. They want to see Patrek executed for his "crimes" and don't like you snooping around on his behalf. You can convince them to back off without a fight if you tell them that Flowers is behind it, or you can battle them in the snows of Castle Black. You need to defeat your brothers to reach the exit and head after Flowers in Mole's Town.

Mole's Town

Legend

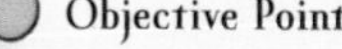
Objective Point

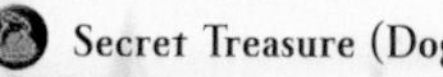
Secret Treasure (Dog)

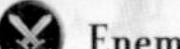
Enemy

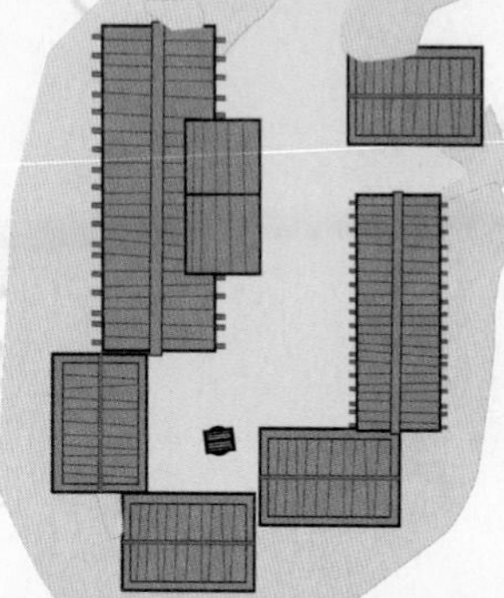

10. Go and find Addam Flowers in the forest of Mole's Town before he reaches the point of no return.

Objective Point A

As soon as you arrive in the forest outside of Mole's Town, you spot Addam Flowers and his old patrol. He's obviously out of his mind, and he kills the last of the patrol before you can reach him.

11. Kill the deranged Addam Flowers.

Objective Point B

When you reach Addam Flowers, he talks about the voices in his head and says the wildlings forced him to eat his fellow brother's heart many years ago when captured. Now the white walkers call to him and ask for more sacrifices.

To end his threat once and for all, kill the deranged Addam Flowers. Alternate stunning him between Alester and Mors and order Dog to knock Flowers down or immobilize him to serve as a break between other abilities. If you keep him off balance, the three of you should slice, bash, and bite Flowers for enough damage to slay your lost brother.

12. Go and report back to Duncan Paege to clear Patrek's name.

Return to Castle Black and let Duncan Paege know that Patrek isn't the criminal in the whole affair. After you relat the story, Patrek is freed.

Patrek thanks you even as you remind him of his responsibility on the Wall. Even though Patrek is unsure of his feelings—his fellow brothers turned their backs on him, after all—he resolves to return to his duty as a sworn brother of the Night's Watch.

Appendix Lists

Achievements

Achievement / Trophy Title	Achievement/ Trophy Type	How to Unlock	Details
Winter Is Coming	Story-related	Finish chapter 1	N/A
Family is Hope...	Story-related	Finish chapter 2	This chapter ends with the quest "For All the Days Gone By"
Dark Wings, Dark Words	Story-related	Finish chapter 3	N/A
Hear Me Roar	Story-related	Finish chapter 4	N/A
Proud to be Faithful	Story-related	Finish chapter 5	N/A
Dead Men Sing No Songs	Story-related	Finish chapter 6	N/A
Here We Stand	Story-related	Finish chapter 7	N/A
Family, Duty, Honor	Story-related	Finish chapter 8	N/A
Unbowed, Unbent, Unbroken	Story-related	Finish chapter 9	N/A
Fire and Blood	Story-related	Finish chapter 10	N/A
Come Try Me	Story-related	Finish chapter 11	N/A
As High As Honor	Story-related	Finish chapter 12	N/A
Growing Strong	Story-related	Finish chapter 13	N/A
Valar Morghulis	Story-related	Finish chapter 14	N/A
The Night is Dark...	Story-related	Finish chapter 15	N/A
Red Priest of R'hllor	Story-related	Finish Alester's story	Unlockable when you chose Alester at the end of the "Bounds" quest
Sworn Brother	Story-related	Finish Mors' Story	Unlockable when you chose Mors at the end of the "Bounds" quest
Platinum Trophy	Story-related	Win all the others trophies of Game of Thrones	Only on PS3.
Disciplinarian	Secondary Objectives	Chapter 1: Confront the four recruits during the training session with Mors	In order to do this, you'll have to chose «I'll show them who's in charge here» when prompted, and win the first 2 fights
Know Your Place	Secondary Objectives	Chapter 2: Protect the nobility with Alester	During the hostage situation, give the nobles' money to the peasants; in the marketplace, give the castle food supply to the peasants; during judgments, choose to kill the people
Man of the People	Secondary Objectives	Chapter 2: Protect the people with Alester	During the hostage situation, take from your own castle funds to supply the peasants ; in the marketplace, kill every peasant; during judgments, choose to release the people
End of the Line	Secondary Objectives	Chapter 4: Don't lose pursuit of the bastard Harry Waters	This achievement will only unlock if you followed the bastard successfully to the Hen House
Bloodhound	Secondary Objectives	Chapter 5: Find all the corrupt brothers of the Night's Watch	You'll have to use the dog and follow the scents of the brothers to uncover their secrets. Bartram and Gwayne are the real culprits, but everyone is hiding something.
Once More Unto the Breach	Secondary Objectives	Chapter 5: Attack the camp without killing the sentries at the start	When prompted, tell Patrek to attack the camp right away.
Am I Not Merciful?	Secondary Objectives	Chapter 6: Save Orys from the City Watch	There are two ways to save Orys. You'll have to promise him to get him back either way, then get him outside, through the guards or successfully use Janos' seal when prompted

Achievement / Trophy Title	Achievement/ Trophy Type	How to Unlock	Details
Desecration	Secondary Objectives	Chapter 6: Find the key in Alester's father's tomb	When looking for the seven keys, go search for Raynald's tomb in the crypts and loot it.
The Butcher Comes to Dinner	Secondary Objectives	Chapter 7: Kill 6 of Lord Harlton's soldiers during the fight at dinner	You are poisonned during this fight. If you get under 10% health, you will faint before you can kill them.
Tis But a Scratch!	Secondary Objectives	Chapter 7: Suffer all the physical abuse during the torture sequence	Make sure to insult your torturers whenever you can.
Swift and Deadly	Secondary Objectives	Chapter 9: End the trial by combat in less than 2 minutes	Here are some dialog options that could help you here : «Words are wind... »; «Keep him talking, catch your breath...»; I'll make him spit out everything he knows»
Unrivaled Strategist	Secondary Objectives	Chapter 10: Take back Riverspring with a total victory	Send Ryman into the marketplace with the bowmen; send Greydon with the pikemen at the gates; send Jon on the docks with the peasants.
Quiet as a Shadow	Secondary Objectives	Chapter 11: Reach Jeyne's room without ever being seen	In order to do this, you'll have to use your dog extensively. Do not engage combat, and make sure to backstab the guard that is fleeing through the door upstairs.
Lesser of Two Evils	Secondary Objectives	Chapter 12: Come to the aid of the Reapers	This achievement will only unlock if you spared Axe or Orys lives (only one will suffice)
My Darkest Hour	Secondary Objectives	Chapter 13: Execute the judgment passed down on the Westfords	When Cerenna runs for the door, follow her and interact with her. When prompted, chose to kill her.
The True Face of the Spider	Secondary Objectives	Lose the final battle	Simply lose the fight versus Valarr in the "Light and Shadow" quest
Thorough	Secondary Objectives	Complete all the secondary objectives of the story	N/A
The Greatest	Secondary Quests	Emerge triumphant in the final arena combat	The final combat, versus Lucifer, is a fight to death
Endless watch	Secondary Quests	Send 10 recruits to the Wall with Mors	N/A
Collector	Secondary Quests	Seize the three objects of value from the Collector with Alester	These three items are all lootable in Mallador Brax's room, after defeating him
Pimp	Secondary Quests	Convince Bethany to return to Chataya's brothel with Alester	When you learn the truth about Bethany occupation, make sure to visit Chataya's house and to speak with her. When confronting Bethany, ask her to go back there; however, this will trigger a fight with Guncer and his men.
Devout Follower	Secondary Quests	Find all the statuettes of the Seven	N/A
Fetch!	Gameplay	Use Mors' dog's sense of smell to find 5 secret objects	One very useful item is hidden upon starting the Warg mode tutorial (in Westruins courtyard)
R'hllor Sees All	Gameplay	Find 10 secrets with the Sight of R'hllor	Castlewood and the Red Keep are great places to unlock this achievement.
Golden Touch	Gameplay	Acquire 1 golden dragon	Completing the "Blood on the Sand" quest will help you here.
Man's best friend	Gameplay	Kill 10 enemies with Mors' dog in warg mode	N/A
Accomplished warrior	Gameplay	Kill 400 enemies	N/A
Merciless	Gameplay	Mete out 5 deathblows	Outdoors are easier for this task; also, make sure to use melee weapon if you want to complete this achievement
Great Teamwork	Gameplay	Finish the game without a single ally (except Mors and Alester) being KO'd	This only acconts for allies, since followers can't get KO'd. If one ally is in trouble, use Mors or Alester as a tank
Warlord	Gameplay	Reach the maximum level	N/A
Master-at-arms	Gameplay	Learn all skills within a character's stance tree	N/A
Master of Light and Flame	Gameplay	Gain all the skills linked to R'hllor's fire with Alester	N/A
Clever dog	Gameplay	Gain all the skills linked to the dog with Mors	N/A

Companions

Companion	Joins In	Stance	Abilities	Weapons	Strength	Agility	Luck	Endurance	Intelligence
Ser Terrence Celtigar	Chapter 1	Defense	Resistance, Self Defense, Targeted Strike	Andal Glaive, Worn Wooden Shield	6	6	6	4	7
Ser Ryman Sarwyck	Chapter 2	Defense	Daze Strike, Quick Fix, Taunt	Battle Mace, Sarwyck Shield	5	4	4	6	4
Patrek	Chapter 5	Domination	Death from Above, Devastation, Upheaval	Rib-crusher	8	3	4	6	6
Ser Valarr Hill	Chapter 6	Domination	Death from Above, Earthquaker, Massacre, Pierce, Upheaval	Valarr's Sword	10	8	6	7	7
Ser Desmond Hardyng	Chapter 8	Intensity	Bully, Calm as Still Water, Fierce as a Wolverine, Retaliation, Smooth as Summer Silk, Sting of the Manticore	Rapier	6	8	6	7	8
Orys	Chapter 8 (if you save him)	Assassination	Deterring Strike, Pommel Strike, Precision Strike, Savage Strike	Misericorde	8	10	8	6	8
Endrew	Chapter 9	Frenzy	Flurry of Blows, Rage, Slash	Turn-Cloak	7	7	4	9	8
Alequo	"Blood on the Sand" side quest	Intensity	Calm as Still Water, Retaliation, Sting of the Manticore, Strong as a Bear	Rapier	6	9	8	6	10
Bayard	"Blood on the Sand" side quest	Assassination	Blinding Dust, Precision Strike, Savage Strike, Sneak Attack	Braquemard	6	9	4	3	7
Ser Symon	"Blood on the Sand" side quest	Defense	Daze Strike, Quick Fix, Resistance, Self Defense	Armor-smasher	3	3	4	8	6
Galbart	"Blood on the Sand" side quest	Domination	Add Injury to Injury, Devastation, Earthquaker, Pierce	Bastard Sword	5	3	3	4	3
Criston	"Rings and Chains" side quest (if you save him)	Assassination	Blinding Dust, Discourteous Kick	None	4	7	6	3	5

Equipment

Weapons

Damage		Type	Bonus	Cost		
Min	Max			Golden Dragons	Silver Stags	Groats
19.0	24.2	Perforating		0	0	0
20.8	26.4	Perforating		0	8	3
22.0	28.0	Perforating		0	10	5
23.1	29.5	Perforating		0	12	11
25.5	32.5	Perforating		0	26	14
39.2	50.0	Perforating		0	145	2
44.0	56.0	Perforating		1	126	15
46.4	59.0	Perforating		1	201	9
51.1	65.1	Perforating	Attack speed +8%	2	105	0
52.3	66.5	Perforating		2	142	8
64.2	81.6	Perforating		6	200	10
66.5	84.7	Perforating		7	170	10
71.3	90.7	Perforating	Damage x10 against shadows	15	0	0
21.2	28.6	Perforating		0	0	0
24.5	33.1	Perforating		0	8	11
27.1	36.7	Perforating		0	13	6
35.7	48.3	Perforating		0	24	2
50.3	68.1	Perforating		1	136	5
52.9	71.6	Perforating		2	22	14
55.6	75.2	Perforating	Deflection +10%	2	60	0

Damage		Type	Bonus	Cost		
Min	Max			Golden Dragons	Silver Stags	Groats
64.5	75.7	Perforating	All energy is recovered when your teammate is KO.	3	0	0
63.5	85.9	Perforating		2	193	8
68.9	93.2	Perforating		6	146	4
71.5	96.7	Perforating		7	112	8
75.5	102.1	Perforating	For each dodge, the opponent who attacked you is stunned 3s.	5	0	0
30.8	35.4	Cutting		0	0	0
36.5	42.1	Cutting		0	8	15
40.0	46.0	Cutting		0	9	14
42.4	48.8	Cutting	Chance to inflict Bleeding (6s) with each attack: 1%	0	180	0
44.3	50.9	Cutting		0	15	0
52.0	59.8	Cutting		0	24	2
63.2	72.8	Cutting	Hit chance +5%; chance to inflict Bleeding (7 sec) with each attack: 2%	1	105	0
65.5	75.3	Cutting		1	99	12
71.2	82.0	Cutting		1	180	6
92.4	106.4	Cutting		2	193	8
104.0	119.6	Cutting		6	200	10
107.8	124.0	Cutting		7	170	10
109.7	126.3	Cutting	Energy +20 for each opponent killed	5	30	0
111.6	128.4	Cutting		8	7	8
111.7	128.5	Cutting		8	19	11
115.5	132.9	Cutting	Damage x10 against shadows	15	0	0
29.1	37.1	Cutting		0	0	0
31.0	39.4	Cutting		0	7	13
34.6	44.0	Cutting		0	8	15
39.6	50.4	Cutting		0	14	5
40.1	51.1	Cutting	Chance to inflict Knocked Down (4s) on a stunned opponent with each attack: 25%	0	15	10
47.3	60.3	Cutting		0	23	3
63.8	81.2	Cutting		1	109	2
73.0	92.8	Cutting	Chance to inflict Scared (7s) with each critical hit: 50%	1	200	0
78.3	99.7	Cutting		2	33	12
89.2	113.6	Cutting		2	206	4
92.9	118.3	Cutting		6	119	1
100.2	127.6	Cutting		7	141	9
109.3	139.1	Cutting	Damage x10 against shadows	15	0	0
32.4	37.3	Blunt		0	0	0
36.5	41.9	Blunt		0	8	7
38.5	44.3	Blunt		0	8	15
46.6	53.6	Blunt		0	15	0
56.7	65.3	Blunt		0	25	0
75.0	86.2	Blunt		1	126	15
83.0	95.6	Blunt		2	12	9
93.2	107.2	Blunt		2	168	3
99.2	114.2	Blunt		6	64	11
111.4	128.2	Blunt	For each critical hit, all the opponents in a range of 3 meters around your target will receive normal damage	4	60	0
115.4	132.8	Blunt		7	199	11
121.6	139.8	Blunt	Damage x10 against shadows	15	0	0
33.6	42.7	Blunt		0	0	0
37.8	48.0	Blunt		0	8	7
45.8	58.2	Blunt		0	14	5
60.9	77.5	Blunt		0	25	14
70.4	89.6	Blunt		2	193	8
71.4	90.8	Blunt		1	99	12
84.0	106.8	Blunt		2	1	14
100.3	127.7	Blunt		2	193	8

Damage		Type	Bonus	Cost		
Min	Max			Golden Dragons	Silver Stags	Groats
111.2	141.6	Blunt		6	173	7
117.6	149.6	Blunt		7	170	10
125.9	160.3	Blunt	Damage x10 against shadows	15	0	0
27.3	31.5	Perforating		0	7	8
27.4	31.5	Perforating		0	0	0
29.1	33.5	Perforating		0	8	0
32.6	37.5	Perforating		0	12	6
42.8	49.2	Perforating		0	22	5
51.3	59.1	Perforating		1	63	3
77.0	88.6	Perforating		2	54	12
85.6	98.4	Perforating		3	9	6
89.0	102.4	Perforating	Critical hit chance +10% when your health is lower than 30%	10	60	0
93.0	107.0	Perforating	Critical damage +10%; chance to inflict Immobilized (5 sec) with each attack	10	0	0
94.1	108.3	Perforating		7	17	13
101.0	116.2	Perforating		8	48	12
28.5	37.8	Perforating		0	0	0
35.6	47.2	Perforating		0	9	6
40.9	54.3	Perforating		0	15	0
56.9	75.5	Perforating		0	28	9
61.9	82.1	Perforating		1	109	2
65.9	87.3	Perforating		1	180	6
80.2	106.2	Perforating		2	155	1
88.6	117.4	Perforating		6	91	14
103.3	136.9	Perforating		8	19	11
106.8	141.6	Perforating	Damage x10 against shadows	15	0	0
41.7	50.9	Cutting		0	0	0
57.2	70.0	Cutting		0	10	5
62.5	76.3	Cutting		0	15	10
72.9	89.1	Cutting		0	25	0
85.9	104.9	Cutting		1	90	15
98.9	120.9	Cutting		1	190	11
117.2	143.2	Cutting		2	155	1
135.5	165.6	Cutting	Hit chance +6%; critical hit chance +3%	4	20	0
138.0	168.6	Cutting		6	173	7
148.4	181.4	Cutting		7	199	11
156.2	190.9	Cutting	Damage x10 against shadows	15	0	0
40.7	54.0	Cutting		0	0	0
45.8	60.8	Cutting		0	8	7
56.0	74.2	Cutting		0	14	5
58.6	77.6	Cutting	Critical damage +8%	0	30	0
63.6	84.4	Cutting	Chance of critical hit +3%	0	38	12
68.7	91.1	Cutting		0	24	2
91.7	121.5	Cutting		1	118	2
98.9	131.1	Cutting		1	201	9
114.6	151.8	Cutting		2	155	1
140.1	185.7	Cutting		7	17	13
147.7	195.7	Cutting		8	19	11
152.8	202.6	Cutting	Damage x10 against shadows	15	0	0
42.4	53.9	Blunt		0	0	0
53.0	67.4	Blunt		0	9	6
54.3	69.1	Blunt		0	9	10
66.2	84.2	Blunt		0	16	4
76.7	97.7	Blunt		0	25	14
92.7	117.9	Blunt		1	109	2

Damage		Type	Bonus	Cost		
Min	Max			Golden Dragons	Silver Stags	Groats
108.5	138.1	Blunt		2	12	9
119.2	151.6	Blunt		2	155	1
132.4	168.4	Blunt		6	91	14
144.2	183.6	Blunt		7	126	9
158.4	201.6	Blunt	Damage x10 against shadows	15	0	0
36.0	44.0	Blunt		0	9	6
44.7	54.6	Blunt		0	0	0
55.8	68.2	Blunt		0	9	6
67.0	81.8	Blunt		0	15	10
78.2	95.6	Blunt		0	25	0
100.5	122.9	Blunt		1	118	2
111.7	136.5	Blunt		2	1	14
122.4	149.6	Blunt		2	142	8
145.2	177.4	Blunt		6	146	4
156.3	191.1	Blunt		7	170	10
167.5	204.7	Blunt	Damage x10 against shadows	15	0	0
32.9	37.8	Ranged		0	0	0
39.1	44.9	Ranged		0	8	15
40.1	46.1	Ranged		0	9	2
47.2	54.4	Ranged		0	15	0
53.4	61.4	Ranged		0	23	3
76.0	87.4	Ranged		1	126	15
82.1	94.5	Ranged		2	1	14
84.3	96.9	Ranged	Aiming speed +8%; Accuracy +5%	2	15	0
94.5	108.7	Ranged		2	168	3
107.1	123.3	Ranged		5	135	15
109.8	126.4	Ranged		6	186	9
112.9	129.9	Ranged		7	141	9
121.2	139.4	Ranged		8	150	0
34.3	42.0	Ranged		0	0	0
40.8	49.8	Ranged		0	8	15
53.6	65.6	Ranged		0	16	4
60.1	73.5	Ranged		0	25	0
73.0	89.2	Ranged		1	99	12
87.9	107.5	Ranged		2	12	9
90.2	110.2	Ranged	Damage +25% on heavy armor; critical hit chance +5% with a perforating type bolt	2	40	0
100.8	123.2	Ranged		2	180	15
107.3	131.1	Ranged		6	91	14
119.7	146.3	Ranged		7	170	10
128.7	157.3	Ranged		8	195	0
x	x	None	Default arrows (when the player equips a ranged weapon without a projectile)	0	0	0
x	x	Blunt		0	2	0
x	x	Cutting		0	2	0
x	x	Perforating		0	2	0
x	x	Blunt	Chance to inflict Stunned (3s) with each shot: 1%	0	20	0
x	x	Cutting	Chance to inflict Bleeding (6s) with each shot: 2%	0	20	0
x	x	Perforating	Chance to inflict Immobilized (5s) with each attack: 2%	0	20	0
x	x	Blunt	Chance to inflict Stunned (3s) with each shot: 2%	0	100	0
x	x	Cutting	Chance to inflict Bleeding (6s) with each attack: 4%	0	100	0
x	x	Perforating	Chance to inflict Immobilized (5s) with each attack: 4%	0	100	0
x	x	Blunt	Chance to inflict Stunned (3s) with each shot: 3%	1	65	0
x	x	Cutting	Chance to inflict Bleeding (6s) with each shot: 6%	1	65	0
x	x	Perforating	Chance to inflict Immobilized (5s) with each attack: 6%	1	65	0
x	x	Perforating	Damage x10 against shadows	5	0	0
x	x	None	Default bolts (when the player equips a ranged weapon without a projectile)	0	0	0

Damage		Type	Bonus	Cost		
Min	Max			Golden Dragons	Silver Stags	Groats
x	x	Blunt		0	2	0
x	x	Cutting		0	2	0
x	x	Perforating		0	2	0
x	x	Blunt	Chance to inflict Stunned (3s) with each shot: 1%	0	20	0
x	x	Cutting	Chance to inflict Bleeding (6s) with each shot: 2%	0	20	0
x	x	Perforating	Chance to inflict Immobilized (5s) with each attack: 2%	0	20	0
x	x	Blunt	Chance to inflict Stunned (3s) with each shot: 2%	0	100	0
x	x	Cutting	Chance to inflict Bleeding (6s) with each attack: 4%	0	100	0
x	x	Perforating	Chance to inflict Immobilized (5s) with each attack: 4%	0	100	0
x	x	Blunt	Chance to inflict Stunned (3s) with each shot: 3%	1	65	0
x	x	Cutting	Chance to inflict Bleeding (6s) with each shot: 6%	1	65	0
x	x	Perforating	Chance to inflict Immobilized (5s) with each attack: 6%	1	65	0
x	x	Perforating	Damage x10 against shadows	5	0	0

Belt Items

Class	Name	Uses	Substance	Description	Effect	Cost		
						Golden Dragons	Silver Stags	Groats
Container	Flask	3	x	Holds up to 3 uses of a substance.	x	0	25	0
Container	Gourd	4	x	Holds up to 4 uses of a substance.	x	0	75	0
Content	Flammable Oil	x	Combustible	Allows Alester to set fire to a weapon or to make several enemies flammable targets.	Flammable (20s): Chance of becoming On Fire: x2	0	18	0
Content	Wildfire	x	Combustible	Used to set a weapon or an opponent on fire.	Damage: 250 health points: On Wildfire 1s	0	100	0
Content	Laurel Oil	x	Oil	Improves mobility and joint problems, aiding recovery when Immobilized.	Heals Immobilized	0	0	8
Content	Firemilk	x	Oil	Firemilk is a reddish liquor that heals Bleeding.	Heals Bleeding	0	1	0
Content	Sourleaf Oil	x	Oil	Sourleaf oil prevents you from being Stunned or knocked down.	Sourleaf Oil (10 s): Resistance at 100% for Stunned and knocked down	0	4	0
Content	Hop Oil	x	Oil	Hops are plants that affect the nervous system. This oil aids recovery from being Scared.	Heals Scared	0	5	0
Content	Balm Oil	x	Oil	Counteracts all known poisons.	Cure for all known poisons	0	7	0
Content	Water	x	Potion	Restores some energy.	Energy Recovery changes to 10% per second during 4s.	0	3	0
Content	Tyroshi Alcohol	x	Potion	Tyroshi alcohol warms you up, increasing bravado and damage resistance.	Tyroshi Alcohol (15s) Attack speed +20%; Damage resistance +10%	0	6	0
Content	Dreamwine	x	Potion	This wine-based potion is a painkiller that also helps to heal minor injuries.	Restores 220 health points	0	8	0
Content	Milk of the Poppy	x	Potion	A concoction that helps recover some health.	Restores 300 health points	0	15	0
Content	Wine of Courage	x	Potion	This Astapori beverage makes you Invincible for a short while.	Invincible (6s): You no longer feel the blows	0	25	0
Content	Maester's Mixture	x	Potion	Recover a significant amount of health.	Restores 500 health points	0	35	0
Content	Blindeye	x	Poison	Blinds your enemies so they fight with less accuracy.	Blindeye (14s): Hit chance -50%	0	5	0
Content	Hemlock	x	Poison	Slows the opponent's movements for a few moments.	Hemlock poison: Attack speed -30%; hit chance -20%	0	8	0
Content	Sweetsleep	x	Poison	This poison tires opponents so much that they become Stunned.	Stunned (4s)	0	13	0
Content	Basilisk Venom	x	Poison	This poison will turn an enemy into a Madman, causing them to attack anyone.	Madman (12s): The opponent will attack anyone.	0	15	0
Content	Manticore Venom	x	Poison	This powerful poison spreads rapidly through the blood and affects human tissue. It will only work if your opponent is Bleeding.	If your opponent is Bleeding: Damage: 30 health points/ second; Attack speed -25%	0	20	0

Class	Name	Uses	Substance	Description	Effect	Cost		
						Golden Dragons	Silver Stags	Groats
Content	Aconitine	x	Poison	Aconites are a breed of plant that can harm humans. In combat, aconitine poisoning will prevent a target from using their abilities.	Scared (10s): Your opponent is unable to use his abilities.	0	23	0
Content	Strangler	x	Poison	This poison gradually chokes the life out of your opponent until the fight is over, inflicting more and more damage as time passes.	Cumulative damage: +3 health points/second (max at 60/s)	0	25	0

Armor

Class	Name	Type	Health	Energy Cost	Deflection Penalty	Bonus	Cost		
							Golden Dragons	Silver Stages	Groats
Helm	Straw hat	None	20	2	1.2		0	2	13
Helm	Old hood of the Night's Watch	None	32	2	1.8		0	4	13
Helm	Old hood	None	28	1.8	1.6		0	5	0
Helm	Peasant hood	None	17	1.9	1.4		0	7	13
Helm	Leather hood	Light	65	3.9	4.4		0	7	13
Helm	Red priest hood	Light	62	3.7	4.2		0	7	13
Helm	Wildling hood	Light	61	3	4		0	7	0
Helm	Worn iron helmet	Light	70	4	4.5		0	9	9
Helm	Vale of Arryn leather hood	Light	76.7	3.51	4		0	14	5
Helm	Sellsword leather hood	Light	68.9	3.77	4.3		0	14	5
Helm	Sarwyck hood	Light	72.8	3.64	4.2		0	20	13
Helm	Gold Cloak studded leather helmet	Light	85	3.64	3.8		0	100	12
Helm	Studded leather helmet	Light	88.4	3.51	3.6		0	117	0
Helm	Castlewood studded leather helmet	Light	96.2	3.25	3.4		0	149	8
Helm	Bloodseeker iron helmet	Light	104	3.38	3.1		1	154	1
Helm	Light steel helmet	Light	107.9	3.25	3		1	186	9
Helm	Lannister leather helmet	Light	116	3	2.7		2	41	9
Helm	The Three Wats' hat	Light	115	3.4	3.2	Bargaining chance +10%	3	30	0
Helm	High Priest Benerro's hood	Light	115	3	2	Critical hit chance +8%; chance to resist to the state On Fire +15%	3	163	0
Helm	Lann the Clever's helmet	Light	120	2.5	2	Chance to inflict Blindeye (8s) with each attack: 16%	4	20	0
Helm	Rusty iron helmet	Intermediate	55	5.4	7		0	4	6
Helm	Wildling mail coif	Intermediate	75	4.6	5		0	9	6
Helm	Iron mail helmet	Intermediate	78	5.2	6.5		0	10	6
Helm	Sellsword iron helmet	Intermediate	83.2	5.07	6.4		0	17	9
Helm	Sarwyck iron helmet	Intermediate	88.4	4.94	6.3		0	24	11
Helm	Vale of Arryn kettle hat	Intermediate	93.6	4.81	6.1		0	31	14
Helm	Toregg's helmet	Intermediate	90	4	3	Damage Resistance +3%; Bargaining chance -1%	0	38	2
Helm	Gold Cloak iron helmet	Intermediate	104	4.94	5.9		0	115	5
Helm	Reinforced kettle hat	Intermediate	109.2	4.81	5.7		0	133	4
Helm	Castlewood kettle hat	Intermediate	119.6	4.55	5.5		0	169	0
Helm	Sarwyck mail coif	Intermediate	125	4	5	Critical damage resistance +7%	0	173	1
Helm	Bloodseeker leather helmet	Intermediate	130	4.68	5.2		1	199	6
Helm	Gold-trimmed iron helmet	Intermediate	135.2	4.55	5.1		2	25	5
Helm	Lannister iron helmet	Intermediate	146	4.29	4.8		2	96	14

Class	Name	Type	Health	Energy Cost	Deflection Penalty	Bonus	Cost		
							Golden Dragons	Silver Stages	Groats
Helm	Rusty Sarwyck barbute	Heavy	46	8	15		0	9	1
Helm	Barbute	Heavy	91	6	13		0	13	0
Helm	Wildling heavy helmet	Heavy	94	8	15		0	13	5
Helm	Sellsword barbute	Heavy	97	6.37	12.7		0	20	13
Helm	Sarwyck barbute	Heavy	104	6.24	12.4		0	28	10
Helm	Vale of Arryn beaked helm	Heavy	110	6.11	12.2		0	36	6
Helm	Gold Cloak helm	Heavy	123	6.24	11.8		0	130	0
Helm	Gold Cloak helm	Heavy	127	6	12.3		0	0	0
Helm	Visored sallet	Heavy	130	6.11	11.6		0	149	8
Helm	Castlewood sallet with a visor	Heavy	143	5.85	11.3		0	188	8
Helm	Guardian helm	Heavy	143	5.85	11.3	Chance to resist to the state Stunned +50%	0	188	7
Helm	Bloodseeker knight's helmet	Heavy	156	5.98	10.8		2	35	0
Helm	Knight's helm	Heavy	162	5.85	10		2	74	1
Helm	Lannister plate helmet	Heavy	176	5.59	10		2	151	14
Helm	Barristan Selmy's jousting helmet	Heavy	183	6	11	Health +10%; critical damage +5%; Deflection +3%	7	12	0
Chest	Peasant clothes	None	350	9	6		0	15	10
Chest	Tattered pants	None	170	1.3	0.2		0	28	2
Chest	Wildling leather armor	Light	180	13	14		0	18	12
Chest	Leather tunic	Light	200	12	13.6		0	24	0
Chest	Studded leather tunic	Light	215	12	13.7		0	24	0
Chest	Red priest clothing	Light	200	12	13.6		0	24	0
Chest	Vale of Arryn leather armor	Light	236	10.8	12.4		0	44	0
Chest	Sellsword leather armor	Light	212	11.6	13.2		0	44	0
Chest	Sarwyck leather armor	Light	224	11.2	13		0	64	0
Chest	Wildling soft fur	Light	350	6	5		0	175	0
Chest	Gold Cloak leather armor	Light	260	11.2	11.6		1	100	0
Chest	Studded leather armor	Light	272	10.8	11.2		1	150	0
Chest	Castlewood leather armor	Light	296	10	10.4		2	40	0
Chest	Studded leather armor	Light	296	10	10.4		2	40	0
Chest	Bloodseeker leather armor	Light	320	10.4	9.6		5	70	0
Chest	Mail and leather armor	Light	332	10	9.2		5	170	0
Chest	Lannister leather armor	Light	356	9.2	8.4		6	160	0
Chest	Thoros of Myr's robe	Light	350	8	9	Chance to inflict Flammable (7s) to your opponent each time he attacks you: 20%	11	130	0
Chest	Wildling coat of mail	Intermediate	230	18	22		0	31	4
Chest	Night's Watch armor	Intermediate	240	16	20		0	32	0
Chest	Sellsword coat of mail	Intermediate	256	15.6	19.6		0	54	0
Chest	Sarwyck coat of mail	Intermediate	272	15.2	19.2		0	76	0
Chest	Vale of Arryn coat of mail	Intermediate	288	14.8	18.8		0	98	0
Chest	Alester Sarwyck's armor	Intermediate	335	15	18	Chance to resist to the state On Fire +10%	0	125	10
Chest	Sarwyck reinforced coat of mail	Intermediate	290	13	17		1	102	8
Chest	Gold Cloak coat of mail	Intermediate	320	15.2	18		1	145	0
Chest	Gold Cloak coat of mail	Intermediate	320	15.2	18		0	0	0

Class	Name	Type	Health	Energy Cost	Deflection Penalty	Bonus	Cost: Golden Dragons	Cost: Silver Stages	Cost: Groats
Chest	Lord's steel coat of mail	Intermediate	336	14.8	17.6		1	200	0
Chest	Castlewood chainmail	Intermediate	368	14	16.8		2	100	0
Chest	Bloodseeker coat of mail	Intermediate	400	14.4	16		6	0	0
Chest	Reinforced coat of mail	Intermediate	416	14	15.6		6	110	0
Chest	Stark coat of mail	Intermediate	432	13.6	15.6		7	10	0
Chest	Lannister coat of mail	Intermediate	448	13.2	14.8		7	120	0
Chest	Old Targaryen king's armor	Intermediate	490	12	15	If your opponent is Bleeding: Chance to gain +30% of attack speed (10s) with each attack: 20%	10	180	0
Chest	Red Viper's chainmail	Intermediate	410	14	15	Chance to inflict Hemlock (6s) to your opponent each time he attacks you: 10%	12	10	0
Chest	Night's Watch breastplate	Heavy	280	20	40		0	40	0
Chest	Wildling heavy chest	Heavy	270	25	41		0	40	0
Chest	Sellsword breastplate	Heavy	300	19.6	39.2		0	64	0
Chest	Rusty Sarwyck breastplate	Heavy	190	21	42		0	71	14
Chest	Gorn's armor	Heavy	300	19	38	Health recovery +15%; Bargaining chance -3%	0	81	4
Chest	Sarwyck breastplate	Heavy	320	19.2	38.5		0	88	0
Chest	Vale of Arryn breastplate	Heavy	340	18.8	37.6		0	112	0
Chest	Westford armor	Heavy	410	20	36	Damage resistance +2%	0	187	8
Chest	Wildling padded fur	Heavy	495	15	28		0	200	0
Chest	Gold Cloak breastplate	Heavy	380	19.2	36.4		1	190	0
Chest	Warrior's breastplate	Heavy	400	18.8	35.6		2	40	0
Chest	Tyrell breastplate	Heavy	420	18.4	35.6	Energy recovery +10%	2	100	0
Chest	Castlewood breastplate	Heavy	440	18	34.8		2	160	0
Chest	Bloodseeker armor	Heavy	480	18.4	33.2		6	140	0
Chest	Knight's breastplate	Heavy	500	18	32.4		7	50	0
Chest	Lannister breastplate	Heavy	540	17.2	30.8		8	80	0
Chest	Brynden Rivers' breastplate	Heavy	560	18	31	Damage resistance +4%; Agility +1	14	100	0
Chest	Jon Connington's breastplate	Heavy	558	19	33.8	Chance to inflict Provoked (8s) with each attack: 20%	15	194	0
Gloves	Wilding vambraces	Light	55	3.3	3.7		0	6	4
Gloves	Studded leather gloves	Light	60	3.6	4.4		0	7	3
Gloves	Leather gloves	Light	60	3.6	4.1		0	7	3
Gloves	Vale of Arryn leather gloves	Light	70.8	3.24	3.7		0	13	3
Gloves	Sellsword leather gloves	Light	63.6	3.48	4		0	13	3
Gloves	Sarwyck leather gloves	Light	67.2	3.36	3.8		0	19	3
Gloves	Leather vambraces	Light	78	3.3	3.7		0	24	5
Gloves	Gold Cloak leather gloves	Light	78	3.36	3		0	92	15
Gloves	Gold Cloak leather gloves	Light	78	3.36	3		0	0	0
Gloves	Leather vambraces	Light	81.6	3.24	3.4		0	107	15
Gloves	Castlewood leather vambraces	Light	89	3	3.1		0	137	15
Gloves	People's Friend	Light	75	2.5	3	Each dodge recover 20% of energy to your teammate and your allies	1	8	12
Gloves	Bloodseeker leather gloves	Light	96	3.12	2.9		1	125	15
Gloves	Padded leather gloves	Light	99.6	3	2.8		1	155	15
Gloves	Lannister leather gloves	Light	107	2.76	2		2	5	15
Gloves	Wildling mail gauntlets	Intermediate	68	4.1	5.4		0	8	12

Class	Name	Type	Health	Energy Cost	Deflection Penalty	Bonus	Cost		
							Golden Dragons	Silver Stages	Groats
Gloves	Mail and leather gloves	Intermediate	72	4.8	6		0	9	10
Gloves	Sellsword mail gauntlets	Intermediate	76.8	4.68	5.9		0	16	3
Gloves	Sarwyck mail gauntlets	Intermediate	81.6	4.56	5.7		0	22	13
Gloves	Vale of Arryn mail gauntlets	Intermediate	86.4	4.44	5.6		0	29	6
Gloves	Gold Cloak mail gauntlets	Intermediate	96	4.56	5.4		0	106	9
Gloves	Warrior's mail gauntlets	Intermediate	100.8	4.44	5.3		0	122	15
Gloves	Castlewood mail gauntlets	Intermediate	110.4	4.2	5		0	156	0
Gloves	Bloodseeker mail gauntlets	Intermediate	120	4.32	4.8		1	168	2
Gloves	Knight's mail gauntlets	Intermediate	124.8	4.2	4.7		1	200	15
Gloves	Stark mail gauntlets	Intermediate	130	4.1	4.7		2	24	0
Gloves	Lannister mail gauntlets	Intermediate	135	3.96	4.4		2	56	14
Gloves	Davos Seaworth's gloves	Intermediate	140	4	4.6	Chance of bonus loot: +8%; Damage +10% on an opponent who doesn't attack you	3	192	0
Gloves	Wildling heavy gloves	Heavy	82	5	10		0	11	4
Gloves	Worn plate gauntlets	Heavy	84	6	12		0	12	0
Gloves	Sellsword plate gauntlets	Heavy	90	5.88	11.8		0	19	3
Gloves	Sarwyck plate gauntlets	Heavy	96	5.76	11.6		0	26	6
Gloves	Vale of Arryn plate gauntlets	Heavy	102	5.64	11.3		0	33	10
Gloves	Gold Cloak plate gauntlets	Heavy	114	5.76	10.9		0	120	0
Gloves	Warrior's plate gauntlets	Heavy	120	5.64	10.7		0	137	15
Gloves	Castlewood plate gauntlets	Heavy	132	5.4	10.4		0	174	0
Gloves	Gerold Hightower's gauntlets	Heavy	138	5.28	10.2	Strength +1	0	184	8
Gloves	Bloodseeker plate gauntlets	Heavy	144	5.52	10		2	0	0
Gloves	Knight's gauntlets	Heavy	150	5.4	9.7		2	35	15
Gloves	Lannister plate gauntlets	Heavy	162	5.16	9.2		2	108	2
Gloves	Strong Belwas' gauntlets	Heavy	152	5.6	11	Chance of critical hit +2%; chance to inflict Stunned (2 sec) with each attack: 2%	4	72	0
Boots	Leather shoes	None	35	2	1.8		0	9	0
Boots	Gold Cloak's leather boots	Light	98	4.2	4.4		0	0	0
Boots	Wildling leather boots	Light	70	3	4		0	8	2
Boots	Studded leather boots	Light	75	4.5	5.1		0	9	0
Boots	Flexible leather boots	Light	72	4	4.7		0	9	6
Boots	Vale of Arryn leather boots	Light	88	4.05	4.7		0	16	8
Boots	Sellsword leather boots	Light	79	4.35	5		0	16	8
Boots	Sarwyck leather boots	Light	84	4.2	4.8		0	24	0
Boots	Leather boots	Light	75	4.5	5.1		0	30	6
Boots	Gold Cloak's leather boots	Light	98	4.2	4.4		0	116	4
Boots	Studded leather boots	Light	102	4.05	4.2		0	135	0
Boots	Castlewood studded leather boots	Light	111	3.75	3.9		0	172	8
Boots	Bloodseeker leather boots	Light	120	3.9	3.6		2	0	0

Class	Name	Type	Health	Energy Cost	Deflection Penalty	Bonus	Cost		
							Golden Dragons	Silver Stages	Groats
Boots	Studded leather boots	Light	124	3.75	3		2	37	8
Boots	Lannister leather boots	Light	134	3.45	3.2		2	112	8
Boots	Syrio Forel's dueling boots	Light	140	3	2.5	Deflection +8%; Dodge +4%	4	75	0
Boots	Wildling mail chausses	Intermediate	80	3	6		0	11	4
Boots	Mail chausses	Intermediate	90	6	7.5		0	12	0
Boots	Sellsword mail chausses	Intermediate	96	5.85	7.4		0	20	4
Boots	Sarwyck mail chausses	Intermediate	102	5.7	7.3		0	28	8
Boots	Vale of Arryn mail chausses	Intermediate	108	5.55	7.1		0	36	12
Boots	Gold Cloak's mail chausses	Intermediate	120	5.7	6.8		0	133	2
Boots	Warrior's mail chausses	Intermediate	126	5.55	6.6		0	153	12
Boots	Castlewood mail chausses	Intermediate	138	5.25	6.3		0	195	0
Boots	Bloodseeker mail chausses	Intermediate	150	5.4	6		2	52	8
Boots	Knight's mail chausses	Intermediate	156	5.25	5.9		2	93	12
Boots	Stark mail chausses	Intermediate	162	5.1	5.9		2	135	0
Boots	Lannister mail chausses	Intermediate	168	4.95	5.6		2	176	4
Boots	Turnover boots	Intermediate	170	4.9	5.3	Energy cost -10%; 1 in 6 chance to receive Knocked Down (3s) for each failed attack	4	187	8
Boots	Wildling heavy boots	Heavy	95	6	14		0	13	12
Boots	Iron boots	Heavy	105	7	15		0	15	0
Boots	Sellsword boots	Heavy	112	7.35	14.7		0	24	0
Boots	Sarwyck plate boots	Heavy	112	7.35	14.5		0	33	0
Boots	Vale of Arryn plate boots	Heavy	127	7.05	15		0	42	0
Boots	Gold Cloak's plate boots	Heavy	143	7.2	13.7		0	150	0
Boots	Warrior's plate boots	Heavy	150	7.05	13.4		0	172	8
Boots	Castlewood plate boots	Heavy	165	6.75	13.1		1	7	8
Boots	Valarr's plate boots	Heavy	180	6.9	12		2	105	0
Boots	Bloodseeker plate boots	Heavy	180	6.9	12		2	105	0
Boots	Knight's boots	Heavy	187	6.75	12.2		2	150	0
Boots	Lannister plate boots	Heavy	203	6.45	11.6		3	30	0
Cloak	Wildling cloak	Light	27	2	2.2		0	3	12
Cloak	Old cloak	Light	28	1.9	2.1		0	4	13
Cloak	Red priest cloak	Light	28	1.3	1.4		0	5	5
Cloak	Sellsword cloak	Light	31.8	1.74	2		0	6	10
Cloak	Sarwyck cloak	Light	33.6	1.68	2		0	9	10
Cloak	Vale of Arryn cloak	Light	32	1.62	1.9		0	12	10
Cloak	Lord's cloak	Light	34	1.6	1.8		0	40	10
Cloak	Recruiter's cloak	Light	35	1.3	1.7	Dodge +3% (affects only Mors)	0	0	0
Cloak	City Watch cloak	Light	39	1.7	1.6		0	53	4
Cloak	City Watch cloak	Light	39	1.7	1.6		0	0	0
Cloak	Knight's cloak	Light	40.8	1.7	1.62		0	61	8
Cloak	Tyrell cloak	Light	39	1.5	1.4	Energy Recovery per second +1	0	62	8
Cloak	Castlewood cloak	Light	44.4	1.5	1.6		0	69	0
Cloak	Alester's cloak	Light	33	1.4	1.5		0	80	3
Cloak	Sarwyck Giltwaters	Light	34	1.7	1.9	Bargaining chance +6%	0	89	6
Cloak	Lord's cloak	Light	49	1.4	1.3		0	183	2
Cloak	Lannister cloak	Light	52	1.5	1.3		1	3	0
Cloak	Myrish silk cloak	Light	53	1.6	1	Health increases by 2% for every deflection; Health increases by 5% for every dodge	2	196	8

Class	Name	Type	Health	Energy Cost	Deflection Penalty	Bonus	Cost		
							Golden Dragons	Silver Stages	Groats
Cloak	Ilyn Payne's executioner's cloak	Light	55	1.8	1.5	Chance of 5% to execute your opponent when he has less than 20% health (does not work on elites and boss)	3	54	0
Cloak	Recruiting officer's cloak	Light	56	1.7	1	After each Dodge, your next attack will be a critical hit.	3	120	0
Shield	Worn small wooden shield	x	55	4.2	4.8		0	0	0
Shield	Small wooden shield	x	70	4.2	4.8		0	25	2
Shield	Small iron shield	x	84	5.6	7		0	33	9
Shield	Worn large shield	x	98	7	14		0	42	0
Shield	Sarwyck shield	x	105	6.86	13.7		0	92	7
Shield	Vale of Arryn great shield	x	119	6.58	13.2		0	117	9
Shield	Gold cloak small shield	x	91	3.92	4.1		0	130	2
Shield	Gold cloak shield	x	112	5.32	6.3		0	149	1
Shield	Worn warrior's shield	x	95.2	3.78	3.9		0	151	2
Shield	Gold cloak large shield	x	133	6.72	12.7		0	168	0
Shield	Warrior's shield	x	117.6	5.18	6.2		0	172	2
Shield	Worn knight's shield	x	140	6.58	12.5		0	193	2
Shield	Castlewood shield	x	154	6.3	12.2		1	33	9
Shield	Small ornate shield	x	116	3.5	3.2		1	46	2
Shield	Large shield	x	145.6	4.9	5.5		1	77	10
Shield	Bloodseeker shield	x	168	6.44	11.6		1	84	0
Shield	Knight's shield	x	175	6.3	11.3		1	109	2
Shield	Lannister shield	x	172	6	10.8		1	159	9
Shield	Baratheon guard shield	x	160	5	12	For the Resistance defensive ability: The duration of the effect increases from 10s to 15s	2	0	0
Shield	Tytos Lannister's shield	x	175	6.16	11.9	Damage Resistance +4%	3	0	0
Shield	Lord Commander Qorgyle's shield	x	185	9	12	Chance to resist to the state Stunned +30%	5	0	0

Jewels

Name	Description	Bonus	Cost		
			Golden Dragons	Silver Stags	Groats
Seal of Knowledge	This seal is used by the masters of the Citadel to seal scholarly documents. As they are rare, they can fetch a good price.		0	12	0
Silver ring	A ring of good quality.	Health recovery +10%	0	34	6
Gold ring	A gaudy ring, worn by wealthy merchants.	Damage +5%; hit chance +3%	0	46	14
Steel signet ring	A fine ring, worn by nobles or men-at-arms.	For each opponent killed:-Restores 30 health points	0	148	7
Gold signet ring	A beautiful gold-plated ring, worn by powerful men.	For every dodge: chance of critical hit +5% (max of +30%)	1	102	8
Amber seal	An engraved amber seal worn by wealthy lords with lands.	Strength +1; hit chance +5%; Deflection +5%	7	80	0
Diamond seal	A very precious seal, worn only by the wealthiest lords of Westeros.	Endurance +1; Intelligence +1; Luck +1; Energy recovery +20%	15	0	0
Gawen's fixed locket	The locket that was found in King's Landing. It has been meticulously fixed and cleaned of traces of blood.	Health max +80	0	0	0
Mors Westford's collar	Forged in the Westerlands, this collar is all that remains of his old life as a knight.	Damage +4%	0	32	14
Red priest ring	Alester has not parted from this ring since he became a red priest.	Hit chance +7%	0	41	4
Neck ring of the First Men	Neck ring worn by the last hero.	Luck +1	0	92	14
Ring of the Lioness	A ring engraved by smiths of House Lannister for Queen Cersei.	Bargaining chance +8%; critical hit chance +2%	0	100	0

Name	Description	Bonus	Cost		
			Golden Dragons	Silver Stags	Groats
House Harlton signet	Forged by Martin for Harlton when his previous House signet was stolen.	Bargaining chance +10%; Dodge +2%	1	0	0
Baratheon signet ring	A ring engraved with a crowned stag.	Energy recovery +15%	1	1	14
Cerenna's amber pendant	A gift that Mors gave to his wife. It brings back fond memories (affects only Mors).	Damage Resistance +3%	1	51	14
Raynald Sarwyck's collar	Raynald inherited this collar of the Sarwyck family, which is worn for official ceremonies.	Health Recovery +8/s	1	71	4
Symbol of defiance		Damage +5% below 25% of health	2	64	6
Wildling bracelet	Your dog obeys the finger and the eye.	Dog command recharge speed +14%; Dog attack speed +16%; Dog dodge +10%	2	126	14
Master pyromancer's ring	An old ring with a large ruby, which sparkles in proximity to an open flame.	Burning weapon duration +2s	3	26	4
Ashes of the Seven	These ashes are a symbol of Alester's devotion to R'hllor (affects only Alester).	Energy recovery +30%	10	0	0
Glory of the Seven	The Glory of the Seven represents the sense of duty and unfailing devotion of your family (affects only Mors).	Health max +120; Energy cost -25%	10	0	0
Strangler	This poison gradually chokes the life out of your opponent until the fight is over, inflicting more and more damage as time passes.	Cumulative damage: +3 health points/second (max at 60/s)	0	25	0

Quests Objects

Name	Quests	Description	Cost		
			Golden Dragons	Silver Stags	Groats
A ranger's personal belongings	Quest 1	The bag of a Sworn Brother containing his personal belongings and equipment.	x	x	x
Icemark keys	Quest 1	The keys to Icemark, which Mormont gave to Cregan to enable him to patrol in the ancient fortress abandoned by the Night's Watch.	x	x	x
Letter from Jon Arryn	Quest 3	Letter from Jon Arryn written to the hero of Stag's Mount.	x	x	x
Key to the Red Keep's cells	Quest 4		x	x	x
Letter from Falena	Quest 4	A woman's letter, addressed to Gawen.	x	x	x
Letter from Gawen	Quest 4	A note bearing Gawen's signature that became wrinkled during its turbulent voyage.	x	x	x
Hen's keys	Quest 5		x	x	x
Bartram's saddlebag	Quest 6	Bartram's scent is on this leather bag, which contains lots of supplies and 20 silver stags.	0	24	5
Key to the master bedchamber of Mole's Town brothel	Quest 7	This small and well-used key gives access to the most spacious bedchamber in Mole's Town's whorehouse.	x	x	x
Gawen's broken locket	Quest 8	This broken locket used to belong to Dorna Sarwyck but was left to Gawen upon her death.	x	x	x
Key to Orys' cell	Quest 8		x	x	x
Key to the arena private entrance	Quest 8	A dark gray key.	x	x	x
Key to the sewer drain	Quest 8	A small rusty key that opens a drain in the sewers.	x	x	x
Letter to Commander Janos	Quest 8		x	x	x
Reapers' master key	Quest 8	An old and damaged key.	x	x	x
Letter from Falena	Quest 8	A letter from Gawen's mistress, found on his body.	x	x	x
Letter to the commander of the City Watch	Quest 8	Correspondence between Valarr and the commander of the City Watch, Janos Slynt.	x	x	x
Bunch of keys to Riverspring Castle	Quest 9	A set containing many keys.	x	x	x
Raynald's master key	Quest 9		x	x	x
The Brotherhood documents	Quest 9	These encrypted documents have probably been written by Raynald Sarwyck.	x	x	x

Name	Quests	Description	Cost		
			Golden Dragons	Silver Stags	Groats
The Crone's key	Quest 9		x	x	x
The Father's key	Quest 9		x	x	x
The Maiden's key	Quest 9		x	x	x
The Mother's key	Quest 9		x	x	x
The Smith's key	Quest 9		x	x	x
The Stranger's key	Quest 9		x	x	x
The Warrior's key	Quest 9		x	x	x
The Collector must be killed	Quest 9	A missive from Harlton for the attention of Raynald Sarwyck.	x	x	x
Minutes of the Shadow Council	Quest 9	An official document of Harlton's Brotherhood.	x	x	x
A guard's helm	Quest 11	This full helmet belonged to one of Castlewood's guards.	x	x	x
Archives of the Brotherhood	Quest 11	These encrypted documents contain the names of all members of the organization.	x	x	x
Castlewood executioner's keys	Quest 11	A bunch of dirty and rusty keys.	x	x	x
Heart's bane	Quest 11	An extremely powerful poison.	x	x	x
Key to Castlewood's high tower	Quest 11	A wrought-iron key made for an intricate lock.	x	x	x
Keys to Castlewood Keep	Quest 11	Heavy wrought-iron keys.	x	x	x
Ointments	Quest 11	A salve to treat injuries as well as an infusion of dreamwine to ease pain.	x	x	x
The hunting party	Quest 11	An official document of Harlton's Brotherhood.	x	x	x
Concerns	Quest 11	A letter from Raynald Sarwyck.	x	X	x
Missive from beyond the narrow sea	Quest 11	An official document of Harlton's Brotherhood.	x	x	x
Letter from Marianne	Quest 11	A loose sheet of paper has been slipped inside the book that Lady Marianne had sent to you.	x	x	x
Jorah's signet ring	Quest 13	A gleaming ring of solid gold engraved with the Blood-seekers' emblem.	x	x	x
Key to Riverspring's cells	Quest 13	A heavy key showing the Sarwyck family emblem.	x	x	x
Harlton's bunch of keys	Quest 14		x	x	x
Key to Castlewood cellar	Quest 14		x	x	x
Key to Castlewood's southeast tower	Quest 14	A little copper key.	x	x	x
Key to Mole's Town crime scene	Quest 14		x	x	x
Key to the sewers	Quest 15	A small and poorly forged iron key.	x	x	x
Silver key	Quest 15	A finely wrought silver key that opens the secret hideout of Petyr and Stevron, the pyromancers.	x	x	x
Letter from Valarr to the pyromancers	Quest 15	A letter of fine quality bearing the seal of the Blood-seekers.	x	x	x
The Crone	Side Quest 1: The Faith of Our Ancestors	The Crone symbolizes wisdom and the experience of age.	x	x	x
The Father	Side Quest 1: The Faith of Our Ancestors	This figurine depicts the Father, a bearded man in the prime of his life and wearing a crown.	x	x	x
The Maiden	Side Quest 1: The Faith of Our Ancestors	This statuette depicts the Maiden, a beautiful young woman with perfect form.	x	x	x
The Mother	Side Quest 1: The Faith of Our Ancestors	This statuette depicts the Mother, a middle-aged woman with a kind smile.	x	x	x
The Smith	Side Quest 1: The Faith of Our Ancestors	This statuette depicts the Smith wielding a hammer in his muscled arms.	1	20	0
The Stranger	Side Quest 1: The Faith of Our Ancestors	The Stranger is the eternal outcast. He represents death and comes to take the faithful to the other side.	x	x	x

Name	Quests	Description	Cost		
			Golden Dragons	Silver Stags	Groats
The Warrior	Side Quest 1: The Faith of Our Ancestors	The Warrior is the protector of the Faith of the Seven.	x	x	x
Jonos' loot	Side Quest 5: The Black Bloodhound	An extraordinary mess containing written notes of debts owed signed by most of the Night's Watch as well as several hundred copper coins.	0	115	10
Moon tea	Side Quest 7: Self-Made Girl	A cloth sachet that emits a strong scent of herbs.	x	x	x
Ser Gyles' purse	Side Quest 7: Self-Made Girl	A leather purse containing the coin that Ser Gyles owes Chataya. It is surprisingly heavy.	x	x	x
Bethany's plea for help	Side Quest 7: Self-Made Girl	A message that Bethany requested be delivered to Ser Gyles Langward.	x	x	x
Crumpled letter	Side Quest 7: Self-Made Girl	A letter written by the hand of Ser Gyles, addressed to Bethany.	x	x	x
Key to the Collector's cellars	Side Quest 10: Avenge Riverspring		x	x	x
Key to the Collector's slave cells	Side Quest 10: Avenge Riverspring		x	x	x
A most rewarding transaction	Side Quest 10: Avenge Riverspring	A trading document.	x	x	x
Initiation of Collector into the Shadow Council	Side Quest 10: Avenge Riverspring	An official document of Harlton's Brotherhood.	x	x	x
Seizure	Side Quest 10: Avenge Riverspring	A missive for the Collector.	x	x	x
A message from the Wall	Side Quest 13: Not So Wild	A missive that has suffered from the elements. It has been carried by a raven over many a land since leaving Castle Black.	x	x	x

Quests

Quest Name	Type	Location	Quest Giver	Experience	Special Rewards
For This Night and All Nights to Come	Primary Quest 1	Castle Black	Lord Commander Mormont	1,500	Quest Rewards
The Faith of Our Ancestors	Side Quest 1	Common Hall	Walder	900	62 Silver Stags, Ashes of the Seven (Alester) or Glory of the Seven (Mors)
Their Watch Is Ending	Side Quest 2	Icemark	Cregan	100	Quest Rewards
For All the Days Gone By	Primary Quest 2	Riverspring	Automatic	1,825	Quest Rewards
Between a Hunter and His Prey	Primary Quest 3	Icemark	Automatic	2,000	Quest Rewards
Treasure Hunt	Side Quest 3	The Gift	Ondrew	200	50 Silver Stags
The Lion's Will	Primary Quest 4	King's Landing	Automatic	1,260	Quest Rewards
Beauty and the Beast	Primary Quest 5	Castle Black	Lord Commander Mormont	1,650	Quest Rewards
The Crown's Dogs	Primary Quest 6	Throne Room of the Red Keep	Queen Cersei	1,500	Quest Rewards
Silence in the Ranks	Side Quest 4	Throne Room of the Red Keep	Ser Uthor Donnerly	200	Ring of the Lioness
Stray Dogs	Primary Quest 7	Castle Black	Lord Commander Mormont	1,440	Quest Rewards
The Black Bloodhound	Side Quest 5	Common Hall	Addam Flowers	100	None
New Blood	Side Quest 6	Common Hall	Lord Commander Mormont	600	62 Silver Stags, Recruiter's Cloak
A New Hope	Primary Quest 8	Throne Room of the Red Keep	Automatic	1,250	Quest Rewards
Self-Made Girl	Side Quest 7	King's Landing	Hubb	250	93 Silver Stags, the Maiden
Blood on the Sand	Side Quest 8	King's Landing	Ossifer	0	8 Golden Dragons
Legacy	Primary Quest 9	Riverspring	Automatic	1,500	Quest Rewards
Rings and Chains	Side Quest 9	Riverspring Castle	Elyana	240	93 Silver Stags
Avenge Riverspring	Side Quest 10	Tunnels of Riverspring	Documents in secret Brotherhood chamber	320	187 Silver Stags, Gerold Hightower's Gauntlets, The Stranger
Promise	Primary Quest 10	Westford Cottage	Automatic	1,350	Quest Rewards
Crossroads	Primary Quest 11	Castlewood	Automatic	1,580	Quest Rewards
The Maggot in the Apple	Side Quest 11	Castlewood Castle	Gawen	100	Fewer enemies in "Crossroads" quest
Breaking Point	Primary Quest 12	Riverspring	Automatic	1,640	Quest Rewards
Safer Streets	Side Quest 12	Riverspring	Harwyn	100	None
Fight Fire with Fire	Primary Quest 13	Tunnels of Riverspring	Automatic	1,000	Quest Rewards
Bounds	Primary Quest 14	Riverspring Castle	Automatic	2,485	Quest Rewards
Not So Wild	Side Quest 13	Riverspring	Harwyn	985	Wilding Bracelet (if Sabraque survives)
Rituals and Litanies	Side Quest 14	Castle Black	Duncan Paege	850	Shadow Fiend
Light and Shadow	Primary Quest 15	King's Landing	Automatic	1,250	Quest Rewards
Old Scar	Primary Quest 16	Westford Cottage	Automatic	0	None
Ice and Fire	Primary Quest 17	Throne Room of the Red Keep	Automatic	500	None

STANCES

Stances	Names	Required Weapons	Ability Types	Descriptions	Effects	Bonus Effects
Assassination	Sneak Attack	One-handed weapon	Damage	Take advantage of an unsuspecting opponent to inflict significant damage.	- Damage x1.8	"If your opponent is not targeting you: - Damage x3"
Assassination	Deterring Strike	One-handed weapon	Area Damage	Unleash a swift circular attack that sends your opponents (within a range of 3 meters) fleeing. This ability is executed from your current position.	"- Damage x0.7 - Your opponents will attack your teammate (if you have one)."	62 Silver Stags, Ashes of the Seven (Alester) or Glory of the Seven (Mors)
Assassination	Blinding Dust	One-handed weapon	Interrupt	Stun and disorient your opponent by precisely tossing dust into their eyes.	- Stunned (2s)	
Assassination	Precision Strike	One-handed weapon	Damage over time	Land a well-aimed strike that is intended to weaken the target over time with blood loss.	"- Damage x1.2 - Bleed (4s)"	"If your opponent is already Bleeding: - Bleed (10s)"
Assassination	Unbowing	One-handed weapon	Defensive	Ignore damage for a short period of time when on the brink of death.	- You become Invincible (5s) when you have 10% health remaining.	
Assassination	Poisoned weapon	One-handed weapon	Poison	Apply Hemlock to your blade. Your next attack will poison your opponent.	"Hemlock poison (10s): - Attack speed -30% - Hit chance -20%"	
Assassination	Pommel Strike	One-handed weapon	Damage, Disarmament	Strike your opponent with the pommel of your sword.	- Damage x1.6	"If your opponent is in Counter-Attack - Disarmed"
Assassination	Savage Strike	One-handed weapon	Interrupt, Damage	Crown your opponent with a vicious blow.	- Damage x1.9	"If your opponent is Stunned: - Damage x3.2"
Assassination	Apothecary	x	Passive	You have learned the vagaries of poisoning and can now apply them to gain a great advantage.	- Sneak Attack will cause max damage to a opponent poisoned with Hemlock even when he is targeting you.	
Assassination	Assassin's Dance	x	Passive	You are free to focus on inflicting devastating strikes when not targeted by an opponent.	If no opponents are targeting you:- Chance of Critical Hit: +5%-Critical Damage +10%	
Assassination	Contagion	x	Passive	Your Hemlock poison can be spread to other opponents.	With every blow to an opponent poisoned by Hemlock:- Chance of 50% that Hemlock will spread (8s) to another opponent who is in a range of 4 meters around your opponent.	
Assassination	Guile	x	Passive	You take advantage of any opportunity during a fight.	- Damage +10% on opponents having the state Stunned, Knocked down or fighting an ally.	
Assassination	Thirst For Life	x	Passive	Your will to survive allows you to find a way out when things look grim.	When your health is lower than 50%:- Dodge +6%	

Assassination	Vicious	x	Passive	You tear into an inattentive opponent.	- Chance to inflict Bleeding (7s) with each attack on an opponent not attacking you: 15%	
Hardened Killer	Brutally Efficient	x	Passive	You finish off beaten enemies swiftly and more efficiently.	- Chance to kill an opponent with less than 50% health: 10%	
Hardened Killer	Energy Bonus	x	Passive	You are able to use more abilities in combat.	- Your energy increases from 100 to 110.	
Hardened Killer	Expert Poisoner	x	Passive	You have become a master in the use of poisons.	- Poisoned weapon will now inflict poison on your next three hits.	
Hardened Killer	Hardened Killer	x	Passive	You have grown more efficient at finishing off your opponents.	- Chance of Critical Hit on opponents with less than 30% of health: +7%	
Hardened Killer	Initiative	x	Passive	You have learned to end fights quickly and fight hard at the start of combat to gain the upper hand immediately.	You get the state Initiative (10s) at the start of each combat:- Damage +10%- Attack Speed +10%	
Hardened Killer	Intelligence Bonus	x	Passive	Your knowledge gained over time and in battle has boosted your intellect.	- Intelligence +1	
Hardened Killer	Ultimate Survival	x	Passive	Your keenly honed survival instincts help you recognize and escape dangerous situations.	When you use the ability Unbowing :- Invincible is now activated at 20% of health remaining (instead of 10%).	
Intensity	Bully	One-handed weapon	Support	Taunt your enemies so they rush towards you (within a range of 6 meters).	- Provoked (10s)	
Intensity	Calm as Still Water	One-handed weapon	Interrupt, Damage	Effortlessly find a flaw in your opponent's defense and knock him down.	"- Damage x0.8 - Knocked down 3s"	
Intensity	Retaliation	One-handed weapon	Damage	You are in a defensive position to strike back, ideal if you are surrounded.	"Counter-Attack (6s): - Dodge +10% - Damage x1.5 from each incoming attack. - Damage x2.5 from each dodge you succeed."	
Intensity	Fierce as a Wolverine	One-handed weapon	Damage	Disorient your opponent with a savage attack to reduce his accuracy.	"- Damage x1.5 - Hit chance -30% for the next attack of your opponent."	
Intensity	Light as a Feather	One-handed weapon	Immobilize, Damage	Immobilize your opponent by striking him in the legs.	- Damage x1.2- Immobilized (8s)	
Intensity	Quick as a Snake	One-handed weapon	Area Damage	Strike all the enemies surrounding you (within a range of 3 meters). This ability is executed from you current position.	- Damage x1	
Intensity	Strong as a Bear	One-handed weapon	Interrupt, Damage	Stun your opponent by striking them in the face.	"- Damage x1.2 - Stunned (3s)"	
Intensity	Sting of the Manticore	One-handed weapon	Damage	Strike a death blow to an opponent who has been knocked down.	- Damage x1.5	"If your opponent is Knocked down: - Damage x2 - Bleeding (4s)"

Stances	Names	Required Weapons	Ability Types	Descriptions	Effects	Bonus Effects
Intensity	Anticipation	x	Passive	You can read your enemies' movements, making it easier to ward off their predictable attacks.	- Deflection +1% with each attack received (max +25%).	
Intensity	Cocksure	x	Passive	Your confidence increases with every dodge you perform.	- Damage +5% after each dodge (max of +25%).	
Intensity	Opportunist	x	Passive	You know how to take advantage of beneficial situations when they arise.	If your opponent is Knocked down:- Guaranteed Critical Hit	
Intensity	Recuperative Defense	x	Passive	You are still able to deflect blows while recovering your energy.	- Deflection +20% when using the recovery ability.	
Intensity	Smooth as Summer Silk	x	Passive	You have learned how to move more fluidly and have a greater chance of successfully performing dodges when provoking enemies.	When using the ability Bully:- Deflection +8% (10s)- Dodge +12% (10s)	
Intensity	Vicious Circle	x	Passive	Your attacks are becoming more and more powerful.	- Chance of a Critical Hit +2% with each Critical Hit performed (max of +20%)	
Master Water Dancer	Agility Bonus	x	Passive	Your training as a water dancer has made you more agile.	- Agility +1	
Master Water Dancer	Energy Bonus	x	Passive	You are able to use more abilities in combat.	- Your energy increases from 100 to 110.	
Master Water Dancer	Hard Target	x	Passive	You have now mastered the art of dodging.	- 1 in 3 Deflections will automatically be a dodge	
Master Water Dancer	Master Water Dancer	x	Passive	A water dancer bases his strategy on fluidity and reacting. In this manner, he can find flaws in his opponent's defense.	- Chance to inflict Bleeding (7s) with each attack: 5%.- Health +5% with each dodge.	
Master Water Dancer	Sharp Sting of the Manticore	x	Passive	You take advantage of your enemies' moments of weakness to try and finish them off.	When your opponent is Knocked down, the impact of the ability Sting of the Manticore is increased:- Damage changes to x3- Bleeding increases from 4s to 8s.	
Master Water Dancer	Slippery as an Eel	x	Passive	You have an increased ability to dodge when you are looking for opportunities to counter-attack.	When you use the ability Retaliation:- Your dodge increases from +10% to +20%.	
Master Water Dancer	Surgical Precision	x	Passive	Your extremely accurate attacks help you exploit even the smallest of weaknesses in the opponent's armor.	If using a cutting or perforating weapon:- The ability Quick as a Snake inflicts Bleeding (6s)	
Dexterity	Smoke Bomb	Bow, crossbow	Support	Conceal yourself from your opponents in a cloud of smoke (if you do not have a teammate, your opponents will continue to attack you).	- Loss of aggressiveness	
Dexterity	Explosive Missile	Bow, crossbow	Area Interrupt, Damage	Hurl an explosive projectile at your opponent. All opponents fighting within 3 meters of the target are affected.	"- Damage: 120 health points - Stunned 3s"	
Dexterity	Focus	Bow, crossbow	Support	Take time to regain your energy while focusing on your enemies.	"- Forced to not attack for 2s - Energy gain: 25/100"	

Dexterity	Discourteous Kick		Interrupt, Damage	Kick your opponent in the groin.	"- Damage: 75 health points - Bleeding (12s)"	
Dexterity	Paralyzing Powder	Bow, crossbow	Immobilize	Throw paralyzing powder at the opponents facing you (within a 120° cone over 4 meters).	- Immobilized (7s)	
Dexterity	Poisoned Missile	Bow, crossbow	Poison	Apply Hemlock to your projectile. Your attack will poison your opponent.	"Hemlock poison (10s): - Attack speed -30% - Hit chance -20%"	
Dexterity	Rapid Fire	Bow, crossbow	Support, damage	Shoot frantically at your opponent.	"- Attack Speed +25% against your target - The effect will stop if an attack misses or if you change targets"	
Dexterity	Head Shot	Bow, crossbow	Interrupt, Damage	Take time to aim at your opponent's head.	"- Damage x1.7 - Knocked down (3s)"	
Dexterity	Chirurgeon	x	Passive	You are able to target your opponent's wound.	If your opponent is Bleeding:- Chance of Critical Hit: +20%- Each Critical Hit will Immobilize the opponent (7s)	
Dexterity	Deft Reloads	x	Passive	Your time spent training allows you to reload your weapon more quickly.	- Reload Speed +10%	
Dexterity	Impact	x	Passive	Your missiles hit with greater force, which increases the chance of immobilizing your opponent.	- Chance to inflict Immobilized (8s) with each attack: 5%.	
Dexterity	Sequential Shot	x	Passive	You become more accurate when repeatedly firing at the same target, inflicting more critical hits.	- Hit chance +3% with each attack on the same target- Critical Hit for every 5 attacks ??on the same target	
Dexterity	Skilled Marksman	x	Passive	You require less time to aim at your opponents.	- Aiming Speed +15%	
Dexterity	Target Practice	x	Passive	You need less time to shoot at immobilized enemies.	If your opponent is Immobilized:- Attack Speed +20%	
Elite Archer	Agility Bonus	x	Passive	Your experience acquired while fighting at a distance has helped increase your agility.	- Agility +1	
Elite Archer	Dead Eye	x	Passive	Your critical strikes are now very precise.	- Chance to inflict Dead Eye with each Critical Hit: 50%Dead Eye:- Hit chance -10%	
Elite Archer	Elite Archer	x	Passive	You have become an expert in fighting at a distance.	- Critical Damage +5%- Hit chance +10%- Deflection +5%- Energy recovery +5%	
Elite Archer	Energy Bonus	x	Passive	You are able to use more abilities in combat.	- Your energy increases from 100 to 110.	
Elite Archer	Fire Volley	x	Passive	Your skill with ranged weapons allows you to launch projectiles much quicker.	- The attack speed provided by the ability Rapid Fire increases from +25% to +30%.	
Elite Archer	Point Blank	x	Passive	You have become very accurate and effective when an opponent engages in hand-to-hand combat.	If your opponent is using a melee weapon:- Chance to inflict Stunned (5s) with each attack: 5%.	
Elite Archer	Top Shot	x	Passive	You have become one of the finest marksmen in all the land, able to place your shots precisely where you want them.	- Chance of Critical Hit: +5%	

Stances	Names	Required Weapons	Ability Types	Descriptions	Effects	Bonus Effects
Domination	Earthquaker	Two-handed weapon	Area Interrupt	Make the ground shake to stun all nearby opponents (within a range of 4 meters). This ability is executed from your current position.	- Stunned (2s)	
Domination	Devastation	Two-handed weapon	Area Damage	Perform a massive strike against all opponents in front of you (within a 160° cone over 3 meters).	- Damage x1.3	
Domination	Headbutt	All	Interrupt, Damage	Grab your opponent and headbutt him.	- Damage x1	"If your opponent is Stunned: - Damage x2"
Domination	Upheaval	Two-handed weapon	Interrupt, Damage	Knock your opponent to the ground with a violent blow.	"- Damage x1.3 - Knocked down (3s)"	
Domination	Massacre	Two-handed weapon	Area Damage	Unleash a wild swing that strikes all enemies (within a range of 3 meters). This ability is executed from your current position.	- Damage x1.1	
Domination	Pierce	Two-handed weapon	Damage	Pierce through your opponent's armor and cause them to bleed.	"- Damage x1.2 - Bleeding (5s)"	"If your opponent has medium armor: - Bleeding (10s)"
Domination	Add Injury to Injury	Two-handed weapon	Damage	Direct an attack at your opponent's existing wound.	- Damage x1.2	"If your opponent is Bleeding: - Damage x1.8"
Domination	Death From Above	Two-handed weapon	Damage	Raise your weapon to the skies and strike your opponent in the face.	- Damage x1.2	"If your opponent is Knocked down: - Damage x2.4"
Domination	Born to Fight	x	Passive	Your strike your enemies with greater force.	- 1 in 5 hits will be a critical hit.	
Domination	Butcher	x	Passive	You are ruthless and cause greater damage to enemies who are Stunned or Knocked Down.	If your opponent is Stunned or Knocked down:- Damage +10%	
Domination	Ferocity	x	Passive	Your have unmatched physical strength thanks to your training.	- When inflicting Stunned and Knocked down, they now last +1s	
Domination	Hard Head	x	Passive	You are more resistant to stun attacks.	- Chance to resist Stunned: +20%.	
Domination	The Sight of Blood	x	Passive	Your unquenchable thirst for violence is further fueled by the sight of blood.	After each kill:- Damage +5%- Attack Speed +3%	
Domination	Unflinching	x	Passive	Your excellent physical condition helps you withstand attacks that would normally knock you over.	- Chance to resist Knocked down: +25%.	
Elite Warrior	Body of a Warrior	x	Passive	Your use of two-handed weapons has helped you gain extremely well-developed muscles.	- Damage resistance +6%	
Elite Warrior	Energy Bonus	x	Passive	You are able to use more abilities in combat.	- Your energy increases from 100 to 110.	
Elite Warrior	Eternal Rest	x	Passive	Your strength you gained in combat helps you knock down several enemies.	- The ability Massacre now knocks down (2s) opponents who have the state Immobilized.	

Elite Warrior	Gruesome	x	Passive	You can re-open your enemies' wounds with greater ease.	The ability Add Injury to Injury inflicts more damage to an opponent who has the state Bleeding:- Damage x2	
Elite Warrior	Shockwave	x	Passive	Your attacks now shake the very ground you stand on.	The ability Earthquaker now inflicts damage:- Damage x0.5	
Elite Warrior	Strength Bonus	x	Passive	Your have become stronger as a result of the rigors of serving on the Wall.	- Strength +1	
Elite Warrior	Strong Constitution	x	Passive	You have toughened your body to the point that some poisons no longer have an effect on you.	- Hemlock, Blindeye and Manticore's venom no longer affect you	
Frenzy	Bloody Frenzy	Two weapons (one-handed)	Support	Whip yourself and all your allies into a rage.	"Bloody Frenzy (15s): - Damage +6% - Attack speed +8%"	
Frenzy	Flurry of Blows	Two weapons (one-handed)	Damage	Hammer your opponent with blow after blow.	"- Hit 1: Damage x1.2 - Hit 2: Damage x1.4 - Hit 3: Damage x2"	
Frenzy	Fury	Two weapons (one-handed)	Support	Become enraged for a short period and go Berserk if your health drops below 50%.	"Berserk (25s): - Attack Speed +20% - Damage +12% - Loss of control"	
Frenzy	Rage	Two weapons (one-handed)	Area Damage	Attack all your enemies (within a range of 3 meters). This ability is executed from your current position.	- Damage x1.2	
Frenzy	Slash	Two weapons (one-handed)	Prolonged Damage	Slash your opponent to make him bleed.	"- Damage x1.2 - Bleeding (7s)"	
Frenzy	Cutthroat	Two weapons (one-handed)	Interrupt, Damage	Attempt to slit your opponent's throat. The lower your opponent's health, the less chance he has of dodging.		"- Damage x4 - Bleeding 7s - Knocked down 4s"
Frenzy	Vicious Hit	Two weapons (one-handed)	Damage	Make the most of your opponent's blood loss to inflict serious damage and stun him.	- Damage x1.4	"If your opponent is Bleeding: - Damage x2.2 - Stunned (4s)"
Frenzy	Victorious Assault	Two weapons (one-handed)	Damage	Mercilessly attack an opponent who has been Knocked down.	- Damage x0.8	"If your opponent is Knocked down: - Damage x2.8 - Health +15%"
Frenzy	Revenge	x	Passive	You avenge every critical blow you receive.	- When you receive a Critical Hit, your next attack will inflict Bleeding (8s)	
Frenzy	Self-Control	x	Passive	You are able to walk the knife's edge between madness and clarity of thought in combat.	When you are under Berserk:- You no longer lose control of your character.- You steal 40 health points to your opponent with each attack.	

Stances	Names	Required Weapons	Ability Types	Descriptions	Effects	Bonus Effects
Frenzy	Tireless	x	Passive	Your abilities require less energy as your armor takes damage.	- Energy Cost -10% with each 20% of health lost.	
Frenzy	Tough Nut	x	Passive	You've learned from all the bad hits you've taken and have figured out how to protect yourself from similar attacks.	- Damage resistance +4% with each Critical Hit received (max of +20%)	
Frenzy	Trance	x	Passive	You enter into a trance when about to die.	- Energy Recovery +10% when you have less than 50% health.	
Frenzy	Warrior's Aura	x	Passive	You and your allies become invigorated each time you succeed in interrupting an opponent.	For each time you interrupt an opponent's ability:- Critical Hit chance +5% for you and all your allies (max at +25%)	
Berserker	Desensitization	x	Passive	You are no longer affected by pain, allowing you to better inflict it onto others.	- Damage +5% with each 20% of health lost (max of +20%).	
Berserker	Energy Bonus	x	Passive	You are able to use more abilities in combat.	- Your energy increases from 100 to 110.	
Berserker	Frenzied Fury	x	Passive	Your attack speed when Enraged (ability: Fury) is now increased.	When you are Enraged :- Attack speed +10%	
Berserker	Killer Instinct	x	Passive	Your incredible will to win pushes you beyond normal limits until you have crushed your enemies beneath your boot.	- Critical Damage +8%- Critical hit chance +3%	
Berserker	Luck Bonus	x	Passive	Your combat experience now helps you tip the scales in a number of imperceptible ways.	- Luck +1	
Berserker	Rain of Blood	x	Passive	Your penchant for violence manifests itself more and more over the course of a fight.	- The ability Cutthroat now inflicts Bleeding for 15s (instead of 7s).	
Berserker	Sacred Fury	x	Passive	Sacred Fury is the final state of the Berserker, a cross between man and wild beast.	While going Berserk, your rage is is fueled by pain. With each attack received:- Attack Speed +2% (max of +20%).- Critical hit chance +3% (max of +30%).	
Defense	Shield Strike	Shield	Interrupt, Damage	Upend your opponent with a violent blow from your shield.	"- Damage x1 - Stunned (4s)"	"If your opponent has no shield: - Knocked down (3s)"
Defense	Daze Strike	Shield	Interrupt, Damage	Stun your opponent by slamming your shield into his face.	"- Damage x0.7 - Stunned (2s)"	
Defense	Targeted Strike	Sword, axe, mace (one-handed)	Interrupt, Damage	Strike your opponent in an open wound.	- Damage x1.4	"If your opponent is already Bleeding: - Damage x2.5"
Defense	Taunt	Sword, axe, mace (one-handed)	Support	Deride all opponents with your rapier wit to incite them to attack you (within a range of 10 meters).	- Provoked (13s)	
Defense	Quick Fix	Sword, axe, mace (one-handed)	Defensive	Patch up your armor to repair battle damage.	- Health +20%	

Defense	Resistance	Shield	Defensive	Temporarily increase your damage resistance.	"Resistance (10s) - Damage resistance +35%"	
Defense	Self Defense	Sword, axe, mace (one-handed)	Damage	Unleash a series of strikes.	"- Hit 1: Damage x1 - Hit 2: Damage x1.2"	"If your opponent attacks you: - Hit 3: damage x1.6"
Defense	Massive Strike	Sword, axe, mace (one-handed)	Area Damage	Smash your opponents all around you (within a range of 3 meters). This ability is executed from your current position.	"- Damage x1.2 - Chance to inflict Bleeding (6s) to each opponent: 25%."	
Defense	Clenched Teeth	x	Passive	You have developed a high tolerance for pain.	- Health Recovery +10% for each Critical Hit received (max of +50%).	
Defense	Fighting Spirit	x	Passive	Your fighting spirit inspires your nearby comrades.	- Damage +5% for your allies.	
Defense	Flawless Armor	x	Passive	You are more resistant to attacks while recovering.	- Damage Resistance +40% when using the recovery ability.	
Defense	Physical Strength	x	Passive	You are tougher and your enemies have greater difficulty in overpowering you.	- Chance to resist Stunned or Knocked down: +10%.	
Defense	Stalwart Defender	x	Passive	You defend better when the odds are stacked against you.	When 3 or more enemies are attacking you:- Dodge +6%- Chance of Critical Hit: +7%	
Defense	Tactician	x	Passive	You show your true potential when surrounded, and all members of your team, yourself included, inflict more damage.	- Damage +10% when 3 or more opponents attack you	
Elite Knight	Endurance Bonus	x	Passive	Your duties defending Westeros as part of the Night's Watch have toughened you up.	- Endurance +1	
Elite Knight	Energy Bonus	x	Passive	You are able to use more abilities in combat.	- Your energy increases from 100 to 110.	
Elite Knight	Enhancing Health	x	Passive	You can withstand more attacks before succumbing.	- Health max +75	
Elite Knight	Natural Recovery	x	Passive	You have grown accustomed to long and challenging fights.	- Health Recovery +20% for every 10s spent in combat (max of +100%).	
Elite Knight	Punishing Blows	x	Passive	You have learned how to make your attacking abilities more brutally effective.	For the abilities Self Defense and Massive Strike:- Chance to inflict the state Bleeding (6s) with each use: 35%.	
Elite Knight	Shield Expert	x	Passive	Your shield has become like an extension of your body, and all shield related abilities are improved.	For the abilities Daze Strike and Shield Strike:- Damage x2- Stunned +1sFor the ability Resistance:- Damage Resistance +15%	
Elite Knight	Unwavering Mental Fortitude	x	Passive	You have gained incredible mental strength. Finishing off an opponent makes you even more difficult to kill.	- Each opponent killed gives you 100 Health Points.	
Skinchanger	Attack	All	Attack	Command your dog to attack the targeted enemy.		
Skinchanger	Takedown	All	Interrupt	Order your dog to jump on a foe and knock them to the ground.	- Knocked down (3s)	

Stances	Names	Required Weapons	Ability Types	Descriptions	Effects	Bonus Effects
Skinchanger	Disarm	All		Command your dog to bite a foe's hand in order to disarm them.	"If your opponent is in Counter-Attack: - Disarmed"	
Skinchanger	Immobilize	All	Immobilize, Interrupt	Command your dog to bite a foe's legs.	- Immobilized (10s)	
Skinchanger	Intimidation	All	Support	Command your dog to terrorize a foe and prevent him from using his abilities.	- Scared (8s)	
Skinchanger	Throat Lunge	All	Interrupt, Damage	Command your dog to leap at a foe's throat. Only a shield can repel this attack.	"If your opponent does not have a shield: - Damage x4"	
Skinchanger	Remove Shield	All		Order your dog to snatch the shield out of a foe 's hand.	"If your opponent has a shield: - Disarmed"	
Skinchanger	Wild	All	Support	Command your dog to to let out a monstrous bark, which will awaken the animal spirit in you and all allies.	"For you, your teammate and your allies: - Energy Recovery changes to 3% per second for 9s."	
Skinchanger	Barking	x	Passive	Your dog's bark is deeper and more threatening.	- Duration +3s for Wild and Intimidation.	
Skinchanger	Cave Canem	x	Passive	You have greater control when skinchanging and can rip targets' throats out quicker.	During Skinchanger mode:- Kill speed +20%.	
Skinchanger	Energy	x	Passive	Your dog now succumbs to fatigue more slowly.	- Speed of command recharge +10%	
Skinchanger	Fighting Dog	x	Passive	Your dog has benefited from intensive attack training.	- Damage +30%	
Skinchanger	Harassment	x	Passive	Your dog has become more effective in battle as a result of the combat experience he's gained.	- When the dog kills an opponent, its abilities are instantly recharged.	
Skinchanger	Reflexes	x	Passive	Your dog has become better at dodging attacks.	- Deflection +10%	
Skinchanger	Sharp Fangs	x	Passive	Your dog's attacks are more deadly.	- The abilities Throat Lunge, Remove Shield and Disarm now cause Bleeding (8s).	
Skinchanger	Toughness	x	Passive	Your dog can now withstand more hits in combat.	- Health +20%	
R'hllor	Flaming Weapon	Swords, one-handed weapons and ranged weapons	Support	Use a flask of flammable oil to set your weapon alight.	"- Flaming Weapon (10s)With a ranged weapon: - Burning Projectile"	
R'hllor	Accelerated Combustion	All	Damage over time, interrupt	Increase the burn rate on an opponent who is already on fire.	"If your opponent has the state On Fire or On Wildfire: - Combustion (5s)"	
R'hllor	Explosion	All	Area Interrupt, Damage	Cause a 3 meter radius explosion on an opponent who is On Fire or On Wildfire.	"If your opponent has the state On Fire or On Wildfire: - Damage: 150 health points - Stunned 3s"	

R'hllor	Flame of Life	All	Defensive	Use the Flame of Life to revive a teammate who has been knocked out.	- Revival with 30% health.	
R'hllor	Regenerative Heat	All	Defensive	Generate heat that helps increase health recovery.	"Regenerative Heat (10s) - Health Recovery increased (+2%/s) - Energy Recovery inactive"	
R'hllor	Dazzling Light	All	Disorder	Invoke R'hllor's light to blind your enemies (within a range of 5 meters). They will have trouble distinguishing their allies from their opponents.	- Madman 10s	
R'hllor	R'hllor's Blade	Swords, one-handed weapons and ranged weapons	Damage	Using your mastery of fire, set your weapon alight without using flammable oil.	"- Flaming Weapon 10sWith a ranged weapon: - Burning Projectile"	
R'hllor	Wildfire Weapon	Swords, one-handed weapons and ranged weapons	Damage, Interrupt	Use wildfire to set your weapon on fire. Wildfire inflicts greater damage and spreads twice as fast as traditional fire.	"- Wildfire weapon 13sWith a ranged weapon: - Wildfire Shot"	
R'hllor	Breath of Life	x	Passive	Increases the amount of health recovered when Flame of Life is used.	- Revival with 50% health (instead of 30%).	
R'hllor	Ignition	x	Passive	Your ability Accelerated Combustion is even quicker and inflicts more damage.	When using the ability Accelerated Combustion:- Damage +60%	
R'hllor	Incombustible	x	Passive	You are more resistant to fire. Damage is decreased significantly and wildfire attacks no longer interrupt you.	- Fire damage suffered -50%.	
R'hllor	Inferno	x	Passive	Your Explosion ability inflicts more damage and spreads fire over a wider area.	When using the ability Explosion :- Damage +15%- Range of effect increased to 5 meters	
R'hllor	R'hllor's Fire	x	Passive	Your mastery of fire has improved, and you can set your weapon alight for a longer period of time.	- Flaming Weapon and R'hllor's Blade last +5s	
R'hllor	R'hllor's Flames	x	Passive	Your Regenerative Heat ability is less restrictive and lasts longer.	- No longer prevents you from regaining energy and lasts +5s	
R'hllor	Rebirth	x	Passive	When you are knocked out, R'hllor gives you a second chance...	- After your first knock out each fight, you are automatically revived with 25% health.	
R'hllor	Vial of Last Resort	x	Passive	When you are knocked out, you make a last-ditch attempt to knock your enemies out as well by leaving wildfire behind (affecting enemies within a range of 4 meters).	- Damage: 100 health points- On Wildfire 6s	

TRAITS

Name	Cost	Description	Effect
Born Leader	4	Your leadership skills motivate your teammate and your allies.	Damage +7% for your teammate and your allies
Acrobat	3	Your keen sense of balance allows you to deflect blows more skillfully.	Deflection +6%
Leech	3	The sight of blood fuels your desire for battle.	If your opponent is Bleeding: Damage +15%
Art of Medicine	2	You are a master of the curative arts.	The health gained from a healing flask is increased by 15%
Brute	2	Your overwhelming might is too much for enemies, giving you a chance to stun them.	Chance to inflict the state Stunned (3s) with each attack: 2%
Gifted	2	Your aptitude for learning allows you to pick up skills more quickly than most.	Two extra skill points earned per level
Master of Poisons	2	Your knowledge of toxins allows you to wield them more skillfully than most.	Poison Impact Duration +3 sec
Accurate	1	You strike with precision, able to probe and exploit the chinks in your opponent's armor.	Chance to inflict Bleeding 1% for each blow (for 6s)
Adventurer	1	Your senses are well developed.	Chance of bonus loot +5%
Ambidextrous	1	You are particularly comfortable with a weapon in each hand.	Critical hit chance +2% with two weapons
Assassin	1	You are comfortable handling small blades (daggers and short-swords).	Attack Speed +2% with a dagger or a shortsword
Bruiser	1	Your physical strength makes you more effective at using two-handed heavy weapons.	Damage +2% with a two-handed weapon
Dexterous	1	Your natural dexterity gives you an innate proficiency with a ranged weapon.	Hit chance +2% with a ranged weapon
Honed Reflexes	1	Countless battles have tuned your reflexes so finely that you can now avoid the worst situations without even thinking.	Critical hit Damage Resistance +10%
Parry	1	You are an expert at parrying attacks with your shield.	Damage resistance +2% using a shield
Bad Leader	4	Your poor leadership skills discourage your teammate and your allies.	Damage -7% for your teammate and your allies
Greyscale	3	This disease, which causes your flesh to harden, makes your dodges less effective.	Deflection -6%
Hematophobia	3	Your fear of blood makes you less effective against bleeding enemies.	If your opponent has the state Bleeding: Damage -15%
Asthmatic	2	Your asthma makes you slightly more fatigued when you perform strenuous tasks. Each ability you use in combat will cost you a little more energy.	Energy Cost +8%
Clumsy	2	You are not very good at handling flasks, a trait that could have dire consequences in tense situations.	Chance of failure of 15% each time you use a flask
Gout	2	This arthritic condition inflames your joints and makes moving difficult.	Attack Speed -5%
Witless	2	You're not the sharpest blade in the armory.	Two fewer skill points gained per level
Allergic	1	Your allergies make you more acutely affected by poisons.	Poison Effect Duration +3 sec
Collapsed Lung	1	A previous injury in battle has claimed the use of one of your lungs.	Energy recovery -6%
Half Pint	1	Due to your small frame, you're less able to shrug off blows.	Damage resistance -2%
Hemophiliac	1	This condition hinders the clotting ability of your blood, meaning that you bleed a lot. Best to avoid contact with sharp objects if at all possible.	Damage received by the state Bleeding x2

Name	Cost	Description	Effect
Inattentive	1	You are less likely to deliver critical hits.	Critical hit -3%
Paranoid	1	Your mind is constantly envisioning the worst possible scenario, a fear that manifests even larger when numerous foes attack you.	Hit chance -10% when three opponents attack you
Psychopath	1	Your need to kill makes you unstable.	Deflection -5% for each opponent finished off by someone else other than you
Pyrophobia	1	A crippling fear of flames causes fire attacks to burn you even hotter than they would a normal person.	Damage taken by fire +0,2
Art of Escape	x	You kept your word and freed Orys, the leader of the Reapers, from the dungeons of the City Watch of King's Landing.	Deflection +1%
Back From Beyond the Grave	x	After Valarr had locked you away in your father's tomb, you emerged alive.	Endurance +1
Back From the Seven Hells	x	You came back to life after the kiss of fire given by Alester.	Endurance +1
Bloodhound	x	You tracked down all the brothers in Mole's Town who were lured in by Jared's coin.	Dog Damage +5%
Dogged Investigator	x	You uncovered the truth about your brother Gawen's past during your reunion.	One extra skill point earned per level
Expeditious	x	You killed Gendel in cold blood when he was at your mercy in the abandoned fort of Icemark.	Chance of critical hit +1%
Fanatic	x	You extolled the virtues of your god at every opportunity during the rioting in Riverspring.	Chance to resist to the states On Fire and On Wildfire +5%
Fast Talker	x	You misled your torturers when you were imprisoned by Lord Harlton.	Intelligence +1
God of Flame	x	Using diplomacy, you managed to make Weymar talk, your prisoner at the potter's in King's Landing.	Critical Damage +1%
God of Shadow	x	You let Valarr torture and kill Weymar, your prisoner at the potter's in King's Landing.	Chance of critical hit +1%
Habit	x	You fought all Lord Harlton's men under the influence of poison after dinner at Castlewood.	Damage Resistance to critical hits +2%.
Indestructible	x	You survived Gorn's formidable horde in the abandoned fort of Icemark.	Damage Resistance +1%
Indomitable Will	x	You stood up to your torturers, enduring horrific treatment while imprisoned by Lord Harlton.	Damage Resistance +6%-Endurance -1
Justice Is Blind	x	You killed Orys, the leader of the Reapers, who was locked up in the tower of the City Watch of King's Landing.	Critical Damage +1%
Kindhearted	x	You released Marianne, the niece of Lord Harlton.	Chance of critical hit +1%
Ladykiller	x	You killed Marianne, the niece of Lord Harlton.	Critical Damage +2%
Morbid Curiosity	x	You opened your father's tomb in the Riverspring crypts.	Chance of loot +2%
Nimble	x	You caught the young man on the run during a chase in King's Landing.	Deflection +1%
No Surrender, No Retreat	x	You piled up Gorn's men into a towering mound at the abandoned fort of Icemark and fought until your body gave out.	Health max +5
Nostalgic	x	Memories came flooding back during your first meeting with Varys.	One extra skill point earned per level.
Opportunistic	x	You recruited Yohn's men, who had been captured by the Lord Commander of the Night's Watch.	Damage +2% for your allies.
Resourceful	x	You obtained a City Watch of King's Landing uniform without spending a single groat.	Chance of bonus loot +1%
Sadistic	x	You tortured Gendel at length when he was at your mercy in the abandoned fort of Icemark.	Critical Damage +3%
Sarwycks' Vengeance	x	You will take vengeance no matter what. As for the child...	Chance of critical hit +4%

Name	Cost	Description	Effect
Stray Dog	x	You were officially made a recruiter by the Lord Commander of the Night's Watch.	Damage +2% to your allies
Talkative	x	You demonstrated your oratory skills during your meeting with Queen Cersei.	Deflection +1%
Unimpeachable Morals	x	You defeated all of Yohn's men who had been captured by the Lord Commander of the Night's Watch.	Damage Resistance +1%
Unwavering	x	You never succumbed to Valarr's taunts during your trial by combat.	Deflection +1%
Westfords' Vengeance	x	You will take vengeance and save the child, no matter what.	Health Recovery +4%

GAME OF THRONES

PRIMA Official Game Guide

Written by Michael Searle

Product Manager: Fernando Bueno and Paul Giacomotto
Design & Layout: Jamie Knight, Rick Wong and Kari Keating
Maps: 99 Lives
Copyeditor: Carrie Andrews

Special Thanks from Prima Games- Robyn Mukai and Tim Pivnicny were instrumental in the creation and approval of this game guide. Thanks for all your hard work and support. Others who helped with the production of this guide- Sally Ortiz, Jeremy Cail, Michiko Shiikuma. Thanks to Cyanide for making such a fun project to work on. Thanks to Home Box Office, Inc. taking time from your busy schedule to review our guide and the approvals of course.

Special thanks from the author- Michael would like to thank his family for their unconditional support during this long quest for excellence, the creative teams at Atlus and Prima for helping to forge a guide tempered by passion and experience, and George R. R. Martin for his imagination and wit in creating one of the finest worlds I've ever had the pleasure of reading.

ISBN: 978-0-307-89439-7

Printed in the United States of America

Prima Games
An Imprint of Random House, Inc.

3000 Lava Ridge Court, St. 100 • Roseville, CA 95661
www.primagames.com